Haskell
The Craft of Functional Programming

INTERNATIONAL COMPUTER SCIENCE SERIES

Consulting Editor: **A D McGettrick** *University of Strathclyde*

Haskell
The Craft of
Functional
Programming

Second edition

Simon Thompson

Harlow, England • London • New York • Boston • San Francisco • Toronto • Sydney • Singapore • Hong Kong
Tokyo • Seoul • Taipei • New Delhi • Cape Town • Madrid • Mexico City • Amsterdam • Munich • Paris • Milan

Pearson Education Limited
Edinburgh Gate
Harlow
Essex CM20 2JE
England

and Associated Companies throughout the world

Visit us on the World Wide Web at:
http://www.pearsoned.co.uk

© Addison Wesley Longman Limited 1999

Cover designed by Designers & Partners, Oxford
Typeset in 10/12 pt Times by 56
Printed in Great Britain by Henry Ling Limited, at the Dorset Press, Dorchester, DT1 1HD

First published 1999

ISBN-10: 0-201-34275-8
ISBN-13: 978-0-201-34275-8

British Library Cataloguing-in-Publication Data
A catalogue record for this book is available from the British Library

Library of Congress Cataloging-in Publication Data
Thompson, Simon.
Haskell: the craft of functional programming / Simon Thompson. – 2nd ed.
        p.   cm.
   Includes bibliographical references and index.
   ISBN 0-201-34275-8
   1. Functional programming (Computer science). I. Title.
QA76.62.T497   1999
005.13'3–dc21
                                                                98-51704
                                                                      CIP

Trademark Notice
Macintosh and Power Macintosh are trademarks of Apple Computer, Inc. UNIX is Licensed through X/Open Company Ltd. Windows and Windows 95 are trademarks of Microsoft Corporation.

15 14 13 12 11
07 06 05

To Alice

and Rory

Contents

....

Preface

Computer technology changes with frightening speed; the fundamentals, however, remain remarkably static. The architecture of the standard computer is hardly changed from the machines which were built half a century ago, even though their size and power are incomparably different from those of today. In programming, modern ideas like object-orientation have taken decades to move from the research environment into the commercial mainstream. In this light, a functional language like Haskell is a relative youngster, but one with a growing influence to play.

- Functional languages are increasingly being used as **components** of larger systems like Fran (Elliott and Hudak 1997), in which Haskell is used to describe reactive graphical animations, which are ultimately rendered in a lower-level language. This inter-operation is done without sacrificing the semantic elegance which characterizes functional languages.

- Functional languages provide a **framework** in which the crucial ideas of modern programming are presented in the clearest possible way. This accounts for their widespread use in teaching computing science and also for their influence on the design of other languages. A case in point is the design of G-Java, the generics of which are directly modelled on polymorphism in the Haskell mould.

This book provides a tutorial introduction to functional programming in Haskell. The remainder of the preface begins with a brief explanation of functional programming and the reasons for studying it. This is followed by an explanation of the approach taken in the book and an outline of its contents. Perhaps most importantly for readers of the first edition, the changes in approach and content in this second edition are then discussed. A final section explains different possible routes through the material.

What is functional programming?

Functional programming offers a high-level view of programming, giving its users a variety of features which help them to build elegant yet powerful and general libraries of functions. Central to functional programming is the idea of a function, which computes a result that depends on the values of its inputs.

An example of the power and generality of the language is the map function, which is used to transform every element of a list of objects in a specified way. For example, map can be used to double all the numbers in a sequence of numbers or to invert the colours in each picture appearing in a list of pictures.

The elegance of functional programming is a consequence of the way that functions are defined: an equation is used to say what the value of a function is on an arbitrary input. A simple illustration is the function addDouble which adds two integers and doubles their sum. Its definition is

```
addDouble x y = 2*(x+y)
```

where x and y are the inputs and 2*(x+y) is the result.

The model of functional programming is simple and clean: to work out the value of an expression like

```
3 + addDouble 4 5
```

the equations which define the functions involved in the expression are used, so

```
3 + addDouble 4 5
⤳   3 + 2*(4+5)
⤳   . . .
⤳   21
```

This is how a computer would work out the value of the expression, but it is also possible to do exactly the same calculation using pencil and paper, making transparent the implementation mechanism.

It is also possible to discuss how the programs behave in general. In the case of addDouble we can use the fact that x+y and y+x are equal for all numbers x and y to conclude that addDouble x y and addDouble y x are equal for all x and y. This idea of proof is much more tractable than those for traditional imperative and object-oriented (OO) languages.

Haskell and Hugs

This text uses the programming language Haskell, which has freely available compilers and interpreters for most types of computer system. Used here is the Hugs interpreter which provides an ideal platform for the learner, with its fast compile cycle, simple interface and free availability for Windows, Unix and Macintosh systems.

Haskell began life in the late 1980s as an intended standard language for lazy functional programming, and since then it has gone through various changes and modifications. This text is written in Haskell 98, which consolidates work on Haskell thus far, and which is intended to be stable; future extensions will result in Haskell 2 some years down the line, but it is expected that implementations will continue to support Haskell 98 after that point.

While the book covers most aspects of Haskell 98, it is primarily a programming text rather than a language manual. Details of the language and its libraries are contained in the language and library reports available from the Haskell home page,

```
http://www.haskell.org/
```

Why learn functional programming?

A functional programming language gives a simple model of programming: one value, the result, is computed on the basis of others, the inputs.

Because of its simple foundation, a functional language gives the clearest possible view of the central ideas in modern computing, including abstraction (in a function), data abstraction (in an abstract data type), genericity, polymorphism and overloading. This means that a functional language provides not just an ideal introduction to modern programming ideas, but also a useful perspective on more traditional imperative or object-oriented approaches. For example, Haskell gives a direct implementation of data types like trees, whereas in other languages one is forced to describe them by pointer-linked data structures.

Haskell is not just a good 'teaching language'; it is a practical programming language, supported by having extensions such as interfaces to C functions and component-based programming, for example. Haskell has also been used in a number of real-world projects. More information about these extensions and projects can be found in the concluding chapter.

Who should read this book?

This text is intended as an introduction to functional programming for computer science and other students, principally at university level. It can be used by beginners to computer science, or more experienced students who are learning functional programming for the first time; either group will find the material to be new and challenging.

The book can also be used for self-study by programmers, software engineers and others interested in gaining a grounding in functional programming.

The text is intended to be self-contained, but some elementary knowledge of commands, files and so on is needed to use any of the implementations of Haskell. Some logical notation is introduced in the text; this is explained as it appears. In Chapter 19 it would help to have an understanding of the graphs of the $\log$, n^2 and 2^n functions.

The approach taken here

There is a tension in writing about a programming language: one wants to introduce all the aspects of the language as early as possible, yet not to over-burden the reader with too much at once. The first edition of the text introduced ideas 'from the bottom up', which meant that it took more than a hundred pages before any substantial example could be discussed.

The second edition takes a different approach: a case study of 'pictures' introduces a number of crucial ideas informally in the first chapter, revisiting them as the text proceeds. Also, Haskell has a substantial library of built-in functions, particularly over lists, and this edition exploits this, encouraging readers to use these functions before seeing the details of their definitions. This allows readers to progress more quickly, and also accords with practice: most real programs are built using substantial libraries of pre-existing code, and it is therefore valuable experience to work in this way from the start. A section containing details of the other changes in the second edition can be found later in this preface.

Other distinctive features of the approach in the book include the following.

- The text gives a thorough treatment of reasoning about functional programs, beginning with reasoning about list-manipulating functions. These are chosen in preference to functions over the natural numbers for two reasons: the results one can prove for lists seem substantially more realistic, and also the structural induction principle for lists seems to be more acceptable to students.

- The Picture case study is introduced in Chapter 1 and revisited throughout the text; this means that readers see different ways of programming the same function, and so get a chance to reflect on and compare different designs.

- Function design – to be done before starting to code – is also emphasized explicitly in Chapters 4 and 11.

- There is an emphasis on Haskell as a practical programming language, with an early introduction of modules, as well as a thorough examination of the do notation for I/O and other monad-based applications.

- Types play a prominent role in the text. Every function or object defined has its type introduced at the same time as its definition. Not only does this provide a check that the definition has the type that its author intended, but also we view types as the single most important piece of documentation for a definition, since a function's type describes precisely how the function is to be used.

- A number of case studies are introduced in stages through the book: the picture example noted above, an interactive calculator program, a coding and decoding system based on Huffman codes and a small queue simulation package. These are used to introduce various new ideas and also to show how existing techniques work together.

- Support materials on Haskell, including a substantial number of Web links, are included in the concluding chapter. Various appendices contain other backup information including details of the availability of implementations, common Hugs errors and a comparison between functional, imperative and OO programming.

● Other support materials appear on the Web site for the book:

`http://www.cs.ukc.ac.uk/people/staff/sjt/craft2e/`

Outline

The introduction in Chapter 1 covers the basic concepts of functional programming: functions and types, expressions and evaluation, definitions and proof. Some of the more advanced ideas, such as higher-order functions and polymorphism, are previewed here from the perspective of the example of pictures built from characters. Chapter 2 looks at the practicalities of the Hugs implementation of Haskell, loading and running scripts written in traditional and 'literate' styles, and the basics of the module system. It also contains a first exercise using the `Picture` type. These two chapters together cover the foundation on which to build a course on functional programming in Haskell.

Information on how to build simple programs over numbers, characters and Booleans is contained in Chapter 3. The basic lessons are backed up with exercises, as is the case for all chapters from here on. With this basis, Chapter 4 steps back and examines the various strategies which can be used to define functions, and particularly emphasizes the importance of using other functions, either from the system or written by the user. It also discusses the idea of 'divide and conquer', as well as introducing recursion over the natural numbers.

Structured data, in the form of tuples and lists, come in Chapter 5. After introducing the idea of lists, programming over lists is performed using two resources: the list comprehension, which effectively gives the power of `map` and `filter`; and the first-order prelude and library functions. Nearly all the list prelude functions are polymorphic, and so polymorphism is brought in here. Chapter 6 contains various extended examples, and only in Chapter 7 is primitive recursion over lists introduced; a text processing case study provides a more substantial example here.

Chapter 8 introduces reasoning about list-manipulating programs, on the basis of a number of introductory sections giving the appropriate logical background. Guiding principles about how to build inductive proofs are presented, together with a more advanced section on building successful proofs from failed attempts.

Higher-order functions are introduced in Chapters 9 and 10. First functional arguments are examined, and it is shown that functional arguments allow the implementation of many of the 'patterns' of computation identified over lists at the start of the chapter. Chapter 10 covers functions as results, defined both as lambda-expressions and as partial applications; these ideas are examined by revisiting the `Picture` example, as well as through an index case study. This is followed by an interlude – Chapter 11 – which discusses the role of the development life cycle in programming.

Type classes allow functions to be overloaded to mean different things at different types; Chapter 12 covers this topic as well as surveying the various classes built into Haskell. The Haskell type system is somewhat complicated because of the presence of classes, and so Chapter 13 explores the way in which types are checked in Haskell. In general, type checking is a matter of resolving the various constraints put upon the possible type of the function by its definition.

In writing larger programs, it is imperative that users can define types for themselves. Haskell supports this in two ways. Algebraic types like trees are the subject of Chapter 14, which covers all aspects of algebraic types from design and proof to their interaction with type classes, as well as introducing numerous examples of algebraic types in practice. These examples are consolidated in Chapter 15, which contains the case study of coding and decoding of information using a Huffman-style code. The foundations of the approach are outlined before the implementation of the case study. Modules are used to break the design into manageable parts, and the more advanced features of the Haskell module system are introduced at this point.

An abstract data type (ADT) provides access to an implementation through a restricted set of functions. Chapter 16 explores the ADT mechanism of Haskell and gives numerous examples of how it is used to implement queues, sets, relations and so forth, as well as giving the basics of a simulation case study.

Chapter 17 introduces lazy evaluation in Haskell which allows programmers a distinctive style incorporating backtracking and infinite data structures. As an example of backtracking there is a parsing case study, and infinite lists are used to give 'process style' programs as well as a random-number generator.

Haskell programs can perform input and output by means of the IO types. Their members – examined in Chapter 18 – represent action-based programs. The programs are most readily written using the do notation, which is introduced at the start of the chapter, and illustrated through a series of examples, culminating in an interactive front-end to the calculator. The foundations of the do notation lie in monads, which can also be used to do action-based programming of a number of different flavours, some of which are examined in the second half of the chapter.

The text continues with an examination in Chapter 19 of program behaviour, by which we mean the time taken for a program to compute its result, and the space used in that calculation. Chapter 20 concludes by surveying various applications and extensions of Haskell as well as looking at further directions for study. These are backed up with Web and other references.

The appendices cover various background topics. The first examines links with functional and OO programing, and the second gives a glossary of commonly used terms in functional programming. The others include a summary of Haskell operators and Hugs errors, together with help on understanding programs and details of the various implementations of Haskell.

The Haskell code for all the examples in the book, as well as other background materials, can be downloaded from the Web site for the book.

What has changed from the first edition?

The second edition of the book incorporates a number of substantial changes, for a variety of reasons.

`Bottom up' or not?

Most importantly, the philosophy of how to introduce material has changed, and this makes most impact on how lists are handled. The first edition was written with a resolutely 'bottom up' approach, first introducing recursive definitions of monomorphic functions, and only later bringing in the built-in functions of the prelude and the libraries. This edition starts by introducing in Chapter 5 the (first-order) polymorphic list-manipulating functions from the prelude as well as list comprehensions, and only introduces recursive definitions over lists in Chapter 7.

The main reason for this change was the author's (and others') experience that once recursion had been introduced early, it was difficult to get students to move on and use other sorts of definitions; in particular it was difficult to get students to use prelude and library functions in their solutions. This is bad in itself, and gives students only a partial view of the language. Moreover, it rests ill with modern ideas about programming, which emphasize the importance of re-use and putting together solutions to utilize a rich programming environment that provides many of the required building blocks.

Introduction

Another consequence of the first-edition approach was that it took some hundred pages before any substantial examples could be introduced; in this edition there is an example of pictures in Chapter 1 which both forms a more substantial case study and is used to preview the ideas of polymorphism, higher-order functions and type abstraction introduced later in the text. The case study is revisited repeatedly as new material is brought in, showing how the same problems can be solved more effectively with new machinery, as well as illustrating the idea of program verification.

The introduction also sets out more clearly some of the basic concepts of functional programming and Haskell, and a separate Chapter 2 is used to discuss the Hugs system, Haskell scripts and modules and so forth.

Haskell 98

The book now has an emphasis on using the full resources of Haskell 98. Hugs now provides an almost complete implementation of Haskell, and so as far as systems are concerned Hugs is the exclusive subject. In most situations Hugs will probably be the implementation of choice for teaching purposes, and if it is not used, it is only the system descriptions which need to be ignored, as none of the language features described are Hugs-specific.

The treatment of abstract data types uses the Haskell mechanism exclusively, rather than the restricted type synonym mechanism of Hugs which was emphasized in the first edition. The material on I/O now starts with the do notation, treating it as a mini language for describing programs with actions. This is followed by a general introduction to monads, giving an example of monadic computation over trees which again uses the do notation.

Finally, functions in the text are given the same names as they have in the prelude or libraries, which was not always the case in the first edition. Type variables are the customary a, b, ... and list variables are named xs, ys and so on.

Recursion, types and proof

As hinted earlier, recursion is given less emphasis than before.

The material on type checking now takes the approach of looking more explicitly at the constraints put upon types by definitions, and emphasizes this through a sequence of examples. This replaces an approach which stated typing rules but said less about their application in practice.

Students have made the point that proof over lists seems more realistic and indeed easier to understand than proof over the natural numbers. For that reason, proof over lists is introduced in Chapter 8 rather than earlier. This has the advantage that practical examples can be brought in right from the start, and the material on proof is linked with the pictures case study.

Problem solving and patterns of definition

Because of a concern for 'getting students started' in solving problems, there is an attempt to talk more explicitly about strategies for programming, reorganizing and introducing new material in Chapters 4 and 11; this material owes much to Polya's problem-solving approach in mathematics. There is also explicit discussion about various 'patterns of definition' of programs in Section 9.1.

Conclusion and appendices

The new edition contains a concluding chapter which looks to further resources, both printed and on the Web, as well as discussing possible directions for functional programming.

Some material from the appendices has been incorporated into the conclusion, while the appendix that discusses links with other paradigms says rather more about links with OO ideas. The other appendices have been updated, while the one that dealt with 'some useful functions' has been absorbed into the body of the text.

To the reader

This introduction to functional programming in Haskell is designed to be read from start to finish, but some material can be omitted, or read in a different order.

The material is presented in an order that the author finds natural, and while this also reflects some of the logical dependencies between parts of the subject, some material later in the text can be read earlier than it appears. Specifically, the introductions to I/O in the first four sections of Chapter 18 and to algebraic types in the early sections on Chapter 14 can be tackled at any point after reading Chapter 7. Local definitions, given by where and let, are introduced in Chapter 6; they can be covered at any point after Chapter 3.

It is always an option to cover only a subset of the topics, and this can be achieved by stopping before the end; the rest of this section discusses in more detail other ways of trimming the material.

There is a thread on program verification which begins with Chapter 8 and continues in Sections 10.9, 14.7, 16.10 and 17.9; this thread is optional. Similarly, Chapter 19 gives a self-contained treatment of program time and space behaviour which is also optional.

Some material is more technical, and can be omitted on (at least the) first reading. This is signalled explicitly in the text, and is contained in Sections 8.7 and part of Section 13.2.

Finally, it is possible to omit some of the examples and case studies. For example, Sections 6.2 and 6.4 are extended sets of exercises which need not be covered; the text processing (Section 7.6) and indexing (Section 10.8) can also be omitted – their roles are to provide reinforcement and to show the system used on rather larger examples. In the later chapters, the examples in Sections 14.6 and 16.7–16.9 and in Chapter 17 can be skipped, but paring too many examples will run the risk of losing some motivating material.

Chapter 15 introduces modules in the first two sections; the remainder is the Huffman coding case study, which is optional. Finally, distributed through the final chapters are the calculator and simulation case studies. These are again optional, but omission of the calculator case study will remove an important illustration of parsing and algebraic and abstract data types.

Acknowledgements

For feedback on the first edition, I am grateful particularly to Ham Richards, Bjorn von Sydow and Kevin Hammond and indeed to all those who have pointed out errata in that text. In reading drafts of the second edition, thanks to Tim Hopkins and Peter Kenny as well as the anonymous referees.

Emma Mitchell and Michael Strang of Addison-Wesley have supported this second edition from its inception; thanks very much to them.

Particular thanks to Jane for devotion beyond the call of duty in reading and commenting very helpfully on the first two chapters, as well as for her support over the last year while I have been writing this edition. Finally, thanks to Alice and Rory who have more than readily shared our home PC with Haskell.

Simon Thompson
Canterbury, January 1999

Chapter 1

Introducing functional programming

This chapter sets the scene for our exposition of functional programming in Haskell. The chapter has three aims.

- We want to introduce the main ideas underpinning functional programming. We explain what it means to be a function and a type. We examine what it means to find the value of an expression, and how to write an evaluation line-by-line. We look at how to define a function, and also what it means to prove that a function behaves in a particular way.

- We want to illustrate these ideas by means of a realistic example; we use the example of pictures to do this.

● Finally, we want to give a preview of some of the more powerful and distinctive ideas in functional programming. This allows us to illustrate how it differs from other approaches like object-oriented programming, and also to show why we consider functional programming to be of central importance to anyone learning computing science. As we proceed with this informal overview we will give pointers to later chapters of the book where we explain these ideas more rigorously and in more detail.

(1.1) Computers and modelling

In the last fifty years computers have moved from being enormous, expensive, scarce, slow and unreliable to being small, cheap, common, fast and (relatively!) dependable. The first computers were 'stand-alone' machines, but now computers can also play different roles, being organized together into networks, or being embedded in domestic machines like cars and washing machines, as well as appearing in personal computers (PCs), organizers and so on.

Despite this, the fundamentals of computers have changed very little in this period: the purpose of a computer is to manipulate symbolic information. This information can represent a simple situation, such as the items bought in a supermarket shopping trip, or more complicated ones, like the weather system above Europe. Given this information, we are required to perform tasks like calculating the total cost of a supermarket trip, or producing a 24-hour weather forecast for southern England.

How are these tasks achieved? We need to write a description of how the information is manipulated. This is called a **program** and it is written in a **programming language**. A programming language is a formal, artificial language used to give instructions to a computer. In other words the language is used to write the **software** which controls the behaviour of the **hardware**. While the structure of computers has remained very similar since their inception, the ways in which they are programmed have developed substantially. Initially programs were written using instructions which controlled the hardware directly, whereas modern programming languages aim to work closer to the level of the problem – a 'high' level – rather than at the 'low' or machine level.

The programming language is made to work on a computer by an **implementation**, which is itself a program and which runs programs written in the higher-level language on the computer in question.

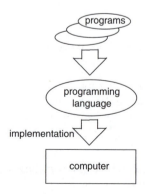

Our task in this text is programming, so we shall be occupied with the upper half of the diagram above, and not the details of implementation (which are discussed in Peyton Jones 1987; Peyton Jones and Lester 1992).

Our subject here is **functional** programming, which is one of a number of different programming styles or **paradigms**; others include object-oriented (OO), structured and logic programming. How can there be different paradigms, and how do they differ? One very fruitful way of looking at programming is that it is the task of **modelling** situations – either real-world or imaginary – within a computer. Each programming paradigm will provide us with different tools for building these models; these different tools allow us – or force us – to think about situations in different ways. A functional programmer will concentrate on the relationships between values, while an OO programmer will concentrate on the objects, say. Before we can say anything more about functional programming we need to examine what it means to be a function.

1.2 What is a function?

A **function** is something which we can picture as a box with some inputs and an output, thus:

The function gives an **output** value which depends upon the **input** value(s). We will often use the term **result** for the output, and the terms **arguments** or **parameters** for the inputs.

A simple example of a function is addition, +, over numbers. Given input values 12 and 34 the corresponding output will be 46.

The process of giving particular inputs to a function is called **function application**, and (12 + 34) represents the application of the function + to 12 and 34.

Addition is a mathematical example, but there are also functions in many other situations; examples of these include

- a function giving the distance by road (*output*) between two cities (*inputs*);

- a supermarket check-out program, which calculates the bill (*output*) from a list of bar codes scanned in (*input*); and

- a process controller, which controls valves in a chemical plant. Its inputs are the information from sensors, and its output the signals sent to the valve actuators.

We mentioned earlier that different paradigms are characterized by the different tools which they provide for modelling: in a functional programming language functions will be the central component of our models. We shall see this in our running example of pictures, which we look at now.

1.3 Pictures and functions

In this chapter, and indeed throughout the book, we will look at an example of two-dimensional pictures, and their representation within a computer system. At this stage we simply want to make the point that many common relationships between pictures are modelled by functions; in the remainder of this section we consider a series of examples of this.

Reflection in a vertical mirror will relate two pictures, and we can model this by a function flipV:

where we have illustrated the effect of this reflection on the 'horse' image

In a similar way we have a function flipH to represent flipping in a horizontal mirror. Another function models the inversion of the colours in a (monochrome) image

Some functions will take two arguments, among them a function to scale images,

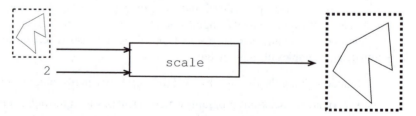

a function describing the superimposition of two images,

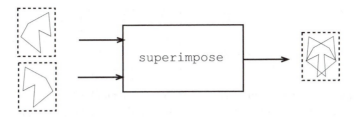

a function to put one picture above another,

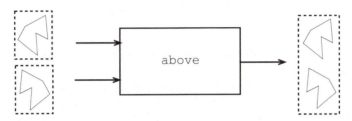

and a function to place two pictures side by side.

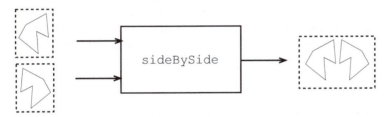

We have now seen what it means to be a function, as well as some examples of functions. Before we explain functional programming, we first have to look at another idea, that of a 'type'.

1.4 Types

The functions which we use in functional programs will involve all sorts of different kinds of value: the addition function + will combine two numbers to give another number; flipV will transform a picture into a picture; scale will take a picture and a number and return a picture, and so on.

A **type** is a collection of values, such as numbers or pictures, grouped together because although they are different – 2 is not the same as 567 – they are the same *sort* of thing, in that we can apply the same functions to them. It is reasonable to find the larger of two numbers, but not to compare a number and a picture, for instance.

If we look at the addition function, +, it only makes sense to add two numbers but not two pictures, say. This is an example of the fact that the functions we have been talking about themselves have a type, and indeed we can illustrate this diagrammatically, thus:

The diagram indicates that + takes two whole numbers (or Integers) as arguments and gives a whole number as a result. In a similar way, we can label the scale function

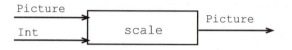

to indicate that its first argument is a Picture and its second is an Int, with its result being a Picture.

We have now explained two of the central ideas in functional programming: a type is a collection of values, like the whole numbers or integers; a function is an operation which takes one or more arguments to produce a result. The two concepts are linked: functions will operate over particular types: a function to scale a picture will take two arguments, one of type Picture and the other of type Int.

In modelling a problem situation, a type can represent a concept like 'picture', while a function will represent one of the ways that such objects can be manipulated, such as placing one picture above another. We shall return to the discussion of types in Section 1.11.

1.5 The Haskell programming language

Haskell (Peyton Jones and Hughes 1998) is the functional programming language which we use in this text. However, many of the topics we cover are of more general interest and apply to other functional languages (as discussed in Chapter 20), and indeed are lessons for programming in general. Nevertheless, the book is of most value as a text on functional programming in the Haskell language.

Haskell is named after Haskell B. Curry who was one of the pioneers of the λ calculus (lambda calculus), which is a mathematical theory of functions and has been an inspiration to designers of a number of functional languages. Haskell was first specified in the late 1980s, and has since gone through a number of revisions before reaching its current 'standard' state.

There are a variety of implementations of Haskell available; in this text we shall use the **Hugs** (1998) system. We feel that Hugs provides the best environment for the learner, since it is freely available for PC, Unix and Macintosh systems, it is efficient and compact and has a flexible user interface.

Hugs is an interpreter – which means loosely that it evaluates expressions step-by-step as we might on a piece of paper – and so it will be less efficient than a compiler which translates Haskell programs directly into the machine language of a computer. Compiling a language like Haskell allows its programs to run with a speed similar to those written in more conventional languages like C and C++. Details of all the different implementations of Haskell can be found in Appendix E and at the Haskell home page, `http://www.haskell.org/`.

From now on we shall be using the Haskell programming language and the Hugs system as the basis of our exposition of the ideas of functional programming. Details of how to obtain Hugs are in Appendix E. All the programs and examples used in the text can be downloaded from the Web page for this book,

`http://www.cs.ukc.ac.uk/people/staff/sjt/craft2e/`

1.6 Expressions and evaluation

In our first years at school we learn to **evaluate** an **expression** like (7 - 3) * 2

expression   value

(7-3)*2 ➤━━━━━━━━➤ 8

evaluation

to give the **value** 8. This expression is built up from symbols for numbers and for functions over those numbers: subtraction – and multiplication *; the value of the expression is a number. This process of evaluation is automated in an electronic calculator.

In functional programming we do exactly the same: we evaluate expressions to give values, but in those expressions we use functions which model our particular problem. For example, in modelling pictures we will want to evaluate expressions whose values are pictures. If the picture

is called `horse`, then we can form an expression by applying the function `flipV` to the horse. This function application is written by putting the function followed by its argument(s), thus: `flipV horse` and then evaluation will give

expression   value

flipV horse ➤━━━━━━━━➤

evaluation

A more complicated expression is

`invertColour (flipV horse)`

the effect of which is to give a horse reflected in a vertical mirror – `flipV horse` as shown above – and then to invert the colours in the picture to give

To recap, in functional programming, we compute by evaluating expressions which use functions in our area of interest. We can see an implementation of a functional language as something like an electronic calculator: we supply an expression, and the system evaluates the expression to give its value. The task of the programmer is to write the functions which model the problem area.

A **functional program** is made up of a series of **definitions** of functions and other values. We will look at how to write these definitions now.

1.7 Definitions

A functional program in Haskell consists of a number of **definitions**. A Haskell definition associates a **name** (or **identifier**) with a value of a particular **type**. In the simplest case a definition will have the form

```
name :: type
name = expression
```

as in the example

```
size :: Int
size = 12+13
```

which associates the name on the left-hand side, `size`, with the value of the expression on the right-hand side, 25, a value whose type is `Int`, the type of whole numbers or integers. The symbol '`::`' should be read as 'is of type', so the first line of the last definition reads '`size` is of type `Int`'. Note also that names for functions and other values begin with a small letter, while type names begin with a capital letter.

Suppose that we are supplied with the definitions of `horse` and the various functions over `Picture` mentioned earlier – we will discuss in detail how to download these and use them in a program in Chapter 2 – we can then write definitions which use these operations over pictures. For example, we can say

```
blackHorse :: Picture
blackHorse = invertColour horse
```

so that the `Picture` associated with `blackHorse` is obtained by applying the function `invertColour` to the `horse`, thus giving

Another example is the definition

```
rotateHorse :: Picture
rotateHorse = flipH (flipV horse)
```

and we can picture the evaluation of the right-hand side like this

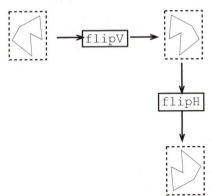

assuming the function `flipH` has the effect of reflecting a `Picture` in a horizontal mirror. The effect of these two reflections is to rotate the picture through 180°.

In Section 1.6 we explained that the Hugs system works rather like a calculator in evaluating expressions. How will it evaluate an expression like

```
size - 17
```

for instance? Using the definition of `size` given earlier, we can replace the left-hand side – `size` – with the corresponding right-hand side – 12+13; this gives us the expression

```
(12+13) - 17
```

and so by doing some arithmetic we can conclude that the value of the expression is 8.

The definitions we have seen so far are simply of constant values; we now turn our attention to how functions are defined.

1.8 Function definitions

We can also define functions, and we consider some simple examples now. To square an integer we can say

```
square :: Int -> Int
square n = n*n
```

where diagrammatically the definition is represented by

The first line of the Haskell definition of `square` declares the type of the thing being defined: this states that `square` is a function – signified by the arrow `->` – which has a single argument of type Int (appearing before the arrow) and which returns a result of type Int (coming after the arrow).

The second line gives the definition of the function: the equation states that when square is applied to an **unknown** or **variable** n, then the result is n*n. How should we read an equation like this? Because n is an arbitrary, or unknown value, it means that the equation holds *whatever the value of* n, so that it will hold whatever integer expression we put in the place of n, having the consequence that, for instance

```
square 5 = 5*5
```

and

```
square (2+4) = (2+4)*(2+4)
```

This is the way that the equation is used in evaluating an expression which uses square. If we are required to evaluate square applied to the expression e, we replace the application square e with the corresponding right-hand side, e*e.

In general a simple function definition will take the form

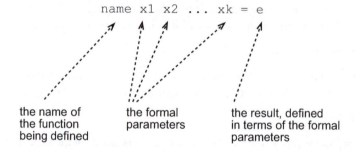

name x1 x2 ... xk = e

the name of the function being defined

the formal parameters

the result, defined in terms of the formal parameters

The variables used on the left-hand side of an equation defining a function are called the **formal parameters** because they stand for arbitrary values of the parameters (or **actual** parameters, as they are sometimes known). We will only use 'formal' and 'actual' in the text when we need to draw a distinction between the two; in most cases it will be obvious which is meant when 'parameter' is used.

Accompanying the definition of the function is a **declaration** of its type. This will take the following form, where we use the function scale over pictures for illustration:

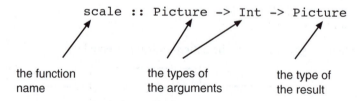

scale :: Picture -> Int -> Picture

the function name

the types of the arguments

the type of the result

In the general case we have

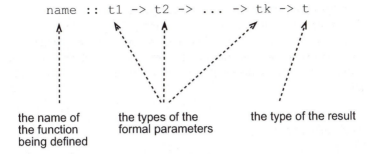

<table>
<tr><td>the name of
the function
being defined</td><td>the types of the
formal parameters</td><td>the type of the result</td></tr>
</table>

The definition of `rotateHorse` in Section 1.7 suggests a general definition of a rotation function. To rotate *any* picture we can perform the two reflections, and so we define

```
rotate :: Picture -> Picture
rotate pic = flipH (flipV pic)
```

We can read the equation thus:

> To `rotate` a picture `pic`, we first apply `flipV` to form `(flipV pic)`; we then reflect this in a horizontal mirror to give `flipH (flipV pic)`.

Given this definition, we can replace the definition of `rotateHorse` by

```
rotateHorse :: Picture
rotateHorse = rotate horse
```

which states that `rotateHorse` is the result of applying the function `rotate` to the picture `horse`.

The pattern of definition of `rotate` – 'apply one function, and then apply another to the result' – is so common that Haskell gives a way of combining functions directly in this way. We define

```
rotate :: Picture -> Picture
rotate = flipH . flipV
```

The '.' in the definition signifies **function composition**, in which the output of one function becomes the input of another. In pictures,

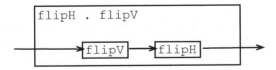

we see the creation of a new function by connecting together the input and output of two given functions: obviously this suggests many other ways of connecting together functions, many of which we will look at in the chapters to come.

The direct combination of functions gives us the first example of the power of functional programming: we are able to combine functions using an operator like '.' just as we can combine numbers using '+'. We use the term '**operator**' here rather than 'function' since '.' is written between its arguments rather than before them; we discuss operators in more detail in Section 3.7.

The direct combination of functions by means of the operator '.' which we have seen here is not possible in other programming paradigms, or at least it would be an 'advanced' aspect of the language, rather than appearing on page 11 of an introductory text.

Type abstraction

Before moving on, we point out another crucial issue which we will explore later in the book. We have just given definitions of

```
blackHorse :: Picture
rotate     :: Picture -> Picture
```

which **use** the type Picture and some functions already defined over it, namely flipH and flipV. We were able to write the definitions of blackHorse and rotate *without knowing anything about* the details of the type Picture or about how the 'flip' functions work over pictures, save for the fact that they behave as we have described.

Treating the type Picture in this way is called **type abstraction**: as users of the type we don't need to concern ourselves with how the type is defined. The advantage of this is that the definitions we give apply *however* pictures are modelled. We might choose to model them in different ways in different situations; whatever the case, the function composition flipH . flipV will rotate a picture through 180°. Chapter 16 discusses this in more detail, and explains the Haskell mechanism to support type abstraction. In the next section we preview other important features of Haskell.

1.9 Looking forward: a model of pictures

We include this section in the first chapter of the book for two reasons. To start with, we want to describe one straightforward way in which Pictures can be modelled in Haskell. Secondly, we want to provide an informal preview of a number of aspects of Haskell which make it a powerful and distinctive programming tool. As we go along we will indicate the parts of the book where we expand on the topics first introduced here.

Our model consists of two-dimensional, monochrome pictures built from **characters**. Characters are the individual letters, digits, spaces and so forth which can be typed at the computer keyboard and which can also be shown on a computer screen. In Haskell the characters are given by the built-in type Char.

This model has the advantage that it is straightforward to view these pictures on a computer terminal window (or if we are using Windows, in the Hugs window). On the other hand, there are other more sophisticated models; details of these can be found at the Web site for the book, mentioned on page 7.

Our version of the horse picture, and the same picture flipped in horizontal and vertical mirrors will be

```
.......##...        ......##....        ...##.......
.....##..#..        .....#.#....        ..#..##.....
...##.....#.        ....#..#....        .#.....##...
..#.......#.        ...#...#....        .#.......#..
..#...#...#.        ..#...#.....        .#...#...#..
..#...###.#.        .#....#..##.        .#.###...#..
.#....#..##.        ..#...###.#.        .##..#....#.
..#...#.....        ..#...#...#.        .....#...#..
...#...#....        ..#.......#.        ....#...#...
....#..#....        ...##.....#.        ....#..#....
.....#.#....        .....##..#..        ....#.#.....
......##....        .......##...        ....##......
```

horse   flipH horse   flipV horse

where we use dots to show the white parts of the pictures.

How are the pictures built from characters? In our model we think of a picture as being made up of a **list** of lines, that is a collection of lines coming one after another in order. Each line can be seen in a similar way as a list of characters. Because we often deal with collections of things when programming, lists are built into Haskell. More specifically, given any type – like characters or lines – Haskell contains a type of lists of that type, and so in particular we can model pictures as we have already explained, using lists of characters to represent lines, and lists of lines to represent pictures.

With this model of Pictures, we can begin to think about how to model functions over pictures. A first definition comes easily; to reflect a picture in a horizontal mirror each line is unchanged, but the order of the lines is reversed: in other words we reverse the list of lines:

```
flipH = reverse
```

where reverse is a built-in function to reverse the order of items in a list. How do we reflect a picture in a vertical mirror? The ordering of the lines is not affected, but instead *each line is to be reversed*. We can write

```
flipV = map reverse
```

since map is the Haskell function which applies a function to each of the items in a list, individually. In the definitions of flipH and flipV we can begin to see the power and elegance of functional programming in Haskell.

- We have used reverse to reverse a list of lines in flipH and to reverse each line in flipV: this is because the same definition of the function reverse can be used over *every* type of list. This is an example of polymorphism, or generic programming, which is examined in detail in Section 5.7.

- In defining flipV we see the function map applied to its argument reverse, *which is itself a function*. This makes map a very general function, as it can have any desired action on the elements of the list, specified by the function which is its argument. This is the topic of Chapter 9.

- Finally, the *result* of applying map to reverse is itself a function. This covered in Chapter 10.

The last two facts show that functions are 'first-class citizens' and can be handled in exactly the same way as any other sort of object like numbers or pictures. The combination of this with polymorphism means that in a functional language we can write very general functions like reverse and map, which can be applied in a multitude of different situations.

The examples we have looked at here are not out of the ordinary. We can see that other functions over pictures have similarly simple definitions. We place one picture above another simply by joining together the two lists of lines to make one list. This is done by the built-in operator ++, which joins together two lists:[1]

```
above = (++)
```

To place two pictures sideBySide we have to join corresponding lines together, thus

```
.......##...    ++    ......##....
.....##..#..    ++    .....#.#....
...##.....#.    ++    ....#..#....
..#.......#.    ++    ...#...#....
..#...#...#.    ++    ..#...#.....
..#...###.#.    ++    .#....#..##.
.#....#..##.    ++    ..#...###.#.
..#...#.....    ++    ..#...#...#.
...#...#....    ++    ..#.......#.
....#..#....    ++    ...##.....#.
.....#.#....    ++    .....##..#..
......##....    ++    .......##...
```

and this is defined using the function zipWith. This function is defined to 'zip together' corresponding elements of two lists using – in this case – the operator ++.

```
sideBySide = zipWith (++)
```

The function superimpose is a rather more complicated application of zipWith, and also we can define invertColour using map. We shall return to these examples in Chapter 10.

1.10 Proof

In this section we explore another characteristic aspect of functional programming: proof. A proof is a logical or mathematical argument to show that something holds *in all circumstances*. For example, given any particular right-angled triangle

---

[1] The operator ++ is surrounded by parentheses (...) in this definition so that it is interpreted as a function; we say more about this in Section 3.7.

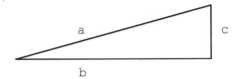

we can check whether or not $a^2=b^2+c^2$ holds. In each case we check, this formula will hold, but this is not in itself enough to show that the formula holds for all a, b and c. A proof, on the other hand, is a general argument which establishes that $a^2=b^2+c^2$ holds whatever right-angled triangle we choose.

How is proof relevant to functional programming? To answer this we will take an example over the Picture type to illustrate what can be done. We saw in Section 1.8 that we can define

```
rotate = flipH . flipV
```

but it is interesting to observe that if we reverse the order in which the flip functions are applied then the composition has the same effect, as illustrated here:

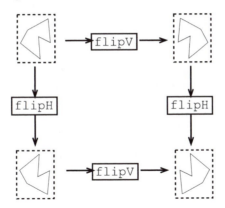

Now, we can express this property as a simple equation between functions:

```
flipH . flipV = flipV . flipH                          (flipProp)
```

Moreover, we can look at our implementations of flipV and flipH and give a logical **proof** that these functions have the property labelled (flipProp) above. The crux of the argument is that the two functions operate independently:

- the function flipV affects each line but leaves the lines in the same order while
- the function flipH leaves each line unaffected, while reversing the order of the list of lines.

Because the two functions affect different aspects of the list it is immaterial which is applied first, since the overall effect of applying the two in either case is to

- reverse each line and reverse the order of the list of lines.

Proof is possible for most programming languages, but it is substantially easier for functional languages than for any other paradigm. Proof of program properties will be a theme in this text, and we start by exploring proof for list-processing functions in Chapter 8.

What benefit is there in having a proof of a property like (flipProp)? It give us *certainty* that our functions have a particular property. Contrast this with the usual approach in computing where we **test** the value of a function at a selection of places; this only gives us the assurance that the function has the property we seek at the test points, and in principle tells us nothing about the function in other circumstances. There are safety-critical situations in which it is highly desirable to be sure that a program behaves properly, and proof has a role here. We are not, however, advocating that testing is unimportant – merely that testing and proof have complementary roles to play in software development.

More specifically, (flipProp) means that we can be sure that however we apply the functions flipH . flipV and flipV . flipH they will have the same effect. We could therefore **transform** a program using flipH . flipV into one using the functions composed in the reverse order, flipV . flipH, and be certain that the new program will have exactly the same effect as the old. Ideas like this can be used to good effect within implementations of languages, and also in developing programs themselves, as we shall see in Section 10.9.

(1.11) Types and functional programming

What is the role of types in functional programming? Giving a type to a function first of all gives us crucial information about how it is to be used. If we know that

```
scale :: Picture -> Int -> Picture
```

we know two things immediately.

- First, scale has two arguments, the first being a Picture and the second an Int; this means that scale can be applied to horse and 3.
- The result of applying scale to this Picture and Int will be a Picture.

The type thus does two things. First, it expresses a **constraint** on how the function scale is applied: it must be applied to a Picture and an Int. Second, the type tells us what the result is if the function is correctly applied: in this case the result is a Picture.

Giving types to functions and other things not only tells us how they can be used; it is also possible to check automatically that functions are being used in the right way and this process – which is called **type checking** – takes place in Haskell. If we use an expression like

```
scale horse horse
```

we will be told that we have made an error in applying scale to two pictures when a picture and a number are what was expected. Moreover, this can be done without knowing the *values* of scale or horse – all that we need to know to perform the check is the *types* of the things concerned. Thus, **type errors** like these are caught before programs are used or expressions are evaluated.

It is remarkable how many errors, due either to mistyping or to misunderstanding the problem, are made by both novice and experienced programmers. A type system therefore helps the user to write correct programs, and to avoid a large proportion of programming pitfalls, both obvious and subtle.

1.12 Calculation and evaluation

We have explained that Hugs can be seen as a general calculator, using the functions and other things defined in a functional program. When we evaluate an expression like

```
23 - (double (3+1))
```
$(\ddagger)$

we need to use the definition of the function:

```
double :: Int -> Int
double n = 2*n
```
(dbl)

This we do by replacing the unknown n in the definition (dbl) by the expression (3+1), giving

```
double (3+1) = 2*(3+1)
```

Now we can replace double (3+1) by 2*(3+1) in ($\ddagger$), and evaluation can continue.

One of the distinctive aspects of functional programming is that such a simple 'calculator' model effectively describes computation with a functional program. Because the model is so straightforward, we can perform evaluations in a **step-by-step** manner; in this text we call these step-by-step evaluations **calculations**. As an example, we now show the calculation of the expression with which we began the discussion.

```
    23 - (double (3+1))
~>  23 - (2*(3+1))                                      using (dbl)
~>  23 - (2*4)                                          arithmetic
~>  23 - 8                                              arithmetic
~>  15                                                  arithmetic
```

where we have used '~>' to indicate a step of the calculation, and on each line we indicate at the right-hand margin how we have reached that line. For instance, the second line of the calculation:

```
~>  23 - (2*(3+1))                                      using (dbl)
```

says that we have reached here using the definition of the double function, (dbl).

In writing a calculation it is sometimes useful to <u>underline</u> the part of the expression which gets modified in transition to the next line. This is, as it were, where we need to focus our attention in reading the calculation. The calculation above will have underlining added thus:

```
23 - (double (3+1))
~→   23 - (2*(3+1))                              using (dbl)
~→   23 - (2*4)                                  arithmetic
~→   23 - 8                                       arithmetic
~→   15                                           arithmetic
```

In what is to come, when we introduce a new feature of Haskell we shall show how it fits into this line-by-line model of evaluation. This has the advantage that we can then explore new ideas by writing down calculations which involve these new concepts.

Summary

As we said at the start, this chapter has three aims. We wanted to introduce some of the fundamental ideas of functional programming; to illustrate them with the example of pictures, and also to give a flavour of what it is that is distinctive about functional programming. To sum up the definitions we have seen,

- a function is something which transforms its inputs to an output;
- a type is a collection of objects of similar sort, such as whole numbers (integers) or pictures;
- every object has a clearly defined type, and we state this type on making a definition;
- functions defined in a program are used in writing expressions to be evaluated by the implementation; and
- the values of expressions can be found by performing calculation by hand, or by using the Hugs interpreter.

In the remainder of the book we will explore different ways of defining new types and functions, as well as following up the topics of polymorphism, functions as arguments and results, data abstraction and proof which we have touched upon in an informal way here.

Chapter 2

Getting started with Haskell and Hugs

Chapter 1 introduced the foundations of functional programming in Haskell. We are now ready to use the Hugs system to do some practical programming, and the principal purpose of this chapter is to give an introduction to Hugs.

In beginning to program we will also learn the basics of the Haskell module system, under which programs can be written in multiple, interdependent files, and which can use the `built-in' functions in the prelude and libraries.

Our programming examples will concentrate on using the `Picture` example introduced in Chapter 1 as well as some simple numerical examples. In support of this we will look at how to download the programs and other background materials for the book, as well as how to obtain Hugs.

We conclude by briefly surveying the kinds of error message that can result from typing something incorrect into Hugs.

2.1 A first Haskell program

We begin the chapter by giving a first Haskell program or **script**, which consists of the numerical examples of Chapter 1. As well as definitions, a script will contain comments.

```
{-##########################################################

        FirstScript.hs

        Simon Thompson, June 1998

        The purpose of this script is
          - to illustrate some simple definitions
            over integers (Int);
          - to give a first example of a script.

##########################################################-}


--        The value size is an integer (Int), defined to be
--        the sum of twelve and thirteen.

size :: Int
size = 12+13


--        The function to square an integer.

square :: Int -> Int
square n = n*n


--        The function to double an integer.

double :: Int -> Int
double n = 2*n


--        An example using double, square and size.

example :: Int
example = double (size - square (2+2))
```

Figure 2.1 An example of a traditional script.

A **comment** in a script is a piece of information of value to a human reader rather than to a computer. It might contain an informal explanation about how a function works, how it should or should not be used, and so forth.

There are two different styles of Haskell script, which reflect two different philosophies of programming.

Traditionally, everything in a program file is interpreted as program text, *except* where it is explicitly indicated that something is a comment. This is the style of

```
###############################################################

    FirstLiterate.lhs

    Simon Thompson, June 1998

    The purpose of this script is
      - to illustrate some simple definitions
        over integers (Int);
      - to give a first example of a literate script.

###############################################################
```

The value size is an integer (Int), defined to be the sum of twelve and thirteen.

```
>        size :: Int
>        size = 12+13
```

The function to square an integer.

```
>        square :: Int -> Int
>        square n = n*n
```

The function to double an integer.

```
>        double :: Int -> Int
>        double n = 2*n
```

An example using double, square and size.

```
>        example :: Int
>        example = double (size - square (2+2))
```

Figure 2.2   An example of a literate script.

FirstScript.hs, in Figure 2.1. Scripts of this style are stored in files with an **extension** '.hs'.

Comments are indicated in two ways. The symbol '--' begins a comment which occupies the part of the line to the right of the symbol. Comments can also be enclosed by the symbols '{-' and '-}'. These comments can be of arbitrary length, spanning more than one line, as well as enclosing other comments; they are therefore called **nested comments**.

The alternative, **literate** approach is to make *everything* in the file commentary on the program, and explicitly to signal the program text in some way. A literate version of the script is given in Figure 2.2, where it can be seen that the program text is on lines beginnning with '>', and is separated from the rest of the text in the file by blank lines. Literate scripts are stored in '.lhs' files.

The two approaches emphasize different aspects of programming. The traditional gives primacy to the program, while the literate approach emphasizes that there is more to programming than simply making the right definitions. Design decisions need to be explained, conditions on using functions and so on need to be written down – this is of benefit both for other users of a program and indeed for ourselves if we re-visit a program we have written some time ago, and hope to modify or extend it. We could see this book itself as an extended 'literate script', since commentary here is interspersed by programs which appear in typewriter font on lines of their own. Typewriter font is also used for URLs and proofs in later chapters.

Downloading the programs

All the programs defined in the book, together with other support material and general Haskell and functional programming links, can be found at the Web site for the book,

```
http://www.cs.ukc.ac.uk/people/staff/sjt/craft2e/
```

The scripts we define are given in literate form.

2.2 Using Hugs

Hugs is a Haskell implementation which runs on both PCs (under Windows 95 and NT) and Unix systems, including Linux. It is freely available via the Haskell home page,

```
http://www.haskell.org/hugs/
```

which is a source of much material on Haskell and its implementations. Further information about downloading and installing Hugs may be found in Appendix E.

In this text we describe the terminal-style interface to Hugs, illustrated in Figure 2.3, because this is common to both Windows and Unix. Experienced PC users should have little difficulty in using the Winhugs system, which gives a Windows-style interface to the Hugs commands, once they have understood how Hugs itself works.

Starting Hugs

To start Hugs on Unix, type hugs to the prompt; to launch Hugs using a particular file, type hugs followed by the name of the file in question, as in

```
hugs FirstLiterate
```

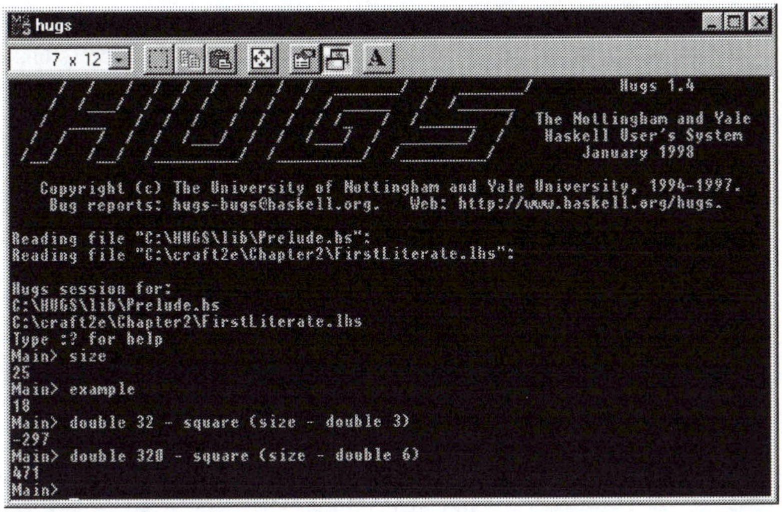

Figure 2.3 A Hugs session on Windows.

On a Windows system, Hugs is launched by choosing it from the appropriate place on the Start menu; to launch Hugs on a particular file, double-click the icon for the file in question.[1]

Haskell scripts carry the extension .hs or .lhs (for literate scripts); only such files can be loaded, and their extensions can be omitted when they are loaded either when Hugs is launched or by a :load command within Hugs.

Evaluating expressions in Hugs

As we said in Section 1.6, the Hugs interpreter will evaluate expressions typed at the prompt. We see in Figure 2.3 the evaluation of size to 25, example to 18 and two more complex expressions, thus

```
Main> double 32 - square (size - double 3)
-297
Main> double 320 - square (size - double 6)
471
Main>
```

where we have indicated the machine output by using a slanted font; user input appears in unslanted form. The **prompt** here, Main>, will be explained in Section 2.4 below.

As can be seen from the examples, we can evaluate expressions which use the definitions in the current script. In this case it is FirstLiterate.lhs (or FirstScript.hs).

---

[1] This assumes that the appropriate registry entries have been made; we work here with the standard installation of Hugs as discussed in Appendix E.

One of the advantages of the Hugs interface is that it is easy to experiment with functions, trying different evaluations simply by typing the expressions at the keyboard. If we want to evaluate a complex expression, it might be sensible to add it to the program, as in the definition

```
test :: Int
test = double 320 - square (size - double 6)
```

All that we then need to do is to type `test` to the *Main>* prompt.

Hugs commands

Hugs commands begin with a colon, ':'. A summary of the main commands follows.

`:load parrot`	Load the Haskell file `parrot.hs` or `parrot.lhs`. The file extension `.hs` or `.lhs` does not need to be included in the filename.
`:reload`	Repeat the last load command.
`:edit first.lhs`	Edit the file `first.lhs` in the default editor. Note that the file extension `.hs` or `.lhs` is needed in this case. See the following section for more information on editing.
`:type exp`	Give the type of the expression `exp`. For example, the result of typing `:type size+2` is `Int`.
`:info name`	Give information about the thing named `name`.
`:find name`	Open the editor on the file containing the definition of `name`.
`:quit`	Quit the system.
`:?`	Give a list of the Hugs commands.
`!com`	Escape to perform the Unix or DOS command `com`.

All the ':' commands can be shortened to their initial letter, giving `:l parrot` and so forth. Details of other commands can be found in the comprehensive on-line Hugs documentation which can be read using a Web browser. On a standard Windows installation it is to be found at

```
C:\hugs\docs\manual-html\manual_contents.html
```

but in general you will need to consult locally to find its location on the system which you are using.

Editing scripts

Hugs can be connected to a 'default' text editor, so that Hugs commands such as `:edit` and `:find` use this editor. This may well be determined by your local set-up. The 'default' default editor on Unix is `vi`; on Windows systems `edit` or `notepad` might be used. Details of how to `:set` values such as the default editor are discussed in Appendix E.

Using the Hugs `:edit` command causes the editor to be invoked on the appropriate file. When the editor is quit, the updated file is loaded automatically. However, it is more convenient to keep the editor running in a separate window and to reload the file by:

● writing the updated file from the editor (without quitting it), and then

● reloading the file in Hugs using :reload or :reload filename.

In this way the editor is still open on the file should it need further modification.

We now give some introductory exercises for using Hugs on the first example programs.

A first Hugs session

Task 1

Load the file FirstLiterate.lhs into Hugs, and evaluate the following expressions

```
square size
square
double (square 2)
$$
square (double 2)
23 - double (3+1)
23 - double 3+1
$$ + 34
13 'div' 5
13 'mod' 5
```

On the basis of this can you work out the purpose of $$?

Task 2

Use the Hugs command :type to tell you the type of each of these, apart from $$.

Task 3

What is the effect of typing each of the following?

```
double square
2 double
```

Try to give an explanation of the results that you obtain.

Task 4

Edit the file FirstLiterate.lhs to include definitions of functions from integers to integers which behave as follows.

- The function should double its input and square the result of that.
- The function should square its input and double the result of that.

Your solution should include declarations of the types of the functions.

(2.3) The standard prelude and the Haskell libraries

We saw in Chapter 1 that Haskell has various built-in types, such as integers and lists and functions over those types, including the arithmetic functions and the list functions map and ++. Definitions of these are contained in a file, the **standard prelude**, Prelude.hs. When Haskell is used, the default is to load the standard prelude, and this can be seen in Figure 2.3 in the line

```
Reading file: "C:\HUGS\lib\Prelude.hs";
```

which precedes the processing of the file FirstLiterate.lhs on which Hugs was invoked.

As Haskell has developed over the last decade, the prelude has also grown. In order to make the prelude smaller, and to free up some of the names used in it, many of the definitions have been moved into **standard libraries**, which can be included when they are needed. We shall say more about these libraries as we discuss particular parts of the language.

As well as the standard libraries, the Hugs distribution includes various contributed libraries which support concurrency, functional animations and so forth. Again, we will mention these as we go along. Other Haskell systems also come with contributed libraries, but all systems support the standard libraries.

In order to use the libraries we need to know something about Haskell modules, which we turn to now.

(2.4) Modules

A typical piece of computer software will contain thousands of lines of program text. To make this manageable, we need to split it into smaller components, which we call modules.

A **module** has a name and will contain a collection of Haskell definitions. To introduce a module called Ant we begin the program text in the file thus:

```
module Ant where
   ...
```

A module may also **import** definitions from other modules. The module Bee will import the definitions in Ant by including an import statement, thus:

```
module Bee where
import Ant
   ...
```

The import statement means that we can use all the definitions in Ant when making definitions in Bee. In dealing with modules in this text we adopt the conventions that

● there is exactly one module per file;
● the file Blah.hs or Blah.lhs contains the module Blah.

The module mechanism supports the libraries we discussed in Section 2.3, but we can also use it to include code written by ourselves or someone else.

The module mechanism allows us to control how definitions are imported and also which definitions are made available or **exported** by a module for use by other modules. We look at this in more depth in Chapter 15, where we also ask how modules are best used to support the design of software systems.

We are now in a position to explain why the Hugs prompt appears as *Main>*. The prompt shows the name of the top-level module currently loaded in Hugs, and in the absence of a name for the module it is called the 'Main' module, discussed in Chapter 15.

In the light of what we have seen so far, we can picture a Hugs session thus:

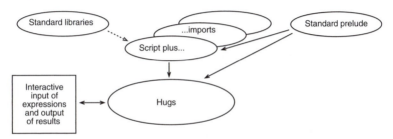

The current script will have access to the standard prelude, and to those modules which it imports; these might include modules from the standard libraries, which are found in the same directory as the standard prelude. The user interacts with Hugs, providing expressions to evaluate and other commands and receiving the results of the evaluations.

The next section revisits the picture example of Chapter 1, which is used to give a practical illustration of modules.

(2.5) A second example: Pictures

The running example in Chapter 1 was of pictures, and in Figure 2.4 we show parts of a script implementing pictures. We have omitted some of the definitions, replacing them with ellipses '...'. The module here is called Pictures, and can be downloaded from the Web page for this text, mentioned on page 22. This module is imported into another module by the statement

```
import Pictures
```

The only new aspect to the example here is the function

```
printPicture :: Picture -> IO ()
```

```
>        module Pictures where

>        type Picture = ....
```

The horse example used in Craft2e, and a completely white picture.

```
>        horse , white :: Picture
>        horse = ....
>        white = ....
```

Getting a picture onto the screen.

```
>        printPicture :: Picture -> IO ()
>        printPicture = ....
```

Reflection in vertical and horizontal mirrors.

```
>        flipV , flipH :: Picture -> Picture
>        flipV = map reverse
>        flipH = reverse
```

One picture above another. To maintain the rectangular property, the pictures need to have the same width.

```
>        above :: Picture -> Picture -> Picture
>        above = (++)
```

One picture next to another. To maintain the rectangular property, the pictures need to have the same height.

```
>        sideBySide :: Picture -> Picture -> Picture
>        sideBySide = zipWith (++)
```

Superimpose two pictures (assumed to be same size).

```
>        superimpose :: Picture -> Picture -> Picture
>        superimpose = ....
```

Invert the black and white in the picture.

```
>        invertColour :: Picture -> Picture
>        invertColour = ....
```

Figure 2.4 A view of the Pictures script.

which is used to display a Picture on the screen. The type IO is a part of the Haskell mechanism for input/output (I/O). We examine this mechanism in detail in Chapter 18; for the present it is enough to know that if horse is the name of the picture used in the earlier examples, then the effect of the function application

```
printPicture horse
```

is the display

```
.......##...
.....##..#..
...##.....#.
..#.......#.
..#...#...#.
..#...###.#.
.#....#..##.
..#...#.....
...#...#....
....#..#....
.....#.#....
......##....
```

first seen in Chapter 1. Any Picture can be printed in a similar way.

In the remainder of this section we present a series of practical exercises designed to use the module Pictures.lhs.

Exercises

2.1 Define a module UsePictures which imports Pictures and contains definitions of blackHorse, rotate and rotateHorse which can use the definitions imported from Pictures.

In the remaining questions you are expected to add other definitions to your module UsePictures.

2.2 How would you make a definition of a black rectangle? How could you do this without using white, but assuming that you have a function superimpose defined as discussed on page 5?

2.3 How could you make the picture

Try to find two different ways of getting the result. It may help to work with pieces of white and black paper.

Using your answer to the first part of this question, how would you define a chess (or checkers) board, which is an 8 × 8 board of alternating squares?

2.4 Three variants of the last picture which involve the 'horse' pictures are

How would you produce these three?

2.5 Give another variant of the 'horse' pictures in the previous question, and show how it could be created. Note: a nice variant is

(2.6) Errors and error messages

No system can guarantee that what you type is sensible, and Hugs is no exception. If something is wrong, either in an expression to be evaluated or in a script, you will receive an **error message**. Try typing

```
2+(3+4
```

to the Hugs prompt. The error here is in the **syntax**, and is like a sentence in English which does not have the correct grammatical structure, such as 'Fishcake our camel'.

The expression has too few parentheses: after the '4', a closing parenthesis is expected, to match with the opening parenthesis before '3'. The error message reflects this by saying that what follows '4' is unexpected:

```
ERROR: Syntax error in expression (unexpected end of input)
```

In a similar way typing 2+(3+4)) results in the message

```
ERROR: Syntax error in input (unexpected ')')
```

Now try typing the following expression.

```
double square
```

This gives a **type** error, since double is applied to the function square, rather than an integer:

```
ERROR: Type error in application
*** expression    : double square
*** term          : square
*** type          : Int -> Int
*** does not match : Int
```

The message indicates that something of type Int was expected, but something of type Int -> Int was present instead. Here double expects something of type Int as its argument, but square of type Int -> Int is found in the place of an integer.

When you get an error message like the one above you need to look at how the **term**, in this case square of type Int -> Int, does not match the **context** in which it is used: the context is given in the second line (double square) and the type required by the context, Int, is given in the last line.

Type errors do not always give rise to such well-structured error messages. Typing either 4 double or 4 5 will give rise to a message like

```
ERROR: ... is not an instance of class ...
```

We will explore the technical details behind these messages in a later chapter; for now it is sufficient to read these as 'Type Error!'.

The last kind of error we will see are **program errors**. Try the expression

```
4 'div' (3*2-6)
```

We cannot divide by zero (what would the result be?) and so we get the message

```
Program error: {primDivInt 4 0}
```

indicating that a division of 4 by 0 has occurred. More details about the error messages produced by Hugs can be found in Appendix F.

Summary

The main aim of this chapter is practical, to acquaint the reader with the Hugs implementation of Haskell. We have seen how to write simple Hugs programs, to load them into Hugs and then to evaluate expressions which use the definitions in the module.

Larger Haskell programs are structured into modules, which can be imported into other modules. Modules support the Haskell library mechanism and we illustrate modules in the case study of Pictures introduced in Chapter 1.

We concluded the chapter with an overview of the possible syntax, type and program errors in expressions or scripts submitted to Hugs.

The first two chapters have laid down the theoretical and practical foundations for the rest of the book, which explores the many aspects of functional programming using Haskell and the Hugs interpreter.

Chapter 3

Basic types and definitions

We have now covered the basics of functional programming and have shown how simple programs are written, modified and run in Haskell. This chapter covers Haskell's most important **basic types** and also shows how to write definitions of functions which have multiple **cases** to cover alternative situations. We conclude by looking at some of the details of the **syntax** of Haskell.

Haskell contains a variety of numerical types. We have already seen the `Int` type in use; we shall cover this and also the type `Float` of **floating-point** fractional numbers.

Often in programming we want to make a choice of values, according to whether or not a particular **condition** holds. Such conditions include tests of whether one number is greater than another; whether two values are equal, and so on. The results of these tests – `True` if the condition holds and `False` if it fails – are called the **Boolean** values, after the nineteeth-century logician George Boole, and they form the Haskell type `Bool`. In this chapter we cover the Booleans, and how they are used to give choices in function definitions by means of **guards**.

Finally, we look at the type of characters – individual letters, digits, spaces and so forth – which are given by the Haskell type `Char`.

The chapter provides reference material for the basic types; a reader may skip the treatment of `Float` and much of the detail about `Char`, referring back to this chapter when necessary.

Each section here contains examples of functions, and the exercises build on these. Looking ahead, this chapter gives a foundation on top of which we look at a variety of different ways that programs can be designed and written, which is the topic of the next chapter.

3.1   The Booleans: `Bool`

The Boolean values `True` and `False` represent the results of tests, which might, for instance, compare two numbers for equality, or check whether the first is smaller than the second. The Boolean type in Haskell is called `Bool`. The Boolean operators provided in the language are:

`&&`	and
`||`	or
`not`	not

Because `Bool` contains only two values, we can define the meaning of Boolean operators by **truth tables** which show the result of applying the operator to each possible combination of arguments. For instance, the third line of the first table says that the value of `False && True` is `False` and that the value of `False || True` is `True`.

t_1	t_2	t_1 `&&` t_2	t_1`||` t_2
T	T	T	T
T	F	F	T
F	T	F	T
F	F	F	F

t_1	`not` t_1
T	F
F	T

Booleans can be the arguments to or the results of functions. We now look at some examples. 'Exclusive or' is the function which returns `True` exactly when one but not both of its arguments have the value `True`; it is like the 'or' of a restaurant menu: you may have vegetarian moussaka or fish as your main course, but not both! The 'built-in or', `||`, is 'inclusive' because it returns `True` if either one or both of its arguments are `True`.

```
exOr :: Bool -> Bool -> Bool
exOr x y = (x || y) && not (x && y)
```

We can picture the function definition using boxes for functions, and lines for values, as we saw in Chapter 1. Lines coming into a function box represent the arguments, and the line going out the result.

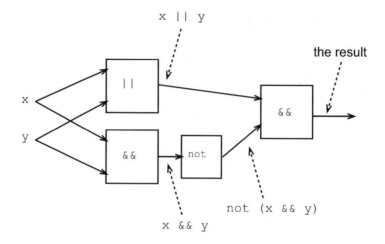

Boolean values can also be compared for equality and inequality using the operators == and /=, which both have the type

```
Bool -> Bool -> Bool
```

Note that /= is the same function as exOr, since both return the result True when exactly one of their arguments is True.

Literals and definitions

Expressions like True and False, and also numbers like 2, are known as **literals**. These are values which are given literally, and which need no evaluation; the result of evaluating a literal is the literal itself.

We can use the literals True and False as arguments, in defining not for ourselves:

```
myNot :: Bool -> Bool
myNot True  = False
myNot False = True
```

We can also use a combination of literals and variables on the left-hand side of equations defining exOr:

```
exOr True  x = not x
exOr False x = x
```

Here we see a definition of a function which uses two equations: the first applies whenever the first argument to exOr is True and the second when that argument is False.

Definitions which use True and False on the left-hand side of equations are often more readable than definitions which only have variables on the left-hand side. This is a simple example of the general **pattern matching** mechanism in Haskell, which we examine in detail in Section 7.1.

3.1 Give another version of the definition of 'exclusive or' which works informally thus: 'exclusive or of x and y will be `True` if either x is `True` and y is `False`, or vice versa'.

3.2 Give the 'box and line' diagram corresponding to your answer to the previous question.

3.3 Using literals on the left-hand side we can make the truth table for a function into its Haskell definition. Complete the following definition of `exOr` in this style.

```
exOr True True  = ...
exOr True False = ...
   ...
```

3.4 Give two different definitions of the `nAnd` function

```
nAnd :: Bool -> Bool -> Bool
```

which returns the result `True` except when both its arguments are `True`. Give a diagram illustrating one of your definitions.

3.5 Give line-by-line calculations of

```
nAnd True True
nAnd True False
```

for each of your definitions of `nAnd` in the previous exercise.

3.2 The integers: `Int`

The Haskell type `Int` contains the integers. The integers are the whole numbers, used for counting; they are written thus:

```
0
45
-3452
2147483647
```

The `Int` type represents integers in a fixed amount of space, and so can only represent a finite range of integers. The value `maxBound` gives the greatest value in the type, which happens to be 2147483647. For the majority of integer calculations these fixed size numbers are suitable, but if larger numbers are required we may use the `Integer` type, which can accurately represent whole numbers of any size.[1]

---

[1] We choose to work with `Int` here because various standard Haskell functions which we introduce later in the chapter use the `Int` type.

We do arithmetic on integers using the following operators and functions; the operations we discuss here also apply to the `Integer` type.

`+`	The sum of two integers.
`*`	The product of two integers.
`^`	Raise to the power; 2^3 is 8.
`-`	The difference of two integers, when infix: `a-b`; the integer of opposite sign, when prefix: `-a`.
`div`	Whole number division; for example `div 14 3` is 4. This can also be written 14 `'div'` 3.
`mod`	The remainder from whole number division; for example `mod 14 3` (or 14 `'mod'` 3) is 2.
`abs`	The absolute value of an integer; remove the sign.
`negate`	The function to change the sign of an integer.

Note that `'mod'` surrounded by **backquotes** is written between its two arguments, is an **infix** version of the function `mod`. Any function can be made infix in this way.

Note: Negative literals

A common pitfall occurs with negative literals. For example the number minus twelve is written as `-12`, but the prefix '`-`' can often get confused with the infix operator to subtract one number from another and can lead to unforeseen and confusing type error messages. For example, the application

`negate -34`

is interpreted as 'negate minus 34' and thus leads to the Hugs error message

`ERROR: a -> a is not an instance of class "Num"`

If you are in any doubt about the source of an error and you are dealing with negative numbers you should enclose them in parentheses, thus: `negate (-34)`. See Section 3.7 for more details.

In what follows we will use the term the **natural numbers** for the non-negative integers: 0, 1, 2, ...

Relational operators

There are ordering and (in)equality relations over the integers, as there are over all basic types. These functions take two integers as input and return a `Bool`, that is either `True` or `False`. The relations are

`>`	greater than (and not equal to)
`>=`	greater than or equal to
`==`	equal to
`/=`	not equal to
`<=`	less than or equal to
`<`	less than (and not equal to)

A simple example using these definitions is a function to test whether three Ints are equal.

```
threeEqual :: Int -> Int -> Int -> Bool
threeEqual m n p = (m==n) && (n==p)
```

3.6 Explain the effect of the function defined here:

```
mystery :: Int -> Int -> Int -> Bool
mystery m n p = not ((m==n) && (n==p))
```

Hint: if you find it difficult to answer this question directly, try to see what the function does on some example inputs.

3.7 Define a function

```
threeDifferent :: Int -> Int -> Int -> Bool
```

so that the result of threeDifferent m n p is True only if all three of the numbers m, n and p are different.

What is your answer for threeDifferent 3 4 3? Explain why you get the answer that you do.

3.8 This question is about the function

```
fourEqual :: Int -> Int -> Int -> Int -> Bool
```

which returns the value True only if all four of its arguments are equal.

Give a definition of fourEqual modelled on the definition of threeEqual above. Now give a definition of fourEqual which *uses* the function threeEqual in its definition. Compare your two answers.

3.9 Give line-by-line calculations of

```
threeEqual (2+3) 5 (11 'div' 2)
mystery (2+4) 5 (11 'div' 2)
threeDifferent (2+4) 5 (11 'div' 2)
fourEqual (2+3) 5 (11 'div' 2) (21 'mod' 11)
```

3.3 Overloading

Both integers and Booleans can be compared for equality, and the same symbol == is used for both these operations, even though they are different. Indeed, == will be used for equality over any type t for which we are able to define an equality operator. This means that (==) will have the type

```
Int  -> Int  -> Bool
Bool -> Bool -> Bool
```

and indeed `t -> t -> Bool` if the type `t` carries an equality.

Using the same symbol or name for different operations is called **overloading**. A number of symbols in Haskell are overloaded, and we will see in Chapter 12 how overloading is handled in the type system of Haskell, and also how users can define their own overloaded operators or names.

(3.4) Guards

Here we explore how conditions or **guards** are used to give alternatives in the definitions of functions. A guard is a Boolean expression, and these expressions are used to express various cases in the definition of a function.

We take as a running example in this section functions which compare integers for size, and start by looking at the example of the function to return the maximum value of two integers. When the two numbers are the same then we call their common value the maximum.

```
max :: Int -> Int -> Int
max x y
  | x >= y      = x
  | otherwise   = y
```

How do we read a definition like this, which appears in the Haskell prelude?

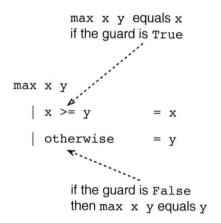

In general, if the first guard (here x>=y) is True then the corresponding value is the result (x in this case). On the other hand, if the first guard is False, then we look at the second, and so on. An `otherwise` guard will hold whatever the arguments, so that in the case of `max` the result is x if x>=y and y otherwise, that is in the case that y>x.

An example in which there are multiple guards is a definition of the maximum of three inputs.

```
maxThree :: Int -> Int -> Int -> Int
maxThree x y z
  | x >= y && x >= z    = x
  | y >= z              = y
  | otherwise           = z
```

How does this definition work? The first guard

```
x >= y && x >= z
```

tests whether x is the maximum of the three inputs; if it is True the corresponding result is x. If the guard fails, then x is not the maximum, so there has to be a choice between y and z. The second guard is therefore

```
y >= z
```

If this holds, the result is y; otherwise the result is z. We will go back to the example of maxThree in Section 4.1.

We first gave a general form for simple function definitions in Chapter 1; we can now strengthen this to give a general form for function definitions with guards in Figure 3.1. Note that the otherwise is not compulsory.

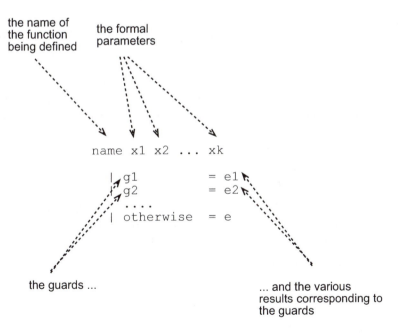

Figure 3.1 The general form for function definitions with guards.

We also saw in Chapter 1 that we can write down line-by-line **calculations** of the values of expressions. How do guards fit into this model? When we apply a function to its arguments we need to know which of the cases applies, and to do this we need to evaluate the guards until we find a guard whose value is True; once we find this, we can evaluate the corresponding result. Taking the example of maxThree, we give two examples in which we perform the evaluation of guards on lines beginning '??'.

```
maxThree 4 3 2
    ?? 4>=3 && 4>=2
    ?? ⇝   True && True
    ?? ⇝   True
  ⇝   4
```

In this example the first guard we try, 4>=3 && 4>=2, gives True and so the result is the corresponding value, 4. In the second example we have to evaluate more than one guard.

```
maxThree 6 (4+3) 5
    ?? 6>=(4+3) && 6>=5
    ?? ⇝   6>=7 && 6>=5
    ?? ⇝   False && True
    ?? ⇝   False
    ?? 7>=5
    ?? ⇝   True
  ⇝   7
```

In this example we first evaluate the first guard, 6>=(4+3) && 6>=5, which results in False; we therefore evaluate the second guard, 7>=5, which gives True, and so the result is 7.

Once we have calculated the value of the second argument, (4+3), we do not re-calculate its value when we look at it again. This is not just a trick on our part; the Hugs system will only evaluate an argument like (4+3) once, keeping its value in case it is needed again, as indeed it is in this calculation. This is one aspect of lazy evaluation, which is the topic of Chapter 17.

Conditional expressions

Guards are conditions which distinguish between different cases in definitions of functions. We can also write general conditional expressions by means of the if...then...else construct of Haskell. The value of

```
if condition then m else n
```

is m if the condition is True and is n if the condition is False, so that the expression if False then 3 else 4 has the value 4, and in general

```
if x >= y then x else y
```

will be the maximum of x and y. This shows that we can write max in a different way thus:

```
max :: Int -> Int -> Int
max x y
    = if x >= y then x else y
```

We tend to use the guard form rather than this, but we will see examples below where the use of if ... then ... else ... is more natural.

Note: Redefining prelude functions

The max function is defined in the prelude, Prelude.hs, and if a definition

max :: Int -> Int -> Int

appears in a script maxDef.hs then this definition will conflict with the prelude definition, leading to the Hugs error message

ERROR "maxDef.hs" (line 3): Definition of variable "max" clashes with import

To redefine the prelude functions max and min, say, the line

import Prelude hiding (max,min)

which overrides the usual import of the prelude should be included at the top of the file maxDef.hs, after its module statement (if any).

Many of the functions defined in this text are in fact included in the prelude, and so this technique needs to be used whenever you want to redefine one of these.

Exercises

3.10 Give calculations of

    max (3-2) (3*8)
    maxThree (4+5) (2*6) (100 'div' 7)

3.11 Give definitions of the functions

    min   :: Int -> Int -> Int
    minThree :: Int -> Int -> Int -> Int

which calculate the minimum of two and three integers, respectively.

3.5 The characters: Char

People and computers communicate using keyboard input and screen output, which are based on sequences of **characters**, that is letters, digits and 'special' characters like space, tab, newline and end-of-file. Haskell contains a built-in type of characters, called Char.

Literal characters are written inside single quotes, thus 'd' is the Haskell representative of the character d. Similarly '3' is the character three. Some special characters are represented as follows

tab	'\t'
newline	'\n'
backslash (\)	'\\'
single quote (')	'\''
double quote (")	'\"'

There is a standard coding for characters as integers, called the ASCII coding. The capital letters 'A' to 'Z' have the sequence of codes from 65 to 90, and the small letters 'a' to 'z' the codes 97 to 122. The character with code 34, for example, can be written '\34', and '9' and '\97' have the same meaning. ASCII has recently been extended to the Unicode standard, which contains characters from fonts other than English.

There are conversion functions between characters and their numerical codes which convert an integer into a character, and vice versa.

```
ord :: Char -> Int
chr :: Int -> Char
```

The coding functions can be used in defining functions over Char. To convert a small letter to a capital an offset needs to be added to its code:

```
offset :: Int
offset = ord 'A' - ord 'a'

toUpper :: Char -> Char
toUpper ch = chr (ord ch + offset)
```

Note that the offset is named, rather than appearing as a part of toUpper, as in

```
toUpper ch = chr (ord ch + (ord 'A' - ord 'a'))
```

This is standard practice, making the program both easier to read and to modify. To change the offset value, we just need to change the definition of offset, rather than having to change the function (or functions) which use it.

Characters can be compared using the ordering given by their codes. So, since the digits 0 to 9 occupy a block of adjacent codes 48 to 57, we can check whether a character is a digit thus:

```
isDigit :: Char -> Bool
isDigit ch = ('0' <= ch) && (ch <= '9')
```

The standard prelude contains a number of conversion functions like toUpper, and discrimination functions like isDigit; details can be found in the file Prelude.hs. Other useful functions over Char are to be found in the library Char.hs.

> **Note: Characters and names**
>
> It is easy to confuse a and 'a'. To summarize the difference, a is a name or a variable, which if defined may have any type whatever, whereas 'a' is a literal character and is therefore of type Char.
>
> In a similar way, it is easy to confuse the number 0 and the character '0'.

Exercises

3.12 Define a function to convert small letters to capitals which returns unchanged characters which are not small letters.

3.13 Define the function

```
charToNum :: Char -> Int
```

which converts a digit like '8' to its value, 8. The value of non-digits should be taken to be 0.

3.6 Floating-point numbers: Float

In Section 3.2 we introduced the Haskell type Int of integers. In calculating we also want to use numbers with fractional parts, which are represented in Haskell by the **floating-point** numbers which make up the type Float. We do not use Float heavily in what follows, and so this section can be omitted on first reading and used as reference material to be consulted when necessary.

Internal to the Haskell system there is a fixed amount of space allocated to representing each Float. This has the effect that not all fractions can be represented by floating-point numbers, and arithmetic over them will not be always be exact. It is possible to use the type of double-precision floating-point numbers, Double for greater precision, or for full-precision fractions built from Integer there is the type Rational. As this is a programming tutorial we restrict our attention to the types Int and Float but we shall survey the numerical types briefly in Chapter 12.

Literal floats in Haskell can be given by decimal numerals, such as

```
0.31426
-23.12
567.347
4523.0
```

The numbers are called floating point because the position of the decimal point is not the same for all Floats; depending upon the particular number, more of the space can be used to store the integer or the fractional part.

Haskell also allows literal floating-point numbers in **scientific notation**. These take the form below, where their values are given in the right-hand column of the table

`+ - *`	`Float -> Float -> Float`	Add, subtract, multiply.
`/`	`Float -> Float -> Float`	Fractional division.
`^`	`Float -> Int -> Float`	Exponentiation $x \hat{} n = x^n$ for a natural number n.
`**`	`Float -> Float -> Float`	Exponentiation $x**y = x^y$.
`==,/=,<,>,` `<=,>=`	`Float -> Float -> Bool`	Equality and ordering operations.
`abs`	`Float -> Float`	Absolute value.
`acos,asin` `atan`	`Float -> Float`	The inverse of cosine, sine and tangent.
`ceiling` `floor` `round`	`Float -> Int`	Convert a fraction to an integer by rounding up, down, or to the closest integer.
`cos,sin` `tan`	`Float -> Float`	Cosine, sine and tangent.
`exp`	`Float -> Float`	Powers of e.
`fromInt`	`Int -> Float`	Convert an `Int` to a `Float`.
`log`	`Float -> Float`	Logarithm to base e.
`logBase`	`Float -> Float -> Float`	Logarithm to arbitrary base, provided as first argument.
`negate`	`Float -> Float`	Change the sign of a number.
`pi`	`Float`	The constant pi.
`signum`	`Float -> Float`	`1.0`, `0.0` or `-1.0` according to whether the argument is positive, zero or negative.
`sqrt`	`Float -> Float`	(Positive) square root.

Figure 3.2   Floating-point operations and functions.

`231.61e7`	231.61×10^7	$= 2,316,100,000$
`231.6e-2`	231.61×10^{-2}	$= 2.3161$
`-3.412e03`	-3.412×10^3	$= -3412$

This representation is more convenient than the decimal numerals above for very large and small numbers. Consider the number 2.1^{444}. This will need well over a hundred digits before the decimal point, and this would not be possible in decimal notation of limited size (usually 20 digits at most). In scientific notation, it will be written as `1.162433e+143`.

Haskell provides a range of operators and functions over `Float` in the standard prelude. The table in Figure 3.2 gives their name, type and a brief description of their behaviour. Included are the

- standard mathematical operations: square root, exponential, logarithm and trigonometric functions;

- functions to convert integers to floating-point numbers: `fromInt`, and vice versa: `ceiling`, `floor` and `round`.

Haskell can be used as a numeric calculator. Try typing the expression which follows to the Hugs prompt:

```
sin (pi/4) * sqrt 2
```

Overloaded literals and functions

In Haskell the numbers 4 and 2 belong to both `Int` and `Float`; they are overloaded, as discussed in Section 3.3. This is also true of some of the numeric functions; addition, for instance, has both the types

```
Int -> Int -> Int
Float -> Float -> Float
```

and the relational operators `==` and so forth are available over all basic types. We shall explore this idea of overloading in more detail when we discuss type classes below in Chapter 12.

Note: Converting integers to floating-point numbers

Although literals are overloaded, there is no automatic conversion from `Int` to `Float`. In general if we wish to add an integer quantity, like `floor 5.6`, to a float, like `6.7`, we will receive an error message if we type

```
(floor 5.6) + 6.7
```

since we are trying to add quantities of two different types. We have to convert the `Int` to a `Float` to perform the addition, thus:

```
fromInt(floor 5.6) + 6.7
```

where `fromInt` takes an `Int` to the corresponding `Float`.

Exercises

3.14 Give a function to return the average of three integers

```
averageThree :: Int -> Int -> Int -> Float
```

Using this function define a function

```
howManyAboveAverage :: Int -> Int -> Int -> Int
```

which returns how many of its inputs are larger than their average value.

The remainder of the questions look at solutions to a quadratic equation

```
a*X² + b*X + c = 0.0
```

where a, b and c are real numbers. The equation has

- two real roots, if b^2 > 4.0*a*c;
- one real root, if b^2 == 4.0*a*c; and
- no real roots, if b^2 < 4.0*a*c.

This assumes that a is non-zero — the case which we call **non-degenerate**. In the degenerate case, there are three sub-cases:

- one real root, if b /= 0.0;
- no real roots, if b == 0.0 and c /= 0.0;
- every real number a root, if b == 0.0 and c == 0.0.

3.15 Write a function

```
numberNDroots :: Float -> Float -> Float -> Int
```

that given the coefficients of the quadratic, a, b and c, will return how many roots the equation has. You may assume that the equation is non-degenerate.

3.16 Using your answer to the last question, write a function

```
numberRoots :: Float -> Float -> Float -> Int
```

that given the coefficients of the quadratic, a, b and c, will return how many roots the equation has. In the case that the equation has every number a root you should return the result 3.

3.17 The formula for the roots of a quadratic is

$$\frac{-b \pm \sqrt{b^2 - 4ac}}{2a}$$

Write definitions of the functions

```
smallerRoot, largerRoot :: Float -> Float -> Float -> Float
```

which return the smaller and larger real roots of the quadratic. In the case that the equation has no real roots or has all values as roots you should return zero as the result of each of the functions.

3.7 Syntax

The syntax of a language describes all the properly formed programs. This section looks at various aspects of the syntax of Haskell, and stresses especially those which might seem unusual or unfamiliar at first sight.

Definitions and layout

A script contains a series of definitions, one after another. How is it clear where one definition ends and another begins? In writing English, the end of a sentence is signalled by a full stop, '.'. In Haskell the **layout** of the program is used to state where one definition ends and the next begins.

Formally, a definition is ended by the first piece of text which lies at the same indentation or to the left of the start of the definition.

When we write a definition, its first character opens up a box which will hold the definition, thus

```
mystery x = x*x
```

Whatever is typed in the box forms part of the definition ...

```
mystery x = x*x

    +x
                +2
```

... until something is found which is on the line or to the left of the line. This closes the box, thus

```
mystery x = x*x

    +x
                +2
```

```
next x = ...
```

In writing a sequence of definitions, it is therefore sensible to give them all the same level of indentation. In our scripts we shall always write top-level definitions starting at the left-hand side of the page, and in literate scripts we will indent the start of each definition by a single 'tab'.

This rule for layout is called the **offside rule** because it is reminiscent of the idea of being 'offside' in soccer. The rule also works for conditional equations such as max and maxThree which consist of more than one clause.

There is, in fact, a mechanism in Haskell for giving an explicit end to part of a definition, just as '.' does in English: the Haskell 'end' symbol is ';'. We can, for instance, use ';' if we wish to write more than one definition on a single line, thus:

```
answer = 42 ;    facSix = 720
```

Note: Layout errors

We see error messages involving ';' even if we have not used it ourselves. If we break the offside rule thus:

```
funny x = x+
1
```

we receive an error message like

```
ERROR .... : Syntax error in expression (unexpected ';')
```

since internally to the system a ';' is placed before the 1 to mark the end of the definition, which does indeed come at an unexpected point.

Recommended layout

The offside rule permits various different styles of layout. In this book for definitions of any size we use the form

```
fun v1 v2 ... vn
  | g1          = e1
  | g2          = e2
  ...
  | otherwise   = er      ( or   | gr      = er)
```

for a **conditional equation** built up from a number of clauses. In this layout, each **clause** starts on a new line, and the guards and results are lined up. Note also that by convention in this text we always specify the type of the function being defined.

If any of the expressions e_i or guards g_i is particularly long, then the guard can appear on a line (or lines) of its own, like this

```
fun v1 v2 ... vn
  | a long guard which may
    go over a number of lines
        = very long expression which goes
          over a number of lines
  | g2        = e2
  ...
```

Names in Haskell

Thus far in the book we have seen a variety of uses of names in definitions and expressions. In a definition like

```
addTwo :: Int -> Int -> Int
addTwo first second = first+second
```

the names or **identifiers** Int, addTwo, first and second are used to name a type, a function and two variables. Identifiers in Haskell must begin with a letter – small or capital – which is followed by an optional sequence of letters, digits, underscores '_' and single quotes.

The names used in definitions of values must begin with a small letter, as must variables and type variables, which are introduced later. On the other hand, capital letters are used to begin type names, such as Int; **constructors**, such as True and False; module names and also the names of type classes, which we shall encounter below.

An attempt to give a function a name which begins with a capital letter, such as

```
Fun x = x+1
```

gives the error message 'Undefined constructor function "Fun"'.

There are some restrictions on how identifiers can be chosen. There is a small collection of **reserved words** which cannot be used; these are

```
case class data default deriving do else if import in infix
infixl infixr instance let module newtype of then type where
```

The special identifiers as, qualified, and hiding have special meanings in certain contexts but can be used as ordinary identifiers.

By convention, when we give names built up from more than one word, we capitalize the first letters of the second and subsequent words, as in 'maxThree'.

The same identifier can be used to name both a function and a variable, or both a type and a type constructor; we recommend strongly that this is *not* done, as it can only lead to confusion.

If we want to **redefine** a name that is already defined in the prelude or one of the libraries we have to **hide** that name on import; details of how to do this are given on page 41.

Haskell is built on top of the Unicode character description standard, which allows symbols from fonts other than those in the ASCII standard. These symbols can be used in identifiers and the like, and Unicode characters – which are described by a 16-bit sequence – can be input to Haskell in the form \u$hhhh$ where each of the h is a hexadecimal (4 bit) digit. In this text we use the ASCII subset of Unicode exclusively.[2]

Operators

The Haskell language contains various operators, like +, ++ and so on. Operators are **infix** functions, so that they are written between their arguments, rather than before them, as is the case for ordinary functions.

In principle it is possible to write all applications of an operator with enclosing parentheses, thus

```
(((4+8)*3)+2)
```

but expressions rapidly become difficult to read. Instead two extra properties of operators allow us to write expressions uncluttered by parentheses.

---

[2] Note that at the time of writing, the Hugs system does not support Unicode characters.

Associativity

If we wish to add the three numbers 4, 8 and 99 we can write either 4+(8+99) or (4+8)+99. The result is the same whichever we write, a property we call the **associativity** of addition. Because of this, we can write

4+8+99

for the sum, unambiguously. Not every operator is associative, however; what happens when we write

4-2-1

for instance? The two different ways of inserting parentheses give

(4-2)-1 = 2-1 = 1   left associative
4-(2-1) = 4-1 = 3   right associative

In Haskell each non-associative operator is classified as either left or right associative. If left associative, any double occurrences of the operator will be parenthesized to the left; if right associative, to the right. The choice is arbitrary, but follows custom as much as possible, and in particular '−' is taken to be left associative.

Binding powers

The way in which an operator associates allows us to resolve expressions like

2^3^2

where the same operator occurs twice, but what is done when two different operators occur, as in the following expressions?

2+3*4
3^4*2

For this purpose the **binding power** or **fixity** of the operators need to be compared. * has binding power 7 while + has 6, so that in 2+3*4 the 3 sticks to the 4 rather than the 2, giving

2+3*4 = 2+(3*4)

In a similar way, ^ with binding power 8 binds more tightly than *, so

3^4*2 = (3^4)*2

A full table of the associativities and binding powers of the predefined Haskell operators is given in Appendix C. In the section 'Do-it-yourself operators' below we discuss how operators are defined in scripts and also how their associativity and binding power can be set or changed by declarations.

> ### Note: Function application
>
> Binding most tightly is function application, which is given by writing the name of the function in front of its argument(s) thus: f v_1 v_2 ... v_n. This binds more tightly than any other operator, so that f n+1 is interpreted as f n plus 1, (f n)+1, rather than f applied to n+1, f (n+1). If in doubt, it is sensible to parenthesize each argument to a function application.
>
> Similarly, as '-' is both an infix and a prefix operator, there is scope for confusion. f -12 will be interpreted as 12 subtracted from f, rather than f applied to -12; the solution again is to bracket the argument.

Operators and functions

Infix operators can be written *before* their arguments, by enclosing the operator in parentheses. We therefore have, for example,

```
(+) :: Int -> Int -> Int
```

so that

```
(+) 2 3 = 2 + 3
```

This conversion is needed later when we make functions into arguments of other functions. We can also convert functions into operators by enclosing the function name in backquotes, thus `name`. We therefore have, using the maximum function defined earlier,

```
2 `max` 3 = max 2 3
```

This notation can make expressions involving **binary** or two-argument functions substantially easier to read.

The fixity and associativity of these operators can be controlled; see Appendix C.

Do-it-yourself operators

The Haskell language allows us to define infix operators directly in exactly the same way as functions. Operator names are built from the operator symbols which include the ASCII symbols

```
! # $ % & * + . / < = > ? \ ^ | : - ~
```

together with the Unicode symbols. An operator name may not begin with a colon.

To define the operator &&& as an integer minimum function, we write

```
(&&&) :: Int -> Int -> Int
x &&& y
  | x > y      = y
  | otherwise  = x
```

The associativity and binding power of the operator can be specified; for details see Appendix C.

Exercises

3.18 Rewrite your solutions to the earlier exercises to use the recommended layout.

3.19 Given the definitions

```
funny x = x+x
 peculiar y = y
```

explain what happens when you remove the space in front of the peculiar.

Summary

This chapter has introduced the base types Int, Float, Char and Bool together with various built-in functions over them. We have seen how Boolean expressions – called guards – allow definitions which have various cases, and this was exemplified by the function returning the maximum of two integer arguments. This definition contains two cases, one which applies when the first argument is the larger and the other when the second is the larger.

Finally, we have seen how the layout of a Haskell program is significant – the end of a definition is implicitly given by the first piece of program text 'offside' of the start of the definition; we have also given an overview of operators in Haskell.

This material, together with what we have seen in earlier chapters, gives us a toolkit which we can use to solve programming problems. In the next chapter we will explore various ways of using that toolkit to solve practical problems.

Chapter 4

Designing and writing programs

In this chapter we step back from discussing the details of Haskell and instead look at how to build programs. We present some general strategies for program design; that is we talk about how programs can be planned *before* we start to write the details. The advice we give here is largely independent of Haskell and will be useful whatever programming language we use.

We follow this by discussing recursion. We begin by concentrating on explaining **why** recursion works, and follow this by looking at **how** to find primitive recursive definitions, extending what we have said about design. We conclude with an optional examination of more general forms of recursion.

Once we have written a definition we need to ask whether it does what it is intended to do. We conclude the chapter by exploring the principles of program testing and examining a number of examples.

4.1 *Where do I start?* Designing a program in Haskell

One theme which we want to emphasize in this book is how we can **design** programs to be written in Haskell. Design is used to mean many different things in computing; the way that we want to think of it is like this:

> **Definition**
>
> Design is the stage before we start writing detailed Haskell code.

In this section we will concentrate on looking at examples, and on talking about the different ways we can try to define functions, but we will also try to give some general advice about how to start writing a program. These are set out as questions we can ask ourselves when we are stuck with a programming problem.

Do I understand what I need to do?

Before we can start to solve a programming problem we need to be clear about what we have to do. Often problems are described in an informal way, and this can mean that the problem either is not fully stated or cannot be solved as it is described.

Suppose we are asked to return the middle of three numbers. It is clear that given the numbers 2, 4 and 3 we should return 3, but when presented with 2, 4 and 2 there are two possible responses.

- We could say that 2 is the middle number because when we write the numbers in order: 2 2 4, then 2 is the number that appears in the middle.
- Alternatively we could say that there is no middle number in this case, since 2 is the lower and 4 the higher, and that we therefore cannot return any result.

What can we learn from this illustration?

- First, that even in simple problems there can be things we have to think about before we start programming.
- Secondly, it is important to realize that there is **no right answer** among the two options given just now: it is up to the person wanting the program written and the programmer to work out between them what is wanted.
- Thirdly, a very good way of thinking about whether we understand the problem is to think about how we expect it to work out in various **examples**.
- Finally, it is worth realizing that often difficulties like this come out at the programming stage, when we have already written a whole lot of definitions; the sooner we spot a problem like this, the more wasted effort we can save.

Another example of this came up in the definition of max in Section 3.4, where we had to say what the function should return when its two arguments were the same. In that case it was sensible to think of the maximum of, say, 3 and 3 as being 3.

Can I say anything about types at this stage?

One thing we can think about at this stage is the types of the various things we are thinking about. We can write

```
middleNumber :: Int -> Int -> Int -> Int
```

as the name and type of the function returning the middle of three numbers without having any idea about how we are going to define the function itself. Nevertheless, it is progress, and also it gives us something to check our definition against when we have written it: if we manage to write a function `middleNumber` but it does not have the type `Int -> Int -> Int -> Int`, then the function cannot be doing what it should.

What do I already know? How can I use this information?

These are crucial questions for a designer of a program. We need to know what resources are available to us for solving the problem at hand: what definitions have we already written which could be useful, what does the language provide in its prelude and libraries? We will obviously learn more about the latter as we go along, but even when we have written only a small number of programs we should always think about how these might help us solve the problem at hand. For instance, in trying to define the function `maxThree` introduced in Section 3.4, we know that we have already got the `max` function, giving the maximum of two numbers.

As well as knowing our resources we also need to know how we can use them; this we look at now. There are two different ways that a definition we already have can be helpful.

We can take the definition of a function as a **model** for what we want to do

In defining `maxThree` we have the resource of already having defined the function `max`. We can think of its definition as a model for how we might define `maxThree`.

In `max` we give the result x on condition that it is the maximum of the two, that is

```
x >= y
```

Our definition of `maxThree` does a similar thing, replacing the condition for two values with the condition for three, namely:

```
x >= y && x >= z
```

This way of using `max` is probably the first to spring to mind, but it is not the only way that `max` can help us in defining `maxThree`.

We can **use** a function we have already defined within the new definition

We are trying to find the maximum of three numbers, and we are already provided with a function `max` to give us the maximum of two. How could we *use* `max` to give us the result we want? We can take the maximum of the first two, and then the maximum of that and the third. In pictures,

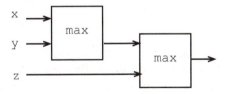

and in Haskell

```
maxThree x y z = max (max x y) z
```

or writing the `max` in its infix form, 'max',

```
maxThree x y z = (x 'max' y) 'max' z
```

Using `max` in this way has some advantages.

The definition of `maxThree` is considerably shorter and easier to read than the original. If at some point we changed the way that `max` was calculated – perhaps making it a built-in function – then this definition would get the benefit of the 'new' `max`. This is not such an advantage in a small example like this, but can be of considerable benefit in a larger-scale system where we can expect software to be modified and extended over its lifetime.

Can I break the problem down into simpler parts?

If we cannot solve a problem as it stands, we can think about breaking it down into smaller parts. This principle of 'divide and conquer' is the basis of all larger-scale programming: we solve aspects of the problem separately and then put them together to give an overall solution.

How do we decide how to break a problem down into parts? We can think of solving a simpler problem and then building the full solution on top, or we can ask ourselves the question here.

What if I had any functions I wanted: which could I use in writing the solution?

This *what if . . . ?* is a central question, because it breaks the problem into two parts. First we have to give the solution *assuming* we are given the auxiliary functions we want and thus without worrying about how they are to be defined. Then, we have separately to define these auxiliary functions.

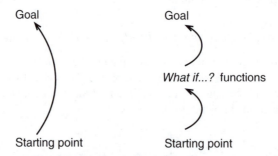

Instead of a single jump from the starting point to the goal, we have two shorter jumps, each of which should be easier to do. This approach is called **top-down** as we start at the top with the overall problem, and work by breaking it down into smaller problems.

This process can be done repeatedly, so that the overall problem is solved in a series of small jumps. We now look at an example; more examples appear in the exercises at the end of the section.

Suppose we are faced with the problem of defining

```
middleNumber :: Int -> Int -> Int -> Int
```

according to the first of the alternatives described on page 54. A model is given by the definition of maxThree, in which we give conditions for x to be the solution, y to be the solution and so on. We can therefore sketch out our solution like this

```
middleNumber x y z
  | condition for x to be solution     = x
  | condition for y to be solution     = y
  ....
```

Now, the problem comes in writing down the conditions, but here we say *what if* we had a function to do this. Let us call it between. It has three numbers as arguments, and a Boolean result,

```
between :: Int -> Int -> Int -> Bool
```

and is defined so that between m n p is True if n is between m and p. We can complete the definition of middleNumber now:

```
middleNumber x y z
  | between y x z     = x
  | between x y z     = y
  | otherwise         = z
```

The definition of the function between is left as an exercise for the reader.

This section has introduced some of the general ideas which can help us to get started in solving a problem. Obviously, because programming is a creative activity there is not going to be a set of rules which will always lead us mechanically to a solution to a problem. On the other hand, the questions posed here will get us started, and show us some of the alternative strategies we can use to plan how we are going to write a program. We follow up this discussion in Chapter 11.

Exercises

4.1 This question is about the function

```
maxFour :: Int -> Int -> Int -> Int -> Int
```

which returns the maximum of four integers. Give three definitions of this function: the first should be modelled on that of maxThree, the second should use the function max and the third should use the functions max and maxThree. For your second and third solutions give diagrams to illustrate your answers. Discuss the relative merits of the three solutions you have given.

4.2 Give a definition of the function

```
between :: Int -> Int -> Int -> Bool
```

discussed in this section. The definition should be consistent with what we said in explaining how middleNumber works. You also need to think carefully about the different ways that one number can lie between two others. You might find it useful to define a function

```
weakAscendingOrder :: Int -> Int -> Int -> Bool
```

so that weakAscendingOrder m n p is True exactly when m, n and p are in weak ascending order, that is the sequence does not go down at any point. An example of such a sequence is 2 3 3.

4.3 Give a definition of the function

```
howManyEqual :: Int -> Int -> Int -> Int
```

which returns how many of its three arguments are equal, so that

```
howManyEqual 34 25 36 = 0
howManyEqual 34 25 34 = 2
howManyEqual 34 34 34 = 3
```

Think about what functions you have already seen – perhaps in the exercises – which you can use in the solution.

4.4 Give a definition of the function

```
howManyOfFourEqual :: Int -> Int -> Int -> Int -> Int
```

which is the analogue of howManyEqual for four numbers. You may need to think *what if . . . ?*.

(4.2) Recursion

Recursion is an important programming mechanism, in which a definition of a function or other object refers to the object itself. This section concentrates on explaining the idea of recursion, and why it makes sense. In particular we give two complementary explanations of how primitive recursion works in defining the factorial function over the natural numbers. In the section after this we look at how recursion is *used* in practice.

Getting started: a story about factorials

Suppose that someone tells us that the factorial of a natural number is the product of all natural numbers from one up to (and including) that number, so that, for instance

```
fac 6 = 1*2*3*4*5*6
```

Suppose we are also asked to write down a table of factorials, where we take the factorial of zero to be one. We begin thus

```
n        fac n
0         1
1         1
2         1*2 = 2
3         1*2*3 = 6
4         1*2*3*4 = 24
```

but we notice that we are repeating a lot of multiplication in doing this. In working out

```
1*2*3*4
```

we see that we are repeating the multiplication of 1*2*3 before multiplying the result by 4

```
1*2*3 *4
```

and this suggests that we can produce the table in a different way, by saying how to start

```
fac 0 = 1
```
                                                                              (fac.1)

which starts the table thus

```
n        fac n
0          1
```

and then by saying how to go from one line to the next

```
fac n = fac (n-1) * n
```
                                                                              (fac.2)

since this gives us the lines

```
n        fac n
0          1
1          1*1 = 1
2          1*2 = 2
3          2*3 = 6
4          6*4 = 24
```

and so on.

What is the moral of this story? We started off describing the table in one way, but came to see that all we needed was the information in (fac.1) and (fac.2).

● (fac.1) tells us the first line of the table, and

● (fac.2) tells us how to get from one line of the table to the next.

The table is just a written form of the factorial function, so we can see that (fac.1) and (fac.2) actually describe the **function** to calculate the factorial, and putting them together we get

```
fac :: Int -> Int
fac n
  | n==0        = 1
  | n>0         = fac (n-1) * n
```

A definition like this is called **recursive** because we actually use fac in describing fac itself. Put this way it may sound paradoxical: after all, how can we describe something in terms of itself? But, the story we have just told shows that the definition is perfectly sensible, since it gives

● a starting point: the value of fac at 0, and

● a way of going from the value of fac at a particular point, fac (n-1), to the value of fac on the next line, namely fac n.

These recursive rules will give a value to fac n whatever the (positive) value n has – we just have to write out n lines of the table, as it were.

Recursion and calculation

The story in the previous section described how the definition of factorial

```
fac :: Int -> Int
fac n
  | n==0        = 1                    (fac.1)
  | n>0         = fac (n-1) * n        (fac.2)
```

can be seen as generating the table of factorials, starting from fac 0 and working up to fac 1, fac 2 and so forth, up to any value we wish.

We can also read the definition in a calculational way, and see recursion justified in another way. Take the example of fac 4

```
fac 4
⤳   fac 3 * 4
```

so that (fac.2) replaces one goal – fac 4 – with a simpler goal – finding fac 3 (and multiplying it by 4). Continuing to use (fac.2), we have

```
fac 4
⤳   fac 3 * 4
⤳   (fac 2 * 3) * 4
⤳   ((fac 1 * 2) * 3) * 4
⤳   (((fac 0 * 1) * 2) * 3) * 4
```

Now, we have got down to the simplest case (or **base case**), which is solved by (fac.1).

```
⤳   (((1 * 1) * 2) * 3) * 4
⤳   ((1 * 2) * 3) * 4
⤳   (2 * 3) * 4
⤳   6 * 4
⤳   24
```

In the calculation we have worked from the goal back down to the base case, using the **recursion step** (fac.2). We can again see that we get the result we want, because the recursion step takes us from a more complicated case to a simpler one, and we have given a value for the simplest case (zero, here) which we will eventually reach.

We have now seen in the case of fac two explanations for why recursion works.

● The **bottom-up** explanation says that the fac equations can be seen to generate the values of fac one-by-one from the base case at zero.

● A **top-down** view starts with a goal to be evaluated, and shows how the equations simplify this until we hit the base case.

The two views here are related, since we can think of the top-down explanation generating a table too, but in this case the table is generated as it is needed. Starting with the goal of fac 4 we require the lines for 0 to 3 also.

Technically, we call the form of recursion we have seen here **primitive recursion**. We will describe it more formally in the next section, where we examine how to start to find recursive definitions. Before we do that, we discuss another aspect of the fac function as defined here.

Undefined or error values

Our definition of factorial covers zero and the positive integers. What will be the effect of applying fac to a negative number? On evaluating fac (-2) in Hugs we receive the error message

```
Program error: {fac (-2)}
```

because fac is not defined on the negative numbers. We could if we wished extend the definition to zero, on the negative numbers, thus

```
fac n
  | n==0       = 1
  | n>0        = fac (n-1) * n
  | otherwise  = 0
```

or we could include our own error message, as follows

```
fac n
  | n==0       = 1
  | n>0        = fac (n-1) * n
  | otherwise  = error "fac only defined on natural numbers"
```

so that when we evaluate `fac (-2)` we receive the message

`Program error: fac only defined on natural numbers`

The error message here is a Haskell string, as discussed in Chapter 5.

4.5 Define the function `rangeProduct` which when given natural numbers m and n returns the product

`m*(m+1)*...*(n-1)*n`

You should include in your definition the type of the function, and your function should return 0 when n is smaller than m.
Hint: you do not need to use recursion in your definition, but you may if you wish.

4.6 As `fac` is a special case of `rangeProduct`, write a definition of `fac` which *uses* `rangeProduct`.

4.3 Primitive recursion in practice

This section examines how primitive recursion is used in practice by examining a number of examples.

The pattern of primitive recursion says that we can define a function from the natural numbers 0, 1, ... by giving the value at zero, and by explaining how to go from the value at n−1 to the value at n. We can give a **template** for this

```
fun n
  | n==0        = ....                          (prim)
  | n>0         = .... fun (n-1) ....
```

where we have to supply the two right-hand sides.

How can we decide whether a function can be defined in this way? Just as we did earlier in the chapter, we frame a question which summarizes the essential property we need for primitive recursion to apply.

What if *we were given the value* `fun (n-1)`. *How could we define* `fun n` *from it?*

We see how this form of recursion works in practice by looking at some examples.

1. Suppose first that we are asked to define the function to give us powers of two for natural numbers

`power2 :: Int -> Int`

so that power2 n is 2^n, that is 2 multiplied by itself n times. The template is

```
power2 n
    | n==0          = ....
    | n>0           = .... power2 (n-1) ....
```

In the zero case the result is 1, and in general 2^n is 2^{n-1} multiplied by 2, so we define

```
power2 n
    | n==0          = 1
    | n>0           = 2 * power2 (n-1)
```

2. As the next example we take the function

```
sumFacs :: Int -> Int
```

so that

```
sumFacs n = fac 0 + fac 1 + ... + fac (n-1) + fac n
```

If we are told that sumFacs 4 is 34 then we can work out sumFacs 5 in one step: we simply add fac 5, that is 120, giving the result 154. This works in general, and so we can fill in the template like this:

```
sumFacs :: Int -> Int
sumFacs n
    | n==0          = 1
    | n>0           = sumFacs (n-1) + fac n
```

In fact this pattern works for any function f of type Int -> Int in the place of fac, so we can say

```
sumFun :: (Int -> Int) -> Int -> Int
sumFun f n
    | n==0          = f 0
    | n>0           = sumFun f (n-1) + f n
```

where the function whose values are being added is itself an argument of the sumFun function. A sample calculation using sumFun is

```
sumFun fac 3
 ↝   sumFun fac 2 + fac 3
 ↝   sumFun fac 1 + fac 2 + fac 3
 ↝   sumFun fac 0 + fac 1 + fac 2 + fac 3
 ↝   fac 0 + fac 1 + fac 2 + fac 3
 ↝   ...
 ↝   10
```

and we can define sumFacs from sumFun thus:

```
sumFacs n = sumFun fac n
```

We briefly introduced the idea of functions as data in Chapter 1, and we will revisit it in detail in Chapter 9. As we mentioned in Chapter 1, having functions as arguments is powerful and sumFun gives a good example: one definition serves to sum the values of *any* function of type Int -> Int over the range of arguments from 0 to n.

3. As a last example we look at a geometrical problem. Suppose we want to find out the maximum number of pieces we can get by making a given number of straight-line cuts across a piece of paper. With no cuts we get one piece; what about the general case? Suppose we have n-1 lines already, and that we add one more.

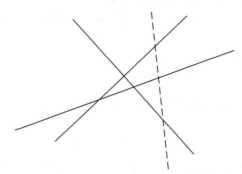

We will get the most new regions if we cross each of these lines; because they are straight lines, we can only cut each one once. This means that the new line crosses exactly n of the regions, and so splits each of these into two. We therefore get n new regions by adding the nth line. Our function definition is given by filling in the template (prim) according to what we have said.

```
regions :: Int -> Int
regions n
  | n==0        = 1
  | n>0         = regions (n-1) + n
```

Exercises

4.7 Using the addition function over the natural numbers, give a recursive definition of multiplication of natural numbers.

4.8 The integer square root of a positive integer n is the largest integer whose square is less than or equal to n. For instance, the integer square roots of 15 and 16 are 3 and 4, respectively. Give a primitive recursive definition of this function.

4.9 Given a function f of type Int -> Int give a recursive definition of a function of type Int -> Int which on input n returns the maximum of the values f 0, f 1, ..., f n. You might find the max function defined in Section 3.4 useful.

To test this function, add to your script a definition of some values of f thus:

```
f 0 = 0
f 1 = 44
f 2 = 17
f _ = 0
```

and so on; then test your function at various values.

4.10 Given a function f of type Int -> Int give a recursive definition of a function of type Int -> Bool which on input n returns True if one or more of the values f 0, f 1, ..., f n is zero and False otherwise.

4.11 Can you give a definition of regions which instead of being recursive *uses* the function sumFun?

4.12 [Harder] Find out the maximum number of pieces we can get by making a given number of flat (that is planar) cuts through a solid block. It is *not* the same answer as we calculated for straight-line cuts of a flat piece of paper.

4.4) General forms of recursion

As we explained in Section 4.2, a recursive definition of a function such as fac would give the value of fac n using the value fac (n-1). We saw there that fac (n-1) is *simpler* in being closer to the base case fac 0. As long as we preserve this property of becoming simpler, different patterns of recursion are possible and we look at some of them in this section. These more general forms of recursion are called **general recursion**. In trying to use recursion to define a function we need to pose the question:

In defining f n which values of f k would help me to work out the answer?

Examples

1. The sequence of Fibonacci numbers starts with 0 and 1, and subsequent values are given by adding the last two values, so that we get 0+1=1, 1+1=2 and so forth. This can be given a recursive definition as follows

```
fib :: Int -> Int
fib n
   | n==0        = 0
   | n==1        = 1
   | n>1         = fib (n-2) + fib (n-1)
```

where we see in the general case that fib n depends upon not only fib (n-1) but also fib (n-2).

This gives a clear description of the Fibonacci numbers, but unfortunately it gives a very inefficient program for calculating them. We can see that calculating fib n requires us to calculate both fib (n-2) and fib (n-1), and in calculating fib (n-1) we will have to calculate fib (n-2) *again*. We look at ways of overcoming this problem in Section 5.2.

2. Dividing one positive integer by another can be done in many different ways. One of the simplest ways is repeatedly to subtract the divisor from the number being divided, and we give a program doing that here. In fact we will define two functions

```
remainder :: Int -> Int -> Int
divide    :: Int -> Int -> Int
```

which separately give the division's remainder and quotient.

In trying to find a definition it often helps to look at an example. Suppose we want to divide 37 by 10. We expect that

```
remainder 37 10 = 7
divide    37 10 = 3
```

If we subtract the divisor, 10, from the number being divided, 37, how are the values related?

```
remainder 27 10 = 7
divide    27 10 = 2
```

The remainder is the same, and the result of the division is one less. What happens at the base case? An example is

```
remainder 7 10 = 7
divide    7 10 = 0
```

Using these examples as a guide, we have

```
remainder m n
  | m<n         = m
  | otherwise   = remainder (m-n) n

divide m n
  | m<n         = 0
  | otherwise   = 1 + divide (m-n) n
```

These definitions also illustrate another important point: a general recursive function does not always give an answer; instead an evaluation may go on forever. Look at what happens if we evaluate

```
remainder 7 0
⤳    remainder (7-0) 0
⤳    remainder 7 0
⤳    ....
```

This calculation will loop for ever, and indeed we should expect problems if we try to divide by zero! However, the problem also appears if we try to divide by a negative number, for instance

```
divide 4 (-4)
⤳    divide (4-(-4)) (-4)
⤳    divide 8 (-4)
⤳    ...
```

The lesson of this example is that in general there is no guarantee that a function defined by recursion will always **terminate**. We will have termination if we use primitive recursion, and other cases where we are sure that we always go from a more complex case to a simpler one; the problem in the example here is that subtracting a negative number increases the result, giving a more complex application of the function.

4.13 Give a recursive definition of a function to find the highest common factor of two positive integers.

4.14 Suppose we have to raise 2 to the power n. If n is even, 2*m say, then

$$2^n = 2^{2*m} = (2^m)^2$$

If n is odd, 2*m+1 say, then

$$2^n = 2^{2*m+1} = (2^m)^2*2$$

Give a recursive function to compute 2^n which uses these insights.

4.5 Program testing

Just because a program is accepted by the Haskell system, it does not mean that it necessarily does what it should. How can we be sure that a program behaves as it is intended to? One option, first aired in Section 1.10, is to prove in some way that it behaves correctly. Proof is, however, an expensive business, and we can get a good deal of assurance that our programs behave correctly by testing the program on selected inputs. The art of testing is then to choose the inputs to be as comprehensive as possible. That is, we want to test data to represent all the different 'kinds' of input that can be presented to the function.

How might we choose test data? There are two possible approaches. We could simply be told the **specification** of the function, and devise test data according to that. This is called **black box** testing, as we cannot see into the box which contains the function. On the other hand, in devising **white box** tests we can use the form of the function definition itself to guide our choice of test data. We will explore these two in turn, by addressing the example of the function which is to return the maximum of three integers,

```
maxThree :: Int -> Int -> Int -> Int
```

Black box testing

How can we make a rational choice of test data for a function, rather than simply picking (supposedly) random numbers out of the air?

What we need to do is try to partition the inputs into different **testing groups** where we expect the function to behave in a similar way for all the values in a given group. In picking the test data we then want to make sure that we choose at least one representative from each group.

We should also pay particular attention to any **special cases**, which will occur on the 'boundaries' of the groups. If we have groups of positive and negative numbers, then we should pay particular attention to the zero case, for instance.

What are the testing groups for the example of maxThree? There is not a single right answer to this, but we can think about what is likely to be relevant to the problem and what is likely to be irrelevant. In the case of maxThree it is reasonable to think that the size or sign of the integers will not be relevant: what will determine the result is their relative ordering. We can make a first subdivision this way

- all three values different;
- all three values the same;
- two items equal, the third different. In fact, this represents two cases
  - two values equal to the maximum, one other;
  - one value equal to the maximum, two others.

We can then pick a set of test data thus

```
6 4 1
6 6 6
2 6 6
2 2 6
```

If we test our definition in Section 3.4 with these data then we see that the program gives the right results. So too does the following program:

```
mysteryMax :: Int -> Int -> Int -> Int
mysteryMax x y z
   | x > y && x > z      = x
   | y > x && y > z      = y
   | otherwise           = z
```

so should we conclude that mysteryMax computes the maximum of the three inputs? If we do, we are wrong, for we have that

```
mysteryMax 6 6 2 ⇝   2
```

This is an important example: it tells us that **testing alone cannot assure us that a function is correct**. How might we have spotted this error in designing our test data? We could have said that not only did we need to consider the groups above, but that we should have looked at all the different possible orderings of the data, giving

- all three values different: six different orderings;
- all three values the same: one ordering;
- two items equal, the third different. In each of the two cases we consider three orderings.

The final case generates the test data 6 6 2 which find the error.

We mentioned special cases earlier: we could see this case of two equal to the maximum in this way. Clearly the author of mysteryMax was thinking about the general case of three different values, so we can see the example as underlining the importance of looking at special cases.

White box testing

In writing white box test data we will be guided by the principles which apply to black box testing, but we can also use the form of the program to help us choose data.

⬤ If we have a function containing guards, we should supply data for each case in the definition. We should also pay attention to 'boundary conditions' by testing the equality case when a guard uses >= or >, for example.

⬤ If a function uses recursion we should test the zero case, the one case and the general case.

In the example of `mysteryMax` we should be guided to the data 6 6 2 since the first two inputs are at the boundaries of the guards

x > y && x > z   y > x && y > z

We take up the ideas discussed in this section when we discuss proof in Chapter 8.

Exercises

4.15 Devise test data for a function

```
allEqual :: Int -> Int -> Int -> Bool
```

intended to test whether its three integer inputs are equal.

4.16 Use the test data from the previous question to test the function

```
solution m n p = ((m+n+p)==3*p)
```

Discuss your results.

4.17 The function

```
allDifferent :: Int -> Int -> Int -> Bool
```

should return `True` only if all its inputs are different. Devise black box test data for this function.

4.18 Test the following function

```
attempt m n p = (m/=n) && (n/=p)
```

using the test data written in the previous question. What do you conclude on the basis of your results?

4.19 Devise test data for a function

```
howManyAboveAverage :: Int -> Int -> Int -> Int
```

which returns how many of its three integer inputs are larger than their average value.

4.20 Devise test data for a function to raise two to a positive integer power.

Summary

This chapter has introduced some general principles of program design.

● We should think about how best to use what we already know. If we have already defined a function f we can make use of it in two ways.

– We can *model* our new definition on the definition of f.

– We can *use* f in our new definition.

● We should think about how to break the problem into smaller, more easily solved, parts. We should ask *What if I had ...?*.

● We can use recursion to define functions.

We also explained the basics of recursion, and saw how it is used in practice to define a variety of functions. We shall see many more illustrations of this when we look at recursion over lists in Chapter 7.

We concluded by showing that it was possible to think in a principled way about designing test data for function definitions rather than simply choosing the first data that came to mind.

Chapter 5

Data types: tuples and lists

Thus far we have looked at programs which work over the basic types such as `Int`, `Float` and `Bool`, and we have also seen how to approach the design of programs in general. However, in practical problems we will want to represent more complex things, as we saw with our `Picture` example in Chapter 1.

This chapter introduces two ways of building compound data in the Haskell language; these are the **tuple** and the **list**, and together they suffice to let us represent many different kinds of `structured' information. We shall meet other ways of defining data types for ourselves in Chapters 14 and 16.

We concentrate here on explaining the facilities that Haskell provides for defining and manipulating tuples and lists. The repertoire for tuples is small, but for lists the langauge provides many predefined functions and operations. As well as these we can use the `list comprehension' notation to write down descriptions of how lists may be formed from other lists.

In order to describe properly the prelude functions on lists we need to explain **polymorphism**, which is the mechanism by which a Haskell function can act over more than one type: the `length` function on lists can be used over any list type, for instance.

After laying the foundations in this chapter we look at a collection of examples in the chapter to come.

(5.1) Introducing tuples, lists and strings

Both tuples and lists are built up by combining a number of pieces of data into a single object, but they have different properties. In a tuple, we combine a predetermined number of values of predetermined types – which might be different – into a single object. In a list we combine an arbitrary number of values – all of the same type – into a single object.

An example can help to clarify the difference. Suppose we are trying to make a simple model of a supermarket, and as part of that model we want to record the contents of someone's shopping basket. A given item has a name and a price (in pence), and we therefore need somehow to combine these two pieces of information. We do this in a tuple, such as

```
("Salt: 1kg",139)
("Plain crisps",25)
```

where in each tuple a `String` is combined with an `Int`. The literal `String` of characters, written between double quotes, gives the name of the item, and the `Int` gives its price. The `String` is in fact a list of characters, and we discuss that type in Section 5.9.

The values `("Salt: 1kg",139)` and `("Plain crisps",25)` belong to the **tuple type**

```
(String,Int)
```

Every member of this type will have two components – a `String` and an `Int` – as specified in the type `(String,Int)`. If we are given a member of this type we can therefore predict what type its components will have, and this means that we can check that these components are used in an appropriate way: we can check that we deal with the second half as an `Int` and not a `Bool`, for example. We therefore keep the property, first mentioned in Chapter 1, that we can type-check all programs prior to execution, and so any type errors in a program can be found before a program is actually executed.

How are the contents of the basket represented? We know that we have a collection of items, but we do not know in advance how many we have; one basket might contain ten items, another one three. Each item is represented in the same way, as a member of the `(String,Int)` type, and so we represent the contents of the basket by a **list** of these, as in the list

```
[ ("Salt: 1kg",139) , ("Plain crisps",25) , ("Gin: 1lt",1099) ]
```

This is a member of the **list type**

```
[ (String,Int) ]
```

Other members of this list type include the empty list, [], and the basket above with a second packet of crisps replacing the gin:

```
[ ("Salt: 1kg",139) , ("Plain crisps",25) , ("Plain crisps",25) ]
```

Since every member of the list has the same type, we can predict the type of any item chosen from the list. Compare this with a list whose members could have different types: if we choose the first element of such a list we cannot predict its type, and so we lose the ability to type-check programs before they are run. Because we want to keep this important property, Haskell is designed so that lists have to contain elements of the same type, but different lists will contain elements of different types.

We can give names to types in Haskell, so that types are made easier to read. In our example we name the two types

```
type ShopItem = (String,Int)
type Basket   = [ShopItem]
```

where the keyword `type` introduces the fact that this is the definition of a type rather than a value. We can also tell this because the type names `ShopItem` and `Basket` begin with capital letters, as noted in Section 3.7. Built into the system is the definition

```
type String = [Char]
```

so Haskell treats strings as a special case of the list type. Names such as `ShopItem` and `String` are **synonyms** for the types which they name.

We now look at tuple types in more detail, and examine some examples of how tuples are used in practice.

5.2) Tuple types

The last section introduced the idea of tuple types. In general a tuple type is built up from components of simpler types. The type

$$(t_1,t_2,\ldots,t_n)$$

consists of tuples of values

$$(v_1,v_2,\ldots,v_n)$$

in which v_1::t_1, ..., v_n::t_n. In other words, each component v_i of the tuple has to have the type t_i given in the corresponding position in the tuple type.

The reason for the name 'tuple' is that these objects are usually called pairs, triples, quadruples, quintuples, sextuples and so on. The general word for them is therefore 'tuple'. In other programming languages, these types are called records or structures; see Appendix A for a more detailed comparison.

We can model a type of supermarket items by the `ShopItem` type defined by

```
type ShopItem = (String,Int)
```

and we saw above that its members include items like ("Gin, 1lt",1099).

A type definition like this is treated as shorthand in Haskell – wherever a name like ShopItem is used, it has exactly the same effect as if (String,Int) had been written. Definitions like this make programs more readable and also lead to more comprehensible type error messages.

How else are tuple types used in programs? We look at a series of examples now.

Examples

1. First, we can use a tuple to return a compound result from a function, as in the example where we are required to return both the minimum and the maximum of two Ints

```
minAndMax :: Int -> Int -> (Int,Int)
minAndMax x y
    | x>=y        = (y,x)
    | otherwise   = (x,y)
```

2. Secondly, suppose we are asked to find a (numerical) solution to a problem when it is uncertain whether a solution actually exists in every case: this might be the question of where a straight line meets the horizontal or x-axis, for instance.

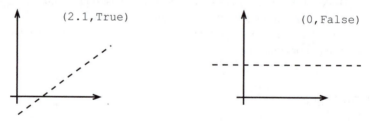

One way of dealing with this is for the function to return a (Float,Bool) pair. If the boolean part is False, this signals that no solution was found; if it is like (2.1,True), it indicates that 2.1 is indeed the solution.

Pattern matching

Next we turn to look at how functions can be defined over tuples. Functions over tuples are usually defined by **pattern matching**. Instead of writing a variable for an argument of type (Int,Int), say, a **pattern**, (x,y) is used.

```
addPair :: (Int,Int) -> Int
addPair (x,y) = x+y
```

On application the components of the pattern are matched by the corresponding components of the argument, so that on applying the function addPair to the argument (5,8) the value 5 is matched to x, and 8 to y, giving the calculation

```
addPair (5,8)
⤳   5+8
⤳   13
```

Patterns can contain literals and nested patterns, as in the examples

```
addPair (0,y) = y
addPair (x,y) = x+y

shift :: ((Int,Int),Int) -> (Int,(Int,Int))
shift ((x,y),z) = (x,(y,z))
```

Functions which pick out particular parts of a tuple can be defined by pattern matching. For the ShopItem type, the definitions might be

```
name  :: ShopItem -> String
price :: ShopItem -> Int

name  (n,p) = n
price (n,p) = p
```

Haskell has these **selector functions** on pairs built in. They are

```
fst (x,y) = x
snd (x,y) = y
```

Given these selector functions we can avoid pattern matching if we so wish. For instance, we could redefine addPair like this

```
addPair :: (Int,Int) -> Int
addPair p = fst p + snd p
```

but generally a pattern-matching definition is easier to read than one which uses selector functions instead.

Examples

3. We first introduced the Fibonacci numbers

```
0, 1, 1, 2, 3, 5, ... , u, v, (u+v), ...
```

in Section 4.4, where we gave an inefficient recursive definition of the sequence. Using a tuple we can give an efficient solution to the problem. The next value in the sequence is given by adding the previous two, so what we do is to write a function which returns *two consecutive values* as a result. In other words we want to define a function fibPair so that it has the property that

```
fibPair n = (fib n , fib (n+1))
```

then given such a pair, (u,v) we get the next pair as $(v,u+v)$, which is exactly the effect of the fibStep function:

```
fibStep :: (Int,Int) -> (Int,Int)
fibStep (u,v) = (v,u+v)
```

This gives us the definition of the 'Fibonacci pair' function

```
fibPair :: Int -> (Int,Int)
fibPair n
  | n==0        = (0,1)
  | otherwise   = fibStep (fibPair (n-1))
```

and we can define

```
fastFib :: Int -> Int
fastFib = fst . fibPair
```

where recall that '.' composes the two functions, passing the output of fibPair to the input of fst, which picks out its first component.

Note: One pair or two arguments?

It is important to distinguish between the functions

```
fibStep :: (Int,Int) -> (Int,Int)
fibStep (x,y) = (y,x+y)
```

```
fibTwoStep :: Int -> Int -> (Int,Int)
fibTwoStep x y = (y,x+y)
```

fibStep has a single argument which is a pair of numbers, while fibTwoStep has two arguments, each of which is a number. We shall see later that the second function can be used in a more flexible way than the first; for the moment it is important to realize that there is a difference, and that type errors will result if we confuse the two and write

```
fibStep 2 3                    fibTwoStep (2,3)
```

We say more about the relationship between these two functions in Section 10.7.

Exercises

5.1 Give a definition of the function

```
maxOccurs :: Int -> Int -> (Int,Int)
```

which returns the maximum of two integers, together with the number of times it occurs. Using this, or otherwise, define the function

```
maxThreeOccurs :: Int -> Int -> Int -> (Int,Int)
```

which does a similar thing for three arguments.

5.2 Give a definition of a function

```
orderTriple :: (Int,Int,Int) -> (Int,Int,Int)
```

which puts the elements of a triple of three integers into ascending order. You might like to use the maxThree, middle and minThree functions defined earlier.

5.3 Define the function which finds where a straight line crosses the x-axis. You will need to think about how to supply the information about the straight line to the function.

5.4 Design test data for the preceding exercises; explain the choices you have made in each case. Give a sample evaluation of each of your functions.

(5.3) Our approach to lists

Lists are a remarkably expressive data type. We can represent a text as a list of lines, each of which is a list of words; we can represent a collection of information, like a supermarket bill, as a list of individual items of data; we can represent a collection of readings from a measuring device as a list of Floats, to mention but three potential applications.

At the same time, there are many different things which we can do to lists, some of which first came out in our implementation of Pictures by lists in Chapter 1. Given a list we can split it up according to various criteria, we can sort it, select items from it and transform all its members in a particular way. We can combine lists by joining them together or by coalescing corresponding elements. We can combine all the members of a list together – by taking their sum, maximum or conjunction, say – among many other operations. Haskell contains many built-in list functions and operators in the standard prelude Prelude.hs and also in the library module List.hs.

Because Haskell has so many list functions built in, we can approach our discussion of lists in two very different ways. We could argue that we should start by defining list-manipulating functions for ourselves, and only use library functions after we have understood their definitions.[1] On the other hand, we could adopt a 'toolkit' approach, and simply discuss the library functions and how they can be used. What we aim to do here is to combine the two approaches, often introducing and using functions before they are defined explicitly, but then looking 'under the bonnet' to see how these functions are defined and how we can define other functions for ourselves.

In order fully to appreciate the general operations on lists we have to examine how generic or **polymorphic** functions are handled in Haskell – which we look at in Section 5.7 – as well as the notion of **higher-order functions**, see Section 9.2.

In the remainder of this chapter we introduce the main facilities for list manipulation within Haskell; in the chapters which follow we use these prelude functions, as well as seeing how to define these and other functions for ourselves.

---

[1] This was essentially the approach taken in the first edition of this book.

(5.4) Lists in Haskell

A list in Haskell is a collection of items from a given type. For every type t there is a Haskell type [t] of lists from t.

```
[1,2,3,4,1,4] :: [Int]
[True]        :: [Bool]
```

We read these as '[1,2,3,4,1,4] is a list of Int' and '[True] is a list of Bool'. String is a synonym for [Char] and the two lists which follow are the same.

```
['a','a','b'] :: String
"aab"         :: String
```

We can build lists of items of any particular type, and so we can have lists of functions and lists of lists of numbers, as in

```
[fac,fastFib]       :: [ Int -> Int ]
[[12,2],[2,12],[]] :: [ [Int] ]
```

As can be seen, the list with elements e_1, e_2 to e_n is written by enclosing the elements in square brackets, thus

```
[e1,e2,...,en]
```

As a special case the empty list, [], which contains no items, is an element of every list type.

The order of the items in a list is significant, as is the number of times that an item appears. The three lists of numbers which follow are therefore all different:

```
[1,2,1,2,2]
[2,1,1,2,2]
[2,1,1,2]
```

The first two have length 5, while the third has length 4; the first element of the first list is 1, while the first element of the second is 2. A set is another kind of collection in which the ordering of items and the number of occurrences of a particular item are not relevant; we look at sets in Chapter 16.

There are some other ways of writing down lists of numbers, characters and other enumerated types

- [n .. m] is the list [n,n+1,...,m]; if n exceeds m, the list is empty.

```
[2 .. 7]      = [2,3,4,5,6,7]
[3.1 .. 7.0] = [3.1,4.1,5.1,6.1]
['a' .. 'm'] = "abcdefghijklm"
```

- [n,p .. m] is the list of numbers whose first two elements are n and p and whose last is m, with the numbers ascending in steps of p−n. For example,

```
[7,6 .. 3]          = [7,6,5,4,3]
[0.0,0.3 .. 1.0] = [0.0,0.3,0.6,0.9]
['a','c' .. 'n'] = "acegikm"
```

● In both cases it can be seen that if the step size does not allow us to reach m exactly, the last item of the list is the largest/smallest in the sequence which is less/greater than or equal to m. It can also be the case that rounding errors on Float lead to lists being different from what is anticipated; an example is given in the exercises.

In the next section we turn to a powerful method of writing down lists which we can use to define a variety of list-manipulating functions.

Exercises

5.5 What value has the expression [0, 0.1 .. 1]? Check your answer in Hugs and explain any discrepancy there might be between the two.

5.6 How many items does the list [2,3] contain? How many does [[2,3]] contain? What is the type of [[2,3]]?

5.7 What is the result of evaluating [2 .. 2]? What about [2,7 .. 4]? Try evaluating [2,2 .. 2]; to **interrupt evaluation** in Hugs under Windows or Unix you need to type Ctrl-C.

5.5 List comprehensions

One of the distinct features of a functional language is the list comprehension notation, which has no parallels in other paradigms.

In a list comprehension we write down a description of a list in terms of the elements of another list. From the first list we **generate** elements, which we **test** and **transform** to form elements of the result. We will describe list comprehensions with a single generator in this section; Section 17.3 covers the general case. Nevertheless, the simple case we look at here is very useful in writing a variety of list-processing programs. We introduce the topic by a series of examples.

Examples

1. Suppose that the list ex is [2,4,7], then the list comprehension

[2*n | n<-ex]   (1)

will be

[4,8,14]

as it contains each of the elements n of the list ex, doubled: 2*n. We can read (1) as saying

'Take all 2*n where n comes from ex.'

where the symbol <- is meant to resemble the mathematical symbol for being an element, '∈'. We can write the evaluation of the list comprehension in a table, thus:

```
[ 2*n | n <- [2,4,7] ]
```

```
   n   =   2   4    7
 2*n   =   4   8   14
```

2.   In a similar way,

```
[ isEven n | n<-ex ] ⤳    [True,True,False]
```

if the function isEven has the definition

```
isEven :: Int -> Bool
isEven n = (n 'mod' 2 == 0)
```

In list comprehensions n<-ex is called a **generator** because it generates the data from which the results are built. On the left-hand side of the '<-' there is a variable, n, while on the right-hand side we put the list, in this case ex, from which the elements are taken.

3.   We can combine a generator with one or more **tests**, which are Boolean expressions, thus:

```
[ 2*n | n <- ex , isEven n , n>3 ]
```
(2)

(2) is paraphrased as

'Take all 2*n where n comes from ex, n is even and greater than 3.'

Again, we can write the evaluation in tabular form.

```
[ 2*n | n <- [2,4,7] , isEven n , n>3 ]
```

```
        n   =   2   4   7
 isEven n   =   T   T   F
      n>3   =   F   T
      2*n   =       8
```

The result of (2) will therefore be the list [8], as 4 is the only even element of [2,4,7] which is greater than 3.

4.   Instead of placing a variable to the left of the arrow '<-', we can put a pattern. For instance,

```
addPairs :: [(Int,Int)] -> [Int]
addPairs pairList = [ m+n | (m,n) <- pairList ]
```

Here we choose all the pairs in the list pairList, and add their components to give a single number in the result list. For example,

```
[ m+n | (m,n) <- [(2,3),(2,1),(7,8)] ]
```

```
   m   =   2   2    7
   n   =   3   1    8
 m+n   =   5   3   15
```

giving the result

```
addPairs  [(2,3),(2,1),(7,8)]  ~>   [5,3,15]
```

5. We can add tests in such a situation, too:

```
addOrdPairs :: [(Int,Int)] -> [Int]
addOrdPairs pairList = [ m+n | (m,n) <- pairList , m<n ]
```

so that with the same input example,

```
[ m+n | (m,n) <- [(2,3),(2,1),(7,8)] , m<n ]
```

m	=	2	2	7
n	=	3	1	8
m<n	=	T	F	T
m+n	=	5		15

giving

```
addOrdPairs [(2,3),(2,1),(7,8)]  ~>   [5,15]
```

since the second pair in the list, $(2,1)$, fails the test.

6. Note that we can simply test elements, with the effect that we filter some of the elements of a list, according to a Boolean condition. To find all the digits in a string we can say

```
digits :: String -> String
digits st = [ ch | ch<-st , isDigit ch ]
```

where the prelude function

```
isDigit :: Char -> Bool
```

is True on those characters which are digits: '0', '1' up to '9'.

7. A list comprehension can form a part of a larger function definition. Suppose that we want to check whether all members of a list of integers are even, or all are odd. We can write

```
allEven xs = (xs == [x | x<-xs, isEven x])
allOdd xs  = ([] == [x | x<-xs, isEven x])
```

We will see list comprehensions in practice in the next section when we examine a simple library database.

Exercises

5.8 Give a definition of a function

```
doubleAll :: [Int] -> [Int]
```

which doubles all the elements of a list of integers.

5.9 Give a definition of a function

```
capitalize :: String -> String
```

which converts all small letters in a String into capitals, leaving the other characters unchanged. How would you modify this function to give

```
capitalizeLetters :: String -> String
```

which behaves in the same way except that all non-letters are removed from the list? You should check the Char.hs library to see whether it contains any functions useful in solving this problem.

5.10 Define the function

```
divisors :: Int -> [Int]
```

which returns the list of divisors of a positive integer (and the empty list for other inputs). For instance,

```
divisors 12 ⤳ [1,2,3,4,6,12]
```

A prime number n is a number whose only divisors are 1 and n. Using divisors or otherwise define a function

```
isPrime :: Int -> Bool
```

which checks whether or not a positive integer is prime (and returns False if its input is not a positive integer).

5.11 Define the function

```
matches :: Int -> [Int] -> [Int]
```

which picks out all occurrences of an integer n in a list. For instance,

```
matches 1 [1,2,1,4,5,1] ⤳ [1,1,1]
matches 1 [2,3,4,6]     ⤳ []
```

Using matches or otherwise, define a function

```
elem :: Int -> [Int] -> Bool
```

which is `True` if the `Int` is an element of the list, and `False` otherwise. For the examples above, we have

```
elem 1 [1,2,1,4,5,1]  ⤳   True
elem 1 [2,3,4,6]      ⤳   False
```

Since `elem` is a prelude function, you need to hide it as described on page 41.

5.6 A library database

This section presents a simple model of the loan data kept by a library, and illustrates how list comprehensions are used in practice.

A library uses a database to keep a record of the books on loan to borrowers; we first look at which type to use to model the database, and then look at the functions which extract information from a database. This is followed by a discussion of how to model changes to the database, and we conclude by exploring how the database functions can be tested.

Types

In modelling this situation, we first look at the types of the objects involved. People and books are represented by strings

```
type Person = String
type Book   = String
```

The database can be represented in a number of different ways. Three among a number of possibilities are

- We can record each loan as a (`Person`,`Book`) pair;
- we could associate with each person the list of books that they have borrowed, using a pair (`Person`,`[Book]`), or
- we could record a list of borrowers with each book, thus: (`[Person]`,`Book`),

Here we choose to make the database a list of (`Person`,`Book`) pairs. If the pair (`"Alice"` , `"Asterix"`) is in the list, it means that `"Alice"` has borrowed the book called `"Asterix"`. We therefore define

```
type Database = [ (Person , Book) ]
```

We have chosen this representation because it is simple, and also treats people and books in the same way, rather than grouping data in an asymmetrical way.

An example object of this type is

```
exampleBase :: Database
exampleBase
= [ ("Alice" , "Tintin")   , ("Anna" , "Little Women") ,
    ("Alice" , "Asterix") , ("Rory" , "Tintin") ]
```

After defining the types of the objects involved, we consider the functions which work over the database.

- Given a person, we want to find the book(s) that he or she has borrowed, if any.

- Given a book, we want to find the borrower(s) of the book, if any. (It is assumed that there may be more than one copy of any book.)

- Given a book, we want to find out whether it is borrowed.

- Given a person, we may want to find out the number of books that he or she has borrowed.

Each of these **lookup** functions will take a Database, and a Person or Book, and return the result of the query. Their types will be

```
books       :: Database -> Person -> [Book]
borrowers   :: Database -> Book -> [Person]
borrowed    :: Database -> Book -> Bool
numBorrowed :: Database -> Person -> Int
```

Note that borrowers and books return lists; these can contain zero, one or more items, and so in particular an empty list can signal that a book has no borrowers, or that a person has no books on loan.

Two other functions need to be defined. We need to be able to model a book being loaned to a person and a loaned book being returned. The functions modelling these will take a database, plus the loan information, and return a *different* database, which is the original with the loan added or removed. These **update** functions will have type

```
makeLoan   :: Database -> Person -> Book -> Database
returnLoan :: Database -> Person -> Book -> Database
```

Defining the lookup functions

We concentrate on the definition of the function

```
books :: Database -> Person -> [Book]
```

which forms a model for the other lookup functions. For the exampleBase, we have

```
books exampleBase "Alice" = [ "Tintin" , "Asterix" ]
books exampleBase "Rory"  = [ "Tintin" ]
```

How are these found? In the "Alice" case we need to run through the list exampleBase finding all the pairs whose first component is "Alice"; for each of these we return the second component. As a list comprehension, we have

```
[ book | (person,book) <- exampleBase , person=="Alice" ]
```

person	=	"Alice"	"Anna"		"Alice"	"Rory"
book	=	"Tintin"	"Little Women"		"Asterix"	"Tintin"
(person==	=	T	F		T	F
"Alice")						
book	=	"Tintin"			"Asterix"	

We make this into a general function by saying

```
books       :: Database -> Person -> [Book]                 (books.1)
books dBase findPerson
  = [ book | (person,book) <- dBase , person==findPerson ]
```

Note that in this definition Person is a type while person is a variable of type Person.

As we said at the start, books forms a model for the other lookup functions, which we leave as an exercise.

Defining the update functions

The database is modified, or updated, by the functions makeLoan and returnLoan. Making a loan is done by adding a pair to the database, which can be done simply by adding an extra pair to the front of the list of pairs.

```
makeLoan   :: Database -> Person -> Book -> Database
makeLoan dBase pers bk = [ (pers,bk) ] ++ dBase
```

We have used the ++ operator here to join two lists, namely the one element list [(pers,bk)] and the 'old' database dBase.

To return a loan, we need to check through the database, and to remove the pair (pers,bk). We therefore run through all the pairs in the database, and retain those which are not equal to (pers,bk), thus

```
returnLoan   :: Database -> Person -> Book -> Database
returnLoan dBase pers bk
  = [ pair | pair <- dBase , pair /= (pers,bk) ]
```

Note that we have used a simple variable pair rather than a pattern to run over the pairs in the dBase. This is because we do not need to deal with the components separately; all we do is check whether the whole pair is equal to the pair (pers,bk). On the other hand we could use a pattern thus:

```
[ (p,b) | (p,b) <- dBase , (p,b) /= (pers,bk) ]
```

and get exactly the same result.

As we have defined it, the returnLoan function will remove *all* pairs (pers,bk) from the database. We will return to this point in the exercises in Section 9.3.

Testing

A Haskell interpreter acts like a calculator, and this is useful when we wish to test functions like those in the library database. Any function can be tested by typing expressions to the Hugs prompt. For example,

```
makeLoan [] "Alice" "Rotten Romans"
```

To test more substantial examples, it is sensible to put test data into a script, so we might include the definition of exampleBase as well as various tests

```
test1 :: Bool
test1 = borrowed exampleBase "Asterix"

test2 :: Database
test2 = makeLoan exampleBase "Alice" "Rotten Romans"
```

and so on. Adding them to the script means that we can repeatedly evaluate them without having to type them out in full each time. Another device which can help is to use $$, which is short for 'the last expression evaluated'. The following sequence makes a loan, then another, then returns the first.

```
makeLoan exampleBase "Alice" "Rotten Romans"
makeLoan $$ "Rory" "Godzilla"
returnLoan $$ "Alice" "Rotten Romans"
```

Note: Variables in list comprehensions

There is an important pitfall to do with the behaviour of variables in list comprehensions. The definition (books.1) of books above might appear to be over-complicated. We might imagine that we could say

```
books dBase findPerson
  = [ book | (findPerson,book) <- dBase ]                (books.2)
```

The effect of this is to return all the books borrowed by *all* borrowers, not just the particular borrower findPerson.

The reason for this is that the findPerson in (findPerson,book) is a *new* variable, and not the variable on the left-hand side of the definition, so in fact (books.2) has the same effect as

```
books dBase findPerson = [ book | (new,book) <- dBase ]
```

where it is clear that there is no constraint on the value of new to be equal to findPerson.

Exercises

5.12 Go through the calculation of

```
books exampleBase "Charlie"
books exampleBase "Rory"
```

5.13 Define the functions borrowers, borrowed and numBorrowed. To define numBorrowed you will probably need the length function which returns the length of a list.

5.14 Give calculations of

```
returnLoan exampleBase "Alice" "Asterix"
returnLoan exampleBase "Alice" "Little Women"
```

5.15 Discuss how you would implement the database functions had you used the representation [(Person,[Book])] rather than [(Person,Book)] for the database.

(5.7) Generic functions: polymorphism

Before looking in detail at the functions on lists provided in the Haskell prelude and library we need to look at the idea of **polymorphism**, which literally means 'has many shapes'. A function is polymorphic if it 'has many types', and this is the case for many list-manipulating functions. An example is the length function, which returns the length of a list, an Int. This function can be applied to any type of list, so that we can say

```
length :: [Bool] -> Int
length :: [[Char]] -> Int
```

and so forth. How do we write down a type for length which encapsulates this? We say

```
length :: [a] -> Int
```

where a is a **type variable**. Any identifier beginning with a small letter can be used as a type variable; conventionally, letters from the beginning of the alphabet, a, b, c, ... are used. Just as in the definition

```
square x = x*x
```

the variable x stands for an arbitrary value, so a type variable stands for an *arbitrary type*, and so we can see all the types like

```
[Bool] -> Int          [[Char]] -> Int
```

as coming about by replacing the variable a by particular types: here Bool and [Char]. Types like [Bool] -> Int are called **instances** of the type [a] -> Int, and because every type for length is an instance of [a] -> Int we call this type the **most general type** for length.

The type of the function to join together two lists, ++, is

```
[a] -> [a] -> [a]
```

The variable a stands for 'an arbitrary type', but we should be clear that all the a's stand for the same type, just as in

```
square x = x*x
```

the x's all stand for the same (arbitrary) value. Instances of [a]->[a]->[a] will include

```
[Int]->[Int]->[Int]
```

but *not* the type

```
[Int]->[Bool]->[Char]
```

This makes sense: we cannot expect to join a list of numbers and a list of Booleans to give a string!

On the other hand, the functions zip and unzip convert between pairs of lists and lists of pairs, and their types involve two type variables:

```
zip   :: [a] -> [b] -> [(a,b)]
unzip :: [(a,b)] -> ([a],[b])
```

Now, instances of the type of zip include

```
[Int]->[Bool]->[(Int,Bool)]
```

where a and b are replaced by different types (Int and Bool, here). It is, of course, possible to replace both variables by the same type, giving

```
[Int]->[Int]->[(Int,Int)]
```

and the general type [a] -> [a] -> [(a,a)].

Types and definitions

How is a polymorphic function defined? Consider the definition of the identity function,

```
id x = x
```

which returns its argument unchanged. In the definition there is nothing to **constrain** the type of x – all we know about x is that it is returned directly from the function. We know, therefore, that the output type is the same as the input, and so the most general type will be

```
id :: a -> a
```

At work here is the principle that a function's type is as general as possible, consistent with the constraints put upon the types by its definition. In the case of the id function, the only constraint is that the input and output types are the same.

In a similar way, in defining

```
fst (x,y) = x
```

neither x nor y is at all constrained, and so they can come from different types a and b, giving the type

```
fst :: (a,b) -> a
```

A final example is given by

```
mystery (x,y) = if x then 'c' else 'd'
```

Here we see that x is used as a Bool in the if x then ..., whereas y is not used at all, and so is not constrained in the definition, giving mystery the type

```
(Bool,a) -> Char
```

We shall examine the definitions of many of the prelude functions in Chapter 7, and see there that, as outlined above, a function or other object will have as general as possible a type, consistent with the constraints put upon the types by its definition. We look in more depth at the mechanics of type checking in Chapter 13.

Hugs can be used to give the most general type of a function definition, using the :type command. If you have given a type declaration for the function, this can be commented out before asking for the type.

Polymorphism and overloading

Polymorphism and overloading are both mechanisms by which the same function name can be used at different types, but they have an important difference.

A polymorphic function like fst has the same definition, namely

```
fst (x,y) = x
```

at all types, so that it is the **same** function at all its instances.

On the other hand, an overloaded name like == has different definitions over different types, so that the same name is being used to mean **different** but similar functions at different types. For example, == over Int is built in, whereas over pairs it will be defined by

```
(n,m) == (p,q)
  = (n==p) && (m==q)
```

More details about overloading can be found in Chapter 12.

Exercises

5.16 Give the most general types for the functions snd and sing defined by

```
snd (x,y) = y
sing x = [x]
```

5.17 Explain why

```
[[a]] -> [[a]]
```

is a type for `id` but why it is not the most general type for this function.

5.18 Earlier in the chapter we saw the example of

```
shift :: ((Int,Int),Int) -> (Int,(Int,Int))
shift ((x,y),z) = (x,(y,z))
```

What is the most general type for `shift`, if the type declaration is omitted?

5.8 Haskell list functions in `Prelude.hs`

Armed with the insight provided by the previous section we can look at the descriptions of the polymorphic list operations from `Prelude.hs` given in Figure 5.1. In this table we give the name of the function or operator, its type, a brief description of its effect and an example, as in the description of `length`

```
length       [a] -> Int                    The length of the list.
                                            length "word" ⤳ 4
```

As well as the polymorphic functions in Figure 5.1, the standard prelude provides various operations over specific types; some of these can be seen in Figure 5.2. The types of the functions `sum` and `product`, which are overloaded, will be discussed further in Chapter 12.

The importance of types

The single most useful piece of information about a function is its **type**, and this is particularly true when we look at the polymorphic types of functions in a library like Figure 5.1. Suppose we are looking for a function to make a list from a number of copies of a single element. It must take the item and a count and give a list, so its type will be one of

```
Int -> a -> [a]                a -> Int -> [a]
```

Looking at Figure 5.1 we can quickly locate one function, `replicate`, which does have one of these types and is indeed the function which we seek. If we want a function to reverse a list it will have type `[a] -> [a]` and although there is more than one function with this type, the search is very much narrowed by looking at types.

This insight is not confined to functional languages, but is of particular use when a language supports polymorphic or **generic** functions and operators as we have seen here.

:	`a -> [a] -> [a]`	Add a single element to the front of a list.
		`3:[2,3]` ⤳ `[3,2,3]`

++	`[a] -> [a] -> [a]`	Join two lists together.
		`"Ron"++"aldo"` ⤳ `"Ronaldo"`

!!	`[a] -> Int -> a`	`xs!!n` returns the nth element of `xs`, starting at the beginning and counting from 0.
		`[14,7,3]!!1` ⤳ `7`

concat	`[[a]] -> [a]`	Concatenate a list of lists into a single list.
		`concat [[2,3],[],[4]]` ⤳ `[2,3,4]`

length	`[a] -> Int`	The length of the list.
		`length "word"` ⤳ `4`

head,last	`[a] -> a`	The first/last element of the list.
		`head "word"` ⤳ `'w'`
		`last "word"` ⤳ `'d'`

tail,init	`[a] -> [a]`	All but the first/last element of the list.
		`tail "word"` ⤳ `"ord"`
		`init "word"` ⤳ `"wor"`

replicate	`Int -> a -> [a]`	Make a list of n copies of the item.
		`replicate 3 'c'` ⤳ `"ccc"`

take	`Int -> [a] -> [a]`	Take n elements from the front of a list.
		`take 3 "Peccary"` ⤳ `"Pec"`

drop	`Int -> [a] -> [a]`	Drop n elements from the front of a list.
		`drop 3 "Peccary"` ⤳ `"cary"`

splitAt	`Int -> [a] -> ([a],[a])`	Split a list at a given position.
		`splitAt 3 "Peccary"` ⤳ `("Pec","cary")`

reverse	`[a] -> [a]`	Reverse the order of the elements.
		`reverse [2,1,3]` ⤳ `[3,1,2]`

zip	`[a]->[b]->[(a,b)]`	Take a pair of lists into a list of pairs.
		`zip [1,2] [3,4,5]` ⤳ `[(1,3),(2,4)]`

unzip	`[(a,b)] -> ([a],[b])`	Take a list of pairs into a pair of lists.
		`unzip [(1,5),(3,6)]` ⤳ `([1,3],[5,6])`

Figure 5.1   Some polymorphic list operations from `Prelude.hs`.

and	`[Bool] -> Bool`	The conjunction of a list of Booleans. `and [True,False]` ↝ `False`
or	`[Bool] -> Bool`	The disjunction of a list of Booleans. `or [True,False]` ↝ `True`
sum	`[Int] -> Int` `[Float] -> Float`	The sum of a numeric list. `sum [2,3,4]` ↝ `9`
product	`[Int] -> Int` `[Float] -> Float`	The product of a numeric list. `product [0.1,0.4 .. 1]` ↝ `0.028`

Figure 5.2 Some monomorphic list operations from `Prelude.hs`.

Further functions

We have not described all the functions in the prelude for two different reasons. First, some of the general functions are **higher-order** and we postpone discussion of these until Chapter 9; secondly, some of the functions, such as zip3, are obvious variants of things we have discussed here. Similarly, we have not chosen to enumerate the functions in the library List.hs; readers should consult the library file itself, which contains type information and comments about the effects of the functions.

In the next chapter we explore how to use the prelude functions in making our own definitions of functions; before that we discuss strings, an example of a list type.

5.9 The String type

The String type is a special case of lists,

```
type String = [Char]
```

and all the polymorphic prelude functions in Figure 5.1 can be used over strings. In Section 3.5 we showed how to write the special characters such as newline and tab using the 'escapes' '\n' and '\t'. These characters can form part of strings, as in the examples

```
"baboon"
""
"\99a\116"
"gorilla\nhippo\nibex"
"1\t23\t456"
```

If we evaluate one of these strings in Hugs, the result is exactly the same as the input. In order to resolve the escape characters and to lose the double quotes we have to perform an output operation. This is done using the primitive Haskell function

```
putStr :: String -> IO ()
```

with the effect of putting the argument string on the screen. Applying putStr to the strings above gives output as follows:

```
baboon

cat
gorilla
hippo
ibex
1       23      456
```

Strings can be joined together using ++, so that "cat"++"\n"++"fish" prints as

```
cat
fish
```

Note: Names, strings and characters

It is easy to confuse a, 'a' and "a". To summarize the difference,

a	is a name or a variable, if defined it may have any type whatever;
'a'	is a character;
"a"	is a string, which just happens to consist of a single character.

Similarly, there is a difference between

emu	a Haskell name or variable;
"emu"	a string.

Other functions over strings can be found in the library String.hs.

Strings and values

Built into Haskell are the overloaded functions show and read, which convert from a value to a String and vice versa; for instance,

```
show (2+3)           ↝   "5"
show (True || False) ↝   "True"
```

In the opposite direction, the function read is used to convert a string to the value it represents, so that

```
read "True" ↝   True
read "3"    ↝   3
```

In some situations it will not be clear what should be the result type for read – it is then possible to give a type to the application, as in

```
(read "3") :: Int
```

the result of which will be 3 and its type, Int.

A full explanation of the types of read and show can be found in Chapter 12.

5.19 Define a function to convert small letters to capitals which returns unchanged characters which are not small letters.

5.20 Define a function

```
romanDigit :: Char -> String
```

which converts a digit to its representation in Roman numerals, so at '7' it will have the value "VII" and so on.

5.21 Define a function

```
onThreeLines :: String -> String -> String -> String
```

which takes three strings and returns a single string which when printed shows the three strings on separate lines.

5.22 Define a function

```
onSeparateLines :: [String] -> String
```

which takes a list of strings and returns a single string which when printed shows the strings on separate lines.

5.23 Give a function

```
duplicate :: String -> Int -> String
```

which takes a string and an integer, n. The result is n copies of the string joined together. If n is less than or equal to 0, the result should be the empty string, "", and if n is 1, the result will be the string itself.

5.24 Give a function

```
pushRight :: String -> String
```

which takes a string and forms a string of length linelength by putting spaces at the front of the string. If linelength were 12 then pushRight "crocodile" would be " crocodile". How would you make linelength a parameter of this function?

5.25 Can you criticize the way the previous function is specified? Look for a case in which it is not defined what it should do – it is an exceptional case.

5.26 Define a function

```
fibTable :: Int -> String
```

which produces a table of Fibonacci numbers. For instance, the effect of putStr
(fibTable 6) should be

n	fib n
0	0
1	1
2	1
3	2
4	3
5	5
6	8

5.27 Define functions to give more readable output from the database operations of
Section 5.6.

Summary

This chapter has introduced the structured types of tuples and lists, and explained their
differences: in a given tuple type, $(t_1, \ldots t_n)$ the elements all have the same form,
namely $(v_1, \ldots v_n)$, with each component v_i being a member of the corresponding
type t_i. The list type $[t]$ on the other hand contains elements $[e_1, \ldots, e_n]$ of
different lengths but in which all the values e_i have the same type t.

Over tuples we introduced the notion of pattern matching – in which a pattern such
as (x,y) could be used to stand for an arbitrary member of a pair type – and saw how
this led to more readable definitions.

The bulk of the chapter was an account of the facilities which Haskell provides for
working with lists. These include

- various ways of writing lists of elements of base type, including ranges like [2,4..12];
- list comprehensions, in which the members of a list are generated, tested and transformed from the elements of another list, as exemplified by

  [toUpper ch | ch <- string , isAlpha ch]

  which selects the alphabetic characters from string, and converts them to upper
  case;
- the functions provided by the standard prelude and the List.hs library;
- String as the list type [Char].

In order to understand the prelude functions it was necessary to discuss polymorphism,
by which a function can have 'many types'. Types of functions like this are described
by using type variables, as in

reverse :: [a] -> [a]

which states that reverse can be applied to a list of any type (a is a type variable),
returning a member of the same list type.

In the chapters to come we will use the list functions given here in making our own
definitions, as well as seeing how the prelude and library functions are themselves
defined.

Chapter 6

Programming with lists

The purpose of this chapter is threefold.

● We revisit and extend the `Picture` example in order to illustrate some of the ideas which we introduced in the previous chapter.

● We discuss the mechanism for making definitions **local** to a function or expression. This becomes important when we start to write more substantial programs, as it makes them both more readable and potentially more efficient.

● We introduce two extended sets of exercises to stretch the reader rather more than the small exercises we have given thus far. The two case studies are

  – an extension of `Pictures` to give them a position (in space); and

  – a billing program for a supermarket checkout, which has to produce a formatted bill from the list of bar codes scanned in at a checkout.

The chapter following this discusses how we implement the primitive functions over lists using recursion; readers may skip forward to this, reading only Sections 6.1 and 6.3 on `Pictures` and local definitions.

6.1 The `Picture` example, revisited

In this section we revisit the `Picture` example, first introduced in Chapter 1 and re-examined in Section 2.5. What we do here is to look at how to implement some of the operations over the `Picture` type

```
type Picture = [[Char]]
```

Some of the operations are defined as library functions. To flip a picture in a horizontal mirror, we simply have to reverse the order of the lines of the picture:

```
flipH :: Picture -> Picture
flipH = reverse
```

and to place one picture above another it is sufficient to join the two lists of lines together:

```
above :: Picture -> Picture -> Picture
above = (++)
```

where we have enclosed the operator ++ in parentheses to make it a (prefix) function.

How do we flip a picture in a vertical mirror? We have to reverse each of the lines, that is we have to transform each member of a list in some way. This is one of the features of a list comprehension, so we can say

```
flipV :: Picture -> Picture
flipV pic
  = [ reverse line | line <- pic ]
```

and we can read off from this program its intended effect:

> "reverse every line in the pic".

This is an example of the general operation of applying a function f to every element of a list xs, given by the list comprehension

```
[ f x | x <- xs ]
```

We shall see that this operation is itself a higher-order function in Chapter 9 below.

Next we explore how to place two pictures side by side. What we want to do is to join up the corresponding lines of the two pictures, as illustrated on page 14. How can we accomplish this? We can see this as like flipV, in that we want to do something to every pair of lines – namely join them with ++ – but we need to associate corresponding lines before we do this. That is exactly the purpose of the prelude function zip, which takes two lists and pairs corresponding elements, and so we can say

```
sideBySide :: Picture -> Picture -> Picture
sideBySide picL picR
  = [ lineL ++ lineR | (lineL,lineR) <- zip picL picR ]
```

The effect of zip is to chop the list of pairs to the shorter of the two inputs, and so sideBySide will clip the bottom lines off whichever picture is the longer; if they are the same length, then there is no clipping. We can also use the higher-order zipWith to define sideBySide; we revisit this in Chapter 9.

In our pictures, white is represented by the dot '.' and black by the hash symbol '#'. To invert the colour of a single character we define

```
invertChar :: Char -> Char
invertChar ch
  = if ch=='.' then '#' else '.'
```

The characters '.' and '#' are swapped by this definition (and any other character is transformed into '.', too). Now, how do we invert the colours in a whole picture? We need to invert each character in a line, using

```
invertLine :: [Char] -> [Char]
invertLine line
  = [ invertChar ch | ch <- line ]
```

and we want to apply this to all the lines in the picture

```
invertColour :: Picture -> Picture
invertColour pic
  = [ invertLine line | line <- pic ]
```

We could if we wish write this as a single definition, thus

```
invertColour :: Picture -> Picture
invertColour pic
  = [ [ invertChar ch | ch <- line ] | line <- pic ]
```

but our use of the auxiliary function invertLine makes the previous definition more readable.

In the next section we extend our model of pictures to give them a position as well as some pictorial content.

Exercises

6.1 Define a function

```
superimposeChar :: Char -> Char -> Char
```

so that the superimposition of '.' with itself gives '.' while any other combination of characters gives '#'.

6.2 Define a function

```
superimposeLine :: [Char] -> [Char] -> [Char]
```

which takes two lines – which you can assume are of the same length – and superimposes their corresponding characters using superimposeChar, so that, for example,

```
superimposeLine ".##." ".#.#" = ".###"
```

You may want to use zip in your solution.

6.3 In a similar way to superimposeLine, define the function

```
superimpose :: Picture -> Picture -> Picture
```

which superimposes two pictures, which you may assume have the same dimensions.

6.4 Using the function putStr :: String -> IO () and any other functions you might need, define the function

```
printPicture :: Picture -> IO ()
```

so that the effect of printPicture [".##.", ".#.#", ".###", "####"] is that

```
.##.
.#.#
.###
####
```

is printed at the terminal window.

6.5 An alternative representation of Picture is the type

```
[[Bool]]
```

where True and False represent black and white points in a picture. How would you have to modify the functions working over Picture to accommodate this change? What are the advantages and disadvantages of the two representations?

6.6 [Harder] Define a function

```
rotate90 :: Picture -> Picture
```

which rotates a picture through 90° clockwise. For instance, the effect of rotate90 on the picture in the previous exercise would be to give

```
#...
####
##.#
###.
```

Hint: you need to make a line of the new picture by picking out the ith elements in each of the lines of the original picture, reflected in a horizontal mirror.

6.7 Using rotate90 or otherwise, define a function which rotates a picture through 90° *anti*clockwise.

6.8 [Harder] Define the function

```
scale :: Picture -> Int -> Picture
```

which scales the input picture by the integer provided as the second argument. For instance, if `exPic` is the picture

```
#.#
..#
```

then the result of `scale exPic 2` should be

```
##..##
##..##
....##
....##
```

In the case of a zero or negative scale factor, you should return an empty picture.

6.2 Extended exercise: positioned pictures

The pictures that we have modelled using the type `Picture` are not anchored at any particular point in space: we can think of them concretely as being on pieces of paper which can be joined together, superimposed, rotated and so on.

A different model of pictures gives each picture a `Position` in space: we can then think of moving these pictures, of superimposing two of these pictures to give another picture, and so on.

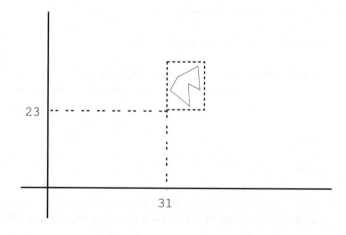

Figure 6.1 An example `Image`.

Basics

How can we represent pictures with positions? First we need to think about how we model positions on an *integer* grid. A Position is given by a pair of integers,

```
type Position = (Int,Int)
```

We will use the term Image for a picture with a position, and so we define

```
type Image = (Picture,Position)
```

An example, in which we position the horse with its bottom left-hand corner or **reference point** at position (31,23), is given in Figure 6.1.

The remainder of this section is a collection of exercises to write functions which manipulate these Images; you can use any of the list functions introduced in the previous chapter and also the functions over Picture which we have already defined.

Exercises

6.9 Define a function

```
makeImage :: Picture -> Position -> Image
```

which makes an Image from a Picture and a Position.

6.10 Define a function

```
changePosition :: Image -> Position -> Image
```

which takes an Image and returns a new Image whose Picture is unchanged but whose Position is given by the second argument to changePosition.

6.11 Give a definition of the function

```
moveImage :: Image -> Int -> Int -> Image
```

so that the effect of moveImage img xMove yMove is to move img by xMove in the horizontal (x) direction and by yMove in the vertical (y) direction.

6.12 Define a function

```
printImage :: Image -> IO ()
```

whose action is the analogue of printPicture for pictures.

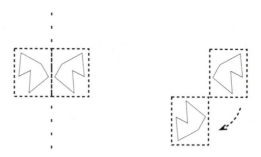

Figure 6.2   The geometrical view of `flipV` and `rotate`.

Transformations

We can extend the transformations over the type `Picture` to the `Image` type, but we need to think about the effect of these transformations on the position. One way to lift the transformations from pictures to images is simply to say that the pictures stay in the same position – we call this the **naive** view.

   If we think of reflections and rotations going on in space, then the results are more likely to be as shown in Figure 6.2, where we see that the position of the resulting image has changed. Rotation is about the reference point, and reflection is in the horizontal or vertical line through the reference point; in general these operations will change the reference point. We call this the **geometrical** view of the transformations.

Exercises

6.13 Implement for `Image` the analogues of `flipH`, `flipV`, `rotate` and `rotate90` under the naive view of how to lift the transformations.

6.14 Implement for `Image` the analogues of `flipH`, `flipV`, `rotate` and `rotate90` under the geometrical view.

Superimposition

When pictures have positions, superimposition can be more complex. Consider the example illustrated in Figure 6.3; here we see one way of superimposing the two images is to use `Picture` superimposition on two pictures which have first been 'padded out' with white space as shown in the figure.

Exercises

6.15 Define functions to 'pad out' a `Picture` with an amount of white space, as shown in Figure 6.3.

You will need to think carefully about the intended effect of the functions before you start to implement them. You will need to have function parameters for the amount of padding to the left, right, bottom and top of the image.

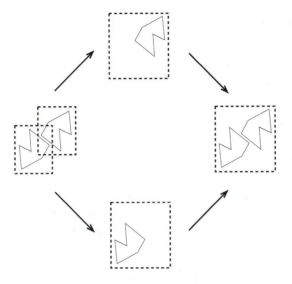

Figure 6.3 Superimposing two Images.

Note, in particular, that the Position of an Image might change as a result of padding.

6.16 Using the padding functions, define a superimposition function for the Image type.

6.17 How would you use Image superimposition to give analogues of above and sideBySide for Images?

(6.3) Local definitions

Before going any further, we need to discuss one further aspect of function definitions. Each (conditional) equation can be followed by a list of definitions which are **local** to the function or other object being defined. These definitions are written after the keyword where; we look first at some examples, before turning to some formalities about the 'visibility' of local definitions, calculation and so forth.

Examples

1. A simple example is given by a function which is to return the sum of the squares of two numbers.

```
sumSquares :: Int -> Int -> Int
```

The result of the function will be the sum of two values, sqN and sqM, so that

```
sumSquares n m
  = sqN + sqM
```

The definition of these two values can be done in the `where` clause which follows the equation, thus

```
sumSquares n m
  = sqN + sqM
    where
    sqN = n*n
    sqM = m*m
```

In such a simple example, it is perhaps hard to see the point of making the local definitions, but in practice many situations occur when a local definition or definitions make a solution both more readable and more efficient. We look at such an example now.

2.   Take the example of the function

```
addPairwise :: [Int] -> [Int] -> [Int]
```

which adds corresponding elements of the two lists, dropping any elements which fail to have a 'partner'. For instance,

```
addPairwise [1,7] [8,4,2] = [9,11]
```

This can be defined by analogy with `sideBySide` in Section 6.1 thus

```
addPairwise intList1 intList2
  = [ m + n | (m,n) <- zip intList1 intList2 ]
```

Now suppose that we are asked to make sure that any elements without a partner are added to the end of the list. This will be the function

```
addPairwise' :: [Int] -> [Int] -> [Int]
```

whose effect on an example will be

```
addPairwise' [1,7] [8,4,2,67] = [9,11,2,67]
```

How can we approach this problem? Using the functions `take` and `drop` first introduced in Figure 5.1 we are able to split up the argument lists.

If `minLength` is the minimum of the two list lengths, then the front part of the result is given by

```
addPairwise (take minLength intList1) (take minLength intList2)
```

What remains? The remains will be

```
drop minLength intList1
drop minLength intList2
```

at least one of which will be [], and so we can collect all the elements 'without partners' simply by joining these two lists together. The function we want can therefore be given by the definition

```
addPairwise' intList1 intList2
  = front ++ rear
    where
    minLength = min (length intList1) (length intList2)
    front     = addPairwise (take minLength intList1)
                            (take minLength intList2)
    rear      = drop minLength intList1 ++ drop minLength intList2
```

Now, we have a gain in efficiency because minLength will only be calculated once, even though it is *used* four times in the definition. We also have a definition which is easier to read: we see that the result has two parts, front and rear, and we can read their definitions separately.

We can, in fact, make a further efficiency gain, by replacing separate calls to take and drop by a single call to splitAt, also introduced in Figure 5.1, as in

```
addPairwise' intList1 intList2
  = front ++ rear
    where
    minLength       = min (length intList1) (length intList2)
    front           = addPairwise front1 front2
    rear            = rear1 ++ rear2
    (front1,rear1) = splitAt minLength intList1
    (front2,rear2) = splitAt minLength intList2
```

In this example we see a third use of a where clause. We can put a pattern – like (front1,rear1) – on the left-hand side of a definition; the result of this is to associate the names front1 and rear1 with the corresponding components of the expression on the right-hand side – in this case the split of the list intList1.

A pattern match of this form is called **conformal**, as the expression on the right-hand side of the definition has to conform to the pattern on the left, otherwise the definition fails.

Another important point in this example is that the order of different definitions is irrelevant. In particular it is possible to use a value before it is defined: the definitions of front and rear precede those of front1 and rear1 which they use. This is equally true for scripts in general, in which the order of the top-level definitions is irrelevant.

Layout

In definitions with where clauses, the layout is significant. The offside rule is used by the system to determine the end of each definition in the where clause.

The where clause must be found in the definition to which it belongs, so that the where must occur somewhere to the right of the start of the definition. Inside the where clause, the same rules apply as at the top level: it is therefore important that the definitions are aligned vertically – if not, an error will result. Our recommended layout is therefore

```
f p1 p2 ··· pk
  | g1              = e1
    ···
  | otherwise     = er
    where
    v1  a1 ··· an = r1
    v2 = r2
    ....
```

The where clause here is attached to the whole of the conditional equation, and so is attached to all the clauses of the conditional equation.

This example also shows that the local definitions can include functions – here v_1 is an example of a local function definition. We have given type declarations for all top-level definitions; it is also possible to give type declarations for where-defined objects in Haskell. In cases where the type of a locally defined object is not obvious from its context, our convention is to include a declaration of its type.

let expressions

It is also possible to make definitions local to an expression. For instance, we can write

```
let x = 3+2 in x^2 + 2*x - 4
```

giving the result 31. If more than one definition is included in one line they need to be separated by semi-colons, thus:

```
let x = 3+2 ; y = 5-1 in x^2 + 2*x - y
```

We shall find that we use this form only occasionally.

Scopes

A Haskell script consists of a sequence of definitions. The **scope** of a definition is that part of the program in which the definition can be used. All definitions at the top-level in Haskell have as their scope the whole script that they are defined in: that is, they can be used in all the definitions the script contains. In particular they can be used in definitions which occur before theirs in the script, as in

```
isOdd, isEven :: Int -> Bool

isOdd n
  | n<=0        = False
  | otherwise   = isEven (n-1)
```

```
isEven n
  | n<0          = False
  | n==0         = True
  | otherwise    = isOdd (n-1)
```

Local definitions, given by `where` clauses, are not intended to be 'visible' in the whole of the script, but rather just in the conditional equation in which they appear. The same is true of the variables in a function definition: their scope is the whole of the conditional equation in which they appear.

Specifically, in the example which follows, the scope of the definitions of sqx, sqy and sq and of the variables x and y is given by the large box; the smaller box gives the scope of the variable z.

```
maxsq x y
```

```
  | sqx > sqy       = sqx
  | otherwise       = sqy

     where
     sqx  = sq x
     sqy  = sq y

     sq :: Int -> Int
     sq z =  z*z
```

In particular it is important to see that

- the variables appearing on the left-hand side of the function definition – x and y in this case – can be used in the local definitions; here they are used in sqx and sqy;
- local definitions can be used before they are defined: sq is used in sqx here;
- local definitions can be used in results and in guards as well as in other local definitions.

It is possible for a script to have two definitions or variables with the same name. In the example below, the variable x appears twice. Which definition is in force at each point? The *most local* is the one which is used.

```
maxsq x y
```

```
  | sq x > sq y    = sq x
  | otherwise      = sq y

     where

     sq x =  x*x
```

In the example, we can think of the inner box *cutting a hole* in the outer, so that the scope of the outer x will exclude the definition of sq. When one definition is contained inside another the best advice is that different variables and names should be used for the inner definitions unless there is a very good reason for using the same name twice.

Finally note that it is not possible to have multiple definitions of the same name at the same level; one of them needs to be hidden if a clash occurs due to the combination of a number of modules.

Calculation

The way in which calculations are written can be extended to deal with `where` clauses. The `sumSquares` function in the previous section gives, for example

```
sumSquares 4 3
= sqN + sqM
  where
  sqN = 4*4 = 16
  sqM = 3*3 = 9
= 16 + 9
= 25
```

The values of the local definitions are calculated beneath the `where` if their values are needed. All local evaluation below the `where` is indented. To follow the top-level value, we just have to look at the calculation at the left-hand side.

The vertical lines which appear are used to link the successive steps of a calculation when these have intermediate `where` calculations. The lines can be omitted.

Exercises

6.18 Define the function

```
maxThreeOccurs :: Int -> Int -> Int -> (Int,Int)
```

which returns the maximum of three integers paired with the number of times it occurs among the three. A natural solution first finds the maximum, and then investigates how often it occurs among the three. Discuss how you would write your solution if you were not allowed to use `where`-definitions.

6.19 Give sample calculations of

```
maxThreeOccurs 4 5 5
maxThreeOccurs 4 5 4
```

using your definition of `maxThreeOccurs` from the previous question.

6.4 Extended exercise: supermarket billing

This collection of exercises looks at supermarket billing.[1] The idea is to use the list-manipulating techniques presented in Chapter 5. In particular we will be using list

---

[1] I am grateful to Peter Lindsay *et al.* of the Department of Computer Science at the University of New South Wales, Australia, for the inspiration for this example, which was suggested by their lecture notes.

comprehensions and also the prelude functions mentioned there. We will also expect local definitions – as explained in Section 6.3 – to be used when appropriate.

The problem

A scanner at a supermarket checkout will produce from a basket of shopping a list of bar codes, like

```
[1234,4719,3814,1112,1113,1234]
```

which has to be converted to a bill

```
                    Haskell Stores


         Dry Sherry, 1lt..........5.40
         Fish Fingers.............1.21
         Orange Jelly.............0.56
         Hula Hoops (Giant).......1.33
         Unknown Item.............0.00
         Dry Sherry, 1lt..........5.40


         Total...................13.90
```

We have to decide first how to model the objects involved. Bar codes and prices (in pence) can be modelled by integers; names of goods by strings. We say therefore that

```
type Name    = String
type Price   = Int
type BarCode = Int
```

The conversion will be based on a **database** which links bar codes, names and prices. As in the library, we use a list to model the relationship.

```
type Database = [ (BarCode,Name,Price) ]
```

The example database we use is

```
codeIndex :: Database
codeIndex = [ (4719, "Fish Fingers" , 121),
              (5643, "Nappies" , 1010),
              (3814, "Orange Jelly", 56),
              (1111, "Hula Hoops", 21),
              (1112, "Hula Hoops (Giant)", 133),
              (1234, "Dry Sherry, 1lt", 540)]
```

The object of the script will be to convert a list of bar codes into a list of (Name,Price) pairs; this then has to be converted into a string for printing as above. We make the type definitions

```
type TillType = [BarCode]
type BillType = [(Name,Price)]
```

and then we can say that the functions we wish to define are

```
makeBill    :: TillType -> BillType
```

which takes a list of bar codes to a list of name/price pairs,

```
formatBill  :: BillType -> String
```

which takes a list of name/price pairs into a formatted bill, and

```
produceBill :: TillType -> String
```

which will combine the effects of makeBill and formatBill, thus

```
produceBill = formatBill . makeBill
```

The length of a line in the bill is decided to be 30. This is made a constant, thus

```
lineLength :: Int
lineLength = 30
```

Making lineLength a constant in this way means that to change the length of a line in the bill, only one definition needs to be altered; if 30 were used in each of the formatting functions, then each would have to be modified on changing the line length. The rest of the script is developed through the sequences of exercises which follow.

Formatting the bill

First we develop the formatBill function from the bottom up: we design functions to format prices, lines, and the total, and using these we finally build the formatBill function itself.

Exercises

6.20 Given a number of pence, 1023 say, the pounds and pence parts are given by 1023 'div' 100 and 1023 'mod' 100. Using this fact, and the show function, define a function

```
formatPence :: Price -> String
```

so that, for example, formatPence 1023 = "10.23"; you need to be careful about cases like "12.02".

6.21 Using the formatPence function, define a function

```
formatLine   :: (Name,Price) -> String
```

which formats a line of a bill, thus

```
formatLine ("Dry Sherry, 1lt",540)
              = "Dry Sherry, 1lt..........5.40\n"
```

Recall that '\n' is the newline character, that ++ can be used to join two strings together, and that length will give the length of a string. You might also find the replicate function useful.

6.22 Using the formatLine function, define

```
formatLines :: [ (Name,Price) ] -> String
```

which applies formatLine to each (Name,Price) pair, and joins the results together.

6.23 Define a function

```
makeTotal :: BillType -> Price
```

which takes a list of (Name,Price) pairs, and gives the total of the prices. For instance,

```
makeTotal [(" ... ",540),(" ... ",121)] = 661
```

6.24 Define the function

```
formatTotal :: Price -> String
```

so that, for example,

```
formatTotal 661 = "\nTotal....................6.61"
```

6.25 Using the functions formatLines, makeTotal and formatTotal, define

```
formatBill :: BillType -> String
```

so that on the input

```
[("Dry Sherry, 1lt",540),("Fish Fingers",121),
("Orange Jelly",56),("Hula Hoops (Giant)",133),
("Unknown Item",0),("Dry Sherry, 1lt",540)]
```

the example bill at the start of the section is produced.

Making the bill: bar codes into names and prices

Now we have to look at the database functions which accomplish the conversion of bar codes into names and prices.

6.26 Define a function

```
look :: Database -> BarCode -> (Name,Price)
```

which returns the (Name,Price) pair corresponding to the BarCode in the Database. If the BarCode does not appear in the database, then the pair ("Unknown Item", 0) should be the result.

Hint: using the ideas of the library database you might find that you are returning a *list* of (Name,Price) rather than a single value. You can assume that each bar code occurs only once in the database, so you can extract this value by taking the head of such a list *if it is non-empty*.

6.27 Define a function

```
lookup :: BarCode -> (Name,Price)
```

which uses look to look up an item in the particular database codeIndex. This function clashes with a function lookup defined in the prelude; consult page 41 for details of how to handle this.

6.28 Define the function

```
makeBill   :: TillType -> BillType
```

which applies lookup to every item in the input list. For instance, when applied to [1234,4719,3814,1112,1113,1234] the result will be the list of (Name,Price) pairs given in Exercise 6.25. Note that 1113 does not appear in codeIndex and so is converted to ("Unknown Item",0).

This completes the definition of makeBill and together with formatBill gives the conversion program.

Extending the problem

We conclude with some further exercises.

6.29 You are asked to add a discount for multiple buys of sherry: for every two bottles bought, there is a 1.00 discount. From the example list of bar codes

```
[1234,4719,3814,1112,1113,1234]
```

the bill should be as illustrated in Figure 6.4. You will probably find it helpful to define functions

```
                    Haskell Stores

           Dry Sherry, 1lt...........5.40
           Fish Fingers..............1.21
           Orange Jelly..............0.56
           Hula Hoops (Giant)........1.33
           Unknown Item..............0.00
           Dry Sherry, 1lt...........5.40

           Discount..................1.00

           Total....................12.90
```

Figure 6.4   Bills with `multibuy' discounts.

```
makeDiscount :: BillType -> Int
formatDiscount :: Int -> String
```

which you can use in a redefined

```
formatBill :: BillType -> String
```

6.30 Design functions which update the database of bar codes. You will need a function to add a `BarCode` and a (`Name`,`Price`) pair to the `Database`, while at the same time removing any other reference to the bar code already present in the database.

6.31 Re-design your system so that bar codes which do not appear in the database give no entry in the final bill. There are (at least) two ways of doing this.

  ● Keep the function `makeBill` as it is, and modify the formatting functions, or
  ● modify the `makeBill` function to remove the 'unknown item' pairs.

6.32 [Project] Design a script of functions to analyse collections of sales. Given a list of `TillType`, produce a table showing the total sales of each item. You might also analyse the bills to see which *pairs* of items are bought together; this could assist with placing items in the supermarket.

Summary

This chapter has introduced the idea of local definitions, most importantly the `where` clauses attached to the conditional equations in function definitions. We illustrated the way in which these definitions are used to make definitions more readable, and also to avoid re-computation of results, like the `minLength` in the example `addPairwise'`. We gave a general template for the layout of function definitions including guards and `where` clauses.

We also saw how the combination of list comprehensions and the built-in functions from the prelude give us a powerful repertoire of tools with which to build definitions over particular list types. This was evident in the `Picture` example as well as in the case studies, and these also gave an opportunity to see the way in which a larger program was built as a collection of related functions.

Chapter 7

Defining functions over lists

We have already seen how to define a variety of functions over lists using a combination of list comprehensions and the built-in list processing functions in the Haskell prelude. This chapter looks `under the bonnet' and explains how functions over lists can be defined by means of recursion. This will allow us to define the prelude functions we have already been using, as well as letting us look at a wider class of applications, including sorting and a case study of text processing.

The chapter begins with a summary of the mechanism of pattern matching, and continues with a justification and explanation of recursion echoing the discussion in Chapter 4. We then explore a variety of examples both of functions defined by primitive recursion and of more general recursive functions, and conclude with the case study mentioned earlier.

7.1 Pattern matching revisited

We have seen that function definitions take the form of conditional equations like

```
mystery :: Int -> Int -> Int
```

```
mystery x y
  | x==0        = y
  | otherwise   = x
```

where a choice of two alternatives is made by guards; we can rewrite this into two equations, thus

```
mystery 0 y = y                                          (mystery.1)
mystery x y = x                                          (mystery.2)
```

where we distinguish between the two cases by using a pattern – here the literal 0 – instead of a variable. Just as for guards, the equations are applied **sequentially**, and so (`mystery.2`) will only be used in cases that (`mystery.1`) does not apply.

Another aspect of this definition is that y is not used on the right-hand side of (`mystery.2`). Because of this we do not need to give a name to the second argument in this case, and so we can replace the variable y with the **wildcard** '_' which matches anything, thus

```
mystery 0 y = y
mystery x _ = x
```

We have therefore seen that pattern matching can be used for distinguishing between certain sorts of **cases** in function definitions. We have also seen pattern matching used to **name the components** of tuples, as in

```
joinStrings :: (String,String) -> String
joinStrings (st1,st2) = st1 ++ "\t" ++ st2
```

where the variables st1 and st2 will be matched with the components of any argument.

In working with lists the two aspects of distinguishing cases and extracting components are used together, as we see in the next section.

Summarizing patterns

A pattern can be one of a number of things:

- A **literal value** such as 24, 'f' or True; an argument matches this pattern if it is equal to the value.
- A **variable** such as x or longVariableName; any argument value will match this.
- A **wildcard** '_'; any argument value will match this.
- A **tuple pattern** $(p_1,p_2,\ldots,p_n)$. To match this, an argument must be of the form $(v_1,v_2,\ldots,v_n)$, and each v_k must match p_k.
- A **constructor** applied to a number of patterns; we will examine this case in the next section and in Chapter 14 below.

In a function definition we have a number of conditional equations, each of which will have a left-hand side in which the function is applied to a number of patterns. When the function is applied we try to match the arguments with the patterns in sequence, and we use the first equation which applies; pattern matching in Haskell is thus **sequential**, in a similar way to the conditions expressed by guards.

7.2 Lists and list patterns

Every list is either **empty**, [], or is non-empty. In the latter case – take the example [4,2,3] – then it can be written in the form x:xs, where x is the first item in the list and xs is the remainder of the list; in our example, we have 4:[2,3]. We call 4 the **head** of the list and [2,3] the **tail**.

What is more, every list can be built up from the empty list by repeatedly applying ':', and indeed Haskell lists are represented in that way internally. Our example list can be thought of as being built step-by-step from the right, thus

```
[]        3:[] = [3]        2:[3] = [2,3]        4:[2,3] = [4,2,3]
```

and we can write the list using ':' repeatedly thus:

```
4:2:3:[]
```

Note that here we use the fact that ':' is **right associative**, so that for any values of x, y and zs,

```
x:y:zs = x:(y:zs)
```

It is also not hard to see that 4:2:3:[] is the *only* way that [4,2,3] can be built using ':'. The operator ':', of type

```
a -> [a] -> [a]
```

therefore has a special role to play for lists: it is a **constructor** for lists, since every list can be built up in a unique way from [] and ':'. For historical reasons we sometimes call this constructor **cons**. Not all functions are constructors: ++ can be used to build lists, but this construction will not be unique, since, for example

```
[1] ++ [2,3] = [1,2,3] = [1,2] ++ [3]
```

Pattern-matching definitions

If we want to make a definition covering all cases of lists we can write

```
fun xs = ....
```

but more often than not we will want to distinguish between empty and non-empty cases, as in the prelude functions

```
head               :: [a] -> a
head (x:_)          = x

tail               :: [a] -> [a]
tail (_:xs)         = xs

null               :: [a] -> Bool
null []             = True
null (_:_)          = False
```

where head takes the first item in a non-empty list, tail takes all but the head of a non-empty list and null checks whether or not a list is empty.

In the definition of null the pattern (_:_) will match any non-empty list, but it gives no names for the head and tail; when we need to name one of these, as in tail, then a different pattern, (_:xs), is used.

It has become an informal convention in the Haskell community to write variables over lists in the form xs, ys (pronounced 'exes', 'whyes') and so on, with variables x, y, ... ranging over their elements. We will – when using short variable names – endeavour to stick to that convention.

We can now explain the final case of pattern matching. A **constructor pattern** over lists will either be [] or will have the form (p:ps) where p and ps are themselves patterns.

- A list matches [] exactly when it is empty.
- A list will match the pattern (p:ps) if it is non-empty, and moreover if its head matches the pattern p and its tail the pattern ps.

In the case of the pattern (x:xs), it is sufficient for the argument to be non-empty to match the pattern; the head of the argument is matched with x and its tail with xs.

A pattern involving a constructor like ':' will always be parenthesized, since function application binds more tightly than any other operation.

The case construction

So far we have seen how to perform a pattern match over the arguments of functions; sometimes we might want to pattern match over other values. This can be done by a case expression, which we introduce by means of an example.

Suppose we are asked to find the first digit in the string st, returning '\0' in case no digit is found. We can use the function digits of Section 5.5 to give us the list of all the digits in the string: digits st. If this is not empty, that is if it matches (x:_), we want to return its first element, x; if it is empty, we return '\0'.

We therefore want to pattern match over the value of (digits st) and for this we use a case expression as follows:

```
firstDigit :: String -> Char

firstDigit st
  = case (digits st) of
       []    -> '\0'
       (x:_) -> x
```

A case expression has the effect of distinguishing between various alternatives – here those of an empty and a non-empty list – and of extracting parts of a value, by associating values with the variables in a pattern. In the case of matching e with (x:_) we associate the head of e with x; as we have used a wild-card pattern in (x:_), the tail of e is not associated with any variable.

In general, a case expression has the form

```
case e of
  p₁ -> e₁
  p₂ -> e₂
  ...
  pₖ -> eₖ
```

where e is an expression to be matched in turn against the patterns $p_1, p_2, \ldots, p_k$. If p_i is the first pattern which e matches, the result is e_i where the variables in p_i are associated with the corresponding parts of e.

Exercises

7.1 Give a pattern-matching definition of a function which returns the first integer in a list plus one, if there is one, and returns zero otherwise.

7.2 Give a pattern-matching definition of a function which adds together the first two integers in a list, if a list contains at least two elements; returns the head element if the list contains one, and returns zero otherwise.

7.3 Give solutions to the previous two questions *without* using pattern matching.

7.3 Primitive recursion over lists

Suppose we are to find the sum of a list of integers. Just as we described calculating factorial in Section 4.2, we can think of laying out the values of sum in a table thus:

```
              sum [] = 0
....          sum [5] = 5        ....
....          sum [7,5] = 12      ....
....          sum [2,7,5] = 14      ....
....          sum [3,2,7,5] = 17      ....
....
```

and just as in the case of factorial, we can describe the table by describing the first line and how to go from one line to the next, as follows:

```
sum :: [Int] -> Int
sum []     = 0                                    (sum.1)
sum (x:xs) = x + sum xs                           (sum.2)
```

This gives a definition of sum by **primitive recursion over lists**. In such a definition we give

● a starting point: the value of sum at [], and

● a way of going from the value of sum at a particular point – sum xs – to the value of sum on the next line, namely sum (x:xs).

There is also a calculational explanation for why this form of recursion works; again, this is just like the case put forward in Section 4.2. Consider the calculation of `sum` [3,2,7,5]. Using the equation (`sum`.2) repeatedly we have

```
sum [3,2,7,5]
⤳   3 + sum [2,7,5]
⤳   3 + (2 + sum [7,5])
⤳   3 + (2 + (7 + sum [5]))
⤳   3 + (2 + (7 + (5 + sum [])))
```

and now we can use the equation (`sum`.1) and integer arithmetic to give

```
⤳   3 + (2 + (7 + (5 + 0)))
⤳   17
```

We can see that the recursion used to define `sum` will give an answer on any finite list since each recursion step takes us closer to the 'base case' where `sum` is applied to [].
    In the next section we look at a collection of examples of definitions by primitive recursion.

Exercises

7.4 Define the function

```
product :: [Int] -> Int
```

which gives the product of a list of integers, and returns 1 for an empty list; why is this particular value chosen as the result for the empty list?

7.5 Define the functions

```
and, or :: [Bool] -> Bool
```

which give the conjunction and disjunction of a list of Booleans. For instance,

```
and [False, True] = False
or  [False, True] = True
```

On an empty list `and` gives `True` and `or` gives `False`; explain the reason for these choices.

7.4 Finding primitive recursive definitions

We saw in the last section how primitive recursion over lists works, by means of two explanations: tabulating a function and calculating the result of a function. In this section we present a series of examples of primitive recursive definitions over lists. A template for a primitive recursive definition over lists is

```
fun []     = ....
fun (x:xs) = .... x .... xs .... fun xs ....
```

The crucial question to ask in trying to find a primitive recursive definition is:

What if *we were given the value* `fun xs`. *How could we define* `fun (x:xs)` *from it?*

We explore how definitions are found through a series of examples.

1. By analogy with `sum`, many other functions can be defined by 'folding in' an operator. The prelude functions `product`, `and` and `or` are examples; here we look at how to define the prelude function `concat`,

```
concat :: [[a]] -> [a]                                    (concat.0)
```

with the effect that

```
concat [e1,e2,...,en] = e1++e2++...++en
```

We can begin our definition

```
concat []     = []
concat (x:xs) = ....
```

How do we find `concat (x:xs)` if we are given `concat xs`? Look at the example where `(x:xs)` is the list $[e_1,e_2,\ldots,e_n]$. The value of `concat xs` is going to be

$$e_2{+}{+}\ldots{+}{+}e_n$$

and the result we want is $e_1{+}{+}e_2{+}{+}\ldots{+}{+}e_n$, and so we simply have to join the list x to the front of the joined lists `concat xs`, giving the definition

```
concat []     = []                                        (concat.1)
concat (x:xs) = x ++ concat xs                            (concat.2)
```

Looking at the definition here we can see that `(x:xs)` is a list of lists, since its element is joined to another list in (concat.2); the type of x will be the type of the result. Putting these facts together we can conclude that the type of the input is `[[a]]` and the type of the output is `[a]`; this agrees with the type given in (concat.0).

2. How is the function `++` which we used in the previous example itself defined? Can we use primitive recursion? One strategy we can use is to look at examples, so, taking 2 for x and `[3,4]` for xs we have

```
[2,3,4] ++ [9,8] = [2,3,4,9,8]
  [3,4] ++ [9,8] = [3,4,9,8]
```

so we get `[2,3,4] ++ [9,8]` by putting 2 on the front of `[3,4] ++ [9,8]`. In the case that the first list is empty,

```
[] ++ [9,8] = [9,8]
```

These examples suggest a definition

```
(++) :: [a] -> [a] -> [a]

[]      ++ ys = ys
(x:xs) ++ ys = x:(xs++ys)
```

Note that the type of ++ allows lists of arbitrary type to be joined, as long as the two lists are of the same type.

3.   A third example is to check whether an Int is an element of an Int list,

```
elem :: Int -> [Int] -> Bool
```

Clearly, no value is an element of [], but under what circumstances is x an element of (y:ys)? If you are not sure about how to answer this question, now is the point to stop and look at an example or two.

Returning to the question, since (y:ys) is built by adding y to the front of ys, x can be an element of y:ys either

- by being equal to y, or
- by being an element of ys.

It is this second case where we use the value elem x ys, and we make the following primitive recursive definition of elem.

```
elem x []      = False                            (elem.1)
elem x (y:ys) = (x==y) || (elem x ys)             (elem.2)
```

Note: Repeated variables in patterns

Another candidate definition of elem is

```
elem x (x:ys) = True                              (elem.3)
elem x (y:ys) = elem x ys
```

in which the equality check is done by repeating the variable x on the left-hand side of (elem.3). Unfortunately, repeated variables like this are not permitted in Haskell patterns.

---

4.   Suppose we wish to double every element of an integer list

```
doubleAll :: [Int] -> [Int]
```

The neatest solution is to use a list comprehension

```
doubleAll xs = [ 2*x | x<-xs ]
```

but we could ask whether this can be done 'by hand', as it were, using primitive recursion. Looking at some examples, we expect that

```
  doubleAll [2,3] =    [4,6]
doubleAll [4,2,3] = [8,4,6]
```

so that to double all the elements of (x:xs) we need to double all the elements of xs, and to stick 2*x on the front. Formally, we have

```
doubleAll []     = []                              (doubleAll.1)
doubleAll (x:xs) = 2*x : doubleAll xs              (doubleAll.2)
```

5.   Suppose that we want to select the even elements from an integer list.

```
selectEven :: [Int] -> [Int]
```

Using a list comprehension, we can say

```
selectEven xs = [ x | x<-xs , isEven x ]
```

but can we give a primitive recursive definition of this function? For an empty list, there are no elements to select from,

```
selectEven [] = []                                 (selectEven.1)
```

but what happens in the case of a non-empty list? Consider the examples

```
selectEven [2,3,4] = [2,4] = 2 : selectEven [3,4]
selectEven [5,3,4] =    [4] =     selectEven [3,4]
```

It is thus a matter of taking selectEven xs, and adding x to (the front of) this only when x is even. We therefore define

```
selectEven (x:xs)                                  (selectEven.2)
  | isEven x    = x : selectEven xs
  | otherwise   =     selectEven xs
```

6.   As a final example, suppose that we want to **sort** a list of numbers into ascending order. One way to sort the list

7	3	9	2

is to sort the tail [3,9,2] to give

2	3	9

It is then a matter of inserting the head, 7, in the right place in this list, to give the result

2	3	7	9

This gives the definition of iSort – the 'i' is for **insertion** sort.

```
iSort :: [Int] -> [Int]

iSort []     = []                                  (iSort.1)
iSort (x:xs) = ins x (iSort xs)                    (iSort.2)
```

This is a typical example of top-down definition, first discussed in Section 4.1. We have defined `iSort` assuming we can define `ins`. The development of the program has been in two separate parts, since we have a definition of the function `iSort` using a simpler function `ins`, together with a definition of the function `ins` itself. Solving each sub-problem is simpler than solving the original problem itself.

Now we have to define the function

```
ins :: Int -> [Int] -> [Int]
```

To get some guidance about how `ins` should behave, we look at some examples. Inserting 7 into [2,3,9] was given above, while inserting 1 into the same list gives

1	2	3	9

Looking at these two examples we see that

- in the case of 1, if the item to be inserted is no larger than the head of the list, we cons it to the front of the list;

- In the case of 7, if the item is greater than the head, we insert it in the tail of the list, and cons the head to the result, thus:

$$2 \quad : \boxed{\begin{array}{c|c|c} 3 & 7 & 9 \end{array}}$$

The function can now be defined, including the case that the list is empty.

```
ins x []      = [x]                              (ins.1)
ins x (y:ys)
   | x <= y       = x:(y:ys)                      (ins.2)
   | otherwise    = y : ins x ys                  (ins.3)
```

We now show the functions in action, in the calculation of `iSort [3,9,2]`:

```
iSort [3,9,2]
 ⤳   ins 3 (iSort [9,2])                          by (iSort.2)
 ⤳   ins 3 (ins 9 (iSort [2]))                    by (iSort.2)
 ⤳   ins 3 (ins 9 (ins 2 (iSort [])))             by (iSort.2)
 ⤳   ins 3 (ins 9 (ins 2 []))                     by (iSort.1)
 ⤳   ins 3 (ins 9 [2])                               by (ins.1)
 ⤳   ins 3 (2 : ins 9 [])                            by (ins.3)
 ⤳   ins 3 [2,9]                                     by (ins.1)
 ⤳   2 : ins 3 [9]                                   by (ins.3)
 ⤳   2 : [3,9]                                       by (ins.2)
 ⤳   [2,3,9]
```

Developing this function has shown the advantage of looking at examples while trying to define a function; the examples can give a guide about how the definition might break into cases, or the pattern of the recursion. We also saw how using top-down design can break a larger problem into smaller problems which are easier to solve.

In the next section we look at definitions by more general forms of recursion.

7.6 Using primitive recursion over lists, define a function

```
elemNum :: Int -> [Int] -> Int
```

so that `elemNum x xs` returns the number of times that x occurs in the list `xs`.

Can you define `elemNum` without using primitive recursion, using list comprehensions and built-in functions instead?

7.7 Define a function

```
unique :: [Int] -> [Int]
```

so that `unique xs` returns the list of elements of `xs` which occur exactly once. For example, `unique [4,2,1,3,2,3]` is `[4,1]`. You might like to think of two solutions to this problem: one using list comprehensions and the other not.

7.8 Give primitive recursive definitions of the prelude functions `reverse` and `unzip`.

7.9 Can you use the `iSort` function to find the minimum and maximum elements of a list of numbers? How would you find these elements without using `iSort`?

7.10 Design test data for the `ins` function. Your data should address different possible points of insertion, and also look at any exceptional cases.

7.11 By modifying the definition of the `ins` function we can change the behaviour of the sort, `iSort`. Redefine `ins` in two different ways so that

- the list is sorted in descending order;
- duplicates are removed from the list. For example,

  ```
  iSort [2,1,4,1,2] = [1,2,4]
  ```

  under this definition.

7.12 Design test data for the duplicate-removing version of `iSort`, explaining your choices.

7.13 By modifying the definition of the `ins` and `iSort` functions, define a function to sort lists of pairs of numbers. The ordering should be **lexicographic** – the dictionary ordering. This ordering first looks at the first halves of the pairs; only if these values are equal are the second halves compared. For instance, (2,73) is smaller than (3,0), and this is smaller than (3,2).

7.5 General recursions over lists

Just as we argued in Section 4.4, a recursive definition of a function need not always use the value of the function on the tail; any recursive call to a value on a *simpler* list will be legitimate, and so a number of different patterns of recursion are available for finding function definitions over lists. In trying to use recursion over lists to define a function we need to pose the question:

In defining f (x:xs) *which values of* f ys *would help me to work out the answer?*

---

1. It is possible to use recursion over two arguments simultaneously, an example being the definition of the prelude function zip. Recall that here we turn two lists into a list of pairs,

```
zip :: [a] -> [b] -> [(a,b)]
```

with the examples

```
zip [1,5] ['c','d']     = [(1,'c'), (5,'d')]
zip [1,5] ['c','d','e'] = [(1,'c'), (5,'d')]
```

If each of the lists is non-empty, we form a pair from their heads, and then zip their tails, giving

```
zip (x:xs) (y:ys) = (x,y) : zip xs ys                         (zip.1)
```

but in all other cases – that is when at least one of the lists is empty – the result is empty:

```
zip _ _ = []                                                  (zip.2)
```

Note that we rely on the sequential nature of pattern matching here; we can give the patterns for (zip.2) explicitly if we wish, thus:

```
zip (x:xs) (y:ys) = (x,y) : zip xs ys
zip (x:xs) []     = []
zip []     zs     = []
```

and in the second definition we see the three separate cases given in three separate equations. Using the original definition, an example calculation gives

```
zip [1,5] ['c','d','e']
~>  (1,'c') : zip [5] ['d','e']                           by (zip.1)
~>  (1,'c') : (5,'d') : zip [] ['e']                      by (zip.1)
~>  (1,'c') : (5,'d') : []                                by (zip.2)
~>  (1,'c') : [ (5,'d') ]                                 by defn of :
~>  [ (1,'c') , (5,'d') ]                                 by defn of :
```

Note that we have used the fact that ':' is right associative in writing this calculation.

2. The function take is used to take a given number of values from a list. For instance,

```
take 5  "Hot Rats" = "Hot R"
take 15 "Hot Rats" = "Hot Rats"
```

In this example we do recursion over an Int and a list

```
take :: Int -> [a] -> [a]
```

There are some special cases, when the `Int` is zero, or the list is empty

```
take 0 _       = []                                          (take.1)
take _ []      = []                                          (take.2)
```

What about the general case, when the list is non-empty and the `Int` greater than zero? We take n-1 elements from the tail of the list, and place the head on the front, thus:

```
take n (x:xs)
  | n>0        = x : take (n-1) xs                            (take.3)
```

and in the other cases we give an error

```
take _ _       = error "PreludeList.take: negative argument"
                                                             (take.4)
```

3. As a final example, we look at another method for sorting lists (of integers). The **quicksort** algorithm works by generating *two* recursive calls to sort. Suppose we are to sort the list

$$[4,2,7,1,4,5,6]$$

we can take off the head, 4, and then split the result $[2,7,1,4,5,6]$ into two parts:

$$[2,1,4] \qquad\qquad [7,5,6]$$

The first contains the elements no larger than 4, the second those exceeding 4. We sort these two, giving

$$[1,2,4] \qquad\qquad [5,6,7]$$

and then we get an ordered version of the original list thus

$$[1,2,4] \ ++\ [4] \ ++\ [5,6,7]$$

We can write this now

```
qSort :: [Int] -> [Int]

qSort [] = []                                                (qSort.1)
qSort (x:xs)
  = qSort [ y | y<-xs , y<=x] ++ [x] ++ qSort [ y | y<-xs , y>x]
                                                             (qSort.2)
```

It is striking to see how close this program is to our informal description of the algorithm, and this expressiveness is one of the important advantages of a functional approach.

We can see that this recursion will give an answer for every finite list, since in the recursive calls we apply qSort to two sublists of xs, which are necessarily smaller than (x:xs).

In Chapter 19 we talk about the efficiency of various algorithms, and show that in general quicksort will be more efficient than insertion sort. In the following section we look at a larger example of definitions which use general forms of recursion.

(**Exercises**)————————————————————————————————————

7.14 Using the definition of `take` as a guide, define the prelude functions `drop` and `splitAt`.

7.15 What is the value of `take (-3) []` according to the definition of `take` given earlier? How would you modify the definition so that there is an error reported whenever the `Int` argument is negative?

7.16 How would you define a function `zip3` which zips together three lists? Try to write a recursive definition and also one which *uses* `zip` instead; what are the advantages and disadvantages of the two different definitions?

7.17 How would you modify `qSort` to sort a list into descending order? How would you ensure that `qSort` removed duplicate elements?

7.18 One list is a **sublist** of another if the elements of the first occur in the second, in the same order. For instance, `"ship"` is a sublist of `"Fish & Chips"`, but not of `"hippies"`.

A list is a **subsequence** of another if it occurs as a sequence of elements *next to each other*. For example, `"Chip"` is a subsequence of `"Fish & Chips"`, but not of `"Chin up"`.

Define functions which decide whether one string is a sublist or a subsequence of another string.

(**7.6**) **Example: text processing**

In word processing systems it is customary for lines to be filled and broken automatically, to enhance the appearance of the text. This book is no exception. Input of the form

```
The heat bloomed      in December
  as the    carnival   season
              kicked into   gear.
Nearly helpless with sun and glare, I avoided Rio's brilliant
sidewalks
   and glittering beaches,
panting in dark    corners
and waiting out the inverted southern summer.
```

would be transformed by **filling** to

```
The heat bloomed in December as the
carnival season kicked into gear.
Nearly helpless with sun and glare,
I avoided Rio's brilliant sidewalks
and glittering beaches, panting in
dark corners and waiting out the
inverted southern summer.
```

To align the right-hand margin, the text is **justified** by adding extra inter-word spaces on all lines but the last:

```
The heat bloomed in December as the
carnival  season  kicked into gear.
Nearly helpless with sun and glare,
I avoided Rio's brilliant sidewalks
and glittering beaches, panting  in
dark  corners  and  waiting out the
inverted southern summer.
```

An input file in Haskell can be treated as a string of characters, and so string-manipulating operations play an important role here. Also, since strings are lists, this example will exercise general list functions.

Overall strategy

In this section we give an example of bottom-up program development, thinking first about some of the components we will need to solve the problem, rather than decomposing the solution in a top-down way.

The first step in processing text will be to split an input string into **words**, discarding any white space. The words are then rearranged into lines of the required length. These lines can then have spaces added so as to justify the text. We therefore start by looking at how text is split into words.

Extracting words

We first ask, given a string of characters, how should we define a function to take the first word from the front of a string?

A word is any sequence which does not contain the **whitespace** characters space, tab and newline.

```
whitespace = ['\n','\t',' ']
```

In defining getWord we will use the standard function elem, which tests whether an object is an element of a list. For instance, elem 'a' whitespace is False.

To guide the definition, consider two examples.

- getWord " boo" should be "" as the first character is whitespace;
- getWord "cat dog" is "cat". We get this by putting 'c' on the front of "at", which is getWord "at dog".

The definition is therefore given by:

```
getWord :: String -> String
getWord []    = []                                    (getWord.1)
getWord (x:xs)
  | elem x whitespace    = []                          (getWord.2)
  | otherwise            = x : getWord xs              (getWord.3)
```

Consider an example

```
getWord "cat dog"
~>  'c' : getWord "at dog"                              by (getWord.3)
~>  'c' : 'a' : getWord "t dog"                         by (getWord.3)
~>  'c' : 'a' : 't' : getWord " dog"                    by (getWord.3)
~>  'c' : 'a' : 't' : []                                by (getWord.2)
~>  "cat"
```

In a similar way, the first word of a string can be dropped.

```
dropWord :: String -> String
dropWord []    = []
dropWord (x:xs)
  | elem x whitespace    = (x:xs)
  | otherwise            = dropWord xs
```

It is easy to check that dropWord "cat dog" = " dog". We aim to use the functions getWord and dropWord to split a string into its constituent words. Note that before we take a word from the string " dog", we should remove the whitespace character(s) from the front. The function dropSpace will do this.

```
dropSpace :: String -> String
dropSpace []    = []
dropSpace (x:xs)
  | elem x whitespace    = dropSpace xs
  | otherwise            = (x:xs)
```

How is a string st to be split into words? Assuming st has no whitespace at the start,

● the first word in the output will be given by applying getWord to st;

● the remainder will be given by splitting what remains after removing the first word and the space following it: dropSpace (dropWord st).

The top-level function splitWords calls split after removing any whitespace at the start of the string.

```
type Word = String

splitWords :: String -> [Word]
splitWords st = split (dropSpace st)

split :: String -> [Word]
split [] = []
split st
  = (getWord st) : split (dropSpace (dropWord st))
```

Consider a short example.

```
splitWords "  dog cat"
↝   split "dog cat"
↝   (getWord "dog cat")
            : split (dropSpace (dropWord "dog cat"))
↝   "dog" : split (dropSpace " cat")
↝   "dog" : split "cat"
↝   "dog" : (getWord "cat")
            : split (dropSpace (dropWord "cat"))
↝   "dog" : "cat" : split (dropSpace [])
↝   "dog" : "cat" : split []
↝   "dog" : "cat" : []
↝   [ "dog" , "cat" ]
```

Splitting into lines

Now we have to consider how to break a list of words into lines. As before, we look to see how we can take the first line from a list of words.

```
type Line = [Word]
getLine :: Int -> [Word] -> Line
```

getLine takes two parameters. The first is the length of the line to be formed, and the second the list from which the words are taken. The definition uses length to give the length of a list. The definition will have three cases

- In the case that no words are available, the line formed is empty.

- If the first word available is w, then this goes on the line if there is room for it: its length, length w, has to be no greater than the length of the line, len.
  The remainder of the line is built from the words that remain by taking a line of length len-(length w+1).

- If the first word does not fit, the line has to be empty.

```
getLine len []      = []
getLine len (w:ws)
  | length w <= len    = w : restOfLine
  | otherwise          = []
    where
    newlen      = len - (length w + 1)
    restOfLine  = getLine newlen ws
```

Why is the rest of the line of length len-(length w+1)? Space must be allocated for the word w *and* the inter-word space needed to separate it from the word which follows. How does the function work in an example?

```
getLine 20 ["Mary","Poppins","looks","like",...
↝   "Mary" : getLine 15 ["Poppins","looks","like",...
↝   "Mary" : "Poppins" : getLine 7 ["looks","like",...
```

⤳   "Mary" : "Poppins" : "looks" : getLine 1 ["like",...
⤳   "Mary" : "Poppins" : "looks" : []
⤳   ["Mary" , "Poppins" , "looks"]

A companion function,

```
dropLine :: Int -> [Word] -> Line
```

removes a line from the front of a list of words, just as `dropWord` is a companion to `getWord`. The function to split a list of words into lines of length at most (the constant value) `lineLen` can now be defined:

```
splitLines :: [Word] -> [Line]
splitLines [] = []
splitLines ws
  = getLine lineLen ws
        : splitLines (dropLine lineLen ws)
```

This concludes the definition of the function `splitLines`, which gives filled lines from a list of words.

Conclusion

To fill a text string into lines, we write

```
fill :: String -> [Line]
fill = splitLines . splitWords
```

To make the result into a single string we need to write a function

```
joinLines :: [Line] -> String
```

This is left as an exercise, as is justification of lines.

Exercises

7.19 Define the function `dropLine` specified in the text.

7.20 Give a definition of the function

```
joinLine :: Line -> String
```

which turns a line into printable form. For example,

```
joinLine [ "dog" , "cat" ] = "dog cat"
```

7.21 Using the function `joinLine`, or otherwise, define the function

```
joinLines :: [Line] -> String
```

which joins together the lines, separated by newlines.

7.22 In this case study we have defined separate 'take' and 'drop' functions for words and lines. Redesign the program so that it uses 'split' functions – like the prelude function `splitAt` – instead.

7.23 [Harder] Modify the function `joinLine` so that it justifies the line to length `lineLen` by adding the appropriate number of spaces between the words.

7.24 Design a function

```
wc :: String -> (Int,Int,Int)
```

which when given a text string returns the number of characters, words and lines in the string. The end of a line in the string is signalled by the newline character, `'\n'`. Define a similar function

```
wcFormat :: String -> (Int,Int,Int)
```

which returns the same statistics for the text *after* it has been filled.

7.25 Define a function

```
isPalin :: String -> Bool
```

which tests whether a string is a palindrome – that is whether it is the same read both backwards and forwards. An example is the string

```
Madam I'm Adam
```

Note that punctuation and white space are ignored in the test, and that no distinction is made between capital and small letters. You might first like to develop a test which simply tests whether the string is exactly the same backwards and forwards, and only afterwards take account of punctuation and capital letters.

7.26 [Harder] Design a function

```
subst :: String -> String -> String -> String
```

so that

```
subst oldSub newSub st
```

is the result of replacing the first occurrence in `st` of the substring `oldSub` by the substring `newSub`. For instance,

```
subst "much  " "tall " "How much  is that?"
  = "How tall is that?"
```

If the substring `oldSub` does not occur in `st`, the result should be `st`.

Summary

This chapter has shown how functions can be defined by recursion over lists, and completes our account of the different ways that list-processing functions can be defined. In the chapter we have looked at examples of the design principles which we first discussed in Chapter 4, including 'divide and conquer' and general pieces of advice about designing recursive programs. The text processing case study provides a broadly bottom-up approach to defining a library of functions.

Chapter 8

Reasoning about programs

We gave an introduction to proof in Section 1.10, where we said that a **proof** is an argument that a particular proposition holds. Often a proposition will be **general** in saying that something holds **for all** things of a certain sort. In mathematics we might give a proof of Pythagoras' theorem, which states that there is a relationship $a^2=b^2+c^2$ between the sides of all right-angled triangles.

In programming we can prove that programs have a particular property **for all** input values. A property like this means that we can be certain that the program will behave as we require whatever the conditions. Compare this with program testing: a test assures us that a program behaves as it should on a particular collection of input values; it can only be an act of faith to infer from this that the program behaves as expected on every possible input, and no mathematician would accept a proposition as valid simply because it holds for a limited set of test data.

Central to the application of reasoning within functional programming is the insight that we can read function definitions as logical descriptions of what they do; we discuss this in depth at the start of the chapter. After examining the relationship of reasoning and testing, we look at some background topics in programming and logic, before introducing the central idea of proof by induction over finite lists.

Proofs by induction follow a pattern, and we illustrate this by giving a sequence of examples. We also supply advice on how to go about finding induction proofs. The chapter concludes with a more challenging example of proof, which can be omitted on a first reading.

8.1 Understanding definitions

Suppose that we ask ourselves the seemingly obvious question: 'how do we understand what a function does?' There are various ways of answering this.

- We can evaluate what the function does on particular inputs, using an implementation like Hugs.
- We can do the same thing by hand, performing a line-by-line calculation. This has the advantage of letting us see how the program gets to its result, but the disadvantage of being slow and impractical for all but the smallest of programs.
- We can try to argue about how the program behaves in general.

The third answer, in which we reason about the behaviour of our programs, is the subject of this chapter, which builds on the introduction of Section 1.10.

Consider a simple functional program like

```
length []     = 0                                          (length.1)
length (x:xs) = 1 + length xs                              (length.2)
```

Using the definition we can calculate the length of any particular list like [2,3,1]

```
length [2,3,1]
⤳   1 + length [3,1]                              by (length.2)
⤳   1 + (1 + length [1])                          by (length.2)
⤳   1 + (1 + (1 + length []))                     by (length.2)
⤳   1 + (1 + (1 + 0))                             by (length.1)
⤳   3
```

We can also read (length.1) and (length.2) as **descriptions** of how length behaves in general.

- (length.1) says what length [] is;
- (length.2) says that **whatever values** of x and xs we choose, length (x:xs) will be equal to 1 + length xs.

In the second case we have a **general property** of length: it states something about how length behaves on all non-empty lists. On the basis of these equations we can conclude that

```
length [x] = 1                                             (length.3)
```

How do we do that? We know that (length.2) holds for **all** values of x and xs, and so it will hold in particular when xs is replaced by [], so

```
length [x]
  = length (x:[])                                          by defn of [x]
  = 1 + length []                                          by (length.2)
  = 1 + 0                                                  by (length.1)
  = 1
```

The lesson of this discussion is that we can read a function definition in (at least) two different ways.

● We can take the definition as describing how to compute particular results, such as length [2,3,1].

● We can also take the definition as a **general description** of the behaviour of the function in question.

From this general description we are able to deduce other facts, some like (length.3) being utterly straightforward, and others like

```
length (xs ++ ys) = length xs + length ys                (length.4)
```

expressing more complicated interactions between two or more functions. We will prove (length.4) in Section 8.6.

Another way of looking at the proof of (length.3) above is that we are doing **symbolic evaluation**; rather than evaluating length at a particular value like [2] we have replaced the number 2 with a variable x, but used the evaluation rules in exactly the way that we used them earlier. We will find that symbolic evaluation forms an important part of our proofs, but we will need to use another principle – induction – to do most proofs for recursive functions.

To conclude this introduction, we have seen that functional programs 'describe themselves' in a direct way. If you are familiar with an imperative language like Pascal, C or Java, think how you might convince yourself of the analogues of (length.3) or (length.4) for programs written in that language. It is not straightforward to see how one might state these properties, and even more difficult to envisage how one might prove them valid.

8.2 Testing and proof

When we introduced program testing in Section 4.5 we looked at the example

```
mysteryMax :: Int -> Int -> Int -> Int
mysteryMax x y z
  | x > y && x > z       = x
  | y > x && y > z       = y
  | otherwise            = z
```

which was an attempted solution to the problem of finding the maximum of three integers. We can think of trying to prove that it does this. We need to look at various cases of the ordering of the values. If we first look at the cases

```
x > y && x > z
y > x && y > z
z > x && z > y
```

then in each of these `mysteryMax` will produce the correct solution. In the other cases, at least two of the three arguments are equal. If all three are equal,

```
x == y && y == z
```

the function also operates correctly. Finally, we start to look at the cases where precisely two elements are equal. The function behaves correctly when

```
y == z && z > x
```

but in the case of

```
x == y && y > z
```

we can see that the result will, erroneously, be z.

Now, we can see this process of attempting to prove a result as a general way of testing the function – it is a form of **symbolic testing** which will consider all cases in turn, at least until an error is found. We can thus see that reasoning can give us a powerful way of debugging programs by focusing on the reason why we cannot complete a proof of correctness, as well as the more traditional view that a proof shows that a program meets the requirements put upon it.

On the other hand, as we mentioned in Section 4.5, finding a proof is a difficult enterprise, and so there are clearly roles for both proof and testing in the development of reliable software.

8.3 Definedness, termination and finiteness

Before we say anything more about proof, we need to talk about two aspects of programming upon which we have only touched so far.

Definedness and termination

Evaluating an expression can have one of two outcomes:

- the evaluation can halt, or **terminate**, to give an answer; or
- the evaluation can go on forever.

If we make the definition

```
fact :: Int -> Int
fact n
   | n==0       = 1
   | otherwise  = n * fact (n-1)
```

then examples of the two are given by the expressions

```
fact 2                          fact (-2)
```

since in the latter case

```
fact (-2)
⤳   (-2) * fact (-3)
⤳   (-2) * ((-3) * fact (-4))
⤳   ...
```

In the case that evaluation goes on for ever, we say that the value of the expression is **undefined**, since no defined result is reached. In writing proofs we often have to confine our attention to cases where a value is **defined**, since it is only for defined values that many familiar properties hold. One of the simplest examples is given by the expression

```
0*e
```

which we expect to be 0 irrespective of the value of e. That is certainly so if e has a defined value, but if e is fact (-2), the value of

```
0 * fact (-2)
```

will be undefined and *not* zero.

In many of the proofs we give, we state that results hold for all defined values. This restriction does not cause problems in practice, since the defined cases will be exactly those which interest us in the vast majority of cases. An undefined value *is* of interest when a function does not give a defined value when it is expected to – a case of symbolic debugging.

Finiteness

We have said nothing so far about the order in which expressions are evaluated in Haskell. In fact, Haskell evaluation is **lazy**, so that arguments to functions are only evaluated if their values are actually needed. This gives some Haskell programs a distinctive flavour, which we explore in depth in Chapter 17. What is important for us here is that lazy evaluation allows the definition and use of **infinite** lists like

```
[1,2,3, ... ]
```

and **partially defined** lists. In what follows we will mainly confine our attention to **finite** lists, by which we mean lists which have a defined, finite length and defined elements. Examples are

```
[]              [1,2,3]            [[4,5],[3,2,1],[]]
```

Reasoning about lazy programs is discussed explicitly in Section 17.9 below.

Exercises

8.1 Given the definition of fact above, what are the results of evaluating the following expressions?

```
(4 > 2) || (fact (-1) == 17)
(4 > 2) && (fact (-1) == 17)
```

Discuss the reasons why you think that you obtained these answers.

8.2 Give a definition of a multiplication function

```
mult :: Int -> Int -> Int
```

so that mult 0 (fact (-2)) ⤳ 0. What is the result of mult (fact (-2)) 0 for your function? Explain why this is so.

(8.4) A little logic

In order to appreciate how to reason about functional programs we need not have a background in formal logic. Nevertheless, it is worth discussing two aspects of logic before we proceed with our proofs.

Assumptions in proofs

First, we look at the idea of proofs which contain **assumptions**. Taking a particular example, it follows from elementary arithmetic that if we *assume* that petrol costs 27 pence per litre, then we can prove that four litres will cost £1.08.

What does this tell us? It does *not* tell us outright how much four litres will cost; it only tells us the cost *if the assumption is valid*. To be sure that the cost will be £1.08, we need to supply some evidence that the assumption is justified: this might be another proof — perhaps based on petrol costing £1.20 per gallon — or direct evidence.

We can write what we have proved as a formula,

1 litre costs 27 pence $\Rightarrow$ 4 litres cost £1.08

where the arrow, $\Rightarrow$, which is the logical symbol for **implication**, says that the second proposition **follows from** the first.

As we have seen, we prove an implication like $A \Rightarrow B$ by assuming A in proving B. If we then find a proof of A, then knowing the implication will guarantee that B is also valid.

Yet another way of looking at this is to see a proof of $A \Rightarrow B$ as a *machine* for turning a proof of A into a proof of B. We use this idea in proof by induction, as one of the tasks in building an induction proof is the induction step, where we prove that one property holds assuming another.

Free variables and quantifiers

When we write an equation like

```
square x = x*x
```

it is usually our intention to say that this holds **for all** (defined) values of the free variable x. If we want to make this 'for all' explicit we can use a **quantifier** thus

∀x (square x = x*x)

where we read the universal quantifier, '∀x', as saying 'for all x...'.

We now turn to induction, the main technique we use for proving properties of programs.

(8.5) Induction

In Chapter 7 we saw that a general method for defining lists was primitive recursion, as exemplified by

```
sum :: [Int] -> Int
sum []     = 0                          (sum.1)
sum (x:xs) = x + sum xs                 (sum.2)
```

Here we give a value outright at [], and define the value of sum (x:xs) using the value sum xs. Structural induction is a proof principle which states:

Definition

Principle of structural induction for lists

In order to prove that a logical property P(xs) holds for all **finite** lists xs we have to do two things.

● **Base case.** Prove P([]) outright.

● **Induction step.** Prove P(x:xs) on the *assumption* that P(xs) holds.
In other words P(xs) ⇒ P(x:xs) has to be proved.
The P(xs) here is called the *induction hypothesis* since it is assumed in proving P(x:xs).

It is interesting to see that this is just like primitive recursion, except that instead of building the values of a function, we are building up the parts of a proof. In both cases we deal with [] as a basis, and then build the general thing by showing how to go from xs to (x:xs). In a function definition we define fun (x:xs) using fun xs; in the proof of P(x:xs) we are allowed to use P(xs).

Justification

Just as we argued that recursion was not circular, so we can see proof by induction building up the proof for all finite lists in stages. Suppose that we are given proofs of P([]) and P(xs) ⇒ P(x:xs) for all x and xs and we want to show that P([1,2,3]). The list [1,2,3] is built up from [] using cons thus,

1:2:3:[]

and we can construct the proof of P([1,2,3]) in a way which mirrors this step-by-step construction,

- P([]) holds;

- P([]) $\Rightarrow$ P([3]) holds, since it is a case of P(xs) $\Rightarrow$ P(x:xs);

- Recall our discussion of '$\Rightarrow$' above; if we know that both P([]) $\Rightarrow$ P([3]) and P([]) hold, then we can infer that P([3]) holds.

- P([3]) $\Rightarrow$ P([2,3]) holds, and so for similar reasons we get P([2,3]).

- Finally, because P([2,3]) $\Rightarrow$ P([1,2,3]) holds, we see that P([1,2,3]) holds.

This explanation is for a particular finite list, but will work for any finite list: if the list has n elements, then we will have n+1 steps like the four above. To conclude, this shows that we get P(xs) for every possible **finite** list xs if we know that both requirements of the induction principle hold.

A first example

We have mentioned the definition of sum; recall also the function to double all elements of a list

```
doubleAll []     = []                           (doubleAll.1)
doubleAll (z:zs) = 2*z : doubleAll zs           (doubleAll.2)
```

Now, how would we expect doubleAll and sum to interact? If we sum a list after doubling all its elements, we would expect to get the same result as by doubling the sum of the original list:

```
sum (doubleAll xs) = 2 * sum xs                 (sum+dblAll)
```

Setting up the induction

How are we to prove this for all xs? According to the principle of structural induction we get two induction goals. The first is the base case

```
sum (doubleAll []) = 2 * sum []                 (base)
```

The second is the induction step, in which we have to prove

```
sum (doubleAll (x:xs)) = 2 * sum (x:xs)         (ind)
```

using the induction hypothesis

```
sum (doubleAll xs) = 2 * sum xs                 (hyp)
```

In all proofs that follow we will label the cases by (base), (ind) and (hyp).

The base case

We are required to prove (base): how do we start? The only resources we have are the equations (sum.1), (sum.2), (doubleAll.1) and (doubleAll.2), so we have to concentrate on using these. As we are trying to prove an equation, we can think of simplifying the two sides separately, so working with the left-hand side first,

```
sum (doubleAll [])
  = sum []                                              by (doubleAll.1)
  = 0                                                   by (sum.1)
```

Looking at the right-hand side, we have

```
2 * sum []
  = 2 * 0                                               by (sum.1)
  = 0                                                   by *
```

This shows that the two sides are the same, and so completes the proof of the base case.

The induction step

Here we are required to prove (ind). As in the base case we have the defining equations of doubleAll and sum, but we also can – and usually *should* – use the induction hypothesis (hyp).

We work as we did in the base case, simplifying each side as much as we can using the defining equations. First the left-hand side,

```
sum (doubleAll (x:xs))
  = sum (2*x : doubleAll xs)                            by (doubleAll.2)
  = 2*x + sum (doubleAll xs)                            by (sum.2)
```

and then the right

```
2 * sum (x:xs)
  = 2 * (x + sum xs)                                    by (sum.2)
  = 2*x + 2 * sum xs                                    by arith.
```

Now, we have simplified each side using the defining equations. The last step equating the two is given by the induction hypothesis (hyp), which can be used to carry on the simplification of the left-hand side, giving

```
sum (doubleAll (x:xs))
  = sum (2*x : doubleAll xs)
  = 2*x + sum (doubleAll xs)
  = 2*x + 2 * sum xs                                    by (hyp)
```

and so this final step makes the left- and right-hand sides equal, on the assumption that the induction hypothesis holds. This completes the induction step, and therefore the proof itself.   ∎

We use the box, ∎ , to signify the end of a proof.

Finding induction proofs

Looking at the previous example, we can glean a number of pieces of advice about how to find proofs of properties of recursively defined functions.

- State clearly the goal of the induction and the two sub-goals of the induction proof: (base) and (hyp) ⇒ (ind).
- If any confusion is possible, change the names of the variables in the relevant definitions so that they are different from the variable(s) over which you are doing the induction.
- The only resources available are the definitions of the functions involved and the general rules of arithmetic. Use these to simplify the sub-goals. If the sub-goal is an equation, then simplify each side separately.
- In the case of the induction step, (ind), you should expect to use the induction hypothesis (hyp) in your proof; if you do not, then it is most likely that your proof is incorrect.
- Label each step of your proof with its justification: this is usually one of the defining equations of a function.

In the next section we look at a series of examples.

8.6 Further examples of proofs by induction

In this section we present two more examples of proof by structural induction over finite lists.

Examples

1. `length` **and** `++`

We begin by looking at the example (`length.4`) introduced at the start of the chapter.

```
length (xs ++ ys) = length xs + length ys                (length.4)
```

Recall the definitions of `length` and `++`

```
length []     = 0                                        (length.1)
length (z:zs) = 1 + length zs                            (length.2)
```

```
[]      ++ zs = zs                                       (++.1)
(w:ws)  ++ zs = w:(ws++zs)                               (++.2)
```

where we have chosen new names for the variables so as not to conflict with the variables in the goal.

There is some question about how to proceed with the proof, since (`length.4`) involves two variables, xs and ys. We can be guided by the definitions, where we see that the definition of `++` is made by recursion over the *first* variable. We therefore make the goal a proof of (length.4) for all finite xs and ys by induction over xs; the proof works for all ys as ys is a variable, which stands for an **arbitrary** list, just like the variable x in the earlier proof of (length.3) stood for an arbitrary list element.

Statement   We can now write down the two goals of the induction proof. The base case requires that we prove

length ([] ++ ys) = length [] + length ys   (base)

and in the induction step we have to prove

length ((x:xs) ++ ys) = length (x:xs) + length ys   (ind)

from the inductive assumption

length (xs ++ ys) = length xs + length ys   (hyp)

Base   We look separately at the two sides of (base), left-hand side first,

```
length ([] ++ ys)
  = length ys                                                by (++.1)
```

```
length [] + length ys
  = 0 + length ys                                            by (length.1)
  = length ys
```

which shows their equality.

Induction   First we look at the left-hand side of (ind)

```
length ((x:xs) ++ ys)
  = length (x:(xs ++ ys))                                    by (++.2)
  = 1 + length (xs ++ ys)                                    by (length.2)
```

We cannot simplify this further with the defining equations, but we can use (hyp) to give us

```
  = 1 + length xs + length ys                                by (hyp)
```

Now, looking at the right-hand side of (ind) we get

```
length (x:xs) + length ys
  = 1 + length xs + length ys                                by (length.2)
```

and this shows that (ind) follows from (hyp), completing the second half of the proof and thus the proof itself.   ■

2. `reverse` **and** `++`

What happens when we reverse the join of two lists, xs++ys?

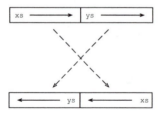

Each list is reversed, and they are swapped. In formal terms,

```
reverse (xs ++ ys) = reverse ys ++ reverse xs            (reverse++)
```

where we define

```
reverse []     = []                                       (reverse.1)
reverse (z:zs) = reverse zs ++ [z]                        (reverse.2)
```

We will try to prove (reverse++) for all finite lists xs and ys by induction over xs.

Statement   The base case is

```
reverse ([] ++ ys) = reverse ys ++ reverse []            (base)
```

and the induction goal is

```
reverse ((x:xs) ++ ys) = reverse ys ++ reverse (x:xs)    (ind)
```

which is to be proved using the assumption

```
reverse (xs ++ ys) = reverse ys ++ reverse xs            (hyp)
```

Base   Simplifying both sides of (base) gives us

```
reverse ([] ++ ys)
  = reverse ys                                            by (++.1)
```

```
reverse ys ++ reverse []
  = reverse ys ++ []                                      by (reverse.1)
```

but we can prove the two equal only if we can show that appending an empty list to the end of a list is an **identity** operation, that is

```
xs ++ [] = xs                                             (++.3)
```

We leave a proof of this by induction over xs as an exercise for the reader.

Induction   Again, we look at the two sides of the equation, left-hand side first.

```
reverse ((x:xs) ++ ys)
  = reverse (x:(xs ++ ys))                              by (++.2)
  = reverse (xs ++ ys) ++ [x]                       by (reverse.2)
  = (reverse ys ++ reverse xs) ++ [x]                   by (hyp)
```

Examining the right-hand side, we have

```
reverse ys ++ reverse (x:xs)
  = reverse ys ++ (reverse xs ++ [x])               by (reverse.2)
```

Now, these two are *almost* equal, except that the joins are bracketed differently. We need another general property of ++, namely that it is **associative**:

```
xs ++ (ys ++ zs) = (xs ++ ys) ++ zs                       (++.4)
```

the proof of which we again leave as an exercise.   ∎

This proof is instructive: it shows that often in proofs we use other theorems or lemmas (the mathematician's term for a 'little theorem') on the way. If we do any serious proof we will build up a library of these lemmas, with (++.3) and (++.4) being basic results about ++ which we will call upon almost without thinking. We would expect this library to resemble the standard prelude: it would contain all those theorems which link the prelude functions and which will be called into use whenever we use prelude functions. Many of the exercises at the end of the section ask you to prove theorems concerning prelude functions.

Exercises

8.3 Prove for all finite xs and ys that

```
sum (xs ++ ys) = sum xs + sum ys                         (sum++)
```

8.4 Prove the two rules for ++:

```
xs ++ [] = xs                                             (++.3)
xs ++ (ys ++ zs) = (xs ++ ys) ++ zs                       (++.4)
```

for all finite xs, ys and zs.

8.5 Show for all finite xs that

```
sum (reverse xs)    = sum xs
length (reverse xs) = length xs
```

What common factors can you see in your two proofs?

8.6 Show for all finite integer lists xs and ys that

```
elem z (xs ++ ys) = elem z xs || elem z ys
```

8.7 Show for all finite lists ps that

```
zip (fst (unzip ps)) (snd (unzip ps)) = ps
```

Under what conditions on xs and ys is it the case that

```
unzip (zip xs ys) = (xs,ys)
```

when unzip is defined by

```
unzip [] = ([],[])
unzip ((x,y):ps)
  = (x:xs,y:ys)
    where
    (xs,ys) = unzip ps
```

Give a proof in that case.

8.8 [Harder] Show for all finite xs and defined n that

```
take n xs ++ drop n xs = xs
```

8.7 Generalizing the proof goal

It is not always easy to build a proof in a straightforward way, by induction over a goal we set ourselves. In this section we explore an example in which we are able to build a proof of the property we seek only after two false starts. The section is more challenging than the rest of the chapter and can safely be omitted on first reading.

The shunting function

The shunt function moves the elements from one list onto another, thus

```
shunt :: [a] -> [a] -> [a]
```

```
shunt []     ys = ys                        (shunt.1)
shunt (x:xs) ys = shunt xs (x:ys)           (shunt.2)
```

Starting with an empty second argument, we have

```
shunt [2,3,1] []
⤳    shunt [3,1] [2]
⤳    shunt [1] [3,2]
⤳    shunt [] [1,3,2]
⤳    [1,3,2]
```

and so we can reverse lists using this function:

```
rev :: [a] -> [a]
rev xs = shunt xs []                                      (rev.1)
```

Now we turn to looking at properties of the rev function.

First proof attempt

Reversing a list twice should give us back the list we started with, and so we aim to prove that

```
rev (rev xs) = xs                                          Q(xs)
```

for all finite lists xs. The base case is easily established, but when we look at the induction step, we meet our first problem:

```
rev (rev (x:xs))
  = shunt (shunt (x:xs) []) []                    by (rev.1)
  = shunt (shunt xs [x]) []                       by (shunt.2)
```

This has no direct relationship to the induction hypothesis, which mentions only the function rev. A clue to the problem is that rev is not the function defined by recursion — it is simply a specialization of shunt. Can we find a *generalization* of Q(xs) which talks explicitly about shunt and which is to be proved by induction?

In general the effect of shunt xs ys is to give

```
(reverse xs) ++ ys
```

If we reverse this list, we should get

```
(reverse ys) ++ xs
```

(try some examples!) and so we should be able to prove that

```
shunt (shunt xs ys) [] = shunt ys xs
```

When ys is replaced by [], we get Q(xs). We therefore aim to prove this generalization.

Second proof attempt

Our aim is to show

```
shunt (shunt xs ys) [] = shunt ys xs
```

for all finite lists xs and ys. In the case that xs is [], the proof is simple. Now we look at the induction step:

```
shunt (shunt (x:xs) ys) []
  = shunt (shunt xs (x:ys)) []                    by (shunt.2)
```

We would now like to claim by induction that this is equal to shunt (x:ys) xs, but to do this we need the induction hypothesis to give the result that

```
shunt (shunt xs (x:ys)) [] = shunt (x:ys) xs
```

rather than

```
shunt (shunt xs ys) [] = shunt ys xs
```

To get around this, we strengthen the induction hypothesis to become

```
shunt (shunt xs zs) [] = shunt zs xs   for all finite lists zs
```

so that in particular it will hold when (x:ys) replaces zs. We now try again.

The successful proof attempt

In logical notation, our goal is to prove

```
∀zs (shunt (shunt xs zs) [] = shunt zs xs)
```

for all finite xs by induction.

Statement   Now we can state what is required. The base case is

```
∀zs (shunt (shunt [] zs) [] = shunt zs [])                    (base)
```

and the induction step is to prove

```
∀zs (shunt (shunt (x:xs) zs) [] = shunt zs (x:xs))            (ind)
```

assuming the induction hypothesis

```
∀zs (shunt (shunt xs zs) [] = shunt zs xs)                    (hyp)
```

Base   In the base case we prove

```
∀zs (shunt (shunt [] zs) [] = shunt zs [])                    (base)
```

by proving it for an arbitrary zs. The left-hand side simplifies to the right-hand side in one step.

```
shunt (shunt [] zs) []
  = shunt zs []                                        by (shunt.1)
```

Induction   As in the base case, we prove

```
∀zs (shunt (shunt (x:xs) zs) [] = shunt zs (x:xs))           (ind)
```

by proving it for an arbitrary zs. Simplifying the left-hand side, we have

```
shunt (shunt (x:xs) zs) []
  = shunt (shunt xs (x:zs)) []                         by (shunt.2)
```

Now, by (hyp), where we take the particular value (x:zs) to replace the universally quantified variable zs,

```
= shunt (x:zs) xs                                          by (hyp)
= shunt zs (x:xs)                                          by (shunt.2)
```

This is the right-hand side, and so the proof is complete for an arbitrary ys, giving a proof of (ind), and completing the induction proof. ∎

This example shows that we may have to generalize what has to be proved in order for induction proofs to work. This seems paradoxical: we are making it harder for ourselves, apparently. We are in one way, but at the same time we make the induction hypothesis *stronger*, so that we have *more* resources to use when proving the induction step.

Exercises

8.9 Prove for all finite lists xs and ys that

```
rev (xs ++ ys) = rev ys ++ rev xs
```

8.10 Using the function

```
facAux :: Int -> Int -> Int
facAux 0 p = p
facAux n p = facAux (n-1) (n*p)
```

we can define

```
fac2 n = facAux n 1
```

Prove that for all defined natural numbers n,

```
fac n = fac2 n
```

Summary

This chapter has shown that we can give Haskell programs a logical reading which allows us to reason about them. Central to reasoning about lists is the principle of structural induction, which does for proof what primitive recursion does for definitions.

We gave a collection of hints about how we can build proofs for functional programs, and illustrated these by giving a number of results for common prelude functions such as sum, ++ and length, as well as exercises involving others.

Chapter 9

Generalization: patterns of computation

Software **reuse** is a major goal of the software industry. One of the great strengths of modern functional programming languages like Haskell is that we can use them to define **general** functions which can be used in many different applications. The Haskell prelude functions over lists, for instance, form a toolkit to which we turn again and again in a host of situations.

We have already seen one aspect of this generality in **polymorphism**, under which the **same** program can be used over many **different** types. The prelude functions over lists introduced in Chapter 5 provide many examples of this including length, ++ and take.

As we said, these functions have the same effect over every argument – length computes the length of a list of any type, for instance. In this chapter we explore a second mechanism, by which we can write functions which embody a **pattern of computation**; two examples of what we mean follow.

● *Transform every element of a list in some way.* We might turn every alphabetic character into upper case, or double every number.

● *Combine the elements of a list using some operator.* We could add together the elements of a numeric list in this way, for example.

How can we write general functions which implement patterns like this? We need to make the transformation or operator into a **parameter** of the general function; in other words we need to have functions as arguments of other functions. These **higher-order functions** are the topic of this chapter. Complementing this is the ability to make functions the **results** of functions; we look at that in the next chapter.

We begin the chapter by examining the patterns of computation over lists which we have encountered so far, and in the remaining sections of the chapter we show how these are realized as higher-order Haskell functions. We also re-examine primitive recursive definitions, and see that they generalize the process of combining the elements of a list using an operator.

We conclude with an example of generalization: taking a function over String into a polymorphic, higher-order function. We do this by identifying the parts of the function which make it specific to String and turning those into a parameter of the function. The example serves as a model for how we can generalize functions in any situation thus making them applicable in many more contexts, so that they become suitable candidates for reuse.

(9.1) Patterns of computation over lists

Many of the definitions of list processing functions we have seen so far fall into a small number of different sorts. In this section we look back over the previous chapters and discuss the patterns which emerge. These patterns are realized as Haskell functions later in the chapter.

Applying to all – mapping

Many functions call for all of the elements of a list to be transformed in some way – this we call **mapping**. We have seen examples of this from the first chapter, where we noted that to flip a picture in a vertical mirror – `flipV` – we needed to `reverse` each line of the `Picture`, which is a list of lines.

We also saw mapping in Chapter 5 in our first example of a list comprehension which was to double every element of a list of integers.

```
doubleAll [2,3,71] = [4,6,142]
```

Other examples include

- taking the second element of each pair in a list of pairs, as we do in the library database;
- in the supermarket billing example, converting every item in a list of bar codes to the corresponding (Name,Price) pair;
- formatting each (Name,Price) pair in a list.

Selecting elements – filtering

Selecting all the elements of a list with a given property is also common. Chapter 5 contains the example of the function which selects the digits from a string

```
digits "29 February 2004" = "292004"
```

Among the other cases we have seen are

- select each pair which has a particular person as its first element;
- select each pair which is *not* equal to the loan pair being returned.

Combining the items – folding

The first example of primitive recursion in Chapter 7 was sum, which computes the total of a list of integers. The total of the list is given by **folding** the function + into the list, thus:

```
sum [2,3,71] = 2+3+71
```

In a similar way,

- ++ can be folded into a list of lists to concatenate it, as is done in the definition of concat;
- && can be folded into a list of Booleans to take their conjunction: this is the prelude function and;
- max can be folded into a list of integers to give their maximum.

Breaking up lists

A common pattern in the text processing example of Chapter 7 is to take or drop items from a list while they have some property. A first example is getWord,

```
getWord "cat dog" = "cat"
```

in which we continue to take characters while they are alphabetic. Other examples include dropWord, dropSpace and getLine. In the last of these the property in question depends not only upon the particular list item but also on the part of the list selected so far.

Combinations

These patterns of definition are often used together. In defining books for the library database, which returns all the books on loan to a given person, we filter out all pairs involving the person, and then take all second components of the results. The strength of list comprehensions is that they give this combination of mapping and filtering, which fits some examples – like the library database – particularly well.

Other combinations of functions are also common.

- In the pictures case study the function invertColour inverts the colour of every character in a Picture by inverting every line; inverting a line requires us to invert every character, so here we have two (nested) uses of mapping.
- Formatting the item part of a supermarket bill involves processing each item in some way, then combining the results, using ++.

Primitive recursion and folding

The form of many definitions is primitive recursive. Sorting by insertion is a classic example:

```
iSort []     = []
iSort (x:xs) = ins x (iSort xs)
```

Haskell provides a mechanism to turn a prefix function like ins into an infix version. The name is enclosed by back quotes, 'ins', so

```
iSort (x:xs) = x 'ins' (iSort xs)
```

and, in a given example, we have

```
iSort [4,2,3] = 4 'ins' 2 'ins' 3 'ins' []
```

Looked at this way, the definition looks like 'ins' folded into the list [4,2,3]. We shall look at this again in Section 9.3.

The last 10%

The different kinds of definition discussed so far have all been primitive recursive: we were able to define the result for (x:xs) in terms of the result for xs. It has been said that at least 90% of all definitions of list processing functions are primitive recursive. Some are not, however; in Chapter 7 notable examples are quicksort and the splitLines function,

```
splitLines [] = []
splitLines ws
  = getLine lineLen ws
        : splitLines (dropLine lineLen ws)
```

For a non-empty list of words ws, the result splitLines ws is defined using a recursive call of splitLines not on the tail of ws but on (dropLine lineLen ws). This form of recursion will terminate because (dropLine lineLen ws) will always be shorter than ws itself, at least in sensible cases where no word in the list ws is longer than the line length lineLen.

(9.2) Higher-order functions: functions as arguments

A Haskell function is **higher-order** if it takes a function as an argument or returns a function as a result, or both. In this section we show how a variety of functions, including some of the patterns discussed in the last section, can be written using functions as arguments.

Mapping – the map function

We can double all the elements in an integer list in two ways, either using a list comprehension,

```
doubleAll :: [Int] -> [Int]
doubleAll xs = [ 2*x | x <- xs ]
```

or using primitive recursion,

```
doubleAll []     = []
doubleAll (x:xs) = 2*x : doubleAll xs
```

In both cases, we can see that the specific operation of multiplying by two is applied to an element of the list in the expression '2*x'.

Suppose that we want to modify every element of a list by another operation – for instance, the function ord that transforms a Char into an Int – we could modify one of the definitions above by replacing the '2*x' by 'ord x' to give a different definition.

Taking this approach would mean that we would write a whole lot of definitions which differ only in the function used to make the transformation. Instead of doing this, we can write a *single* definition in which the function becomes a **parameter** of the definition. Our general definition will be

```
map f xs = [ f x | x <- xs ]
```
(map.0)

or we can give an explicit primitive recursion

```
map f []     = []
map f (x:xs) = f x : map f xs
```
(map.1)
(map.2)

The function to double all the elements of a list can now be given by applying map to two things: the transformation – double – and the list in question.

```
doubleAll xs = map double xs
```

where double x = 2*x. In a similar way, the function to convert all the characters into their codes will be

```
convertChrs :: [Char] -> [Int]
convertChrs xs = map ord xs
```

In the Picture case study to flip a picture in a vertical mirror we can write

```
flipV :: Picture -> Picture
flipV xs = map reverse xs
```

What is the type of map? It takes two arguments – the first is a function, and the second is a list – and it returns a list.

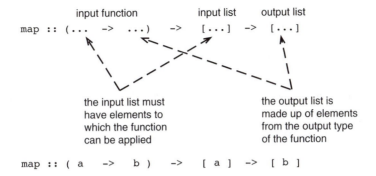

The figure shows how the types of the functions and lists are related, giving map the type

```
map :: (a -> b) -> [a] -> [b]
```

where recall that a and b are type variables, standing for arbitrary types. Instances of the type of map include

```
map :: (Int -> Int) -> [Int] -> [Int]
```

as used in the definition of doubleAll, where map is applied to the function double of type Int -> Int and

```
map :: (Char -> Int) -> [Char] -> [Int]
```

as in the definition of convertChrs.

Modelling properties as functions

Before defining the function to **filter**, or select, those elements of a list having a given property, we need to think about how such properties are to be modelled in Haskell. Take the example of filtering the digits from a string – the function digits mentioned earlier. How is the property of 'being a digit' to be modelled? We have already seen that the prelude contains a function

```
isDigit :: Char -> Bool
```

and we find out whether a particular character like 'd' is a digit or not by applying the function to the character to give a Boolean result, that is True or False.

This is the way that we can model a **property** over any type t. The property is given by a function of type

```
t -> Bool
```

and an element x has the property precisely when f x has the value True. We have already seen the example of isDigit; other examples include

```
isEven :: Int -> Bool
isEven n = (n 'mod' 2 == 0)


isSorted :: [Int] -> Bool
isSorted xs = (xs == iSort xs)
```

where we usually adopt the convention that the names of properties begin with 'is'.

Filtering – the `filter` function

Building on our discussion of properties, we see that the `filter` function will take a property and a list, and return those elements of the list having the property:

```
filter p [] = []                                              (filter.1)
filter p (x:xs)
  | p x          = x : filter p xs                            (filter.2)
  | otherwise    =     filter p xs                            (filter.3)
```

In the case of an empty list, the result is empty. For a non-empty list (x:xs) there are two cases. If the guard condition p x is true then the element x is the first element of the result list; the remainder of the result is given by selecting those elements in xs which have the property p. If p x is False, x is not included, and the result is given by searching xs for elements with property p.

A list comprehension also serves to define `filter`,

```
filter p xs = [ x | x <- xs , p x ]                          (filter.0)
```

where again we see that the condition for inclusion of x in the list is that it has the property p.

Our example `digits` is defined using `filter` as follows

```
digits xs = filter isDigit xs
```

Other applications of `filter` give

```
filter isEven [2,3,4,5]                        ⤳   [2,4]
filter isSorted [[2,3,4,5],[3,2,5],[],[3]] ⤳   [[2,3,4,5],[],[3]]
```

What is the type of `filter`? It takes a property and a list, and returns a list.

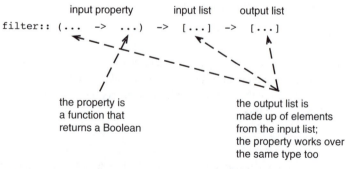

```
            input property        input list       output list
filter:: (...    ->    ...)   ->   [...]   ->   [...]




         the property is                    the output list is
         a function that                     made up of elements
         returns a Boolean                   from the input list;
                                             the property works over
                                             the same type too

filter:: ( a  -> Bool) -> [ a ] -> [ a ]
```

Combining `zip` and `map` – the `zipWith` function

We have already seen the polymorphic function

```
zip :: [a] -> [b] -> [(a,b)]
```

which combines two lists into a list of pairs, where we pair corresponding elements in the two lists. For instance,

```
zip [2,3,4] "Frank" = [(2,'F'),(3,'r'),(4,'a')]
```

What happens if we want to do something to two corresponding elements other than making a pair of them? Recall from Chapter 1 that in our `Picture` case study to define `sideBySide` we wanted to join corresponding lines using (++). To this end we define the `zipWith` function, which combines the effect of zipping and mapping:

```
zipWith f (x:xs) (y:ys) = f x y : zipWith f xs ys
zipWith f _        _     = []
```

In the first case we see that if both lists are non-empty we apply the function f to their heads to give the first element of the result, and zip their tails with f in a similar way. In the second case – when at least one of the inputs is [] – the result is [], just as it was in the definition of `zip`.

Returning to the `Picture` case study, we can then define

```
sideBySide :: Picture -> Picture -> Picture
sideBySide pic1 pic2 = zipWith (++) pic1 pic2
```

What is the type of `zipWith`? The function takes three arguments. The second and third are lists of arbitrary type, [a] and [b] respectively. The result is also a list of arbitrary type, [c]. Now, the first argument is applied to elements of the input lists to give an element of the output list, so it must have type a -> b -> c. Putting this together, we have

```
zipWith :: (a -> b -> c) -> [a] -> [b] -> [c]
```

In the exercises we look further at the examples defined here, as well as introducing other higher-order functions.

Exercises

9.1 Write three line-by-line calculations of `doubleAll [2,1,7]` using the three different definitions of `doubleAll` by means of a list comprehension, primitive recursion and `map`.

9.2 How would you define the `length` function using `map` and `sum`?

9.3 Given the function

```
addUp ns = filter greaterOne (map addOne ns)
```

where

```
greaterOne n = n>1
addOne n     = n+1
```

how would you redefine it using `filter` before `map`, as in

```
addUp ns = map fun1 (filter fun2 ns)
```

9.4 Describe the effect of

```
map addOne (map addOne ns)
```

Can you conclude anything in general about properties of `map f (map g xs)` where f and g are arbitrary functions?

9.5 What is the effect of

```
filter greaterOne (filter lessTen ns)
```

where `lessTen n = n<10`? What about the general case of

```
filter p (filter q xs)
```

where p and q are arbitrary properties?

9.6 Give definitions of functions to take a list of integers, `ns`, and

- return the list consisting of the squares of the integers in `ns`;
- return the sum of squares of items in `ns`;
- check whether all items of the list are greater than zero.

9.7 Using functions defined already wherever possible, write definitions of functions to

- give the minimum value of a function f on inputs 0 to n;
- test whether the values of f on inputs 0 to n are all equal;
- test if all values of f on inputs 0 to n are greater than zero, and,
- check whether the values f 0, f 1 to f n are in increasing order.

9.8 State the type of and define a function `twice` which takes a function from integers to integers and an input integer, and whose output is the function applied to the input twice. For instance, with the `double` function and 7 as input, the result is 28. What is the most general type of the function you have defined?

9.9 Give the type of and define a function `iter` so that

```
iter n f x = f (f (f ... (f x)...))
```

where f occurs n times on the right-hand side of the equation. For instance, we should have

```
iter 3 f x = f (f (f x))
```

and `iter 0 f x` should return x.

9.10 Using `iter` and `double` define a function which on input n returns 2^n; remember that 2^n means one multiplied by two n times.

9.3 Folding and primitive recursion

In this section we look at a particular sort of higher-order function which implements the operation of **folding** an operator or function into a list of values. We will see that this operation is more general than we might first think, and that most primitive recursive functions over lists can, in fact, be defined using a fold.

The functions `foldr1` and `foldr`

Here we look at two sorts of folding function. First we look at a function which folds a function into a non-empty list; in the Haskell prelude this is called `foldr1`; we will discuss why it is called this later in the section.

The definition of `foldr1` will have two cases. Folding f into the singleton list `[a]` gives a. Folding f into a longer list is given by

```
foldr1 f [e₁,e₂,...,eₖ]
  = e₁ 'f' (e₂ 'f' ( ... 'f' eₖ)...)
  = e₁ 'f' (foldr1 f [e₂,...,eₖ])
  = f e₁ (foldr1 f [e₂,...,eₖ])
```

The Haskell definition is therefore

```
foldr1 f [x]    = x                          (foldr1.1)
foldr1 f (x:xs) = f x (foldr1 f xs)          (foldr1.2)
```

and the type of `foldr1` will be given by

```
foldr1 :: (a -> a -> a) -> [a] -> a
```

The type shows that `foldr1` has two arguments.

- The first argument is a binary function over the type a; for example, the function `(+)` over `Int`.
- The second is a list of elements of type a which are to be combined using the operator; for instance, `[3,98,1]`

The result is a single value of type a; in the running example we have

```
foldr1 (+) [3,98,1] = 102
```

Other examples which use `foldr1` include

```
foldr1 (||) [False,True,False] = True
foldr1 (++) ["Freak ", "Out" , "", "!"] = "Freak Out!"
foldr1 min [6] = 6
foldr1 (*) [1 .. 6] = 720
```

The function `foldr1` gives an error when applied to an empty list argument.

We can modify the definition to give an extra argument which is the value returned on the empty list, so giving a function defined on all finite lists. This function is called `foldr` and is defined as follows

```
foldr f s []     = s                          (foldr.1)
foldr f s (x:xs) = f x (foldr f s xs)         (foldr.2)
```

The 'r' in the definition is for 'fold, bracketing to the **right**'. Using this slightly more general function, whose type we predict is

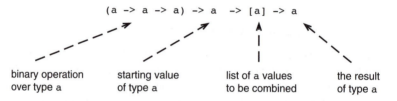

```
         (a -> a -> a) -> a  -> [a] -> a
```

| binary operation | starting value | list of a values | the result |
| over type a | of type a | to be combined | of type a |

we can now define some of the standard functions of Haskell,

```
concat :: [[a]] -> [a]
concat xs = foldr (++) [] xs

and :: [Bool] -> Bool
and bs = foldr (&&) True bs
```

Returning to the start of the section, we can now see why `foldr1` is so called: it is fold function, designed to take a list with at least **one** element. We can also define `foldr1` from `foldr`, thus

```
foldr1 f (x:xs) = foldr f x xs                (foldr1.0)
```

Folding in general – `foldr` again

In fact, the most general type of `foldr` is more general than we predicted. Suppose that the starting value has type b and the elements of the list are of type a, then

```
foldr :: (a -> b -> b) -> b -> [a] -> b
```

We give a full explanation of how this type is derived in Section 13.2.

With this insight about the type of `foldr` we can see that `foldr` can be used to define another whole cohort of list functions. For instance, we can reverse a list thus:

```
rev :: [a] -> [a]
rev xs = foldr snoc [] xs

snoc :: a -> [a] -> [a]
snoc x xs = xs ++ [x]
```

This function is traditionally called `snoc` because it is like 'cons', `:`, in reverse. We can also sort a list in this way

```
iSort :: [Int] -> [Int]
iSort xs = foldr ins [] xs
```

Before we move on, we look for one last time at the definition of `foldr`

```
foldr f s []     = s                          (foldr.1)
foldr f s (x:xs) = f x (foldr f s xs)         (foldr.2)
```

What is the effect of `foldr f s`? We have two cases:

- the value at the empty list is given outright by `s`;
- the value at `(x:xs)` is defined in terms of the value at `xs`, and `x` itself.

This is just like the definition of primitive recursion over lists in Chapter 7.[1] Because of this it is no accident that we can define many of our primitive recursive functions using `foldr`. It is usually mechanical to go from a primitive recursive definition to the corresponding application of `foldr`.

How do the two approaches compare? It is often easier initially to think of a function definition in recursive form and only afterwards to transform it into an application of `foldr`. One of the advantages of making this transformation is that we might then recognize properties of the function by dint of its being a fold. We look at proof for general functions like `map`, `filter` and `foldr` in Section 10.9 and we look at other fold functions in Chapter 19.

Exercises

9.11 How would you define the sum of the squares of the natural numbers 1 to n using map and `foldr`?

9.12 Define a function to give the sum of squares of the positive integers in a list of integers.

9.13 For the purposes of this exercise you should use `foldr` to give definitions of the prelude functions `unZip`, `last` and `init`, where examples of the latter two are given by

```
last "Greggery Peccary" = 'y'
init "Greggery Peccary" = "Greggery Peccar"
```

---

[1] There is an ambiguity in our original characterization. In defining the function g by primitive recursion the value of g `(x:xs)` is defined in terms of both x and xs as well as the value g `xs` itself; this makes primitive recursion slightly more general than folding using `foldr`.

9.14 How does the function

```
mystery xs = foldr (++) [] (map sing xs)
```

behave, where `sing x = [x]` for all x?

9.15 The function `formatLines` is intended to format a list of lines using the function

```
formatLine :: Line -> String
```

to format each line in the list. Define a function

```
formatList :: (a -> String) -> [a] -> String
```

which takes as a parameter a function of type

```
a -> String
```

to format each item of the list which is passed as the second parameter. Show how `formatLines` can be defined using `formatList` and `formatLine`.

9.16 Define a function

```
filterFirst :: (a -> Bool) -> [a] -> [a]
```

so that `filterFirst p xs` removes the first element of xs which does not have the property p. Use this to give a version of `returnLoan` which returns only one copy of a book. What does your function do on a list all of whose elements have property p?

9.17 Can you define a function

```
filterLast :: (a -> Bool) -> [a] -> [a]
```

which removes the last occurrence of an element of a list without property p? How could you define it using `filterFirst`?

9.18 How can you simplify some of your earlier definitions in the light of the higher-order functions you have seen here? You could revisit the 'supermarket billing' exercises and try doing those questions again using the functions you have now seen.

9.4 Generalizing: splitting up lists

As a final example in this chapter we look at how we can generalize the function getWord into a polymorphic, higher-order function. This serves as a model for similar generalizations in many different circumstances.

Many list manipulating programs involve splitting up lists in some way, as a part of their processing. One way of doing this is to select some or all the elements with a particular property – this we have seen with filter. Other ways of processing include taking or dropping elements of the list from the front – this we saw in the text processing example. If we know the number of elements to be dropped, we can use

```
take, drop :: Int -> [a] -> [a]
```

where take n xs and drop n xs are intended to take or drop n elements from the front of the list xs. These functions are defined in Chapter 7.

Also in Chapter 7 we looked at the example of text processing, in which lists were split to yield words and lines. The functions getWord and dropWord defined there were *not* polymorphic, as they were designed to split at whitespace characters.

It is a general principle of functional programming that programs can often be rewritten to use more general polymorphic and/or higher-order functions, and we illustrate that here.

The function getWord was originally defined thus:

```
getWord :: String -> String
getWord []    = []                             (getWord.1)
getWord (x:xs)
  | elem x whitespace    = []                  (getWord.2)
  | otherwise            = x : getWord xs       (getWord.3)
```

What forces this to work over strings is the test in (getWord.2), where x is checked for membership of whitespace. We can generalize the function to have the test – or property – as a parameter.

How is this to be done? Recall that a property over the type a is represented by a function of type (a -> Bool). Making this test a parameter we have

```
getUntil :: (a -> Bool) -> [a] -> [a]
getUntil p []    = []
getUntil p (x:xs)
  | p x        = []
  | otherwise  = x : getUntil p xs
```

in which the test elem x whitespace has been replaced by the test p x, the arbitrary property p applied to x. We can of course recover getWord from this definition:

```
getWord xs
  = getUntil p xs
    where
    p x = elem x whitespace
```

Built into Haskell are the functions `takeWhile` and `dropWhile`, which are like `getUntil` and `dropUntil`, except that they take or drop elements while the condition is `True`. For instance,

```
takeWhile :: (a -> Bool) -> [a] -> [a]
takeWhile p []     = []
takeWhile p (x:xs)
  | p x             = x : takeWhile p xs
  | otherwise       = []
```

`getUntil` can be defined using `takeWhile`, and vice versa.

Exercises

9.19 Give the type and definition of the generalization `dropUntil` of the function `dropWord`.

9.20 How would you define the function `dropSpace` using `dropUntil`? How would you define `takeWhile` using `getUntil`?

9.21 How would you split a string into lines using `getUntil` and `dropUntil`?

9.22 The function `getLine` of Chapter 7 has a polymorphic type – what is it? How could you generalize the test in this function? If you do this, does the type of the function become more general? Explain your answer.

9.23 Can you give generalizations to polymorphic higher-order functions of the text processing functions `getLine`, `dropLine` and `splitLines`?

Summary

This chapter has shown how the informal patterns of definition over lists can be realized as higher-order, polymorphic functions, such as `map`, `filter` and `foldr`. We saw how these functions arose, and also how their types were derived, as well as reviewing the ways in which they could be used to solve problems.

We concluded with an example of how to generalize a function – the particular example was taken from the text processing case study, but the example serves as a model for how to generalize functions in general.

The chapter has focused on how to write functions which take other functions as arguments; where do these arguments come from? One answer is that they are already defined; another is that they come themselves as the results of Haskell functions – this is the topic of the next chapter.

Chapter 10

Functions as values

As we saw in the previous chapter, functions can be arguments of **higher-order** functions. We shall see in this chapter that functions can also be the **results** of other functions and operators. In this way we create functions as values within our programs, rather than simply being able to create them by defining them in a Haskell script.

This machinery allows us to make the results of some functions into the arguments of other higher-order functions, and lets us exploit these general functions to the full. Using this machinery we see that we are able to give what we call function-level definitions of our functions, which use some of the general functions we have seen earlier. These definitions are both more concise and readable than traditional definitions, as well as being more amenable to proof and program transformation.

In this chapter, after showing a number of ways that we can describe functions in Haskell, we show how functions are returned as results of other functions, especially by means of **partial applications** and **operator sections**. We also re-examine some of our examples to see how the ideas fit into programs we built earlier, and in particular we look again at the Picture case study.

A longer example – building an index for a document – is used to show how these new ideas fit into program development. The chapter concludes with some examples of program verification involving higher-order polymorphic objects, where it is shown that the theorems proved about them are reusable in exactly the same way that the functions themselves are reusable.

(10.1) Function-level definitions

One of the reasons that functional programming is called 'functional' is that in such a language we can deal with functions as data, and so treat them much as we might handle integers or lists. Because of this, we will see in this chapter that we can often give a **function-level definition** of a function. What do we mean by this? Rather than explaining how a function operates on one or more parameters, as in the definition

```
rotate :: Picture -> Picture
rotate pic = flipV (flipH pic)                          (rotate.1)
```

a function-level definition gives a direct definition of the function, like

```
rotate = flipV . flipH                                  (rotate.2)
```

In this case we describe `rotate` as the composition of two reflections; of course, the effect of the definitions (`rotate.1`) and (`rotate.2`) is exactly the same, but there are two important advantages of the latter approach. First, the second definition is clearer to read and to modify; we see **explicitly** that the definition is a composition of two functions, rather than having to see it as a consequence of the way the right-hand side is defined in (`rotate.1`).

More importantly, if we state a definition in this form, then we can apply properties of '.' in analysing how `rotate` behaves. This means that in proofs we are able to use properties of composition, as well as being able to see examples of program transformations which will apply because of the form of composition involved. In general these remarks will apply to all higher-order, polymorphic functions, and we see examples of this in Section 10.9 below.

We have already seen other direct definitions, as when we said

```
flipH :: Picture -> Picture
flipH = reverse                                         (flipH.1)
```

We note that this definition has exactly the same effect as saying

```
flipH pic = reverse pic
```

since if we were to use (`flipH.1`) applied to the picture horse, say, the first step of the evaluation would be the step

```
flipH horse
⤳   reverse horse                                        by (flipH.1)
```

in which `flipH` gets replaced by `reverse`.

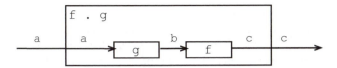

Figure 10.1 Function composition.

(10.2) Function composition

We have already used the Haskell function composition operator, '.'; in this section we look at it in more detail, and in particular examine its type.

One of the simplest ways of structuring a program is to do a number of things one after the other – each part can be designed and implemented separately. In a functional program this is achieved by **composing** a number of functions together: the output of one function becomes the input of another, as in Figure 10.1. The annotations of the arrows in the diagram indicate the types of elements involved.

For any functions f and g, the effect of f . g is given by the definition

(f . g) x = f (g x)   (comp.1)

Not all pairs of functions can be composed. The output of g, g x, becomes the input of f, so that the output type of g must equal the input type of f. In the example of rotate from Section 10.1 we see that the output type of flipH and the input type of flipV are both Picture.

In general, the constraint on which functions can be composed is expressed by giving '.' the type

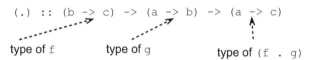

which shows that, if we call the first input f and the second g,

● The input of f and the output of g are of the same type: b.

● The result f . g has the same input type, a, as g and the same output type, c, as f.

Composition is **associative**, that is f . (g . h) is equal to (f . g) . h for all f, g and h. We can therefore write f . g . h unambiguously to mean 'do h, then g, then f'.[1]

Forward composition

The order in f . g is significant, and can be confusing; (f . g) means 'first apply g and then apply f to the result', and so we have to read a composition from right to left in order to appreciate its effect.

---

[1] For technical reasons, the '.' is treated as right associative in the Haskell standard prelude.

The reason we write (f . g) for 'g then f' is that we write arguments to the right of functions. The argument is therefore closer to g than to f, and the order of the functions in (f . g) x is the same as in the nested application, f (g x).

It is simple in Haskell to define an operator for composition which takes its arguments in the opposite order to '.'. This we do thus:

```
infixl 9 >.>
```

```
(>.>) :: (a -> b) -> (b -> c) -> (a -> c)
```

```
g >.> f = f . g
```
(fcomp.1)

This definition has the effect that

```
(g >.> f) x = (f . g) x = f (g x)
```
(fcomp.2)

showing that, as it were, the order of the f and g is swapped before the functions are applied. The rotate example can then be written

```
rotate = flipH >.> flipV
```

which we can read as flipH *then* flipV, with the functions being applied from left to right.

The notation '>.>' contains a '.' to show that it is a form of composition, with the arrows showing the direction in which information is flowing. We will tend to use '>.>' in situations where a number of functions are composed, and it is therefore tiresome to read some lines down the page in order to work out the effect of a function definition.

Pitfalls of composition

There are two pitfalls associated with composition which we need to be aware of:

● There is an error caused by the binding power of function application. It is a common error to write f . g x thinking it means (f . g) applied to x. Because function application binds more tightly than anything else, it is interpreted by the system as f . (g x), which will usually lead to a type error.

For example, evaluating

```
not . not True
```

gives the type error message

```
ERROR: Type error in application
*** expression    : not . not True
*** term          : not True
*** type          : Bool
*** does not match : a -> b
```

since there is an attempt to treat not True as a function to be composed with not. Such a function needs to have type a->b, whereas it actually has type Bool.

In applying a composition we therefore need to be sure that it is parenthesized, as follows:

(not . not) True

● Function application and composition can get confused. Function composition combines two functions, while application combines a function and an argument (which can be a function, of course).

If, for example, f has type Int -> Bool, then

- f . x means f composed with the *function* x; x therefore needs to be of type s -> Int for some type s.

- f x means f applied to the object x, so x must therefore be an integer.

<hr>

Exercises

10.1 Redefine the function printBill from the supermarket billing exercise in Section 6.4 so that composition is used. Repeat the exercise using forward composition, >.>.

10.2 If id is the polymorphic identity function, defined by id x = x, explain the behaviour of the expressions

(id . f)   (f . id)   id f

If f is of type Int -> Bool, at what instance of its most general type a -> a is id used in each case? What type does f have if f id is properly typed?

10.3 Define a function composeList which composes a list of functions into a single function. You should give the type of composeList, and explain why the function has this type. What is the effect of your function on an empty list of functions?

(10.3) Functions as values and results

In this section we begin to look at the ways in which functions can become the results of functions; in the next section we look at the important technique of partial application.

We have already seen that functions can be combined together using the composition operator '.' and the forward composition operator '>.>'; this can be done on the right-hand side of function definitions. The simplest example of this is

twice f = (f . f)   (twice.1)

f is a function, and the result is f composed with itself. For this to work, it needs to have the same input and output type, so we have

```
twice :: (a -> a) -> (a -> a)
```

This states that twice takes one argument, a function of type (a -> a), and returns a result of the same type. For instance, if succ is the function to add one to an integer,

```
succ :: Int -> Int
succ n = n+1
```

then applying twice to it gives the example

```
(twice succ) 12
~> (succ . succ) 12                                          by (twice.1)
~> succ (succ 12)                                            by (comp.1)
~> 14
```

We can generalize twice so that we pass a parameter giving the number of times the functional argument is to be composed with itself

```
iter :: Int -> (a -> a) -> (a -> a)

iter n f
  | n>0        = f . iter (n-1) f                              (iter.1)
  | otherwise  = id                                           (iter.2)
```

This is a standard primitive recursion over the integer argument; in the positive case we take the composition of f with itself n-1 times and compose once more with f. In the zero case we apply f no times, so the result is a function which does nothing to its argument, namely id. We can give a constructive definition using the standard list functions.

```
iter n f = foldr (.) id (replicate n f)                       (iter.3)
```

In this definition we create the list of n copies of f

```
[f,f,...,f]
```

which is then composed by folding in the composition operator to give

```
f . f . ... . f
```

As an example, we can define 2^n as iter n double 1, if double doubles its argument.

Expressions defining functions

How else can we write down expressions which describe functions? In writing a function definition we can use a where clause to make a definition.

Suppose, for example, that given an integer n we are to return the function (from Int to Int) which adds n to its argument, we can say

```
addNum :: Int -> (Int -> Int)
addNum n = addN
           where
           addN m = n+m
```

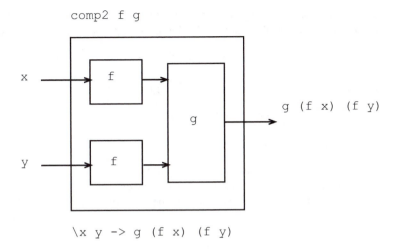

Figure 10.2 Plumbing f and g together.

The result is a function named addN, and addN is itself defined by an equation in the where clause. This method is rather indirect – we say we shall return the function named addN, and then define that function.

Lambda notation

Instead of naming and defining a function that we want to refer to, we can instead write it down directly. In the case of defining addNum we can define the result as

```
\m -> n+m
```

How is this expression to be interpreted?

● Before the arrow are the arguments, in this case the single argument m.
● After the arrow comes the result, here n+m.

That the expression is a function is signalled by its beginning with '\' which is the closest ASCII character to the Greek lambda, λ, which is used in a mathematical theory of functions, called the lambda calculus, for exactly this purpose. The definition of addNum now becomes

```
addNum n = (\m -> n+m)
```

We shall see another way of defining addNum in the next section of this chapter.

Another example which uses the lambda notation is given by the 'plumbing' illustrated in Figure 10.2. The object shown is a function, whose arguments are x and y. The result of the function is

```
g (f x) (f y)
```

so the overall effect is to give a function which applies f to each of its (two) arguments before applying g to the results. The definition states this quite straightforwardly:

```
comp2 :: (a -> b) -> (b -> b -> c) -> (a -> a -> c)

comp2 f g = (\x y -> g (f x) (f y))
```

To add together the squares of 3 and 4 we can write

```
comp2 sq add 3 4
```

where add and sq have the obvious definitions.

In general, a lambda-defined function is an **anonymous** version of the sort of function we have defined earlier. In other words, the function f defined by

```
f x y z = result
```

and the function

```
\x y z -> result
```

have exactly the same effect.

We shall see in the next section that partial application will make many definitions – including those of the functions here – more straightforward. On the other hand the lambda notation is more general, and thus can be used in situations when a partial application could not.

Exercises

10.4 Give calculations of

```
iter 3 double 1
(comp2 succ (*)) 3 4
comp2 sq add 3 4
```

10.5 What is the type and effect of the function

```
\n -> iter n succ
```

10.6 Given a function f of type a -> b -> c, write down a lambda expression that describes the function of type b -> a -> c which behaves like f but which takes its arguments in the other order. Pictorially,

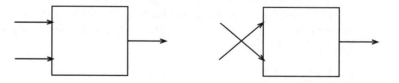

10.7 Using the last exercise, or otherwise, give a definition of the function

```
flip :: (a -> b -> c) -> (b -> a -> c)
```

which reverses the order in which its function argument takes its arguments.

10.8 Using a lambda expression, the Boolean function `not` and the built-in function `elem` describe a function of type

```
Char -> Bool
```

which is `True` only on non-whitespace characters, that is those which are not elements of the list `" \t\n"`.

10.9 Define a function `total`

```
total :: (Int -> Int) -> (Int -> Int)
```

so that `total f` is the function which at value n gives the total

```
f 0 + f 1 + ... + f n
```

10.10 [Harder] Define a function

```
slope :: (Float -> Float) -> (Float -> Float)
```

which takes a function `f` as argument, and returns (an approximation to) its derivative `f'` as result.

10.11 [Harder] Define a function

```
integrate :: (Float -> Float) -> (Float -> Float -> Float)
```

which takes a function `f` as argument, and returns (an approximation to) the two argument function which gives the area under its graph between two end points as its result.

10.4 Partial application

The function `multiply` multiplies together two arguments,

```
multiply :: Int -> Int -> Int
multiply x y = x*y
```

We can view the function as a box, with two input arrows and an output arrow.

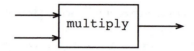

If we apply the function to two arguments, the result is a number; so that, for instance, multiply 2 3 equals 6.

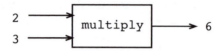

What happens if multiply is applied to **one** argument 2? Pictorially, we have

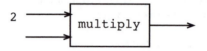

From the picture we can see that this represents a function, as there is still one input arrow to the function awaiting a value. This function will, when given the awaited argument y, return double its value, namely 2*y.

This is an example of a general phenomenon: any function taking two or more arguments can be **partially applied** to one or more arguments. This gives a powerful way of forming functions as results.

To illustrate, we return again to our example in which every element of a list is to be doubled. The function can be defined thus:

```
doubleAll :: [Int] -> [Int]
doubleAll = map (multiply 2)
```

In this definition there are two partial applications:

- multiply 2 is a function from integers to integers, given by applying multiply to one rather than two arguments;
- map (multiply 2) is a function from [Int] to [Int], given by partially applying map.

Partial application is being put to two different uses here.

- In the first case – multiply 2 – the partial application is used to form the function which multiplies by two, and which has to be passed to map to form the doubleAll function;
- the second partial application – of map to multiply 2 – could be avoided by writing the argument to doubleAll

  ```
  doubleAll xs = map (multiply 2) xs
  ```

  but, as was argued in Section 10.1, there are advantages to this form of definition.

In Section 10.3 we saw the example of addNum,

```
addNum n = (\m -> n+m)
```

which when applied to an integer n was intended to return the function which adds n to its argument. With partial application we have a simpler mechanism, as we can say

```
addNum n m = n+m
```

since when addNum is applied to one argument n it returns the function adding n.

The idea of partial application is important. We have already seen that many functions can be defined as **specializations** of general operations like map, filter and so on. These specializations arise by passing a function to the general operation – this function is often given by a partial application, as in the examples from the pictures case study first seen in Chapter 1:

```
flipV       = map reverse
sideBySide = zipWith (++)
```

We return to look at the Picture case study in greater detail in Section 10.5.

It is not always possible to make a partial application, since the argument to which we want to apply the function may not be its first argument. Consider the function

```
elem :: Char -> [Char] -> Bool
```

We can test whether a character ch is a whitespace character by writing

```
elem ch whitespace
```

where whitespace is the string " \t\n". We would like to write the function to test this by partially applying elem to whitespace, but cannot. We could define a variant of elem which takes its arguments in the other order, as in

```
member xs x = elem x xs
```

and write the function as the partial application

```
member whitespace
```

Alternatively, we can write down this function as a

```
\ch -> elem ch whitespace
```

In a similar vein, to filter all non-whitespace characters from a string, we could write either of the partial applications

```
filter (not . member whitespace)
filter (\ch -> not (elem ch whitespace))
```

The types of partial applications

How is the type of a partial application determined? There is a simple rule which explains it.

> **Definition**
>
> **Rule of cancellation**
>
> If the type of a function f is
>
> $$t_1 \rightarrow t_2 \rightarrow \ldots \rightarrow t_n \rightarrow t$$
>
> and it is applied to arguments
>
> $$e_1 :: t_1, \; e_2 :: t_2, \; \ldots, \; e_k :: t_k$$
>
> (where $k \leq n$) then the result type is given by **cancelling** the types t_1 to t_k
>
> $$\cancel{t_1} \rightarrow \cancel{t_2} \rightarrow \ldots \rightarrow \cancel{t_k} \rightarrow t_{k+1} \rightarrow \ldots \rightarrow t_n \rightarrow t$$
>
> which gives the type
>
> $$t_{k+1} \rightarrow t_{k+2} \rightarrow \ldots \rightarrow t_n \rightarrow t$$

For example, using this rule we can see that we get the following types

```
multiply 2         :: Int -> Int
multiply 2 3       :: Int
doubleAll          :: [Int] -> [Int]
doubleAll [2,3]  :: [Int]
```

The syntax of application and ->

Function application is **left associative** so that

```
f x y = (f x) y
f x y ≠ f (x y)
```

The function space symbol '`->`' is **right associative**, so that `a -> b -> c` means

```
a -> (b -> c)
```

and *not*

```
(a -> b) -> c
```

The arrow is not associative. If

```
f :: Int -> Int -> Int
g :: (Int -> Int) -> Int
```

as illustrated

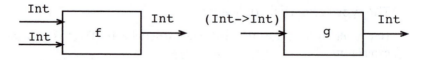

then f will yield a function from Int to Int when given a Int – an example is multiply. On the other hand, when given a function of type Int -> Int, g yields a Int. An example is

```
g :: (Int -> Int) -> Int
g h = (h 0) + (h 1)
```

The function g defined here takes a function h as argument and returns the sum of h's values at 0 and 1, and so g succ will have the value 3.

How many arguments do functions have?

Partial application can appear confusing: in some contexts functions appear to take one argument, and in others more than one. In fact, *every function in Haskell takes exactly one argument*. If this application yields a function, then this function may be applied to a further argument, and so on. Consider the multiplication function again.

```
multiply :: Int -> Int -> Int
```

This is shorthand for

```
multiply :: Int -> (Int -> Int)
```

and so it can therefore be applied to an integer. Doing this gives (for example)

```
multiply 2 :: Int -> Int
```

This can itself be applied to give

```
(multiply 2) 5 :: Int
```

which, since function application is left associative, can be written

```
multiply 2 5 :: Int
```

Our explanations earlier in the book are consistent with this full explanation of the system. We hid the fact that

$$f\ e_1\ e_2\ \ldots\ e_k$$
$$t_1\ \text{->}\ t_2\ \text{->}\ \ldots\ t_n\ \text{->}\ t$$

were shorthand for

$$(\ \ldots((f\ e_1)\ e_2)\ \ldots\ e_k)$$
$$t_1\ \text{->}\ (t_2\ \text{->}\ (\ldots(t_n\ \text{->}\ t)\ldots))$$

but this did no harm to our understanding of how to use the Haskell language. It is to support this shorthand that function application is made left associative and -> is made right associative.

Examples of partial applications will be seen throughout the material to come, and can be used to simplify and clarify many of the preceding examples. Three simple examples are the text processing functions

```
dropSpace = dropWhile (member whitespace)
dropWord  = dropWhile (not . member whitespace)
getWord   = takeWhile (not . member whitespace)
```

where

```
member xs x = elem x xs
```

We look at further examples in the next section, after examining partially applied operators.

Operator sections

The operators of the language can be partially applied, giving what are known as **operator sections**. Examples include

(+2)	The function which adds two to its argument.
(2+)	The function which adds two to its argument.
(>2)	The function which returns whether a number is greater than two.
(3:)	The function which puts the number 3 on the front of a list.
(++"\n")	The function which puts a newline at the end of a string.
("\n"++)	The function which puts a newline at the beginning of a string.

The general rule here is that a section of the operator op will put its argument to the side which completes the application. That is,

```
(op x) y = y op x
(x op) y = x op y
```

When combined with higher-order functions like `map`, `filter` and composition, the notation is both powerful and elegant, enabling us to make a whole lot more function-level definitions. For example,

```
filter (>0) . map (+1)
```

is the function which adds one to each member of a list, and then removes those elements which are not positive.

Exercises

10.12 Use partial applications to define the functions comp2 and total given in Section 10.3 and its exercises.

10.13 Find operator sections sec_1 and sec_2 so that

```
map sec₁ . filter sec₂
```

has the same effect as

```
filter (>0) . map (+1)
```

10.5 Revisiting the `Picture` example

Now that we have been introduced to higher-order functions, and in particular partial application, we can revisit the example of pictures and complete our definitions of the functions over the `Picture` type. The case study was introduced in Chapter 1 and further developed in Sections 2.5 and 6.1.

Recall that a picture is a list of lines, each of which is made up of a list of characters

```
type Picture = [[Char]]
```

We first define reflection in a horizontal mirror, which is given simply by reversing the list of lines,

```
flipH :: Picture -> Picture
flipH = reverse
```

To reflect in a vertical mirror we need to reverse every line – clearly a task for `map`:

```
flipV :: Picture -> Picture
flipV = map reverse
```

To place pictures next to each other we have two functions. To put one picture above the other we join together the two lists of lines

```
above :: Picture -> Picture -> Picture
above = (++)
```

while placing the pictures side-by-side requires corresponding lines to be joined together with `++`, using the function `zipWith` first introduced in Section 9.2.

```
sideBySide :: Picture -> Picture -> Picture
sideBySide = zipWith (++)
```

Among the other functions mentioned were

```
invertColour :: Picture -> Picture
superimpose  :: Picture -> Picture -> Picture
printPicture :: Picture -> IO ()
```

and we give their definitions now. To invert the colour in a picture, we need to invert the colour in every line, so

```
invertColour = map ...
```

where `...` will be the function to invert the colour in a single line. To invert every character in a line – which is itself a list of characters – we will again use `map`. The function mapped is `invertChar`, first defined in Section 6.1. This gives the definition

```
invertColour :: Picture -> Picture
invertColour = map (map invertChar)
```

which we can read as saying

apply map invertChar to every line in the Picture; that is, apply the function invertChar to every character in the Picture, which is a list of lists of characters.

Suppose we are equipped with a function

```
combineChar :: Char -> Char -> Char
```

which superimposes two characters; how are we to use this in superimposing two pictures? Recall the function

```
zipWith :: (a -> b -> c) -> [a] -> [b] -> [c]
```

where zipWith f xs ys produces a list by applying the function f to corresponding elements chosen from xs and ys, so that, for instance

```
zipWith (*) [2,0] [3,1] = [6,0]
```

To superimpose the pictures, we will need to superimpose corresponding lines, so

```
superimpose = zipWith ...
```

where ... will be required to superimpose two single lines.

In doing this, we have to superimpose corresponding characters, so this is again an application of zipWith. What is used to perform the combination of individual characters? The answer is combineChar, and so we have

```
superimpose :: Picture -> Picture -> Picture
superimpose = zipWith (zipWith combineChar)
```

Our final definition is of printPicture, which outputs a Picture to the screen. We have already seen that to output a String we can use the function

```
putStr :: String -> IO ()
```

so it will be sufficient for us to precede application of this by a function to turn the list of lines making up the Picture into a string, in which the lines are separated by newline characters. This we can write as a composition

```
concat . map (++"\n")
```

since the effect of this is first to add a newline character to every line – the role of map (++"\n") – and then to join this list of strings into a single string – the effect of the concat. We therefore define the printing function thus:

```
printPicture :: Picture -> IO ()
printPicture = putStr . concat . map (++"\n")
```

Exercises

In these exercises we suggest further operations over pictures.

10.14 Define a function

```
chessBoard :: Int -> Picture
```

so that chessBoard n is a picture of an n by n chess board.

10.15 How would you implement invertColour, superimpose and printPicture if Picture was defined to be [[Bool]]?

10.16 Define a function

```
makePicture :: Int -> Int -> [(Int,Int)] -> Picture
```

where the list argument gives the positions of the black points in the picture, and the two integer arguments give the width and height of the picture. For example,

```
makePicture 7 5 [(1,3),(3,2)]
```

will have the form

```
.......
...#...
.......
..#....
.......
```

It is evident from this that positions within lines and lines themselves are counted from zero, with line zero being the top line.

10.17 Define a function

```
pictureToRep :: Picture -> ( Int , Int , [(Int,Int)] )
```

which has the reverse effect of makePicture. For example, if pic is

```
....
.##.
....
```

then pictureToRep pic will be (4 , 3, [(1,1),(1,2)])

10.18 If we make the definition

```
type Rep = ( Int , Int , [(Int,Int)] )
```

discuss how you would define functions over Rep to rotate, reflect and superimpose pictures under this alternative representation. Discuss the advantages and disadvantages of this representation in comparison with the original representation given by the Picture type.

10.19 In the light of the discussion in the last four chapters, redo the exercises of Section 6.2, which deal with positioned pictures.

10.6 Further examples

This section explores how partial applications and operator sections can be used to simplify and shorten definitions in a number of other examples. Often it is possible to avoid giving an explicit function definition if we can use a partial application to return a function. Revisiting the examples of Chapter 7 we see that to double all the elements in a list we can write

```
doubleAll :: [Int] -> [Int]
doubleAll = map (*2)
```

using an operator section (*2) to replace the double function, and giving the function definition directly by partially applying map.

To filter out the even elements in a numerical list, we have to check whether the remainder on dividing by two is equal to zero. As a function we can write

```
(==0).('mod' 2)
```

This is the composition of two operator sections: first find the remainder on dividing by two, then check if it is equal to zero. (Why can we not write ('mod' 2 == 0)?) The filtering function can then be written

```
getEvens :: [Int] -> [Int]
getEvens = filter ((==0).('mod' 2))
```

Our final example comes from the list splitting study. We defined

```
getWord xs
  = getUntil p xs
    where
    p x = elem x whitespace
```

The local definition is not now needed, as we can define the function p by an operator section:

```
getWord xs = getUntil ('elem' whitespace) xs
```

Note the way that we partially apply a function to its *second* argument, by forming an operator section. This works because

```
('elem' whitespace) x
= x 'elem' whitespace
= elem x whitespace
```

as required.

Finally, the function getWord can itself be given a direct definition, by partial application thus

```
getWord = getUntil ('elem' whitespace)
```

This definition reads like an informal explanation – to get a word, get characters until a whitespace character is found.

10.7 Currying and uncurrying

In Haskell we have a choice of how to model functions of two or more arguments. We usually represent them in what is called a **curried** form, where they take their arguments one at a time. This is called **currying** after Haskell Curry[2] who was one of the pioneers of the λ-calculus and after whom the Haskell language is named. For instance, a function to multiply two integers would normally be defined thus:

```
multiply :: Int -> Int -> Int
multiply x y = x*y
```

while an **uncurried** version can be given by bundling the arguments into a pair, thus:

```
multiplyUC :: (Int,Int) -> Int
multiplyUC (x,y) = x*y
```

Why do we usually opt for the curried form? There are a number of reasons.

- The notation is somewhat neater; we apply a function to a single argument by juxtaposing the two, f x, and application to two arguments is done by extending this thus: g x y.
- It permits partial application. In the case of multiplication we can write expressions like multiply 2, which returns a function, while this is not possible if the two arguments are bundled into a pair, as is the case for multiplyUC.

We can in any case move between the curried and uncurried representations with little difficulty, and indeed we can define two higher-order functions which convert between curried and uncurried functions.

Suppose first that we want to write a curried version of a function g, which is itself uncurried and of type (a,b) -> c.

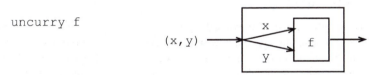

This function expects its arguments as a pair, but its curried version, curry g, will take them separately – we therefore have to form them into a pair before applying g to them:

```
curry :: ((a,b) -> c) -> (a -> b -> c)
curry g x y = g (x,y)
```

curry multiplyUC will be exactly the same function as multiply.

Suppose now that f is a curried function, of type a -> b -> c.

2 In fact the first person to describe the idea was Schönfinkel, but 'Schönfinkeling' does not sound so snappy!

The function `uncurry` `f` will expect its arguments as a pair, and these will have to be separated before `f` can be applied to them:

```
uncurry :: (a -> b -> c) -> ((a,b) -> c)
uncurry f (x,y) = f x y
```

`uncurry multiply` will be exactly the same function as `multiplyUC`. The functions `curry` and `uncurry` are inverse to each other.

Partial application of functions is done on the arguments from left to right, so a function cannot directly be applied to its second argument only. This effect can be achieved indirectly by first transforming the order in which the function takes its arguments and then partially applying it.

```
flip :: (a -> b -> c) -> (b -> a -> c)
flip f x y = f y x
```

`flip map` will takes as its first argument the list and as its second the function to be mapped; it can be applied to its first argument, having the effect of applying `map` to its second only.

Another way of forming the partial application (`'elem'` whitespace) is to use the `flip` function. We have

```
flip elem :: [Char] -> Char -> Bool
```

(among other types) and so we can form the partial application thus:

```
flip elem whitespace
```

We now turn to a more substantial example in which we use the ideas of composition, partial application and operator sections in a variety of ways.

(10.8) Example: creating an index

This section explores a different aspect of text processing from those we have looked at already. How can an index for a document be produced automatically? We use the example to illustrate how higher-order functions are used in many parts of the final program. Polymorphism allows their use at different types, and their function parameters mean that they can be used to different effect in different situations.

To make the example texts shorter, a scaled-down version of the indexing problem is investigated. This is only done for ease of presentation, as all the important aspects of the system are explored here.

Specification

We should first specify what the program is to do. The input is a text string, in which lines are separated by the newline character `'\n'`. The index should give every line on which the word in question occurs. Only words of length at least four letters are to be indexed, and an alphabetical listing of the results produced. Within each entry, a line number should not be duplicated. For example, on the input

```
"cathedral doggerel cathedral\nbattery doggerel cathedral\ncathedral"
```

we would expect to get an index

```
battery        2
cathedral      1, 2, 3
doggerel       1, 2
```

Designing the program

We can represent the index as a list, with each entry being an item. What will a single entry be? It has to associate a collection of line numbers with each word in the text; we can therefore represent each entry by a pair consisting of a list of numbers, of type [Int], and a word, of type String. The top-level function will therefore be

```
makeIndex :: Doc -> [ ([Int],Word) ]
```

where we use the type synonyms

```
type Doc  = String
type Line = String
type Word = String
```

to distinguish the different uses of the string type in the design which follows. Note that these are all the same type; we use the names to make our discussion of types carry more information: the definition of 'Line' can be read as saying 'String thought of as representing a line', for example.

How can the program be designed? We focus on the **data structures** which the program will produce, and we can see the program as working by making a series of modifications to the data with which we begin. This **data-directed** design is common in Haskell functional program development.

At the top level, the solution will be a **composition** of functions. These perform the following operations, in turn.

- Split the text, a Doc, into lines, giving an object of type [Line].

- Pair each line with its line number, giving an object of type [(Int,Line)].

- Split the lines into words, associating each word with the number of the line on which it occurs. This gives a list of type [(Int,Word)].

- Sort this list according to the alphabetical ordering of words (Strings), giving a list of the same type.

- Modify the lists so that each word is paired with a list containing a single line number. This gives a result of type [([Int],Word)].

- Amalgamate entries for the same word into a list of numbers, giving a list of type [([Int],Word)].

- Shorten the list by removing all entries for words of less than four letters, giving a list of type [([Int],Word)].

The definition follows; note that we have used comments to give the type of each component function in the forward composition:

```
makeIndex
  = lines        >.>      --   Doc              -> [Line]
      numLines   >.>      --   [Line]           -> [(Int,Line)]
      allNumWords >.>     --   [(Int,Line)]     -> [(Int,Word)]
      sortLs     >.>      --   [(Int,Word)]     -> [(Int,Word)]
      makeLists  >.>      --   [(Int,Word)]     -> [([Int],Word)]
      amalgamate >.>      --   [([Int],Word)]   -> [([Int],Word)]
      shorten             --   [([Int],Word)]   -> [([Int],Word)]
```

Once the type of each of the functions is given, development of each can proceed independently. The only information necessary to use a function is its *type*, and these types are specified in the definition above. Each of the functions can now be given, in turn.

Implementing the component functions

To split a string into a list of lines it must be split at each occurrence of the newline character, '\n'. How is this written as a function? One solution is to write functions analogous to getWord and dropWord, which together were used earlier in splitWords. Alternatively, we can use the functions getUntil and dropUntil from Chapter 7. A third alternative is to look in the standard prelude where we find the function lines already defined; we therefore use that.

```
lines :: Doc -> [Line]
```

The next function should pair each line with its line number. If the list of lines is linels, then the list of line numbers is

```
[1 .. length linels]
```

Stepping back from the problem, it is apparent that the lists of lines and line numbers need to be combined into a **list of pairs**, by zipping the two lists together. The zip function has already been defined to do exactly this, so the required function is

```
numLines :: [Line] -> [ ( Int , Line ) ]
numLines linels
  = zip [1 .. length linels] linels
```

Now the lines have to be split into words, and line numbers attached. We first consider the problem for a single line.

```
numWords :: ( Int , Line ) -> [ ( Int , Word ) ]
```

Splitting into words can be done by the function splitWords of Chapter 7, modified slightly. When we defined splitWords we preserved any punctuation characters, as these were to appear in the output of the text processor. In contrast here we will modify the definition of whitespace to include punctuation, and so remove the punctuation from the resulting words. We define

```
whitespace :: String
whitespace = " \n\t;:.,\'\"!?()-"
```

Each of these words is then to be paired with the (same) line number. Stepping back from the problem, we see that we have to perform an operation on every item of a list, the list of words making up the line. This is a job for map,

```
numWords (number , line)
  = map (\word -> (number,word)) (splitWords line)
```

or a list comprehension

```
numWords (number , line)
  = [ (number , word) | word <- splitWords line ]
```

To apply this to the whole text, the function numWords has to be applied to every line. This is again done by map, and the individual results joined together or **concatenated**. We make a direct definition of the function, by composing its two parts. First we map the function numWords, then we concatenate the results, using concat.

```
allNumWords :: [ ( Int , Line ) ] -> [ ( Int , Word ) ]
allNumWords = concat . map numWords
```

What has been achieved so far? The text has been transformed into a list of line-number/word pairs, from which an index is to be built. For instance, the text

```
"cat dog\nbat dog\ncat"
```

will be converted to

```
[(1,"cat") , (1,"dog") , (2,"bat") , (2,"dog") , (3,"cat")]
```

The list must next be sorted by word order, and lists of lines on which a word appears be built. The ordering relation on pairs of numbers and words is given by

```
orderPair :: ( Int , Word ) -> ( Int , Word ) -> Bool
orderPair ( n1 , w1 ) ( n2 , w2 )
  = w1 < w2 || ( w1 == w2 && n1 < n2 )
```

The words are compared for dictionary order. For pairs containing the same words, ordering is by line number.

Sorting a list is most easily done by a version of the **quicksort** algorithm. The list is split into parts smaller than and larger than a given element; each of these halves can be sorted separately, and then joined together to form the result.

```
sortLs :: [ ( Int , Word ) ] -> [ ( Int , Word ) ]

sortLs []     = []
sortLs (p:ps) = sortLs smaller ++ [p] ++ sortLs larger
```

The lists smaller and larger are the lists of elements of ps which are smaller (or larger) than the pair p. Note that it is here that duplicate copies are removed – any other occurrence of the pair p in the list ps does not appear in either smaller or larger.

How are the two lists defined? They are given by selecting those elements of ps with given properties: a job for filter, or a list comprehension. Going back to the definition of sortLs,

```
sortLs (p:ps)
  = sortLs smaller ++ [p] ++ sortLs larger
    where
    smaller = [ q | q<-ps , orderPair q p ]
    larger  = [ q | q<-ps , orderPair p q ]
```

After sorting the running example will be

```
[(2,"bat") , (1,"cat") , (3,"cat") , (1,"dog") , (2,"dog")]
```

The entries for the same word need to be accumulated together. First each entry is converted to having a *list* of line numbers associated with it, thus

```
makeLists ::  [ (Int,Word) ] -> [ ([Int],Word) ]
makeLists
  = map mklis
    where
    mklis ( n , st ) = ( [n] , st )
```

For our example, this gives

```
[ ([2],"bat") , ([1],"cat") , ([3],"cat") ,
  ([1],"dog") , ([2],"dog") ]
```

After this, the lists associated with the same words are amalgamated.

```
amalgamate :: [ ([Int],Word) ] -> [ ([Int],Word) ]

amalgamate [] = []
amalgamate [p] = [p]
amalgamate ((l1,w1):(l2,w2):rest)
  | w1 /= w2    = (l1,w1) : amalgamate ((l2,w2):rest)     (amalg.1)
  | otherwise   = amalgamate ((l1++l2,w1):rest)           (amalg.2)
```

The first two equations are simple, with the third doing the work.

- If we have two adjacent entries with different words, case (amalg.1), then we know that there is nothing to add to the first entry – we therefore have to amalgamate entries in the *tail* only.

- If two adjacent entries have the same word associated, case (amalg.2), they are amalgamated and the function is called again on the result. This is because there may be other entries with the same word, also to be amalgamated into the leading entry.

Consider an example

```
amalgamate [ ([2],"bat") , ([1],"cat") , ([3],"cat") ]
 ⇝  ([2],"bat") : amalgamate [([1],"cat"),([3],"cat")] by (amalg.1)
 ⇝  ([2],"bat") : amalgamate [ ([1,3],"cat") ]          by (amalg.2)
 ⇝  ([2],"bat") : [ ([1,3],"cat") ]
 ⇝  [ ([2],"bat") , ([1,3],"cat") ]
```

To meet the requirements, one other operation needs to be performed. 'Small' words of less than four letters are to be removed.

```
shorten
  = filter sizer
    where
    sizer (nl,wd) = length wd > 3
```

Again, the `filter` function proves useful. The index function can now be defined in full:

```
makeIndex :: Doc -> [ ([Int],Word) ]
makeIndex
  = lines >.> numLines >.> allNumWords >.> sortLs >.>
    makeLists >.> amalgamate >.> shorten
```

As was said at the beginning of this section, function composition provides a powerful method for structuring designs: programs are written as a **pipeline** of operations, passing the appropriate data structures between them.

It is easy to see how designs like these can be modified. To take one example, the indexing program above filters out short words only as its final operation. There are a number of earlier points in the chain at which this could have been done, and it is a worthwhile exercise to consider these.

Exercises

10.20 Define the function `lines` using the functions `getUntil` and `dropUntil` from Chapter 9, or the built-in functions `takeWhile` and `dropWhile`. You should be careful that your functions do not give an empty word when there are empty lines in the Doc; this might happen for the examples `"cat\n\ndog"` and `"fish\n"`.

10.21 How would you use lambda expressions to replace the local definitions in `makeLists` and `shorten`? How would you define these functions using list comprehensions?

10.22 In the index for this book, instead of printing an entry like

```
cathedral        3, 5, 6, 7, 9, 10
```

a number of ranges could be given:

```
cathedral          3, 5-7, 9-10
```

How would you redesign your program to do this? Hint: first think about the type of the new index representation and then consider adding another function to the (forward) composition which currently forms the definition of makeIndex.

10.23 How would you re-define sortLs so that duplicate copies of an item are *not* removed? For the index, this means that if a word occurs twice on line 123 say, then 123 occurs twice in the index entry for that word.

10.24 How could the functions getUntil and dropUntil be used in the definition of amalgamate?

10.25 Explain how the function sizer defined locally in shorten can be defined as a composition of built-in functions and operator sections; the role of sizer is to pick the second half of a pair, find its length, and compare the result with 4.

10.26 How is the following definition of the last conditional equation for amalgamate incorrect? Give an example calculation to justify your answer.

```
amalgamate ((l1,w1):(l2,w2):rest)
  | w1 /= w2    = (l1,w1) : amalgamate ((l2,w2):rest)
  | otherwise   = (l1++l2,w1) : amalgamate rest
```

10.27 Give a definition of

```
printIndex :: [ ([Int],Word) ] -> IO ()
```

which gives a neatly laid-out printable version of an index, as shown at the start of the section. You might find it useful to define a function

```
showIndex :: [ ([Int],Word) ] -> String
```

and to use this as a part of your definition of printIndex.

10.28 Modify the program so that words of less than four letters are removed as a part of the definition of allNumWords.

10.29 Modify the makeIndex function so that instead of returning the list of line numbers on which a word occurs, the function returns the total number of times that the word occurs. You will need to make sure that multiple occurrences of a word in a single line are counted. There are two ways of tackling the problem.

- Modify the program as little as is necessary – you could return the length of a list rather than the list itself, for instance.
- Take the program structure as a guide, and write a (simpler) program which calculates the number of occurrences directly.

10.30 Modify the program so that capitalized words like "Dog" are indexed under their uncapitalized equivalents ("dog"). This does not work well for proper names like "Amelia" — what could you do about that?

10.31 The function sortLs is limited to sorting lists of type [(Int,Word)] because it calls the orderPair function. Redefine the function so that it takes the comparison function as a *parameter*. What is its type after this redefinition?

10.32 How would you modify the program if it was to be used to form the index for a Haskell script? Hint: you need to think about what it is sensible to ignore in such an enterprise.

(10.9) Verification and general functions

Verification can take on a different character when we look at higher-order polymorphic functions. We can start to prove equalities between functions, rather than between values of functions, and we shall also see that we are able to prove theorems which resemble their subjects in being general and reusable, and so applicable in many contexts.

Function-level verification

We claimed in Section 10.3 that the function iter is a generalization of twice, since

```
iter 2 f
    = f . iter 1 f                          by (iter.1)
    = f . (f . iter 0 f)                    by (iter.1)
    = f . (f . id)                          by (iter.2)
    = f . f                                 by (compId)
    = twice f                               by (twice.1)
```

In proving this we have used the equality between two functions

```
f . id = f                                             (compId)
```

How is this proved? We examine how each side behaves on an arbitrary argument x

```
(f . id) x
    = f (id x)
    = f x
```

so that for any argument x the two functions have the same behaviour. As black boxes, they are therefore the same. As what interests us here is their behaviour, we say that they are equal. We call this 'black-box' concept of equality **extensional**.

> **Definition**
>
> **Principle of extensionality:**
>
> Two functions f and g are equal if they have the same value at every argument.

This is called extensionality in contrast to the idea of **intensionality** in which we say two functions are the same only if they have the same definitions – we no longer think of them as black boxes; we are allowed to look inside them to see how the mechanisms work, as it were. If we are interested in the results of our programs, all that matters are the values given by functions, not how they are arrived at. We therefore use extensionality when we are reasoning about function behaviour in Haskell. If we are interested in **efficiency** or other performance aspects of programs, then the way in which a result is found *will* be significant, however. This is discussed further in Chapter 19.

Exercises

10.33 Using the principle of extensionality, show that function composition is associative: that is, for all f, g and h,

```
f . (g . h) = (f . g) . h
```

10.34 Show that for all f,

```
id . f = f
```

10.35 Show that the function `flip` defined in Section 10.7 satisfies

```
flip . flip = id
```

Hint: to show this, you might want to prove that for any f,

```
flip (flip f) = f
```

10.36 Two functions f and g are **inverses** if it can be shown that

```
f . g = id              g . f = id
```

Prove that the functions `curry` and `uncurry` of Section 10.7 are inverses. Can you think of other pairs of inverse functions?

10.37 Using induction, prove that for all natural numbers n,

```
iter n id = id
```

10.38 A function f is called **idempotent** if

```
f . f = f
```

Show that the functions `abs` and `signum` are idempotent. Can you think of any other idempotent functions?

Higher-level proofs

Our verification thus far has concentrated on first-order, monomorphic functions. Just as map, `filter` and `fold` generalize patterns of definition, we shall find that proofs about these functions generalize results we have seen already. To give some examples, it is not hard to prove that

```
doubleAll (xs++ys) = doubleAll xs ++ doubleAll ys
```

holds for all finite lists xs and ys. When doubleAll is defined as map (*2) it becomes clear that we have an example of a general result,

```
map f (xs++ys) = map f xs ++ map f ys                    (map++)
```

which is valid for *any* function f. We also claimed in an earlier exercise that

```
sum (xs++ys) = sum xs + sum ys                           (sum.3)
```

for all finite lists xs, ys. The function sum is given by folding in (+),

```
sum = foldr (+) 0
```

and we have, generally, if f is associative, and st is an identity for f, that is,

```
x 'f' (y 'f' z) = (x 'f' y) 'f' z
x 'f' st = x = st 'f' x
```

for all x, y, z then the equation

```
foldr f st (xs++ys) = f (foldr f st xs) (foldr f st ys)   (foldr.3)
```

holds for all finite xs and ys. Obviously (+) is associative and has 0 as an identity, and so (sum.3) is a special case of (fold.3). Now we give three proofs of examples in the same vein.

map and composition

A first example concerns map and composition. Recall the definitions

```
map f []     = []                                        (map.1)
map f (x:xs) = f x : map f xs                            (map.2)
(f . g) x    = f (g x)                                   (comp.1)
```

It is not hard to see that we should be able to prove that

```
map (f . g) xs = (map f . map g) xs                      (map.3)
```

holds for every finite list xs.

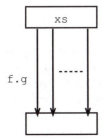
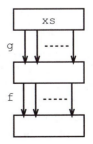

Applying (f . g) to every member of a list should be the same as applying g to every member of the list and then applying f to every member of the result. It is proved just as easily, by structural induction. The (base) case requires the identity to be proved for the empty list.

```
map (f . g) [] = []                                          by (map.1)

(map f . map g) []
  = map f (map g [])                                          by (comp.1)
  = map f []                                                  by (map.1)
  = []                                                        by (map.1)
```

Assuming that

```
map (f . g) xs = (map f . map g) xs                          (hyp)
```

is true, it is now necessary to prove that

```
map (f . g) (x:xs) = (map f . map g) (x:xs)                  (ind)
```

Again, it is enough to analyse each side of the equation.

```
map (f . g) (x:xs)
  = (f . g) x : map (f . g) xs                               by (map.2)
  = f (g x) : map (f . g) xs                                 by (comp.1)

(map f . map g) (x:xs)
  = map f (map g (x:xs))                                     by (comp.1)
  = map f (g x : map g xs)                                   by (map.2)
  = f (g x) : map f (map g xs)                               by (map.2)
  = f (g x) : (map f . map g) xs                             by (comp.1)
```

The induction hypothesis is exactly what is needed to prove the two sides equal, completing the proof of the induction step and the proof itself. ■

Each Haskell list type, besides containing finite lists, also contains infinite and partial lists. In Chapter 17 these will be explained and it will be shown that (map.3) is true for *all* lists xs, and therefore that the functional equation

```
map (f . g) = (map f) . (map g)
```

holds in general.

map and filter

The proof above showed how properties of functional programs could be proved from the definitions of the functions in a straightforward way. The properties can state how the program behaves – that a sorting function returns an ordered list, for instance – or can relate one program to another. This latter idea underlies **program transformation** for functional languages. This section introduces an example called **filter promotion** which is one of the most useful of the basic functional transformations.

```
filter p . map f = map f . filter (p . f)
```

The equation says that a map followed by a filter can be replaced by a filter followed by a map. The right-hand side is potentially more efficient than the left, since the map operation will there be applied to a shorter list, consisting of just those elements with the property (p . f). An example is given by the function first defined in Section 10.4.

```
filter (0<) . map (+1)
```

Instead of mapping first, the function can be replaced by

```
map (+1) . filter ((0<) . (+1))
 = map (+1) . filter (0<=)
```

and it is clear that here the transformed version is more efficient, since the test (0<=) is no more costly than (0<). The proof that

```
(filter p . map f) xs = (map f . filter (p . f)) xs
```

for finite lists xs is by structural induction. First we reiterate the definitions of map, filter and composition.

```
map f []        = []                                          (map.1)
map f (x:xs)    = f x : map f xs                              (map.2)

filter p []     = []                                          (filter.1)
filter p (x:xs)
  | p x         = x : filter p xs                             (filter.2)
  | otherwise   =     filter p xs                             (filter.3)

(f . g) x       = f (g x)                                     (comp.1)
```

The base case consists of a proof of

```
(filter p . map f) [] = (map f . filter (p . f)) []          (base)
```

This is true since

```
(filter p . map f) []
  = filter p (map f [])                          by (comp.1)
  = filter p []                                  by (map.1)
  = []                                           by (filter.1)
```

and

```
(map f . filter (p . f)) []
  = map f (filter (p . f) [])                    by (comp.1)
  = map f []                                      by (filter.1)
  = []                                           by (map.1)
```

In the induction step, a proof of

```
(filter p . map f) (x:xs) = (map f . filter (p . f)) (x:xs)    (ind)
```

is required, using the induction hypothesis

```
(filter p . map f) xs = (map f . filter (p . f)) xs                (hyp)
```

The proof begins with an analysis of the left-hand side of (ind).

```
(filter p . map f) (x:xs)
  = filter p (map f (x:xs))                               by (comp.1)
  = filter p (f x : map f xs)                             by (map.2)
```

There are two[3] cases to consider: whether p (f x) is True or False. Taking the case where p (f x) is True, we continue to examine the left-hand side of (ind), giving

```
  = f x : filter p (map f xs)                           by (filter.2)
  = f x : (filter p . map f) xs                           by (comp.1)
  = f x : (map f . filter (p . f)) xs                        by (hyp)
```

Now we look at the right-hand side of (ind), also assuming that p (f x) is True:

```
(map f . filter (p . f)) (x:xs)
  = map f (filter (p . f) (x:xs))                         by (comp.1)
  = map f (x: (filter (p . f) xs))                      by (filter.2)
  = f x : map f (filter (p . f) xs)                       by (map.2)
  = f x : (map f . filter (p . f)) xs                     by (comp.1)
```

which shows that (ind) holds in the case that p (f x) is True.

A similar chain of reasoning gives the same result in the case where p (f x) is False. This establishes (ind) assuming (hyp), and so together with (base) completes the proof of the filter promotion transformation in the case of finite lists; it holds, in fact, for all lists.   ■

map, reverse and the Picture case study

When we introduced the Picture case study in Chapter 1 we claimed that we could prove that flipV and flipH can be applied in either order to give the same result. Our implementation defines them thus

```
flipH = reverse
flipV = map reverse
```

and we can see informally that

- reverse affects the order of the elements, while leaving the elements unchanged;
- map reverse affects each of the elements, while keeping their order the same.

The second observation is a consequence of the function being a map, and so we make the more general claim that for all finite lists xs and all functions f,

---

[3] We should also think about what happens when p (f x) is undefined; in this case both sides will be undefined, and so equal.

```
map f (reverse xs) = reverse (map f xs)                    (map/reverse)
```

This has the consequence that

```
flipV (flipH xs) = flipH (flipV xs)
```

if we replace f in (map/reverse) by reverse. We will see in Chapter 17 that we can establish (map/reverse) for all lists xs and so conclude that the functional equations hold:

```
map f . reverse = reverse . map f
flipV . flipH   = flipH . flipV
```

We now prove (map/reverse) by induction over xs.

We have seen the definition of map in the previous examples; reverse is defined thus.

```
reverse []     = []                                        (reverse.1)
reverse (z:zs) = reverse zs ++ [z]                         (reverse.2)
```

Statement   We first have to prove the base case:

```
map f (reverse []) = reverse (map f [])                    (base)
```

and then we need to prove the induction step,

```
map f (reverse (x:xs)) = reverse (map f (x:xs))            (ind)
```

assuming the induction hypothesis:

```
map f (reverse xs) = reverse (map f xs)                    (hyp)
```

Base   Looking at the two sides of the base case in turn, we have

```
map f (reverse [])
  = map f []                                         by (reverse.1)
  = []                                               by (map.1)

reverse (map f [])
  = reverse []                                       by (map.1)
  = []                                               by (reverse.1)
```

and this shows that the two sides of the base case equation have the same value, and so we move on to the induction case.

Induction   We start by examining the left-hand side of (ind):

```
map f (reverse (x:xs))
  = map f (reverse xs ++ [x])                        by (reverse.2)
```

Now, it is not hard to prove that

$$\text{map f (ys++zs) = map f ys ++ map f zs} \qquad \text{(map++)}$$

(we leave this proof as an exercise for the reader) and using (map++) we can continue
to simplify the left-hand side

```
    = map f (reverse xs) ++ map f [x]                    by (map++)
    = map f (reverse xs) ++ [f x]                  by (map.1),(map.2)
```

Using the induction hypothesis, we can make one more step,

```
    = reverse (map f xs) ++ [f x]                        by (hyp)
```

Now looking at the right-hand side,

```
reverse (map f (x:xs))
    = reverse (f x : map f xs)                           by (map.2)
    = reverse (map f xs) ++ [f x]                    by (reverse.2)
```

and now we see that the two sides are equal, which establishes the induction step and
so completes the proof. ∎

Libraries of theorems

We have seen in this section that we can prove properties of general functions like map,
filter and foldr. This means that when we define a function which uses map, say,
we can call on a whole library of properties of map, including, for all finite xs and ys:

```
map (f . g) xs          = (map f . map g) xs
(filter p . map f) xs = (map f . filter (p . f)) xs
map f (reverse xs)      = reverse (map f xs)
map f (ys++zs)          = map f ys ++ map f zs
```

We have seen that using the general functions map, filter and others allowed us
to make direct definitions of new functions rather than having to define them 'from
scratch' using recursion. In exactly the same way, these general theorems will mean
that in many cases we can avoid writing an induction proof about our specific function,
and instead simply use one of these theorems.

Exercises

10.39 Prove that for all ys and zs the equation

$$\text{map f (ys++zs) = map f ys ++ map f zs} \qquad \text{(map++)}$$

as was used in the proof of the theorem about map and reverse.

10.40 If f is associative, and st is an identity for f – these notions were defined on
page 195 – then prove that the equation (foldr.3):

```
foldr f st (xs++ys) = f (foldr f st xs) (foldr f st ys)
```

holds for all finite xs and ys.

10.41 Argue that the result

```
concat (xs ++ ys) = concat xs ++ concat ys
```

is a special case of (foldr.3), using

```
concat = foldr (++) []
```

as the definition of concat.

10.42 Prove that for all finite lists xs, and functions f,

```
concat (map (map f) xs) = map f (concat xs)
```

10.43 Prove that over the type Int

```
(0<) . (+1) = (0<=)
```

as is used in the theorem relating map and filter.

10.44 Prove for all finite lists xs that

```
filter p (filter q xs) = filter (p &&& q) xs
```

where the operator &&& is defined by

```
p &&& q = \x -> (p x && q x)
```

Summary

We have seen in this chapter how we can write functions with functions as results. This means that we can create the functions by applying operations like map, filter and foldr within our programs, and that we can indeed treat functions as 'first-class citizens' of our programming language. A consequence of this has been that we are able to explain the definitions of some of the Picture operations first seen in Chapter 1.

The main mechanisms introduced here have allowed us to create functions by applying functions or operators to fewer arguments than we expected, thus creating partial applications and operator sections. We also saw how the Haskell-type system and syntax were adapted to deal with the curried form of function definitions, by which multi-argument functions take their arguments one at a time.

We concluded by showing that we could prove general properties about general functions like map, and thus build up libraries of results about these functions which can potentially be applied whenever the general function is reused.

Program development

In this short chapter which builds on the discussion in Chapter 4 we step back from the details of programming in Haskell to take a more general look at the cycle of stages in which we see a program being developed. Although some of the remarks are specific to Haskell, most are general, and would apply to developing a program in any programming language.

We include a table giving hints about how to proceed in the four steps of understanding, design, implementation and reflection, which owes much to Polya's approach to problem solving in mathematics (Polya 1988). We conclude the chapter by looking at some Haskell illustrations of the general advice given earlier.

11.1 The development cycle

We can see programs being developed in a cycle.

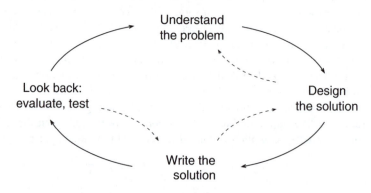

First, we have to **understand the programming problem** that we are trying to solve – we spent some time talking about this in Chapter 4. Once we have done this we can try to **plan** or **design** how we might approach the problem, using all the resources of the programming language, its libraries and also the programs that we have already written. Again in Chapter 4 we argued that we can make considerable progress at this stage before we actually start to **write programs**, which is the next step in the cycle.

Once the program is complete we can **reflect** or **look back** and see how well we have achieved our goal: we might test the program – as outlined in Chapter 4 – or we might at this stage try to prove various properties of the programs we have written. We can also at this point look back at the original problem – was that in fact what the user wanted to solve, or in the light of seeing a running program does the user want to change the specification of the problem?

This clockwise cycle of stages is a simplified model of the way that software is built in practice, from small exercise programs to large-scale industrial projects. Even for the sort of programs we are writing here, **reflecting** on what we are doing is a very important activity, and this is emphasized by the dotted arrows in the cycle diagram.

- As we design a program, we get further insight about how it should be specified: we might find there are cases missed, or questions unanswered by the specification – we need to go back to the specifier and sort these out before we can move on.

- Also at the design stage we might think of competing approaches to solving the problem: we need to think about which will be the better, and maybe we will find that we have to change our approach if our first choice proves to be unworkable.

- In writing the program we may well see how the design could be improved. An example we have seen already concerns the index created in Section 10.8: in that case we kept hold of short words right until the last stage in the composition while we could have got rid of them at a much earlier stage: at the point where the lines were split into words, say.

Especially when we are learning to program it is very good to get into the habit of criticizing our own and other people's programs. Sometimes, indeed, we find that after we have written a program we have gained so much deeper an understanding of the problem and the ways that we might solve it that we throw away our first solution and rewrite it from scratch in order to clean it up and to reflect our better understanding.

It is hard to give general advice about how to write programs, but some of the most important ideas are contained in the table in Figure 11.1. The advice contained there is strongly influenced by Polya's approach to problem solving in mathematics, and his *How To Solve It* (Polya 1988) contains a wealth of suggestions about how to go about looking for solutions to problems, many of which carry over to programming examples. The suggestion of error logging is an integral part of Humphrey's *Personal Software Process* (Humphrey 1996).

In the next section we illustrate some of the points in the development cycle using Haskell programming examples.

Understanding the problem _____

First we need to understand the problem we are trying to solve.

o What are the inputs and outputs to the problem? Are there any special conditions on the inputs or outputs?

o Looking at examples can help to clarify the problem.

o Can the problem be solved? Is the specification complete, or are there aspects which need clarification?

o If there are different possible ways of making sense of it, try to find out from the specifier what was intended.

o Does the problem itself have a structure? Is it made up of a number of parts which could be solved separately? Does a diagram help to describe the problem?

Designing a solution _____

Before writing a program we need to plan how we are going to do it.

o Have you seen a similar problem before? If so, you might use its design as a guide.

o Can you think of a simpler but related problem? If you can solve that, you might use or modify the solution.

o Can you think of a generalization of the problem? This might be easier to solve than the original.

o What is the architecture of the problem? Can you break it up into parts which may be solved (relatively) independently? As well as the parts themselves you will need to think about how the parts fit together.

o Think about how to go from the inputs to the output – a bottom-up approach; use the intermediate data as a guide. Also think about what resources you could be given which would let you solve the problem – this '*what if . . . ?*' approach is top-down.

o Even at the planning stage it is important to know what your resources are. Make sure you check what is provided by your programming language and its libraries. Another important resource consists of the programs which you yourself have already written.

o Design with change in mind. If your program is useful, then it will probably be modified a number of times over its lifetime.

Writing a program _____

To write a program you need to be aware of the resources that your programming language provides. You also need to follow the informal design or plan.

o Haskell has a substantial number of library functions which support programming over lists. Some of these are general polymorphic higher-order functions which can be used in a large variety of situations. Try to use these if you can.   (cont.)

Figure 11.1 The development cycle.

o   We shall see that over other data types we can define similar general functions. It is usually easier to use these functions than to write a solution from scratch.

o   You write your own general functions by abstracting away from the particular. Specifically, the particular – like multiplying by two – can be turned into a function which becomes a parameter to the general function (such as map).

o   Most languages allow you to make definitions with different cases; Haskell also provides pattern matching, which selects parts of an object as well as distinguishing cases.

o   Recursion is a general strategy for designing programs over data types like lists and numbers. To define a recursive function f at argument x you need to ask '*what if I had the value of f at … ?*'.

o   List comprehensions provide an expressive notation for lists.

o   You may need to introduce other functions as you begin to write your definitions. These might appear in where clauses or at the top level of the program.

o   If you cannot define the function you need to, try a simpler one. A solution to this might be a model for what you want, or could be used in the definition of the final function.

Reflection

Looking back on what you have done might affect your program, its design or indeed the specification of the problem itself.

o   Can you test your solution? You need to think of the testing groups over which the program should show similar behaviour, as well as looking hard at any special cases.

o   If your testing reveals errors or 'bugs', try to find their source. Are errors due to accidental mistakes? problems in understanding how the Haskell language works? misunderstanding how to solve the problem? misunderstanding the problem itself? or some other reason?

o   You can learn from the errors you have made; try keeping a log of all the errors that you make, and the reason for them. This should help you not to repeat them.

o   Can you prove that your program does what it should? If not, you can ask why this is, and whether it points to errors in the program or the design.

o   Suppose you were asked to write the same program again. How would you do it differently?

o   Suppose you were asked to modify or extend the program. How easy would that be? If it is difficult, can you think how you might have designed or written the solution differently to accommodate changes more readily?

o   Does the program run in reasonable time? If not, can you see where the bottlenecks are? Can you see how to modify the program to improve its performance?

Figure 11.1   The development cycle (contd).

(11.2) Development in practice

This section looks at the design and programming advice from Chapter 4 and Figure 11.1 by means of a series of programming examples.

Generalizing the problem

Suppose that we are asked to define the lists [1 .. n] for ourselves. A first attempt might try to use recursion, thus

```
[1 .. n] = 1 : [2 .. n]                                    (..1)
```

but the problem here is that [2 .. n] is not an instance of what we are trying to define. The presence of the 2 here suggests that instead of solving the particular problem of lists starting at 1 we should solve the more general problem of defining lists beginning at an arbitrary value. We therefore define [m .. n]:

```
[m .. n]
  | m>n          = []                                      (..2)
  | otherwise    = m : [m+1 .. n]
```

Another solution is given by

```
[1 .. n]
  | 1>n          = []                                      (..3)
  | otherwise    = [1 .. n-1] ++ [n]
```

but (..3) has the disadvantage that it is substantially less efficient than (..2), a topic we pick up in Chapter 19.

Another example of generalization was given in the text processing example in Section 7.6 where we defined a function getLine. The effect of this function is to take a list of words and to return the list of words making up the maximal first line (of length lineLen) which can be built from the words. It was apparent in making the definition that we needed to make the line length a parameter of the definition, so that we defined

```
getLine :: Int -> [Word] -> Line
```

rather than giving it the type [Word] -> Line.

Simplifying the problem

Suppose that we are asked to solve the problem of identifying strings which are palindromes, like

```
"Madam I\'m Adam"
```

One way of approaching the problem is first to think of identifying palindromes where punctuation and capitalization are not considered, such as "ABBA". We might solve this by

```
simplePalCheck :: String -> Bool
simplePalCheck st = (reverse st == st)
```

for instance, but note that there are at least two other different ways we might implement the function `simplePalCheck`. Once we have this function we can then *modify* it to solve the original problem. Alternatively we can *use* this solution to a simplified problem in the full solution:

```
palCheck = simplePalCheck . clean
```

where

```
clean :: String -> String
```

puts all capitals into small letters and removes punctuation. We look at this in the next section.

Design choices

The `clean` function combines mapping (capitals to smalls) and filtering (removing punctuation) and so can be solved thus

```
clean = map toSmall . filter notPunct                    (clean.1)
```

or by means of a list comprehension

```
clean st = [ toSmall ch | ch <- st , notPunct ch ]       (clean.2)
```

How do we choose between these options? One advantage of (`clean.1`) is that we see clearly that we have a function composition, but perhaps (`clean.2`) is more readable.

Auxiliary functions

Suppose we are asked to define when one string is a subsequence of another. By that we mean that the characters of the first string occur next to each other inside the second string, so that `"Chip"` is a subsequence of `"Fish & Chips"`, but not of `"Chin up"`. The function we seek to define is

```
subseq :: String -> String -> Bool
```

and we try to define this by recursion. Starting with the cases of the empty string,

```
subseq []     _  = True
subseq (_:_) [] = False
```

so what is the general case, `subseq (x:xs) (y:ys)`?

- One alternative is that `(x:xs)` is a subsequence of ys, as in
  `subseq "Chip" "Fish & Chips"`
- The other alternative is that `(x:xs)` occurs at the start of `(y:ys)`, as in
  `subseq "Chip" "Chips"`

This latter is not a recursive call to the function we are defining, so we have to say

```
subseq (x:xs) (y:ys)
  = subseq (x:xs) ys || frontseq (x:xs) (y:ys)
```

and write an auxiliary function definition to check this new condition.

```
frontseq :: String -> String -> Bool
frontseq []      _  = True
frontseq (_:_)   [] = False
frontseq (x:xs) (y:ys)
  = (x==y) && frontseq xs ys
```

Exercises

11.1 Give a recursive definition of the range

```
[m,n .. p]
```

11.2 Think of two more ways of implementing the function

```
simplePalCheck :: String -> Bool
```

discussed on page 207.

11.3 Define a function

```
subst :: String -> String -> String ->  String
```

so that the result of subst start find replace is the string start modified so that the first occurrence of find as a subsequence is replaced by replace. If there is no such subsequence, the string should be returned unmodified, so that, for instance,

```
subst "Fish & Chips" "Chip" "Boat" ⤳  "Fish & Boats"
subst "Fish & Chips" "Ship" "Boat" ⤳  "Fish & Chips"
```

Modify the definition so that every occurrence of find is replaced by replace. Explain what your original and modified definitions do in the case of the example

```
subst "Fish & Chips" "" "Boat"
```

Summary

This chapter has explored the idea that program development works in a cycle: first we clarify the specification of the problem to be solved, next we devise a plan of how to solve the problem, and only then do we implement the solution.

At each stage we should reflect on and evaluate what we have done: this aspect is crucial particularly when we are learning to program. For example, being aware of the errors that we make can help us to prevent making them in the future. Also, if we take a problem we have already solved and try to solve it with a new technique we will learn something about the new technique as well as seeing how it fits in with what we have learned already. This is something that we do by continually revisiting the `Picture` case study.

Chapter 12

Overloading and type classes

In looking at Haskell so far we have seen two kinds of function which work over more than one type. A **polymorphic** function such as length has a single definition which works over all its types. **Overloaded** functions like equality, + and show can be used at a variety of types, but with different definitions being used at different types.

The chapter starts with a discussion of the benefits of overloading, before looking at **type classes**, which are collections of types; what the members of a class have in common is the fact that certain functions are defined over the type. For instance, the members of the equality type class, Eq, are those types which carry an equality function, ==. Type classes are thus the mechanism by which overloaded functions can be given types in Haskell.

We shall see how to define type classes and types which belong to these classes – so-called **instances** of the class. We will also see that there is a form of inheritance between type classes, which is related to the inheritance of object-oriented programming. We take this up again in Chapter 16 below.

Haskell's prelude and libraries contain a number of classes and instances, particularly for numeric types – we survey these, referring readers to the Haskell report (Peyton Jones and Hughes 1998) for a full exposition.

Why overloading?

This section looks at the reason for including overloading in Haskell; we do this by looking at a scenario.

Suppose that Haskell did not have overloading, and that we wanted to check whether a particular element is a member of a list of type `Bool`. We would define a function like

```
elemBool :: Bool -> [Bool] -> Bool
elemBool x [] = False
elemBool x (y:ys)
  = (x ==Bool y) || elemBool x ys
```

where we have to write $==_{Bool}$ for the equality function over `Bool`.

Suppose now that we want to check whether an integer is a member of an integer list, then we need to define a *new* function

```
elemInt :: Int -> [Int] -> Bool
```

which differs from `elemBool` only in using $==_{Int}$ instead of $==_{Bool}$. Each time we want to check membership of a list of a different type we will have to define yet another – very similar – function.

One way out of this problem is to make the equality function a parameter of a general function

```
elemGen :: (a -> a -> Bool) -> a -> [a] -> Bool
```

but this gives too much generality in a sense, because it can be used with *any* parameter of type `a -> a -> Bool` rather than just an equality check. Also in this case the parameter has to be written down explicitly each time the function `elemGen` is used, as in

```
elemGen (==Bool)
```

making programs less easy to read.

The alternative is to define a function which uses the overloaded equality,

```
elem :: a -> [a] -> Bool
```

where the type `a` has to be restricted to those types which have an equality. The advantages of this approach are

- **Reuse** The definition of `elem` can be used over all types with equality.
- **Readability** It is much easier to read `==` than $==_{Int}$ and so on. This argument holds particularly for numeric operators, where it is more than tiresome to have to write $+_{Int}$, $*_{Float}$ and so on.

What this discussion shows is that a mechanism is needed to give a type to functions like `elem`: that is precisely the purpose of type classes.

12.2 Introducing classes

The elem function appears to have the type

```
elem :: a -> [a] -> Bool
```

but this type only holds for types a which have an equality function. How is this to be expressed? We need some way of saying whether we have an equality function over a given type. We call the collection of types over which a function is defined a **type class** or simply **class**. For instance, the set of types over which == is defined is the **equality class**, Eq.

Defining the equality class

How do we define a class, such as Eq? We say what is needed for a type a to be in a class. In this case we need a function == defined over a, of type a->a->Bool.

```
class Eq a where
  (==) :: a -> a -> Bool
```

Members of a type class are called its **instances**. Built-in instances of Eq include the base types Int, Float, Bool, Char. Other instances are given by tuples and lists built from types which are themselves instances of Eq; examples include the types (Int,Bool) and [[Char]].

Not all types will necessarily carry an equality; we may choose not to define one, for reasons of information hiding, or there may be no natural way of defining an equality on a particular type. For example, function types like Int -> Int are not instances of Eq, since there is no algorithm which will decide whether two functions over Int have the same behaviour.

It is unfortunate that the term *instance* is used in two quite different ways in Haskell. We talked in Section 5.7 of a type t_1 being an instance of a *type* t_2, when we can substitute for a type variable in t_2 to give t_1. Here we have talked about a type being an instance of a *class*.

Functions which use equality

Many of the functions which we have defined so far use equality over particular types. The function

```
allEqual :: Int -> Int -> Int -> Bool
allEqual m n p = (m==n) && (n==p)
```

decides whether three integers are equal. If we examine the definition itself, it contains nothing which is specific to integers; the only constraint it makes is that m, n and p are compared for equality. Their type can be a for any a *in the type class* Eq. This gives allEqual a most general type thus:

```
allEqual :: Eq a => a -> a -> a -> Bool
allEqual m n p = (m==n) && (n==p)
```

The part before the => is called the **context**. We can read the type as saying that

> if the type a is in the class Eq – that is, if == is defined over the type a – then
> allEqual has type a -> a -> a -> Bool

This means that allEqual can be used at the following types

```
allEqual :: Char -> Char -> Char -> Bool
allEqual :: (Int,Bool) -> (Int,Bool) -> (Int,Bool) -> Bool
```

since both Char and (Int,Bool) belong to Eq, among many other types. What happens if we break this constraint by trying to compare functions for equality? If we define

```
suc :: Int -> Int
suc = (+1)
```

and try to evaluate

```
allEqual suc suc suc
```

we get the message

```
ERROR: Int -> Int is not an instance of class "Eq"
```

which conveys the fact that (Int -> Int) is not in the Eq class, because it is not an instance of that class.

Further equality examples

The elem example in Section 12.1 will have the type

```
elem :: Eq a => a -> [a] -> Bool
```

and so it will be usable at the types

```
Bool -> [Bool] -> Bool
Int  -> [Int]  -> Bool
```

Many of the functions we have defined already use equality in an overloaded way. We can use the Hugs system to deduce the most general type of a function, such as the books function from the library database of Section 5.6, by commenting out its type declaration in the script, thus

```
-- books :: Database -> Person -> [Book]
```

and then by typing

```
:type books
```

to the prompt. The result we get in that case is

```
books :: Eq a => [ (a,b) ] -> a -> [b]
```

which is perhaps a surprise at first. This is less so if we rewrite the definition with books renamed `lookupFirst`, because it looks up all the pairs with a particular first part, and returns their corresponding second parts. Here it is with its variables renamed as well

```
lookupFirst :: Eq a => [ (a,b) ] -> a -> [b]

lookupFirst ws x
  = [ z | (y,z) <- ws , y==x ]
```

Clearly from this definition there is nothing specific about books or people and so it is polymorphic, if we can compare objects in the first halves of the pairs for equality. This condition gives rise to the context Eq a. Finally from Section 5.6, as we saw for books,

```
borrowed    :: Eq b => [ (a,b) ] -> b -> Bool
numBorrowed :: Eq a => [ (a,b) ] -> a -> Int
```

Summary

In this section we have introduced the idea of a class, which is a collection of types — its instances — with the property that certain functions are defined over them. One way we can think of a class is **as an adjective**: any particular type is or is not in the class, just as the weather at any particular moment might or might not be sunny.

We saw how equality could be seen as being defined over all the types in the class Eq. This allows many of the functions defined so far to be given polymorphic type, allowing them to be used over any type in the class Eq. In the following sections we explain how classes and instances are defined in general, and explore the consequences of classes for programming in Haskell.

Exercises

12.1 How would you define the 'not equal' operation, /=, from equality, ==? What is the type of /=?

12.2 Define the function numEqual which takes a list of items, xs say, and an item, x say, and returns the number of times x occurs in xs. What is the type of your function? How could you use numEqual to define member?

12.3 Define functions

```
oneLookupFirst  :: Eq a => [ (a,b) ] -> a -> b
oneLookupSecond :: Eq b => [ (a,b) ] -> b -> a
```

oneLookupFirst takes a list of pairs and an item, and returns the second part of the first pair whose first part equals the item. You should explain what your function does if there is no such pair. oneLookupSecond returns the first pair with the roles of first and second reversed.

(12.3) Signatures and instances

In the last section we saw that the operation of equality, ==, is overloaded. This allows == to be used over a variety of types, and also allows for functions using == to be defined over all instances of the class of types Eq. This section explains the mechanics of how classes are introduced, and then how instances of them may be declared. This allows us to program with classes that we define ourselves, rather than simply using the built-in classes of Haskell.

Declaring a class

As we saw earlier, a class is introduced by a declaration like:

```
class Visible a where
  toString :: a -> String
  size     :: a -> Int
```

The declaration introduces the name of the class, Visible, and then follows a **signature**, that is a list of names and their types. Any type a in the Visible class must carry the two functions in the signature:

- the toString function, which converts an object of the type to a String, and,

- the size function, which returns a measure of the size of the argument, as an integer.

Visible things can be viewed, using the toString function, and we can give an estimate of their size: the size of a list might be its length, while a Boolean might have size one.
     The general form of a class definition will be:

```
class Name ty where
  ... signature involving the type variable ty ...
```

Now, how are types made instances of such a class?

Defining the instances of a class

A type is made a member or **instance** of a class by defining the signature functions for the type. For example,

```
instance Eq Bool where
  True  == True  = True
  False == False = True
  _     == _     = False
```

describes how Bool is an instance of the equality class. The declarations that numeric types like Int and Float are in the equality class (and indeed other built-in classes) involve the appropriate primitive equality functions supplied by the implementation.
     Although we have called the class Eq the equality class, there is no requirement that the == function we define has any of the usual properties of equality apart from having

the same type as equality. It is up to the user to ensure that he or she makes sensible definitions, and documents them adequately.

Taking up our other example, we might say

```
instance Visible Char where
  toString ch  = [ch]
  size _       = 1
```

This shows how characters can be turned into strings – by making them into strings of length one – and gives a measure of their size. We can also make Bool an instance, thus:

```
instance Visible Bool where
  toString True  = "True"
  toString False = "False"
  size _         = 1
```

Suppose the type a is visible: this means that we can estimate the size of a value in a, and turn a value into a string. If presented with a list of values of type a, we can use the toString and size on a to define those functions over [a], so we can declare the following instance

```
instance Visible a => Visible [a] where ....
```

in which the **context** Visible a appears, making clear that we are only making visible lists of objects which are themselves visible. We can complete the definition by saying how we print and give the size of a list of a:

```
instance Visible a => Visible [a] where
  toString = concat . map toString
  size     = foldr (+) 1 . map size
```

To turn a list of a into a String, we turn each element of the list into a string (map toString) and then we concatenate the results, using concat. In a similar way we can estimate the size of a list of a: we take the size of each object (map size), and add one to the total of these sizes by foldr (+) 1.

On the right-hand sides of these definitions we use toString and size over the type a; this shows that we need the context which says that a is a Visible type.

There are some limitations to what can be declared as an instance, in other words on what can appear after the => (if any) in an instance declaration. This must either be a base type like Int, or consist of a type former (or constructor) like [...] or (...,...) applied to distinct type variables.

We will *not* be able, for example, to declare (Float,Float) as an instance; nor can we use named types (introduced by a type definition). More details of the mechanism can be found in the Haskell report (Peyton Jones and Hughes 1998). We shall explore more complex examples in the next part of the book, after we have introduced our own type constructors.

Default definitions

To return to our example of equality, the Haskell equality class is in fact defined by

```
class Eq a where
  (==), (/=) :: a -> a -> Bool
  x /= y      = not (x==y)
  x == y      = not (x/=y)
```

To the equality operation is added inequality, /=. As well as this, there are **default** definitions of /= from == and of == from /=. These definitions have two purposes; they give a definition over all equality types, but as defaults they are **overridden** by an instance declaration.

At any instance a definition of at least one of == and /= needs to be supplied for there to be a proper definition of (in)equality, but a definition of either is sufficient to give both, by means of the defaults.

It is also possible to define both of the operations in an instance delaration , so that if we wanted to define a different version of /= over Bool, we could add to our instance declaration for Bool the line

```
  x /= y      = ... our definition ...
```

If we want to *stop* a default being overridden, we should remove the operation from the class, and instead give its definition at the top level and not in the signature. In the case of the operation /= in Eq we would give the top-level definition

```
x /= y        = not (x == y)
```

which has the type

```
(/=) :: Eq a => a -> a -> Bool
```

and will be effective over all types which carry the == operation.

There are some situations when it is better to give default definitions, which can be overridden, rather than top-level definitions, which cannot. Over the numerical types, for instance, an implementation may well supply all the operations as hardware instructions, which will be much more efficient than the default definitions.

Derived classes

Functions and instances can depend upon types being in classes; this is also true of classes. The simplest example in Haskell is the class of ordered types, Ord. To be ordered, a type must carry the operations >, >= and so on, as well as the equality operations. We say

```
class Eq a => Ord a where
  (<), (<=), (>), (>=) :: a -> a -> Bool
  max, min             :: a -> a -> a
  compare              :: a -> a -> Ordering
```

For a type a to be in the class Ord, we must supply over a definitions of the operations
of Eq as well as the ones in the signature of Ord. Given a definition of < we can supply
default definitions of the remaining operations of Ord. For instance,

```
x <= y     = (x < y || x == y)
x >  y     =  y < x
```

We will explain the type Ordering and the function compare in Section 12.4.

A simple example of a function defined over types in the class Ord is the insertion
sort function iSort of Chapter 7. Its most general type is

```
iSort :: Ord a => [a] -> [a]
```

Indeed, any sorting function (which sorts using the ordering given by <=) would be
expected to have this type.

From a different point of view, we can see the class Ord as **inheriting** the operations
of Eq; inheritance is one of the central ideas of object-oriented programming.

Multiple constraints

In the contexts we have seen so far, we have a single constraint on a type, such as Eq a.
There is no reason why we should not have multiple constraints on types. This section
introduces the notation we use, and some examples where it is needed.

Suppose we wish to sort a list and then show the results as a string. We can write

```
vSort = toString . iSort
```

To sort the elements, we need the list to consist of elements from an ordered type, as
we saw above. To convert the results to a String we need [a] to be Visible; given
the instance declaration on page 216, this will hold if a is visible. We therefore have

```
vSort :: (Ord a,Visible a) => [a] -> String
```

showing that a must be in both the classes Ord and Visible. Such types include Bool,
[Char] and so on.

In a similar way, suppose we are to use lookupFirst, and then make the results
visible. We write

```
vLookupFirst xs x = toString (lookupFirst xs x)
```

We have twin constraints again on our list type [(a,b)]. We need to be able to compare
the first halves of the pairs, so Eq a is required. We also want to turn the second halves
into strings, so needing Visible b. This gives the type

```
vLookupFirst :: (Eq a,Visible b) => [(a,b)] -> a -> String
```

Multiple constraints can occur in an instance declaration, such as

```
instance (Eq a,Eq b) => Eq (a,b) where
  (x,y) == (z,w)  =  x==z && y==w
```

which shows that a pair of types in Eq again belongs to Eq. Multiple constraints can also occur in the definition of a class,

```
class (Ord a,Visible a) => OrdVis a
```

In such a declaration, the class inherits the operations of both Ord and Visible.

In this particular case, the class declaration contains an empty signature. To be in OrdVis, the type a must simply be in the classes Ord and Visible. We could then modify the type of vSort to say

```
vSort :: OrdVis a => [a] -> String
```

The situation when a class is built on top of two or more classes is called **multiple inheritance**; this has consequences for programming style, explored in Section 14.6.

Summary

This section has explained the basic details of the class mechanism in Haskell. We have seen that a class definition specifies a signature, and that in defining an instance of a class we must provide definitions of each of the operations of the signature. These definitions override any default definitions which are given in the class declaration. Contexts were seen to contain one or more constraints on the type variables which appear in polymorphic types, instance declarations and class declarations.

Exercises

12.4 How would you make Bool, pair types, (a,b), and triple types, (a,b,c), into Visible types?

12.5 Write a function to convert an integer into a String, and hence show how Int can be an instance of Visible.

12.6 What is the type of the function

```
compare x y    = size x <= size y ?
```

12.7 Complete the default definitions for the class Ord.

12.8 Complete the following instance declarations:

```
instance (Ord a, Ord b) => Ord (a,b) where ...
instance Ord b => Ord [b] where ...
```

where pairs and lists should be ordered **lexicographically**, like the words in a dictionary.

12.4 A tour of the built-in Haskell classes

Haskell contains a number of built-in classes, which we briefly introduce in this section. Many of the classes are numeric, and are built to deal with overloading of the numerical operations over integers, floating-point reals, complex numbers and rationals (that is integer fractions like $\frac{22}{7}$). Rather than give complete details of the numeric types, we give an exposition of their major features.

Equality: Eq

Equality was described above; to recap, we define it by

```
class Eq a where
  (==), (/=) :: a -> a -> Bool
  x /= y    =  not (x==y)
  x == y    =  not (x/=y)
```

Ordering: Ord

Similarly, we build the ordered class on Eq:

```
class (Eq a) => Ord a where
  compare                :: a -> a -> Ordering
  (<), (<=), (>=), (>) :: a -> a -> Bool
  max, min               :: a -> a -> a
```

The type Ordering contains three values LT, EQ and GT, which represent the three possible outcomes from comparing two elements in the ordering. We shall see how the type Ordering is defined formally in Chapter 14, page 243.

The advantage of using compare is that a single function application decides the exact relationship between two inputs, whereas when using the ordering operators – which return Boolean results – two comparisons might well be necessary. Indeed, we see this in the default definition of compare from == and <=, where two tests are needed to reach the results LT and GT.

```
compare x y
  | x == y    = EQ
  | x <= y    = LT
  | otherwise = GT
```

The defaults also contain definitions of the ordering operators from compare:

```
x <= y       = compare x y /= GT
x <  y       = compare x y == LT
x >= y       = compare x y /= LT
x >  y       = compare x y == GT
```

There are default definitions for all the operations of Ord, but we need to supply an implementation of either compare or <= in order to give an instance of Ord.

Finally we have default definitions for the maximum and minimum operations,

```
max x y
  | x >= y        = x
  | otherwise     = y
min x y
  | x <= y        = x
  | otherwise     = y
```

Most Haskell types belong to these equality and ordering classes: among the exceptions are function types, and some of the abstract data types we meet below in Chapter 16.

Enumeration: Enum

It is useful to generate lists like [2,4,6,8] using the enumeration expression

[2,4 .. 8]

but enumerations can be built over other types as well: characters, floating-point numbers, and so on. The class definition is

```
class (Ord a) => Enum a where
  toEnum            :: Int -> a
  fromEnum          :: a -> Int
  enumFrom          :: a -> [a]              -- [n .. ]
  enumFromThen      :: a -> a -> [a]         -- [n,m .. ]
  enumFromTo        :: a -> a -> [a]         -- [n .. m]
  enumFromThenTo    :: a -> a -> a -> [a]    -- [n,n' .. m]
```

where enumFromTo and enumFromThenTo have default definitions, which we leave as exercises for the reader.

The signature of the class also contains operations fromEnum and toEnum which convert between the type and Int. In the case of Char these conversion functions are also known as ord and chr, where these specializations are given by the definitions:

```
ord :: Char -> Int
ord = fromEnum
```

```
chr :: Int -> Char
chr = toEnum
```

Confusingly, the Haskell report states that 'these functions [toEnum and fromEnum] are not meaningful for all instances of Enum', and using these operations over floating-point values or full precision integers will result in a run-time error.

Full instances of the class include Int, Char, Bool and other finite types like Ordering. Definable over the class are the successor and predecessor functions,

```
succ, pred :: Enum a => a -> a
```

```
succ = toEnum . (+1) . fromEnum
pred = toEnum . (subtract 1) . fromEnum
```

Bounded types: `Bounded`

The Bounded class is specified by the declaration

```
class Bounded a where
  minBound, maxBound :: a
```

and the two values give the minimum and maximum values in these types. The types
Int, Char, Bool, Ordering belong to this class.

Turning values to strings: `Show`

In our introduction to type classes we talked about the class Visible as an example of
a user-defined class. The standard prelude defines the class Show, which contains types
whose values can be written as strings.

```
type ShowS = String -> String

class Show a where
  showsPrec :: Int -> a -> ShowS
  show      :: a -> String
  showList  :: [a] -> ShowS
```

The function showsPrec supports flexible and efficient conversion of large data values,
but in an introductory context, the function

```
show :: a -> String
```

which converts a value into a string is all that is needed. The class contains default
definitions of showsPrec from show and vice versa. Further details about how to
exploit the subtleties of showsPrec can be found in Hudak, Fasel and Peterson (1997).

Most types belong to the class Show; even if values of the type in question cannot be
shown fully, a textutal representation of some sort is given. A function, for example,
will be shown as <<function>>. For other types, example instance declarations might
be

```
instance Show Bool where
  show True  = "True"
  show False = "False"

instance (Show a, Show b) => Show (a,b) where
  show (x,y) = "(" ++ show x ++ "," ++ show y ++ ")"
```

Turning strings to values: `Read`

The class Read contains types whose values can be read from strings. To use the class
it is enough to know about the function

```
read :: (Read a) => String -> a
```

The result of a read may not be properly defined: there needs to be exactly one object of the required type in the input string (which may optionally also contain whitespace or nested comments); in any other case the read will fail with an error. More details of how strings are **parsed** in this way can be found in Section 17.5.

It is also important to see that in many cases the type of the result of the read has to be specified, since it could potentially be of any type in the class Read. For instance, we can write

```
(read "   1   " ):: Int
```

which indicates that in this case we require the result of the read to be an Int.

The class Read complements Show, since strings produced by show are usually readable by read. Many types can be read, but exclusions include function types.

The Haskell numeric types and classes

One of the purposes of the Haskell design was to build a functional programming language which had a strong type system – in which any type errors in definitions and expressions are found before evaluation – yet which contains a rich set of numeric types, as befits a language suitable to substantial 'real world' tasks. Among Haskell's numeric types are

- The fixed precision integers, Int, and the full precision integers, Integer, which represent *all* integers faithfully.

- The floating-point numbers, Float, and the double-precision floating-point numbers, Double.

- Rational numbers, that is fractions, represented as ratios of integers; built-in is the type Rational of Integer fractions.

- Complex numbers, which can be built over other types such as Float.

The design also required that the usual operations like + and / and literals such as 23 and 57.4 would be overloaded. For instance, Int and Integer will carry identical operations[1] and have identical literals, as indeed will Float and Double; a guide to the operations over integers and floats was given in Sections 3.2 and 3.6. This overloading can lead to situations where the type of an expression is undetermined; in such a case we can give an explicit type to an expression, thus:

```
(2+3)::Int
```

The Haskell report (Peyton Jones and Hughes 1998) discusses a mechanism by which a default type can be given to numeric expressions.

Overloading of numeric functions is achieved by defining a collection of classes. Full details of these can be found in the Haskell report (Peyton Jones and Hughes 1998), and in the standard prelude, Prelude.hs; a brief introduction follows here.

The base class to which all numeric types belong is Num, which has the signature

---

[1] Apart from (de)coding of Char, take, drop and so forth.

```
class (Eq a, Show a) => Num a where
  (+), (-), (*)  :: a -> a -> a
  negate         :: a -> a
  abs, signum    :: a -> a
  fromInteger    :: Integer -> a
  fromInt        :: Int -> a

  x - y          = x + negate y
  fromInt        = fromIntegral
```

This signature has the effect that all numeric types carry equality and show functions, together with addition, subtraction, multiplication and related operations. It is also possible to convert an Int or and Integer into a value of any numeric type.

Integer literals are of any numeric type, so that, for example

```
2 :: Num a => a
```

The integer types belong to the class Integral among whose signature functions are

```
quot, rem :: a -> a -> a
div, mod  :: a -> a -> a
```

which give two variants of integer division, 'quot' truncating towards zero, and 'div' truncating below.

Numbers with fractional parts have a substantially richer class structure. Literals of this kind belong to every type in the Fractional class,

```
2.3 :: Fractional a => a
```

which extends Num with fractional division and reciprocal,

```
class (Num a) => Fractional a where
  (/)          :: a -> a -> a
  recip        :: a -> a
  fromRational :: Rational -> a

  recip x      = 1 / x
```

The floating-point numbers in Float and Double belong to the class Floating, which carries the 'mathematical' functions. A part of its signature follows,

```
class (Fractional a) => Floating a where
  pi                :: a
  exp, log, sqrt    :: a -> a
  (**), logBase     :: a -> a -> a
  sin, cos, tan     :: a -> a
  ....
```

and the full signature is to be found in Prelude.hs. Further details of this and the complex and rational types can be found in the prelude, libraries and the Haskell documentation.

————————————————————————————————

12.9 Investigate the Haskell definition of '<' on the types Bool and $(t_1, t_2, \ldots, t_k)$.

12.10 Define a function

```
showBoolFun :: (Bool -> Bool) -> String
```

which displays a Boolean function as a table. Generalize this to

```
showBoolFunGen :: (a -> String) -> (Bool -> a) -> String
```

whose first argument is a function to show elements of a. This argument is used in giving a table of the results of the function. How would you extend your answer to deal with multiple-argument Boolean functions?

12.11 Using your answer to the previous question, or otherwise, describe how you would make Bool -> Bool an instance of the class Show. (Note, however, that this will *not* be legitimate Haskell, since Bool -> Bool is not of the right form for an instance declaration.)

(12.5) Types and classes

This section discusses the relationship between Haskell type classes and the classes of object-oriented programming; it can be omitted on first reading.

The type system of Haskell can be seen as giving monomorphic types to functions. Polymorphic types like

```
show :: Show a => a -> String
```

which involve type classes can be seen as shorthand for collections of typings, such as

```
show :: Bool -> String
show :: Char -> String
```

for each type Bool, Char, ... belonging to the class.

In Haskell a class is a collection of types. Other languages such as C++ make a type and a class the same thing. Under that approach, introducing the class of visible objects would effectively give us a type[2] ShowType. This class would be characterized by having the function

```
show :: ShowType -> String
```

in its interface. The class ShowType would have Bool and Char among its sub-classes (or sub-types). This would allow us to write values like

————————————————————————————

[2] In C++ teminology this would be an abstract base class, with Bool etc. inheriting and being forced to implement the operations of that class.

```
[True,'N',False] :: [ShowType]
```

Moreover, to convert such a list to a `String` we could write

```
concat . map show :: [ShowType] -> String
```

At different items of the list we use *different* versions of the show function; on the first we use the `Bool` function, on the second the `Char` function and so forth. This so-called **dynamic binding** is a powerful feature of many object-oriented languages, including C++, but it is not a feature of Haskell 98; an extension which would allow dynamic binding is described in Läufer (1996).

Returning to our example, what is the type of `concat . map show` in Haskell? It is not hard to see that it is

```
Show a => [a] -> [Char]
```

so that it can be applied to elements of `[Bool]`, `[Char]` and so on, but not to heterogeneous lists like `[True,'N',False]` which are not legitimately typed in Haskell.

Java allows users to define interfaces, which consist of a signature. A part of a class definition can say which interfaces the class implements. This is very like the way in which Haskell types are made instances of type classes, except that in Haskell it is not necessary to make the instance declaration a part of the type definition itself. This has the effect of allowing *post hoc* extensions to the operations supported by a type, in a way which is not possible for a class in Java.

Summary

This chapter has shown how names such as `read` and `show` and operators like `+` can be overloaded to have different definitions at different types. The mechanism which enables this is the system of Haskell classes. A `class` definition contains a signature which contains the names and types of operations which must be supplied if a type is to be a member of the class. For a particular type, the function definitions are contained in an `instance` declaration.

In giving the type of a function, or introducing a class or an instance, we can supply a context, which constrains the type variables occurring. Examples include

```
member :: Eq a => [a] -> a -> Bool
instance  Eq a => Eq [a] where ....
class     Eq a => Ord a  where ....
```

In the examples, it can be seen that `member` can only be used over types in the class Eq. Lists of a can be given an equality, provided that a itself can; types in the class Ord must already be in the class Eq.

After giving examples of the various mechanisms, we looked at the classes in the standard preludes of Haskell, and concluded with a discussion of the relationship between the type classes of Haskell and the classes of object-oriented programming. In the final part of the book we shall revisit classes and see how they are used to structure larger-scale systems.

Checking types

···

Every value in Haskell has a defined type, which might be monomorphic, polymorphic, or involve one or more type class constraints in a context. For example,

```
'w'   :: Char
flip  :: (a -> b -> c) -> (b -> a -> c)
elem  :: Eq a => a -> [a] -> Bool
```

Strong typing means that we can **check** whether or not expressions we wish to evaluate or definitions we wish to use obey the typing rules of the language without any evaluation taking place. The benefit of this is obvious: we can catch a whole lot of errors before we run a program.

Beyond this, types are a valuable form of program documentation: when we look at a definition, the first relevant piece of information about it is its type, since this explains how it is to be used. In the case of a function, we can read off from its type the types of values to which it has to be applied, and also the type of the result of applying it.

Types are also useful in locating functions in a library. Suppose we want to define a function to remove the duplicate elements from a list, transforming [2,3,2,1,3,4] to [2,3,1,4], for instance. Such a function will have type

```
(Eq a) => [a] -> [a]
```

A search of the standard prelude Prelude.hs and the library List.hs reveals just one function of this type, namely nub, which has exactly the effect we seek. Plainly in practice there might be multiple matches (or missed matches because of the choice of parameter order) but nonetheless the types provide a valuable `handle' on the functions in a library.

In this chapter we give an informal overview of the way in which types are checked. We start by looking at how type checking works in a monomorphic framework, in which every properly typed expression has a single type. Building on this, we then look at the polymorphic case, and see that it can be understood by looking at the **constraints** put on the type of an expression by the way that the expression is constructed. Crucial to this is the notion of **unification**, through which constraints are combined. We conclude the chapter by looking at the **contexts** which contain information about the class membership of type variables, and which thus manage **overloading**.

13.1 Monomorphic type checking

In this section we look at how type checking works in a monomorphic setting, without polymorphism or overloading. The main focus here is type-checking function applications. The simplified picture we see here prepares us for Haskell type checking in general, which is examined in the section after this. When discussing polymorphic operations in this section we will use monomorphic instances, indicated by a type subscript or subscripts. For example, we write

```
+_Int   :: Int -> Int -> Int
length_Char :: [Char] -> Int
```

We look first at the way that we type-check expressions, and then look at how definitions are type-checked.

Expressions

In general, an expression is either a literal, a variable or a constant or it is built up by applying a function to some arguments, which are themselves expressions.

The case of function applications includes rather more than we might at first expect. For example, we can see list expressions like [True,False] as the result of applying the constructor function, ':', thus: True:[False]. Also, operators and the if ... then ... else construct act in exactly the same way as functions, albeit with a different syntax.

The rule for type checking a function application is set out in the following diagram, where we see that a function of type s -> t must be applied to an argument of type s. A properly typed application results in an expression of type t.

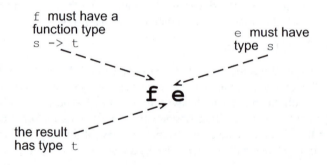

We now look at two examples. First we take ord 'c' $+_{Int}$ 3_{Int}, a correctly typed expression of type Int,

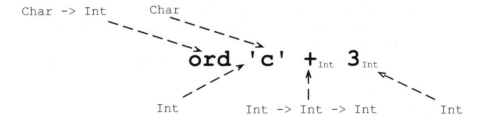

The application of ord to 'c' results in an expression of type Int. The second argument to $+_{Int}$ is also an Int, so the application of $+_{Int}$ is correctly typed, and gives a result of type Int.

   If we modify the example to ord 'c' $+_{Int}$ False, we now see a type error, since a Boolean argument, False, is presented to an operator expecting Int arguments, $+_{Int}$.

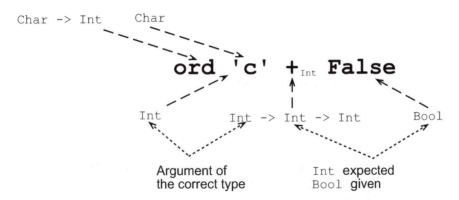

Function definitions

In type-checking a monomorphic function definition such as

```
f :: t1 -> t2 -> ... -> tk -> t                              (fdef)
f p1 p2 ... pk
   | g1      = e1
   | g2      = e2
   ...
   | gl      = el
```

we need to check three things.

- Each of the guards g_i must be of type Bool.
- The value e_i returned in each clause must be of type t.
- The pattern p_j must be consistent with type of that argument, namely t_j.

A pattern is **consistent** with a type if it will match (some) elements of the type. We now look at the various cases. A variable is consistent with any type; a literal is consistent with its type. A pattern (p:q) is consistent with the type [t] if p is consistent with t and q is consistent with [t]. For example, (0:xs) is consistent with the type [Int], and (x:xs) is consistent with any type of lists. The other cases of the definition are similar.

This concludes our discussion of type checking in the monomorphic case; we turn to polymorphism next.

Exercise

13.1 Predict the type errors you would obtain by defining the following functions

```
f n     = 37+n
f True  = 34

g 0 = 37
g n = True

h x
   | x>0        = True
   | otherwise  = 37

k x = 34
k 0 = 35
```

Check your answers by typing each definition into a Haskell script, and loading the script into Hugs. Remember that you can use :type to give the type of an expression.

13.2 Polymorphic type checking

In a monomorphic situation, an expression is either well typed, and has a single type, or is not well typed and has none. In a polymorphic language like Haskell, the situation is more complicated, since a polymorphic object is precisely one which has many types.

In this section we first re-examine what is meant by polymorphism, before explaining type checking by means of **constraint satisfaction**. Central to this is the notion of **unification**, by which we find the types simultaneously satisfying two type constraints.

Polymorphism

We are familiar with functions like

```
length :: [a] -> Int                                              (length)
```

whose types are polymorphic, but how should we understand the type variable a in this type? We can see (length) as shorthand for saying that length has a **set** of types,

```
[Int] -> Int
[(Bool,Char)] -> Int
  . . .
```

in fact containing all the types [t] -> Int where t is a **monotype**, that is a type not containing type variables.

When we apply length we need to determine at which of these types length is being used. For example, when we write

```
length ['c','d']
```

we can see that length is being applied to a list of Char, and so we are using length at type [Char] -> Int.

Constraints

How can we explain what is going on here in general? We can see different parts of an expression as putting different **constraints** on its type. Under this interpretation, type checking becomes a matter of working out whether we can find types which meet the constraints. We have seen some informal examples of this when we discussed the types of map and filter in Section 9.2. We consider some further examples now.

Examples

1. Consider the definition

```
f (x,y) = (x , ['a' .. y])
```

The argument of f is a pair, and we consider separately what constraints there are on the types of x and y. x is completely unconstrained, as it is returned as the first half of a pair. On the other hand, y is used within the expression ['a' .. y], which denotes a range within an enumerated type, starting at the character 'a'. This forces y to have the type Char, and gives the type for f:

```
f :: (a , Char) -> (a , [Char])
```

2. Now we examine the definition

```
g (m,zs) = m + length zs
```

What constraints are placed on the types of m and zs in this definition? We can see that m is added to something, so m must have a numeric type – which one it is remains to be seen. The other argument of the addition is length zs, which tells us two things.

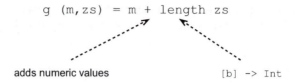

$$g \ (m, zs) \ = \ m \ + \ length \ zs$$

adds numeric values   [b] -> Int

First, we see that zs will have to be of type [b], and also that the result is an Int. This forces + to be used at Int, and so forces m to have type Int, giving the result

g :: (Int , [b]) -> Int

3. We now consider the composition of the last two examples,

h = g . f

In a composition g . f, the output of f becomes the input of g,

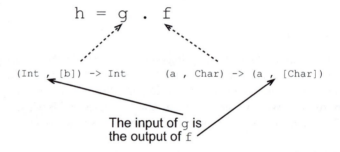

$$h \ = \ g \ . \ f$$

(Int , [b]) -> Int   (a , Char) -> (a , [Char])

The input of g is
the output of f

Here we should recall the meaning of types which involve type variables; we can see them as shorthand for sets of types. The output of f is described by (a , [Char]), and the input of g by (Int , [b]). We therefore have to look for types which meet both these descriptions. We will now look at this general topic, returning to the example in the course of this dicussion.

Unification

How are we to describe the types which meet the two descriptions (a , [Char]) and (Int , [b])?

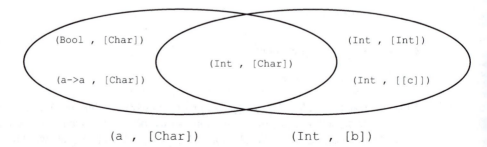

(Bool , [Char])   (Int , [Int])

(Int , [Char])

(a->a , [Char])   (Int , [[c]])

(a , [Char])   (Int , [b])

As sets of types, we look for the intersection of the sets given by (a , [Char]) and (Int , [b]). How can we work out a description of this intersection? Before we do this, we revise and introduce some terminology.

Recall that an **instance** of a type is given by replacing a type variable or variables by type expressions. A type expression is a common instance of two type expressions if it is an instance of each expression. The most general common instance of two expressions is a common instance mgci with the property that every other common instance is an instance of mgci.

Now we can describe the intersection of the sets given by two type expressions. It is called the **unification** of the two, which is the **most general common instance** of the two type expressions.

Examples

3 (contd)   In this example, we have

(a , [Char])   (Int , [b])

(Int , [Char])

with a single type resulting. This gives the function h the following type

h :: (Int , [Char]) -> Int

and this completes the discussion of example 3.

Unification need not result in a monotype. In the example of unifying the types (a, [a]) and ([b],c),

(a , [a])   ([b] , c)

([b] , [[b]])

the result is the type ([b] , [[b]]). This is because the expression (a, [a]) constrains the type to have in its second component a list of elements of the first component type, while the expression ([b] ,c) constrains its first component to be a list. Thus satisfying the two gives the type ([b], [[b]]).

In the last example, note that there are many common instances of the two type expressions, including ([Bool], [[Bool]]) and ([[c]], [[[c]]]), but neither of these examples is the unifier, since ([b], [[b]]) is not an instance of either of them. On the other hand, they are each instances of ([b], [[b]]), as it is the most general common instance, and so the unifier of the two type expressions.

Not every pair of types can be unified: consider the case of [Int] -> [Int] and a -> [a].

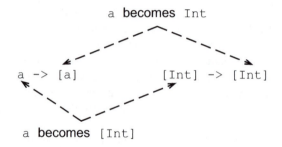

Unifying the argument types requires a to become [Int], while unifying the result types requires a to become Int; clearly these constraints are inconsistent, and so the unification fails.

Type-checking expressions

As we saw in Section 13.1, function application is central to expression formation. This means that type checking also hinges on function applications.

Type-checking polymorphic function application

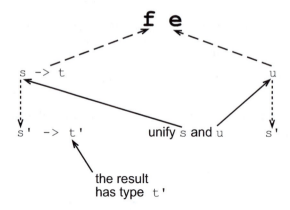

In applying a function f :: s -> t to an argument e :: u we do not require that s and u are equal, but instead that they are unifiable to a type s', say, giving e :: s' and f :: s' -> t'; the result in that case is of type t'. As an example, consider the application map ord where

```
map :: (a -> b) -> [a] -> [b]
ord :: Char -> Int
```

Unifying a -> b and Char -> Int results in a becoming Char and b becoming Int; this gives

```
map :: (Char -> Int) -> [Char] -> [Int]
```

and so

```
map ord :: [Char] -> [Int]
```

As in the monomorphic case, we can use this discussion of typing and function application in explaining type checking all aspects of expressions. We now look at another example, before examining a more technical aspect of type checking.

4. foldr again

In Section 9.3 we introduced the foldr function

```
foldr f s []     = s                        (foldr.1)
foldr f s (x:xs) = f x (foldr f s xs)       (foldr.2)
```

which could be used to fold an operator into a list, as in

```
foldr (+) 0 [2,3,1] = 2+(3+(1+0))
```

so that it appears as if foldr has the type given by

```
foldr :: (a -> a -> a) -> a -> [a] -> a
```

In fact, the most general type of foldr is more general than this. Suppose that the starting value has type b and the elements of the list are of type a

```
foldr :: (... -> ... -> ...) -> b -> [a] -> ...
```

Then we can picture the definition thus:

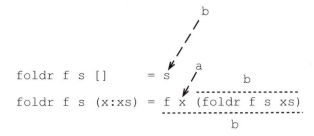

s is the result of the first equation, and so the result type of the foldr function itself will be b, the type of s

```
foldr :: (... -> ... -> ...) -> b -> [a] -> b
```

In the second equation, f is applied to x as first argument, giving

```
foldr :: (a -> ... -> ...) -> b -> [a] -> b
```

The second argument of f is the result of a foldr, and so of type b,

```
foldr :: (a -> b -> ...) -> b -> [a] -> b
```

Finally, the result of the second equation is an application of f; this result must have the same result type as the foldr itself, b.

```
foldr :: (a -> b -> b) -> b -> [a] -> b
```

With this insight about the type of foldr we were able to see that foldr could be used to define another whole cohort of list functions, such as an insertion sort,

```
iSort :: Ord a => [a] -> [a]
iSort = foldr ins []
```

in which ins has the type Ord a => a -> [a] -> [a].

Polymorphic definitions and variables

Here we examine a more technical aspect of how type checking works over polymorphic definitions; it may be omitted on first reading.

Functions and constants can be used at different types in the same expression. A simple instance is

```
expr = length ([]++[True]) + length ([]++[2,3,4])          (expr)
```

The first occurrence of [] is at [Int], whilst the second is at [Bool]. This is completely legitimate, and is one of the advantages of a polymorphic definition. Now suppose that we replace the [] by a variable, and define

```
funny xs = length (xs++[True]) + length (xs++[2,3,4])      (funny)
```

The variable xs is forced to have type [Bool] *and* type [Int]; it is forced to be polymorphic, in other words. This is not allowed in Haskell, as there is no way of expressing the type of funny. It might be thought that

```
funny :: [a] -> Int
```

was a correct type, but this would mean that funny would have all the instance types

```
funny :: [Int] -> Int
funny :: [[Char]] -> Int
    ...
```

which it clearly does not. We conclude that constants and variables are treated differently: constants may very well appear at different incompatible types in the same expression, variables cannot.

What is the significance of disallowing the definition (funny) but allowing the definition (expr)? Taking (expr) first, we have a polymorphic definition of the form [] :: [a] and an expression in which [] occurs twice; the first occurrence is at [Bool], the second at [Int]. To allow these independent uses to occur, we type-check each use of a polymorphic definition with different type variables, so that a constraint on one use does not affect any of the others.

On the other hand, how is the definition of (funny) disallowed? When we type check the use of a variable we will not treat each instance as being of an independent type. Suppose we begin with no constraint on xs, so xs::t, say. The first occurrence of xs forces xs::[Bool], the second requires xs::[Int]; these two constraints cannot be satisfied simultaneously, and thus the definition (funny) fails to type check.

The crucial point to remember from this example is that the definition of a function is not permitted to force any of its arguments to be polymorphic.

Function definitions

In type checking a function definition like (fdef) on page 229 above we have to obey rules similar to the monomorphic case.

- Each of the guards g_i must be of type Bool.
- The value e_i returned in each clause must have a type s_i which is at least as general as t; that is, s_i must have t as an instance.
- The pattern p_j must be **consistent** with type of that argument, namely t_j.

We take up a final aspect of type checking – the impact of type classes – in the next section.

Exercises

13.2 Do the following pairs of types – listed vertically – unify? If so, give a most general unifier for them; if not, explain why they fail to unify.

```
(Int -> b)            (Int,a,a)
(a -> Bool)           (a,a,[Bool])
```

13.3 Show that we can unify (a,[a]) with (b,c) to give (Bool,[Bool]).

13.4 Can the function

```
f :: (a,[a]) -> b
```

be applied to the arguments (2,[3]), (2,[]) and (2,[True]); if so, what are the types of the results? Explain your answers.

13.5 Repeat the previous question for the function

```
f :: (a,[a]) -> a
```

Explain your answers.

13.6 Give the type of f [] [] if f has type

```
f :: [a] -> [b] -> a -> b
```

What is the type of the function h given by the definition

```
h x = f x x ?
```

13.7 How can you use the Haskell system to check whether two type expressions are unifiable, and if so what is their unification? Hint: you can make dummy definitions in Haskell in which the defined value, `zircon` say, is equated with itself:

```
zircon = zircon
```

Values defined like this can be declared to have any type you wish.

13.8 [Harder] Recalling the definitions of `curry` and `uncurry` from Section 10.7, what are the types of

```
curry id
uncurry id
curry (curry id)
uncurry (uncurry id)
uncurry curry
```

Explain why the following expressions do not type-check:

```
curry uncurry
curry curry
```

13.9 [Harder] Give an *algorithm* which decides whether two type expressions are unifiable. If they are, your algorithm should return a most general unifying substitution; if not, it should give some explanation of why the unification fails.

13.3 Type checking and classes

Classes in Haskell restrict the use of some functions, such as ==, to types in the class over which they are defined, in this case Eq. These restrictions are apparent in the **contexts** which appear in some types. For instance, if we define

```
member []     y = False
member (x:xs) y = (x==y) || member xs y
```

its type will be

```
Eq a => [a] -> a -> Bool
```

because x and y of type a are compared for equality in the definition, thus forcing the type a to belong to the equality class Eq.

This section explores the way in which type checking takes place when overloading is involved; the material is presented informally, by means of an example.

Suppose we are to apply the function member to an expression e, whose type is

```
Ord b => [[b]]
```

Informally, e is a list of lists of objects, which belong to a type which carries an ordering. In the absence of the contexts we would unify the type expressions, giving

```
member :: [[b]] -> [b] -> Bool          e :: [[b]]
```

and so giving the application member e the type [b] -> Bool. We do the same here, but we also apply the unification to the contexts, producing the context

```
(Eq [b] , Ord b)                                            (ctx.1)
```

Now, we check and simplify the context.

● The requirements in a context can only apply to type variables, so we need to eliminate requirements like Eq [b]. The only way these can be eliminated is to use the instance declarations. In this case the built-in instance declaration

```
instance Eq a => Eq [a] where ....
```

allows us to replace the requirement Eq [b] with Eq b in (ctx.1), giving the new context

```
(Eq b , Ord b)                                              (ctx.2)
```

We repeat this process until no more instances apply.

If we fail to reduce all the requirements to ones involving a type variable, the application fails, and an error message would be generated. This happens if we apply member to [id];

```
ERROR: a -> a is not an instance of class "Eq"
```

since id is a function, whose type is not it the class Eq.

● We then simplify the context using the class definitions. In our example we have both Eq b and Ord b, but recall that

```
class Eq a => Ord a where ...
```

so that any instance of Ord is automatically an instance of Eq; this means that we can simplify (ctx.2) to

```
Ord b
```

This is repeated until no further simplifications result.

For our example, we thus have the type

```
member e :: Ord b => [b] -> Bool
```

This three-stage process of unification, checking (with instances) and simplification is the general pattern for type checking with contexts in Haskell.

Finally, we should explain how contexts are introduced into the types of the language. They originate in types for the functions in class declarations, so that, for instance, we have

```
toString :: Visible a => a -> String
size     :: Visible a => a -> Int
```

The type checking of functions which use these overloaded functions will propagate and combine the contexts as we have seen above.

We have seen informally how the Haskell type system accommodates type checking for the overloaded names which belong to type classes. A more thorough overview of the technical aspects of this, including a discussion of the 'monomorphism restriction' which needs to be placed on certain polymorphic bindings, is to be found in the Haskell 98 report (Peyton Jones and Hughes 1998).

Exercises

13.10 Give the type of each of the individual conditional equations which follow, and discuss the type of the function which together they define.

```
merge (x:xs) (y:ys)
  | x<y            = x : merge xs (y:ys)
  | x==y           = x : merge xs ys
  | otherwise      = y : merge (x:xs) ys
merge (x:xs) []    = (x:xs)
merge []     (y:ys) = (y:ys)
merge []     []     = []
```

13.11 Define a polymorphic sorting function, and show how its type is derived from the type of the ordering relation

```
compare :: Ord a => a -> a -> Ordering
```

13.12 Investigate the types of the following numerical functions; you will find that the types refer to some of the built-in numeric classes.

```
mult x y = x*y
divide x = x 'div' 2
share x  = x / 2.0
```

Recall that these can be given more restrictive types, such as

```
divide :: Int -> Int
```

by explicitly asserting their types as above.

Summary

The chapter explained how type checking of expressions and definitions is performed in Haskell. Initially this was explored in the monomorphic case, and then expanded to deal with polymorphism. In that case we saw type checking as a process of extracting and consolidating constraints, the latter being given by unification of type expressions which contain type variables. We concluded by examining how to manage contexts in types, and thus how overloading is handled in the Haskell type system.

Algebraic types

So far in our discussion of Haskell we have been able to model entities using

- the base types, `Int`, `Float`, `Bool` and `Char`, and

- composite types: tuple types, $(t_1, t_2, \ldots, t_n)$; list types, $[t_1]$; and function types, $(t_1 \rightarrow t_2)$; where $t_1, \ldots, t_n$ are themselves types.

This gives a wide choice of types and we have seen quite complex structures, like an index for a document, represented by the appropriate combination of types: in the index example, `[ ([Int],[Char]) ]` was used.

However, there are other types which are difficult to model using the constructs we have seen so far. Examples include

- the type of months: January, ..., December;

- the type whose elements are either a number or a string: a house in a street will either have a number or a name, for instance;

- the type of trees, as illustrated in Figure 14.1.

All these types can be modelled by Haskell **algebraic** types, which form the subject of this chapter.

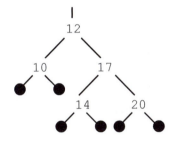

Figure 14.1 An example of a tree of integers.

(14.1) Introducing algebraic types

Algebraic data type definitions are introduced by the keyword `data`, followed by the name of the type, an equals sign and then the **constructors** of the type being defined. The name of the type and the names of constructors begin with capital letters.

We give a sequence of examples of increasing complexity, before discussing the general form of these type definitions.

Enumerated types

The simplest sort of algebraic type is defined by enumerating the elements of the type. For instance,

```
data Temp   = Cold | Hot
data Season = Spring | Summer | Autumn | Winter
```

introduces two types. The type `Temp` has two members, `Cold` and `Hot`, and `Season` has four members. More formally, `Cold` and `Hot` are called the **constructors** of the type `Temp`.

To define functions over these types we use pattern matching: we can match against either a literal or a variable. To describe the (British!) weather we might say

```
weather :: Season -> Temp

weather Summer = Hot
weather _      = Cold
```

Pattern matching is sequential; the first pattern to match an argument will be used. This means that the British weather is only hot in the summer, and it is cold the rest of the year. The built-in Boolean type is defined by

```
data Bool = False | True
```

and the type `Ordering`, used in the class `Ord`, by

```
data Ordering = LT | EQ | GT
```

As we have seen, pattern matching is used to define functions over algebraic types. We can use it to define equality over Temp, for instance,

```
Cold == Cold  = True
Hot  == Hot   = True
_    == _     = False
```

to put Temp into the equality class Eq.

It would be tiresome to have to give a definition of equality for every new type which we introduce, and so the Haskell system can be made to generate definitions of ==, ordering, enumeration and text functions automatically. We discuss the details of this at the end of this section, after looking at some more examples.

Product types

Instead of using a tuple we can define a type with a number of components, often called a **product** type, as an algebraic type. An example might be

```
data People = Person Name Age                        (People)
```

where Name is a synonym for String, and Age for Int, written thus:

```
type Name = String
type Age  = Int
```

The definition of People should be read as saying

> To construct an element of type People, you need to supply two values; one, st say, of type Name, and another, n say, of type Age. The element of People formed from them will be Person st n.

Example values of this type include

```
Person "Electric Aunt Jemima" 77
Person "Ronnie" 14
```

As before, functions are defined using pattern matching. A general element of type People has the form Person st n, and we can use this pattern on the left-hand side of a definition,

```
showPerson :: People -> String
showPerson (Person st n) = st ++ " -- " ++ show n
```

(recall that show gives a textual form of an Int, since Int belongs to the Show class). For instance,

```
showPerson (Person "Electric Aunt Jemima" 77)
 = "Electric Aunt Jemima -- 77"
```

In this example, the type has a single constructor, Person, which is **binary** because it takes two elements to form a value of type People. For the enumerated types Temp and Season the constructors are called **nullary** (or *0-ary*) as they take no arguments.

The constructors introduced by algebraic type definitions can be used just like functions, so that `Person st n` is the result of applying the function `Person` to the arguments st and n; we can interpret the definition (`People`) as giving the **type of the constructor**, here

```
Person :: Name -> Age -> People
```

An alternative definition of the type of people is given by the type synonym

```
type People = (Name,Age)
```

The advantages of using an algebraic type are threefold.

- Each object of the type carries an explicit **label** of the purpose of the element; in this case that it represents a person.
- It is not possible accidentally to treat an arbitrary pair consisting of a string and a number as a person; a person must be constructed using the `Person` constructor.
- The type will appear in any error messages due to mis-typing; a type synonym might be expanded out and so disappear from any type error messages.

There are also advantages of using a tuple type, with a synonym declaration.

- The elements are more compact, and so definitions will be shorter.
- Using a tuple, especially a pair, allows us to reuse many polymorphic functions such as `fst`, `snd` and `unzip` over tuple types; this will not be the case for the algebraic type.

In each system that we model we will have to choose between these alternatives: our decisions will depend exactly on how we use the products, and on the complexity of the system.

The approach here works equally well with unary constructors, so we might say

```
data Age = Years Int
```

whose elements are `Years 45` and so on. It is clear from a definition like this that 45 is here being used as an age in years, rather than some unrelated numerical quantity. The disadvantage is that we cannot use functions defined over `Int` directly over `Age`.

We can use the same name, for instance `Person`, for both the type and the constructor of a type, as in the definition

```
data Person = Person Name Age
```

We choose not to do this, as using the same name for two related but different objects can easily lead to confusion, but it is an idiom used by a number of Haskell programmers.

The examples of types given here are a special case of what we look at next.

Alternatives

A shape in a simple geometrical program is either a circle or a rectangle. These alternatives are given by the type

```
data Shape = Circle Float |                                    (Shape)
             Rectangle Float Float
```

which says that there are two ways of building an element of Shape. One way is to supply the radius of a `Circle`; the other alternative is to give the sides of a `Rectangle`. Example objects of this type are

```
Circle 3.0
Rectangle 45.9 87.6
```

Pattern matching allows us to define functions by cases, as in

```
isRound :: Shape -> Bool
isRound (Circle _)      = True
isRound (Rectangle _ _) = False
```

and also lets us use the components of the elements:

```
area :: Shape -> Float
area (Circle r)      = pi*r*r
area (Rectangle h w) = h*w
```

Another way of reading the definition (Shape) is to say that there are two **constructor functions** for the type Shape, whose types are

```
Circle    :: Float -> Shape
Rectangle :: Float -> Float -> Shape
```

These functions are called constructor functions because the elements of the type are constructed by applying these functions.

Extensions of this type, to accommodate the position of an object, are discussed in the exercises at the end of this section.

The general form of algebraic type definitions

The general form of the algebraic type definitions which we have seen so far is

```
data Typename                                              (Typename)
  = Con₁ t₁₁ ... t₁ₖ₁ |
    Con₂ t₂₁ ... t₂ₖ₂ |
      ....
    Conₙ tₙ₁ ... tₙₖₙ
```

Each Con_i is a constructor, followed by k_i types, where k_i is a non-negative integer which may be zero. We build elements of the type Typename by applying these constructor functions to arguments of the types given in the definition, so that

$$Con_i \ v_{i1} \ \cdots \ v_{ik_i}$$

will be a member of the type Typename if v_{ij} is in t_{ij} for j ranging from 1 to k_i.

Reading the constructors as functions, the definition (Typename) gives the constructors the following types

$$\text{Con}_i \ :: \ t_{i1} \ \text{->} \ \dots \ \text{->} \ t_{ik_i} \ \text{->} \ \text{Typename}$$

In the sections to come, we shall see two extensions of the definitions seen already.

● The types can be **recursive**; we can use the type we are defining, Typename, as (part of) any of the types t_{ij}. This gives us lists, trees and many other data structures.

● The Typename can be followed by one or more type variables which may be used on the right-hand side, making the definition **polymorphic**.

Recursive polymorphic types combine these two ideas, and this powerful mixture provides types which can be reused in many different situations – the built-in type of lists is an example which we have already seen. Other examples are given in the sections which follow.

Before we move on, it is worth contrasting type and data definitions. A synonym given by type is simply a shorthand, and so a synonym type can always be expanded out, and therefore removed from the program. On the other hand, a data definition creates a new type. Because synonyms are simply shorthand, a synonym definition cannot be recursive; data definitions can be and often are recursive, as we shall discover presently.

Deriving instances of classes

As we saw earlier, Haskell has a number of built-in classes including

● Eq, a class giving equality and inequality;

● Ord, built on Eq, giving an ordering over elements of a type;

● Enum, allowing the type to be enumerated, and so giving [n ..   m]-style expressions over the type, and

● Show, allowing elements of the type to be turned into textual form, and Read, which allows values of the type to be read from strings.

When we introduce a new algebraic type, such as Temp or Shape, we might well expect to have equality, enumerations and so on. These can be supplied by the system if we ask for them, thus:

```
data Season = Spring | Summer | Autumn | Winter
              deriving (Eq,Ord,Enum,Show,Read)
```

```
data Shape  = Circle Float |
              Rectangle Float Float
              deriving (Eq,Ord,Show,Read)
```

We can thus compare seasons for equality and order, write expressions of the form

```
[Spring .. Autumn]
```

denoting the list

```
[Spring, Summer, Autumn]
```

and show values of the type. The same applies to Shape, except that we cannot enumerate shapes; being in Enum can only be derived for enumerated types such as Season.

We are not forced to use the derived definitions; we can give our own instances, so that, for example, all circles of negative radius are made equal. The definition of showPerson above could also form a model for making People an instance of the type class Show.

Exercises

14.1 Redefine the function weather:: Season -> Temp so that a guard or an if ... is used rather than pattern matching. Which of the definitions is preferable in your opinion?

14.2 Define the type of months as a Haskell algebraic type. Give a function which takes a month to its appropriate season – in doing this you might want to use the ordering on the type, which is derived as explained above.

14.3 What would be the weather function for New Zealand, which is on a similar latitude to Britain, but in the Southern Hemisphere? What would be the definition for Brazil, which is crossed by the Equator?

14.4 Define a function to give the length of the perimeter of a geometrical shape, of type Shape. What is the type of this function?

14.5 Add an extra constructor to Shape for triangles, and extend the functions isRound, area and perimeter to include triangles.

14.6 Define a function which decides whether a Shape is regular: a circle is regular, a square is a regular rectangle and being equilateral makes a triangle regular.

14.7 Investigate the derived definitions for Temp and Shape: what form do the orderings and the show functions take, for example?

14.8 Define == over Shape so that all circles of negative radius are equated. How would you treat rectangles with negative sides?

14.9 The type Shape takes no account of the position or orientation of a shape. After deciding how to represent points, how would you modify the original definition of Shape to contain the **centre** of each object? You can assume that rectangles lie with their sides parallel to the axes, thus:

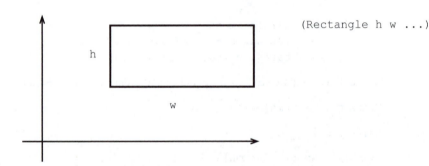

(Rectangle h w ...)

14.10 Calling the new shape type `NewShape`, define a function

> `move :: Float -> Float -> NewShape -> NewShape`

which moves a shape by the two offsets given:

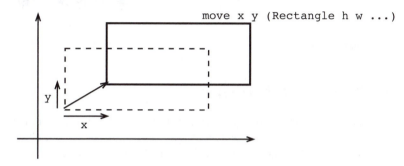

14.11 Define a function to test whether two `NewShapes` overlap.

14.12 Some houses have a number; others have a name. How would you implement the type of 'strings or numbers' used as a part of an address? Write a function which gives the textual form of one of these objects. Give a definition of a type of names and addresses using the type you have defined.

14.13 Reimplement the library database of Section 5.6 to use an algebraic type like `People` rather than a pair. Compare the two approaches to this example.

14.14 The library database of Section 5.6 is to be extended in the following ways.

- CDs and videos as well as books are available for loan.
- A record is kept of the authors of books as well as their titles. Similar information is kept about CDs, but not about videos.
- Each loan has a period: books one month, CDs one week and videos three days.

Explain how you would modify the types used to implement the database, and how the function types might be changed. The system should perform the following operations. For each case, give the types and definitions of the functions involved.

- Find all items on loan to a given person.
- Find all books, CDs or videos on loan to a particular person.
- Find all items in the database due back on or before a particular day, and the same information for any given person.
- Update the database with loans; the constant `today` can be assumed to contain today's date, in a format of your choice.

What other functions would have to be defined to make the system usable? Give their types, but not their definitions.

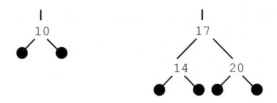

Figure 14.2 Two trees.

Recursive algebraic types

Types are often naturally described in terms of themselves. For instance, an integer expression is either a **literal** integer, like 347, or is given by combining two expressions using an arithmetic operator such as plus or minus, as in (3-1)+3.

```
data Expr = Lit Int |
            Add Expr Expr |
            Sub Expr Expr
```

Similarly, a tree is either nil or is given by combining a value and two sub-trees. For example, the number 12 and the trees in Figure 14.2 are assembled to give the tree in Figure 14.1. As a Haskell type we say

```
data NTree = NilT |
             Node Int NTree NTree
```

Finally, we have already used the type of lists: a list is either empty ([]) or is built from a head and a tail – another list – using the list constructor ':'. Lists will provide a good guide to using recursive (and polymorphic) definitions. In particular they suggest how 'general' polymorphic higher-order functions over other algebraic types are defined, and how programs are verified. We now look at some examples in more detail.

Expressions

The type Expr gives a model of the simple numerical expressions discussed above. These might be used in implementing a simple numerical calculator, for instance.

```
data Expr = Lit Int |
            Add Expr Expr |
            Sub Expr Expr
```

Some examples are

```
2                    Lit 2
2+3                  Add (Lit 2) (Lit 3)
(3-1)+3              Add (Sub (Lit 3) (Lit 1)) (Lit 3)
```

where the informal expressions are listed in the left-hand column, and their Expr forms in the right. Given an expression, we might want to

- evaluate it;
- turn it into a string, which can then be printed;
- estimate its size – count the operators, say.

Each of these functions will be defined in the same way, using **primitive recursion**. As the type is itself recursive, it is not a surprise that the functions which handle the type are also recursive. Also, the form of the recursive definitions follows the recursion in the type definition. For instance, to evaluate an operator expression we work out the values of the arguments and combine the results using the operator.

```
eval :: Expr -> Int
```

```
eval (Lit n)    = n
eval (Add e1 e2) = (eval e1) + (eval e2)
eval (Sub e1 e2) = (eval e1) - (eval e2)
```

Primitive recursive definitions have two parts:

- At the non-recursive, *base* cases – (Lit n) here – the value is given outright.
- At the recursive cases, the values of the function at the sub-expressions from which the expression is formed – eval e1 and eval e2 here – can be used in calculating the result.

The show function has a similar form

```
show :: Expr -> String
```

```
show (Lit n) = show n
show (Add e1 e2)
    = "(" ++ show e1 ++ "+" ++ show e2 ++ ")"
show (Sub e1 e2)
    = "(" ++ show e1 ++ "-" ++ show e2 ++ ")"
```

as does the function to calculate the number of operators in an expression; we leave this as an exercise. Other exercises at the end of the section look at a different representation of expressions for which a separate type is used to represent the different possible operators. Next, we look at another recursive algebraic type, but after that we return to Expr and give an example of a non-primitive-recursive definition of a function to rearrange expressions in a particular way.

Trees of integers

Trees of integers like that in Figure 14.1 can be modelled by the type

```
data NTree = NilT |
              Node Int NTree NTree
```

The null tree is given by NilT, and the trees in Figure 14.2 by

```
Node 10 NilT NilT
Node 17 (Node 14 NilT NilT) (Node 20 NilT NilT)
```

Definitions of many functions are primitive recursive. For instance,

```
sumTree,depth :: NTree -> Int

sumTree NilT          = 0
sumTree (Node n t1 t2) = n + sumTree t1 + sumTree t2

depth NilT            = 0
depth (Node n t1 t2)   = 1 + max (depth t1) (depth t2)
```

with, for example,

```
sumTree (Node 3 (Node 4 NilT NilT) NilT) = 7
depth   (Node 3 (Node 4 NilT NilT) NilT) = 2
```

As another example, take the problem of finding out how many times a number, p say, occurs in a tree. The primitive recursion suggests two cases, depending upon the tree.

● For a null tree, NilT, the answer must be zero.

● For a non-null tree, (Node n t1 t2), we can find out how many times p occurs in the sub-trees t1 and t2 by two recursive calls; we have to make a case split depending on whether p occurs at the particular node, that is depending on whether or not p==n.

The final definition is

```
occurs :: NTree -> Int -> Int

occurs NilT p = 0
occurs (Node n t1 t2) p
  | n==p        = 1 + occurs t1 p + occurs t2 p
  | otherwise   =     occurs t1 p + occurs t2 p
```

The exercises at the end of the section give a number of other examples of functions defined over trees using primitive recursion. We next look at a particular example where a different form of recursion is used.

Rearranging expressions

The next example shows a definition which uses a more general recursion than we have seen so far. After showing why the generality is necessary, we argue that the function we have defined is total: it will give a result on all well-defined expressions.

The operation of addition over the integers is associative, so that the way in which an expression is bracketed is irrelevant to its value. We can, therefore, decide to bracket expressions involving '+' in any way we choose. The aim here is to write a program to turn expressions into right bracketed form, as shown in the following table:

```
(2+3)+4                    2+(3+4)
((2+3)+4)+5                2+(3+(4+5))
((2-((6+7)+8))+4)+5        (2-(6+(7+8)))+(4+5)
```

What is the program to do? The main aim is to spot occurrences of

```
Add (Add e1 e2) e3                                              (AddL)
```

and to transform them to

```
Add e1 (Add e2 e3)                                             (AddR)
```

so a first attempt at the program might say

```
try (Add (Add e1 e2) e3)
  = Add (try e1) (Add (try e2) (try e3))
try ...
```

which is primitive recursive: on the right-hand side of their definition the function `try` is only used on sub-expressions of the argument. This function will have the effect of transforming (AddL) to (AddR), but unfortunately (AddExL) will be sent to (AddExR):

```
((2+3)+4)+5                                                   (AddExL)
(2+3)+(4+5)                                                   (AddExR)
```

The problem is that in transforming (AddL) to (AddR) we may produce another pattern we are looking for at the top level: this is precisely what happens when (AddExL) is transformed to (AddExR). We therefore have to call the function *again* on the result of the rearrangement

```
assoc :: Expr -> Expr

assoc (Add (Add e1 e2) e3)
  = assoc (Add e1 (Add e2 e3))                                 (Add.1)
```

The other cases in the definition make sure that the *parts* of an expression are rearranged as they should be.

```
assoc (Add e1 e2)
  = Add (assoc e1) (assoc e2)                                  (Add.2)
assoc (Sub e1 e2)
  = Sub (assoc e1) (assoc e2)
assoc (Lit n)
  = Lit n
```

The equation (Add.2) will only be applied to the cases where (Add.1) does not apply – this is when e1 is either a Sub or a Lit expression. This is always the case in pattern matching; the *first* applicable equation is used.

When we use primitive recursion we can be sure that the recursion will **terminate** to give an answer: the recursive calls are only made on smaller expressions and so, after a finite number of calls to the function, a base case will be reached.

The assoc function is more complicated, and we need a more subtle argument to see that the function will always give a result. The equation (Add.1) is the tricky one, but intuitively, we can see that some progress has been made – some of the 'weight' of the tree has moved from left to right. In particular, one addition symbol has swapped sides. None of the other equations moves a plus in the other direction, so that after applying (Add.1) a finite number of times, there will be no more exposed addition symbols at the top level of the left-hand side. This means that the recursion cannot go on indefinitely, and so the function always leads to a result.

Syntax: infix constructors

We have seen that functions can be written in infix form; this also applies to constructors. We can, for example, redefine the function assoc thus:

```
assoc ((e1 'Add' e2) 'Add' e3)
  = assoc (e1 'Add' (e2 'Add' e3))
  ...
```

using the infix form of the constructor, given by surrounding it with back-quotes.

When an expression like this is shown, it appears in prefix form, so that the expression (Lit 3) 'Add' (Lit 4) appears as

```
Add (Lit 3) (Lit 4)
```

In a data definition we can define Haskell operators which are themselves constructors. These constructors have the same syntax as operator symbols, except that their first character must be a ':', which is reminiscent of ':', itself an infix constructor. For our type of integer expressions, we might define

```
data Expr = Lit Int |
            Expr :+: Expr |
            Expr :-: Expr
```

When an expression involving operator constructors is printed, the constructors appear in the infix position, unlike the quoted constructors above.

It is left as an exercise to complete the redefinition of functions over Expr under this redefinition of the Expr type.

Mutual recursion

In describing one type, it is often useful to use others; these in turn may refer back to the original type: this gives a pair of **mutually recursive** types. A description of a person might include biographical details, which in turn might refer to other people. For instance:

```
data Person = Adult Name Address Biog |
              Child Name
data Biog   = Parent String [Person] |
              NonParent String
```

In the case of a parent, the biography contains some text, as well as a list of their children, as elements of the type Person.

Suppose that we want to define a function which shows information about a person as a string. Showing this information will require us to show some biographical information, which itself contains further information about people. We thus have two mutually recursive functions:

```
showPerson (Adult nm ad bio)
  = show nm ++ show ad ++ showBiog bio
  ...
showBiog (Parent st perList)
  = st ++ concat (map showPerson perList)
  ...
```

Exercises

14.15 Give calculations of

```
eval (Lit 67)
eval (Add (Sub (Lit 3) (Lit 1)) (Lit 3))
show (Add (Lit 67) (Lit (-34)))
```

14.16 Define the function

```
size :: Expr -> Int
```

which counts the number of operators in an expression.

14.17 Add the operations of multiplication and integer division to the type Expr, and redefine the functions eval, show and size to include these new cases. What does your definition of eval do when asked to perform a division by zero?

14.18 Instead of adding extra constructors to the Expr type, as in the previous question, it is possible to factor the definition thus:

```
data Expr = Lit Int |
            Op Ops Expr Expr

data Ops  = Add | Sub | Mul | Div
```

Show how the functions eval, show and size are defined for this type, and discuss the changes you have to make to your definitions if you add the extra operation Mod for remainder on integer division.

14.19 Give line-by-line calculations of

```
sumTree (Node 3 (Node 4 NilT NilT) NilT)
depth   (Node 3 (Node 4 NilT NilT) NilT)
```

14.20 Complete the redefinition of functions over `Expr` after it has been defined using the infix constructors `:+:` and `:-:`.

14.21 Define functions to return the left- and right-hand sub-trees of an `NTree`.

14.22 Define a function to decide whether a number is an element of an `NTree`.

14.23 Define functions to find the maximum and minimum values held in an `NTree`.

14.24 A tree is reflected by swapping left and right sub-trees, recursively. Define a function to reflect an `NTree`. What is the result of reflecting twice, `reflect . reflect`?

14.25 Define functions

```
collapse, sort :: NTree -> [Int]
```

which turn a tree into a list. The function `collapse` should enumerate the left sub-tree, then the value at the node and finally the right sub-tree; `sort` should sort the elements in ascending order. For instance,

```
collapse (Node 3 (Node 4 NilT NilT) NilT) = [4,3]
sort     (Node 3 (Node 4 NilT NilT) NilT) = [3,4]
```

14.26 Complete the definitions of `showPerson` and `showBiog` which were left incomplete in the text.

14.27 It is possible to extend the type `Expr` so that it contains *conditional* expressions, `If b e1 e2`, where e1 and e2 are expressions, and b is a Boolean expression, a member of the type `BExp`,

```
data Expr = Lit Int |
            Op Ops Expr Expr |
            If BExp Expr Expr
```

The expression

```
If b e1 e2
```

has the value of e1 if b has the value `True` and otherwise it has the value of e2.

```
data BExp = BoolLit Bool |
            And BExp BExp |
            Not BExp |
            Equal Expr Expr |
            Greater Expr Expr
```

The five clauses here give

- Boolean literals, BoolLit True and BoolLit False.
- The conjunction of two expressions; it is True if both sub-expressions have the value True.
- The negation of an expression. Not be has value True if be has the value False.
- Equal e1 e2 is True when the two numerical expressions have equal values.
- Greater e1 e2 is True when the numerical expression e1 has a larger value then e2.

Define the functions

```
eval  :: Expr -> Int
bEval :: BExpr -> Bool
```

by mutual recursion, and extend the function show to show the redefined type of expressions.

(14.3) Polymorphic algebraic types

Algebraic type definitions can contain the type variables a, b and so on, defining polymorphic types. The definitions are as before, with the type variables used in the definition appearing after the type name on the left-hand side of the definition. A simple example is

```
data Pairs a = Pr a a
```

and example elements of the type are

```
Pr 2 3     :: Pairs Int
Pr [] [3] :: Pairs [Int]
Pr [] []   :: Pairs [a]
```

A function to test the equality of the two halves of a pair is given by

```
equalPair :: Eq a => Pairs a -> Bool
equalPair (Pr x y) = (x==y)
```

The remainder of this section explores a sequence of further examples.

Lists

The built-in type of lists can be given by a definition like

```
data List a = NilList | Cons a (List a)
              deriving (Eq,Ord,Show,Read)
```

where the syntax [a], [] and ':' is used for List a, NilList and 'Cons'. Because of this, the type of lists forms a useful paradigm for recursive polymorphic types. In particular, we can see the possibility of defining useful families of functions over such types, and the way in which program verification can proceed by induction over the structure of a type.

Binary trees

The trees of Section 14.2 carry numbers at each node; there is nothing special about numbers, and we can equally well say that they have elements of an arbitrary type at the nodes:

```
data Tree a = Nil | Node a (Tree a) (Tree a)
                deriving (Eq,Ord,Show,Read)
```

The definitions of depth and occurs carry over unchanged:

```
depth :: Tree a -> Int
depth Nil             = 0
depth (Node n t1 t2) = 1 + max (depth t1) (depth t2)
```

as do many of the functions defined in the exercises at the end of Section 14.2. One of these is the function collapsing a tree into a list. This is done by visiting the elements of the tree 'inorder', that is visiting first the left sub-tree, then the node itself, then the right sub-tree, thus:

```
collapse :: Tree a -> [a]
collapse Nil = []
collapse (Node x t1 t2)
  = collapse t1 ++ [x] ++ collapse t2
```

For example,

```
collapse (Node 12
               (Node 34 Nil Nil)
               (Node 3 (Node 17 Nil Nil) Nil))
  = [34,12,17,3]
```

Various higher-order functions are definable, also,

```
mapTree :: (a -> b) -> Tree a -> Tree b
mapTree f Nil = Nil
mapTree f (Node x t1 t2)
  = Node (f x) (mapTree f t1) (mapTree f t2)
```

We shall return to trees in Section 16.7, where particular 'search' trees form a case study.

The union type, Either

Type definitions can take more than one parameter. We saw earlier the example of the type whose elements were either a name or a number. In general we can form a type whose elements come either from a or from b:

```
data Either a b = Left a | Right b
                deriving (Eq,Ord,Read,Show)
```

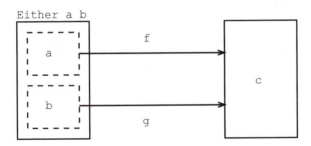

Figure 14.3 Joining together functions.

Members of the 'union' or 'sum' type are (Left x), with x::a, and (Right y) with y::b. The 'name or number' type is given by Either String Int and

```
Left "Duke of Prunes" :: Either String Int
Right 33312           :: Either String Int
```

We can tell whether an element is in the first half of the union by

```
isLeft :: Either a b -> Bool
isLeft (Left _)  = True
isLeft (Right _) = False
```

To define a function from Either a b to Int, say, we have to deal with two cases,

```
fun :: Either a b -> Int
fun (Left x)  = ... x ...
fun (Right y) = ... y ...
```

In the first case, the right-hand side takes x to an Int, so is given by a function from a to Int; in the second case y is taken to an Int, thus being given by a function from b to Int.

Guided by this, we can give a higher-order function which *joins together* two functions defined on a and b to a function on Either a b. The definition follows, and is illustrated in Figure 14.3.

```
either :: (a -> c) -> (b -> c) -> Either a b -> c

either f g (Left x)  = f x
either f g (Right y) = g y
```

If we have a function f::a -> c and we wish to apply it to an element of Either a b, there is a problem: what do we do if the element is in the right-hand side of the Either type? A simple answer is to raise an error

```
applyLeft :: (a -> c) -> Either a b -> c
applyLeft f (Left x)  = f x
applyLeft f (Right _) = error "applyLeft applied to Right"
```

but in the next section we shall explore other ways of handling errors in more detail.

14.28 Investigate which of the functions over trees discussed in the exercises of Section 14.2 can be made polymorphic.

14.29 Define a function `twist` which swaps the order of a union

```
twist :: Either a b -> Either b a
```

What is the effect of `(twist . twist)`?

14.30 How would you define `applyLeft` using the function `either`?

14.31 Show that any function of type `a -> b` can be transformed into functions of type

```
a -> Either b c
a -> Either c b
```

14.32 How could you generalize `either` to `join` so that it has type

```
join :: (a -> c) -> (b -> d) -> Either a b -> Either c d
```

You might find the answer to the previous exercise useful here, if you want to define `join` using `either`.

The trees defined in the text are *binary*: each non-nil tree has exactly two sub-trees. We can instead define general trees with an arbitrary list of sub-trees, thus:

```
data GTree a = Leaf a | Gnode [GTree a]
```

The exercises which follow concern these trees.

14.33 Define functions

- to count the number of leaves in a GTree;
- to find the depth of a GTree;
- to sum a numeric GTree Int;
- to find whether an element appears in a GTree;
- to map a function over the elements at the leaves of a GTree; and
- to flatten a GTree to a list.

14.34 How is the completely empty tree represented as a GTree?

(14.4) Case study: program errors

How should a program deal with a situation which ought not to occur? Examples of such situations include

- attempts to divide by zero, to take the square root of a negative number, and other arithmetical transgressions;
- attempts to take the head of an empty list – this is a special case of a definition over an algebraic type from which one case (here the empty list) is absent.

This section examines the problem, giving three approaches of increasing sophistication. The simplest method is to stop computation and to report the source of the problem. This is indeed what the Haskell system does in the cases listed above, and we can do this in functions we define ourselves using the `error` function,

```
error :: String -> a
```

An attempt to evaluate the expression `error "Circle with negative radius"` results in the message

```
Program error: Circle with negative radius
```

being printed and computation stopping.

The problem with this approach is that all the useful information in the computation is lost; instead of this, the error can be dealt with in some way *without* stopping computation completely. Two approaches suggest themselves, and we look at them in turn now.

Dummy values

The function `tail` is supposed to give the tail of a list, and it gives an error message on an empty list:

```
tail :: [a] -> [a]
tail (_:xs) = xs
tail []     = error "PreludeList.tail: empty list"
```

We could redefine it to say

```
tl :: [a] -> [a]
tl (_:xs) = xs
tl []     = []
```

Now, an attempt to take the tail of *any* list will succeed. In a similar way we could say

```
divide :: Int -> Int -> Int
divide n m
  | (m /= 0)   = n 'div' m
  | otherwise  = 0
```

so that division by zero gives some answer. For `tl` and `divide` there have been obvious choices about what the value in the 'error' case should be; for `head` there is not, and instead we can supply an extra parameter to `head`, which is to be used in the case of the list being empty.

```
hd :: a -> [a] -> a
hd y (x:_) = x
hd y []    = y
```

This approach is completely general; if a function `f` (of one argument, say) usually raises an error when `cond` is `True`, we can define a new function

```
fErr y x
  | cond      = y
  | otherwise = f x
```

This approach works well in many cases; the only drawback is that we have no way of telling when an error has occurred, since we may get the result `y` from either the error or the 'normal' case. Alternatively we can use an error type to trap and process errors; this we look at now.

Error types

The previous approach works by returning a dummy value when an error has occurred. Why not instead return an error *value* as a result? We define the type

```
data Maybe a = Nothing | Just a
                   deriving (Eq,Ord,Read,Show)
```

which is effectively the type a with an extra value `Nothing` added. We can now define a division function `errDiv` thus

```
errDiv :: Int -> Int -> Maybe Int
errDiv n m
  | (m /= 0)  = Just (n 'div' m)
  | otherwise = Nothing
```

and in the general case, where `f` gives an error when `cond` holds,

```
fErr x
  | cond      = Nothing
  | otherwise = Just (f x)
```

The results of these functions are now not of the original output type, a say, but of type `Maybe a`. These `Maybe` types allow us to **raise** an error, potentially. We can do two things with a potential error which has been raised

● we can *transmit* the error through a function, the effect of `mapMaybe`;

● we can *trap* an error, the role of `maybe`.

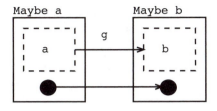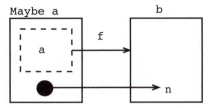

mapMaybe g   maybe n f

Figure 14.4   Error-handling functions.

These two operations are illustrated in Figure 14.4, and we define them now.

The function mapMaybe transmits an error value though the application of the function g. Suppose that g is a function of type a -> b, and that we are to lift it to operate on the type Maybe a. In the case of an argument Just x, g can be applied to the x to give a result, g x, of type b; this is put into Maybe b by applying the constructor function Just. On the other hand, if Nothing is the argument then Nothing is the result.

```
mapMaybe :: (a -> b) -> Maybe a -> Maybe b

mapMaybe g Nothing   = Nothing
mapMaybe g (Just x) = Just (g x)
```

In trapping an error, we aim to return a result of type b, from an input of type Maybe a; we have two cases to deal with

● in the Just case, we apply a function from a to b;
● in the Nothing case, we have to give the value of type b which is to be returned. (This is rather like the value we supplied to hd earlier.)

The higher-order function which achieves this is maybe, whose arguments n and f are used in the Nothing and Just cases respectively.

```
maybe :: b -> (a -> b) -> Maybe a -> b

maybe n f Nothing   = n
maybe n f (Just x) = f x
```

We can see the functions mapMaybe and maybe in action in the examples which follow. In the first, a division by zero leads to a Nothing which passes through the lifting to be trapped – 56 is therefore returned:

```
maybe 56 (1+) (mapMaybe (*3) (errDiv 9 0))
= maybe 56 (1+) (mapMaybe (*3) Nothing)
= maybe 56 (1+) Nothing
= 56
```

In the second, a normal division returns a `Just` 9. This is multiplied by three, and the maybe at the outer level adds one and removes the `Just`:

```
maybe 56 (1+) (mapMaybe (*3) (errDiv 9 1))
= maybe 56 (1+) (mapMaybe (*3) (Just 9))
= maybe 56 (1+) (Just 27)
= 1 + 27
= 28
```

The advantage of the approach discussed here is that we can first define the system without error handling, and afterwards add the error handling, using the `mapMaybe` and maybe functions together with the modified functions to **raise** the error. As we have seen numerous times already, separating a problem into two parts has made the solution of each, and therefore the whole, more accessible.

We revisit the Maybe type in Section 18.8 where we see that it is an example of a more general programming structure, a monad. In particular there we examine the relationship between the function `mapMaybe` and the map function over lists.

Exercises

14.35 Using the functions `mapMaybe` and `maybe`, or otherwise, define a function

```
process :: [Int] -> Int -> Int -> Int
```

so that `process xs n m` takes the nth and mth items of the list of numbers `xs`, and returns their sum. Your function should return 0 if either of the numbers is not one of the indices of the list: for a list of length p, the indices are 0, ..., p−1 inclusive.

14.36 Discuss the advantages and disadvantages of the three approaches to error handling presented in this section.

14.37 What are the values of type `Maybe (Maybe a)`? Define a function

```
squashMaybe :: Maybe (Maybe a) -> Maybe a
```

which will 'squash' `Just (Just x)` to `Just x` and all other values to `Nothing`.

14.38 In a similar way to `mapMaybe`, define the function

```
composeMaybe :: (a -> Maybe b) ->
                (b -> Maybe c) ->
                (a -> Maybe c)
```

which composes two error-raising functions. How could you use `mapMaybe`, the function composition operator and the `squash` function to define `composeMaybe`?

14.39 The Maybe type could be generalized to allow messages to be carried in the Nothing part, thus:

```
data Err a = OK a | Error String
```

How do the definitions of `mapMaybe`, `maybe` and `composeMaybe` have to be modified to accommodate this new definition?

14.5 Design with algebraic data types

Algebraic data types provide us with a powerful mechanism for modelling types which occur both in problems themselves, and within the programs designed to solve them. In this section we suggest a three-stage method for finding the appropriate algebraic type definitions. We apply it in two examples: finding the 'edit distance' between two words, and a simulation problem.

An important moral of the discussion here is that we can start to design data types *independently* of the program itself. For a system of any size we should do this, as we will be more likely to succeed if we can think about separate parts of the system separately.

We shall have more to say about design of data types in the next two chapters.

Edit distance: problem statement

In discussing the stages of design, we follow the example of finding the **edit distance** between two strings. This is the shortest sequence of simple editing operations which can take us from one string to the other.

The example is a version of a practical problem: in keeping a display (of windows or simple text) up-to-date, the speed with which updates can be done is crucial. It is therefore desirable to be able to make the updates from as few elementary operations as possible; this is what the edit distance program achieves in a different context.

We suppose that there are five basic editing operations on a string. We can change one character into another, copy a character without modifying it, delete or insert a character and delete (kill) to the end of the string. We also assume that each operation has the same cost, except a copy which is free.

To turn the string `"fish"` into `"chips"`, we could kill the whole string, then insert the characters one-by-one, at a total cost of six. An optimal solution will copy as much of the string as possible, and is given by

- inserting the character `'c'`,
- changing `'f'` to `'h'`,
- copying `'i'`,
- inserting `'p'`,
- copying `'s'`, and finally
- deleting the remainder of the string, `"h"`.

In the remainder of this section we design a type to represent the editing steps, and after looking at another example of data type design, define a function to give an optimal sequence of editing steps from one string to another.

The analysis here can also be used to describe the difference between two lists of arbitrary type. If each item is a line of a file, the behaviour of the function is similar to the Unix `diff` utility, which is used to give the difference between two text files.

Design stages in the edit distance problem

Now we look at the three stages of algebraic type definition in detail.

● First we have to identify the *types* of data involved. In the example, we have to define

```
data Edit = ...
```

which represents the editing operations.

● Next, we have to identify the different sorts of data in each of the types. Each sort of data is given by a **constructor**. In the example, we can change, copy, delete or insert a character and delete (kill) to the end of the string. Our type definition is therefore

```
data Edit = Change ... |
            Copy ... |
            Delete ... |
            Insert ... |
            Kill ...
```

The '...' show that we have not yet said anything about the types of the constructors.

● Finally, for each of the constructors, we need to decide what its **components** or arguments are. Some of the constructors – `Copy`, `Delete` and `Kill` – require no information; the others need to indicate the new character to be inserted, so

```
data Edit = Change Char |
            Copy |
            Delete |
            Insert Char |
            Kill
            deriving (Eq,Show)
```

This completes the definition.

We now illustrate how other type definitions work in a similar way, before returning to give a solution to the 'edit distance' problem.

Simulation

Suppose we want to model, or **simulate**, how the queues in a bank or Post Office behave; perhaps we want to decide how many bank clerks need to be working at particular times of the day. Our system will take as input the arrivals of customers, and give as output their departures. Each of these can be modelled using a type.

● Inmess is the type of input messages. At a given time, there are two possibilities:

  – No-one arrives, represented by the 0-ary constructor No;
  – Someone arrives, represented by the constructor Yes. This will have components giving the arrival time of the customer, and the amount of time that will be needed to serve them.

Hence we have

```
data Inmess = No | Yes Arrival Service

type Arrival = Int
type Service = Int
```

● Similarly, we have Outmess, the type of output messages. Either no-one leaves (None), or a person is discharged (Discharge). The relevant information they carry is the time they have waited, together with when they arrived and their service time. We therefore define

```
data Outmess = None | Discharge Arrival Wait Service

type Wait = Int
```

We return to the simulation example in Chapter 16.

Edit distance: solution

The problem is to find the lowest-cost sequence of edits to take us from one string to another. We can begin the definition thus:

```
transform :: String -> String -> [Edit]

transform [] [] = []
```

To transform the non-empty string st to [], we simply have to Kill it, while to transform [] to st we have to Insert each of the characters in turn:

```
transform xs [] = [Kill]
transform [] ys = map Insert ys
```

In the general case, we have a choice: should we first use `Copy`, `Delete`, `Insert` or `Change`? If the first characters of the strings are equal we should copy; but if not, there is no obvious choice. We therefore try *all* possibilities and choose the best of them:

```
transform (x:xs) (y:ys)
  | x==y        = Copy : transform xs ys
  | otherwise   = best [ Delete   : transform xs (y:ys) ,
                         Insert y : transform (x:xs) ys ,
                         Change y : transform xs ys ]
```

How do we choose the best sequence? We choose the one with the lowest cost.

```
best :: [[Edit]] -> [Edit]
best [x]    = x
best (x:xs)
  | cost x <= cost b    = x
  | otherwise           = b
    where
    b = best xs
```

The `cost` is given by charging one for every operation except copy, which is equivalent to 'leave unchanged'.

```
cost :: [Edit] -> Int
cost = length . filter (/=Copy)
```

Exercises

The first four questions are designed to make you think about how data types are designed. These questions are not intended to have a single 'right' answer, rather you should satisfy yourself that you have adequately represented the types which appear in your informal picture of the problem.

14.40 It is decided to keep a record of vehicles which will use a particular car park. Design an algebraic data type to represent them.

14.41 If you knew that the records of vehicles were to be used for comparative tests of fuel efficiency, how would you modify your answer to the last question?

14.42 Discuss the data types you might use in a database of students' marks for classes and the like. Explain the design of any algebraic data types that you use.

14.43 What data types might be used to represent the objects which can be drawn using an interactive drawing program? To give yourself more of a challenge, you might like to think about grouping of objects, multiple copies of objects, and scaling.

14.44 How would you modify the edit distance program to accommodate a `Swap` operation, which can be used to transform `"abxyz"` to `"baxyz"` in a single step?

14.45 Write a definition which when given a list of edits and a string st, returns the sequence of strings given by applying the edits to st in sequence.

14.46 Give a calculation of transform "cat" "am". What do you conclude about the efficiency of the transform function?

(14.6) Algebraic types and type classes

We have reached a point where it is possible to explore rather more substantial examples of type classes, first introduced in Chapter 12.

Movable objects

We start by building a class of types whose members are geometrical objects in two dimensions. The operations of the class are those to move the objects in various different ways.

We now work through the definitions, which are illustrated in Figure 14.5. Some moves will be dictated by vectors, so we first define

```
data Vector = Vec Float Float
```

The class definition itself is

```
class Movable a where
  move     :: Vector -> a -> a
  reflectX :: a -> a
  reflectY :: a -> a
  rotate180 :: a -> a
  rotate180 = reflectX . reflectY
```

and it shows the ways in which an object can be moved. First it can be moved by a vector, as in the diagram below.

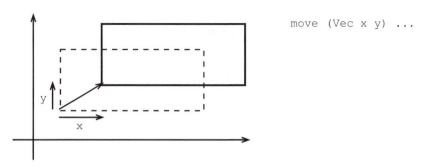

We can also reflect an object in the x-axis (the horizontal axis) or the y-axis (the vertical), or rotate a figure through 180° around the origin (the point where the axes meet). The default definition of rotate180 works by reflecting first in the y-axis and then the x, as we did with the Picture type in Chapter 1.

We can now define a hierarchy of movable objects; first we have the Point,

```
data Vector = Vec Float Float

class Movable a where
  move       :: Vector -> a -> a
  reflectX :: a -> a
  reflectY :: a -> a
  rotate180 :: a -> a
  rotate180 = reflectX . reflectY

data Point = Point Float Float
             deriving Show

instance Movable Point where
  move (Vec v1 v2) (Point c1 c2) = Point (c1+v1) (c2+v2)
  reflectX (Point c1 c2)  = Point c1 (-c2)
  reflectY (Point c1 c2)  = Point (-c1) c2
  rotate180 (Point c1 c2) = Point (-c1) (-c2)

data Figure = Line Point Point |
              Circle Point Float
              deriving Show

instance Movable Figure where
  move v (Line p1 p2) = Line (move v p1) (move v p2)
  move v (Circle p r) = Circle (move v p) r

  reflectX (Line p1 p2) = Line (reflectX p1) (reflectX p2)
  reflectX (Circle p r) = Circle (reflectX p) r

  reflectY (Line p1 p2) = Line (reflectY p1) (reflectY p2)
  reflectY (Circle p r) = Circle (reflectY p) r

instance Movable a => Movable [a] where
  move v   = map (move v)
  reflectX = map reflectX
  reflectY = map reflectY
```

Figure 14.5 Movable objects.

```
data Point = Point Float Float
             deriving Show
```

To make Point an instance of Movable we have to give definitions of move, reflectX and reflectY over the Point type.

```
move (Vec v1 v2) (Point c1 c2) = Point (c1+v1) (c2+v2)
```

Here we can see that the move is achieved by adding the components v1 and v2 to the coordinates of the point. Reflection is given by changing the sign of one of the coordinates

```
reflectX (Point c1 c2) = Point c1 (-c2)
reflectY (Point c1 c2) = Point (-c1) c2
```

For this instance we override the default definition of `rotate180` by changing the sign of both coordinates. This is a more efficient way of achieving the same transformation than the default definition.

```
rotate180 (Point c1 c2) = Point (-c1) (-c2)
```

Using the type of points we can build figures:

```
data Figure = Line Point Point |
              Circle Point Float
```

and in the instance declaration of `Movable` for `Figure` given in Figure 14.5 we use the corresponding operations on `Point`; for example,

```
move v (Line p1 p2) = Line (move v p1) (move v p2)
move v (Circle p r) = Circle (move v p) r
```

This same approach works again when we consider a list of movable objects:

```
instance Movable a => Movable [a] where
  move v  = map (move v)
  reflectX = map reflectX
```

and so on. Using overloading in this way has a number of advantages.

- The code is much easier to read: at each point we write `move`, rather than `movePoint`, and so on.
- We can reuse definitions; the instance declaration for `Movable [a]` makes lists of any sort of movable object movable themselves. This includes lists of points and lists of figures. Without overloading we would not be able to achieve this.

Named objects

Many forms of data contain some sort of name, a `String` which identifies the object in question. What do we expect to be able to do with a value of such a type?

- We should be able to identify the name of a value, and
- we ought to be able to give a new name to a value.

These operations are embodied in the `Named` class:

```
class Named a where
  lookName :: a -> String
  giveName :: String -> a -> a
```

and an example of Named types is given by

```
data Name a = Pair a String
```

the one-constructor type whose two components are of type a and String. The instance declaration for this type is

```
instance Named (Name a) where                          (1)
  lookName (Pair obj nm) = nm
  giveName nm (Pair obj _) = (Pair obj nm)
```

Putting together classes

An important aspect of object-oriented software development is the way in which one class can be built upon another, reusing the operations of the original class on the subclass. In this section we explore how to combine the Movable and Named classes, to give objects which are both movable and named. The section is rather more advanced, and can be omitted on first reading.

Suppose we are to add names to our movable objects – how might this be done? We examine one approach in the text, and another in the exercises.

Our approach is to build the type Name a where elements of type a are movable, that is Movable a holds. We then want to establish that the type Name a is in both the classes Movable and Named. We have shown the latter for *any* type a already in (1) above, so we concentrate on the former.

The crucial insight is that the naming is independent of the named type; any operation on the type can be **lifted** to work over named types thus:

```
mapName :: (a -> b) -> Name a -> Name b

mapName f (Pair obj nm) = Pair (f obj) nm
```

We can then argue that all the operations of the Movable class can be lifted.

```
instance Movable a => Movable (Name a) where            (2)
  move v   = mapName (move v)
  reflectX = mapName reflectX
  reflectY = mapName reflectY
```

Now we already know that Named (Name a) by (1) above, so if we define a class combining these attributes

```
class (Movable b, Named b) => NamedMovable b           (3)
```

we can declare the instance

```
instance Movable a => NamedMovable (Name a)
```

This last instance is established by showing that the two constraints of (3) hold when b is replaced by Name a, but this is exactly what (1) and (2) say given the constraint Movable a.

```
data Name a = Pair a String

exam1 = Pair (Point 0.0 0.0) "Dweezil"

instance Named (Name a) where                                    (1)
  lookName (Pair obj nm) = nm
  giveName nm (Pair obj _) = (Pair obj nm)

mapName :: (a -> b) -> Name a -> Name b

mapName f (Pair obj nm) = Pair (f obj) nm

instance Movable a => Movable (Name a) where                     (2)
  move v   = mapName (move v)
  reflectX = mapName reflectX
  reflectY = mapName reflectY

class (Movable b, Named b) => NamedMovable b                     (3)

instance Movable a => NamedMovable (Name a)
```

Figure 14.6   Named movable objects.

This completes the demonstration that NamedMovable (Name a) holds when we know that Movable a. It is worth realising that this demonstration is produced automatically by the Haskell system – we only need to type what is seen in Figure 14.6.

This section has begun to illustrate how classes can be used in the software development process. In particular we have shown how our movable objects can be named in a way which allows reuse of all the code to move the objects.

Exercises

14.47 A different way of combining the classes Named and Movable is to establish the instance

```
instance (Movable b,Named c) => NamedMovable (b,c)
```

This is done by giving the instances

```
instance Movable b => Movable (b,c) where ....
instance Named c   => Named (b,c) where ....
```

Complete these instance declarations.

14.48 Show that the method of the previous question can be used to combine instances of *any* two classes.

14.49 The example in the final part of this section shows how we can combine an arbitrary instance of the Movable class, a, with a *particular* instance of the Named class, String. Show how it can be used to combine an arbitrary instance of one class with a particular instance of another for *any* two classes whatever.

14.50 Extend the collection of operations for moving objects to include scaling and rotation by an arbitrary angle. This can be done by re-defining Movable or by defining a class MovablePlus over the class Movable. Which approach is preferable? Explain your answer.

14.51 Design a collection of classes to model bank accounts. These have different forms: current, deposit and so on, as well as different levels of functionality. Can you reuse the Named class here?

(14.7) Reasoning about algebraic types

Verification for algebraic types follows the example of lists, as first discussed in Chapter 8. The general pattern of structural induction over an algebraic type states that the result has to be proved for each constructor; when a constructor is recursive, we are allowed to use the corresponding induction hypotheses in making the proof. We first give some representative examples in this section, and conclude with a rather more sophisticated proof.

Trees

Structural induction over the type Tree of trees is stated as follows.

Structural induction over trees

To prove the property P(tr) for all finite tr of type Tree t we have to do two things.

Nil **case**	Prove P(Nil).
Node **case**	Prove P(Node x tr1 tr2) for all x of type t assuming that P(tr1) and P(tr2) hold already.

The advice of Chapter 8 about finding proofs can easily be carried over to the situation here. Now we give a representative example of a proof. We aim to prove for all finite trees tr that

```
map f (collapse tr) = collapse (mapTree f tr)        (map-collapse)
```

which states that if we map a function over a tree, and then collapse the result we get the same result as collapsing before mapping over the list. The functions we use are defined as follows

```
map f []     = []                                           (map.1)
map f (x:xs) = f x : map f xs                               (map.2)

mapTree f Nil = Nil                                         (mapTree.1)
mapTree f (Node x t1 t2)
   = Node (f x) (mapTree f t1) (mapTree f t2)               (mapTree.2)

collapse Nil = []                                           (collapse.1)
collapse (Node x t1 t2)
   = collapse t1 ++ [x] ++ collapse t2                      (collapse.2)
```

Base   In the Nil case, we simplify each side, giving

```
map f (collapse Nil)
   = map f []                                      by (collapse.1)
   = []                                            by (map.1)

collapse (mapTree f Nil)
   = collapse Nil                                  by (mapTree.1)
   = []                                            by (collapse.1)
```

This shows that the base case holds.

Induction   In the Node case, we have to prove:

```
map f (collapse (Node x tr1 tr2))
   = collapse (mapTree f (Node x tr1 tr2))                   (ind)
```

assuming the two induction hypotheses:

```
map f (collapse tr1) = collapse (mapTree f tr1)             (hyp.1)
map f (collapse tr2) = collapse (mapTree f tr2)             (hyp.2)
```

Looking at (ind), we can simplify the left-hand side thus

```
map f (collapse (Node x tr1 tr2))
   = map f (collapse tr1 ++ [x] ++ collapse tr2)    by (collapse.2)
   = map f (collapse tr1) ++ [f x] ++ map f (collapse tr2)
                                                    by (map++)
   = collapse (mapTree f tr1) ++ [f x] ++
     collapse (mapTree f tr2)                       by (hyp1,hyp2)
```

The final step is given by the two induction hypotheses, that the result holds for the two subtrees tr1 and tr2. The result (map++) is the theorem

```
map g (ys++zs) = map g ys ++ map g zs                       (map++)
```

discussed in Chapter 10. Examining the right-hand side now, we have

```
collapse (mapTree f (Node x tr1 tr2))
  = collapse (Node (f x) (mapTree f tr1)
                         (mapTree f tr2))          by (mapTree.2)
  = collapse (mapTree f tr1) ++ [f x] ++
    collapse (mapTree f tr2)                       by (collapse.2)
```

and this finishes the proof in the Node case. As this is the second of the two cases, the proof is complete.   ■

The Maybe type

Structural induction for the type Maybe t becomes proof by cases – because the type is not recursive, in none of the cases is there an appeal to an induction hypothesis. The rule is

Structural induction over the Maybe type

To prove the property P(x) for all defined[1] x of type Maybe t we have to do two things:

> Nothing **case**   Prove P(Nothing).
> Just **case**   Prove P(Just y) for all defined y of type t.

Our example proof is that, for all defined values x of type Maybe Int,

```
maybe 2 abs x ≥ 0
```

Proof   The proof has two cases. In the first x is replaced by Nothing:

```
maybe 2 abs Nothing
  = 2 ≥ 0
```

In the second, x is replaced by Just y for a defined y.

```
maybe 2 abs (Just y)
  = abs y ≥ 0
```

In both cases the result holds, and so the result is valid in general.   ■

Other forms of proof

We have seen that not all functions are defined by primitive recursion. The example we saw in Section 14.2 was of the function assoc, which is used to rearrange arithmetic expressions represented by the type Expr. Recall that

```
assoc (Add (Add e1 e2) e3)
  = assoc (Add e1 (Add e2 e3))                     (assoc.1)
assoc (Add e1 e2) = Add (assoc e1) (assoc e2)      (assoc.2)
assoc (Sub e1 e2) = Sub (assoc e1) (assoc e2)      (assoc.3)
assoc (Lit n)     = Lit n                          (assoc.4)
```

---

[1] When the type is not recursive, the induction principle gives a proof for all defined objects. An object of this type is defined if it is Nothing, or Just y for a defined y.

with (`assoc.1`) being the non-primitive recursive case. We would like to prove that the rearrangement does not affect the value of the expression:

```
eval (assoc ex) = eval ex                              (eval-assoc)
```

for all finite expressions ex. The induction principle for the Expr type has three cases.

Lit **case**	Prove P(`Lit n`).
Add **case**	Prove P(`Add e1 e2`), assuming P(`e1`) and P(`e2`)
Sub **case**	Prove P(`Sub e1 e2`), assuming P(`e1`) and P(`e2`)

To prove (`eval-assoc`) for all finite expressions, we have the three cases given above. The Lit and Sub cases are given, respectively, by (`assoc.4`) and (`assoc.3`), but the Add case is more subtle. For this we will prove

```
eval (assoc (Add e1 e2)) = eval (Add e1 e2)            (eval-Add)
```

by induction on the number of Adds which are left-nested at the top level of the expression e1 – recall that it was by counting these and noting that `assoc` preserves the total number of Adds overall that we proved the function would always terminate. Now, if there are no Adds at the top-level of e1, the equation (`assoc.2`) gives (`eval-Add`). Otherwise we rearrange thus:

```
eval (assoc (Add (Add f1 f2) e2)))
= eval (assoc (Add f1 (Add f2 e2)))                    by (assoc.1)
```

and since f1 contains fewer Adds at top level,

```
= eval (Add f1 (Add f2 e2))
= eval (Add (Add f1 f2) e2)                      by associativity of +
```

which gives the induction step, and therefore completes the proof. ∎

This result shows that verification is possible for functions defined in a more general way than primitive recursion.

(**Exercises**)──

14.52 Prove that the function `weather` from Section 14.1 has the same behaviour as

```
newWeather = makeHot . isSummer
```

when

```
makeHot True  = Hot
makeHot False = Cold
isSummer = (==Summer)
```

where recall that (`==Summer`) is an operator section whose effect is to test whether its argument is equal to Summer.

14.53 Is it the case that the `area` of each `Shape` from Section 14.1 is non-negative? If so, give a proof; if not, give an example which shows that it is not the case.

14.54 If we define the `size` of an `NTree` thus

```
size NilT            = 0
size (Node x t1 t2) = 1 + size t1 + size t2
```

then prove that for all finite `nTrees`, `tr`,

```
size tr < 2^(depth tr)
```

14.55 Show for all finite `NTrees` `tr` that

```
occurs tr x = length (filter (==x) (collapse tr))
```

The next two exercises refer back to the exercises of Section 14.3.

14.56 Prove that the function `twist` has the property that

```
twist . twist = id
```

14.57 Explain the principle of structural induction for the type `GTree`. Formulate and prove the equivalent of the theorem relating `map`, `mapTree` and `collapse` for this type of trees.

Summary

Algebraic types sharpen our ability to model types in our programs: we have seen in this chapter how simple, finite types like `Temp` can be defined, as well as the more complex `Either` and recursive types. Many of these recursive types are varieties of tree: we looked at numerical trees; elements of the type `Expr` can also be thought of as trees representing the underlying structure of arithmetical expressions.

The type of lists gives a guiding example for various aspects of algebraic types.

● The definition of the type is recursive and polymorphic, and many polymorphic higher-order functions can be defined over lists – this carries over to the various types of tree and the error type, `Maybe`, for example.

● There is a simple principle for reasoning over lists, structural induction, which is the model for structural induction over algebraic types.

The chapter also gives guidelines for defining algebraic types. The definition can be given in three parts: first the type name is identified, then the constructors are named, and finally their component types are specified. As in other aspects of program development, this separation of concerns assists the system developer to produce simple and correct solutions.

Having introduced algebraic data types we are able to give more substantial examples of classes and their instances. We can see that the overloading that classes bring makes code both easier to read and more amenable to reuse; we can see in particular how software can be extended in a way that requires little modification to the code.

In the chapters to come, algebraic types will be an integral part of the systems we develop, and indeed in the next case study we exhibit various aspects of these types. We shall also explore a different approach to types: abstract data types, and see how this approach complements and contrasts with the use of algebraic data types.

Chapter 15

Case study: Huffman codes

....

We use the case study in this chapter as a vehicle to illustrate many of the features of the previous chapters – polymorphism, algebraic types and program design – and to illustrate the **module system** of Haskell, which is discussed first.

15.1 Modules in Haskell

As we first saw in Section 2.4, a module consists of a number of definitions (of types, functions and so on), with a clearly defined **interface** stating what the module **exports** to other modules which use or **import** it.

Using modules to structure a large program has a number of advantages.

● Parts of the system can be built separately from each other. Suppose we want to monitor traffic on a network: one module might produce the statistics, while another displays them in a suitable form. If we agree which statistics are to be presented (their type etc.), that is we agree the interface, then development of the two parts of the system can go on independently.

● Parts of a system can be compiled separately; this is a great advantage for a system of any complexity.

● Libraries of components can be reused, by importing the appropriate modules containing them.

In the definition of Haskell, there is no identification between modules and files. Nonetheless, we choose here to write one module per file.

Now we look at the details of Haskell modules, before giving our example which exhibits the system in action.

Module headers

Each module is named, so an example named `Ant` might be

```
module Ant where

data Ants  = ...
anteater x = ...
```

Note that the definitions all begin in the column under the keyword `module`; it is safest to make this the leftmost column of the file, or in the case of a literate script, one tab-stop in from the leftmost column.

Our convention for file names is that a module `Ant` resides in the Haskell file `Ant.hs` or `Ant.lhs`.

Importing a module

The basic operation on modules is to `import` one into another, so in defining `Bee` we might say

```
module Bee where

import Ant

beeKeeper = ...
```

This means that the **visible** definitions from `Ant` can be used in `Bee`. By default the visible definitions in a module are those which appear in the module itself. If we define

```
module Cow where

import Bee
```

the definitions of `Ants` and `anteater` will not be visible in `Cow`. They can be made visible either by importing `Ant` explicitly, or by using the export controls discussed below to modify exactly what is exported from `Bee`.

The main module

Each system of modules should contain a top-level module called Main, which gives a definition to the name main. In a compiled system, this is the expression which is evaluated when the compiled code is executed; in an interpreter like Hugs, it is of less significance. Note that a module with no explicit name is treated as Main.

Export controls

As we explained when import was introduced, the default is that all top-level definitions of a module are exported.

- This may be too much: we might wish not to export some auxiliary functions, such as the shunt function below

```
reverse :: [a] -> [a]
reverse = shunt []

shunt :: [a] -> [a] -> [a]
shunt ys []     = ys
shunt ys (x:xs) = shunt (x:ys) xs
```

  since its only role is in defining the reverse function.

- On the other hand, it might be too little: we perhaps want to export some of the definitions we imported from other modules. The modules Ant, Bee and Cow above provide an example of this.

We can control what is exported by following the name of the module with a list of what is to be exported. For instance, we say in the case of Bee

```
module Bee ( beeKeeper, Ants(..), anteater ) where ...
```

The list contains names of defined objects, such as beeKeeper, and also data types like Ants. In the latter case we follow the type name with (..) to indicate that the constructors of the type are exported with the type itself; if this is omitted, then the type acts like an **abstract data type**, which we investigate further in the next chapter. The (..) is not necessary for a type definition.

Such a list works on a definition-by-definition basis; we can also state that all the definitions in a module are to be exported, as in

```
module Bee ( beeKeeper, module Ant ) where ...
```

or equivalently

```
module Bee ( module Bee , module Ant ) where ...
```

where preceding the name of a module by the keyword module is shorthand for all the names defined within the module. The simple header

```
module Fish where
```

is therefore equivalent to

```
module Fish ( module Fish ) where
```

Import controls

We can control how objects are to be imported, just as we can control their export. We do this by following the `import` statement with a list of objects, types or classes. For instance, if we choose not to import `anteater` from `Ant` we can write

```
import Ant ( Ants(..) )
```

stating that we want just the type `Ants`; we can alternatively say which names we wish to *hide*:

```
import Ant hiding ( anteater )
```

Suppose that in our module we have a definition of `bear`, and also there is an object named `bear` in the module `Ant`. How can we gain access to *both* definitions? The answer is that we use the **qualified** name `Ant.bear` for the imported object, reserving `bear` for the locally defined one. A qualified name is built from the name of a module and the name of an object in that module, separated by a full stop. Note that there should be *no* white space between the '`.`' and the two names, so as to avoid confusion with the composition operator. To use qualified names we should make the import thus:

```
import qualified Ant
```

In the qualified case we can also state which particular items are to be imported or hidden, just as in the unqualified case above. It is possible to use a local name for an imported module, as in

```
import Insect as Ant
```

which gives the local name `Insect` to the imported module `Ant`.

The standard prelude

The standard prelude, `Prelude.hs`, is implicitly imported into every module. If we wish we can modify this import, perhaps `hiding` one or more bindings thus

```
module Eagle where
```

```
import Prelude hiding (words)
```

so that we can give our own definition of the name `words`. If we import `Eagle` into another module, this module will also have explicitly to hide the import of `words` from the prelude if conflicting definitions are to be avoided, and so we see that a re-definition of a prelude function cannot be done 'invisibly', as it were.

If we also wish to have access to the original definition of `words` we can make a qualified import of the prelude,

```
import qualified Prelude
```

and use the original `words` by writing its qualified name `Prelude.words`.

Further details

Further information about the Haskell module system can be found in the language report (Peyton Jones and Hughes 1998); note that some of the details will be different in particular implementations.

Exercises

15.1 Can you get the effect of export controls using `import`? Can you get the effect of the qualifications of `import` using export controls? Discuss why both directives are included in the language.

15.2 Explain why you think it is the default that `imported` definitions are not themselves exported.

15.3 It is proposed to add the following option to the `module` export control and the `import` statement. If the item `-module Dog` appears, then none of the definitions in the module `Dog` is exported or imported. Discuss the advantages and disadvantages of this proposal. How would you achieve the effect of this feature in the existing Haskell module system?

(15.2) Modular design

Any computer system which is used seriously will be modified during its lifetime, either by the person or team who wrote it, or more likely by others. For this reason, all systems should be designed with *change* in mind.

We mentioned this earlier when we said that systems should be **documented**, with types given to all top-level definitions, and comments accompanying each script and substantial definition. Another useful form of description is to link each definition with proofs which concern it; if we know some of the logical properties of a function, we have a more solid conception of its purpose.

Documentation makes a script easier to understand, and therefore change, but we can give **structure** to a collection of definitions if they are split among modules or scripts, each script concerning a separate part of the overall system. The directives which link the files tell us how the parts of the system fit together. If we want to modify a particular part of a system, we should therefore be able to modify a single module (at least initially), rather than starting by modifying the whole of the system as a single unit.

How should we begin to design a system as a collection of modules? The pieces of advice which follow are aimed to make modification as straightforward as possible.

- Each module should have a **clearly identified role**.

- Each module should do **one** thing only. If a module has two separate purposes, these should be split between two separate modules. The chance of a change to one affecting the other is thereby reduced.

- Each part of the system should be performed by one module: each module should do one thing completely; it should be self-contained, in other words. If performing one part of the whole is split between two modules, then either their code should be merged, or there should be a module defined with the single purpose of bringing the two components together.

- Each module should export only what is necessary. It is then clearer what the effect of an import is: precisely the functions which are needed are imported. This process is often called **information hiding** in software engineering, which is itself the general study of principles for programming in the large.

- Modules should be **small**. As a rule of thumb, no module should be larger than can be printed on two or three sides of paper.

We have also mentioned design for **reuse**, particularly in the context of polymorphic types and higher-order functions. The module will be the unit of reuse, and a library will be accessed by means of an import statement. Similar principles apply to the design of libraries. Each library should have a clearly defined purpose, like implementing a type together with basic operations over the type. In addition, we can say that

- on including a general-purpose module, it is possible to suppress the definitions which are not used;

- a qualified import can be used to avoid the name-clashes which can often occur: despite the (infinite) choice of names for functions, in practice we tend to choose from a very small subset!

The advice here might seem dry – what has been said is illustrated in the case study which follows. In the next chapter we will return to the idea of information hiding when we meet abstract data types. In the remainder of this chapter we examine the case study of Huffman coding, the foundations of which we explore now.

(15.3) Coding and decoding

Electronic messages of various kinds are sent between machines and people by the billion each day. Such messages are usually sent as sequences of binary 'bits'. For the transmission to be swift, the messages need to be coded as efficiently as possible. The area we explore here is how to build codes – translations of characters into sequences of bits – which produce messages as compact as possible.

Trees can be used to code and decode messages. Consider as an example the tree

We can see this as giving codes for the letters a, b and t by looking at the **routes** taken to reach the letters. For example, to get to b, we go *right* at the top node, and *left* at the next:

which gives b the code RL. Similarly, L codes a, and RR the letter t.

The codes given by trees are **prefix codes**; in these codes no code for a letter is the start (or prefix) of the code for another. This is because no route to a leaf of the tree can be the start of the route to another leaf. For more information about Huffman codes and a wealth of general material on algorithms, see Cormen, Leiserson and Rivest (1990).

A message is also **decoded** using the tree. Consider the message RLLRRRRLRR. To decode we follow the route through the tree given, moving right then left, to give the letter b,

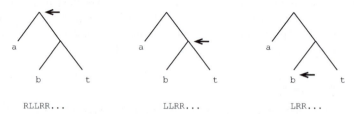

where we have shown under each tree the sequence of bits remaining to be decoded. Continuing again from the top, we have the codes for a then t,

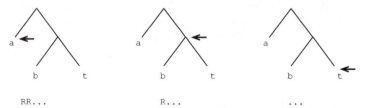

so the decoded message begins with the letters bat.

In full, the message is battat, and the coded message is ten bits long. The codes for individual characters are of different lengths; a is coded in one bit, and the other characters in two. Is this a wise choice of code in view of a message in which the letter t predominates? Using the tree

the coded message becomes RRRLLLRLL, a nine-bit coding. A Huffman code is built so that the most frequent letters have the shortest sequences of code bits, and the less frequent have more 'expensive' code sequences, justified by the rarity of their occurrence; Morse code is an example of a Huffman code in common use.

The remainder of the chapter explores the implementation of Huffman coding, illustrating the module system of Haskell.

Exercises

15.4 What is the coding of the message `battat` using the following tree?

Compare the length of the coding with the others given earlier.

15.5 Using the first coding tree, decode the coded message RLLRLRLLRR. Which tree would you expect to give the best coding of the message? Check your answer by trying the three possibilities.

15.4 Implementation – I

We now begin to implement the Huffman coding and decoding, in a series of Haskell modules. The overall structure of the system we develop is illustrated at the end of the chapter in Figure 15.4.

As earlier, we first develop the types used in the system.

The types – Types.lhs

The codes are sequences of bits, so we define

```
data Bit   =  L | R deriving (Eq,Show)
type HCode = [Bit]
```

and in the translation we will convert the Huffman tree to a table for ease of coding.

```
type Table = [ (Char,HCode) ]
```

The Huffman trees themselves carry characters at the leaves. We shall see presently that during their formation we also use information about the frequency with which each character appears; hence the inclusion of integers both at the leaves and at the internal nodes.

```
data Tree = Leaf Char Int |
            Node Int Tree Tree
```

The file containing the module is illustrated in Figure 15.1. The name of the file, with an indication of its purpose, is listed at the start of the file; each of the definitions is preceded by a comment as to its purpose.

```
Types.lhs
```

The types used in the Huffman coding example.

The interface to the module Types is written out
explicitly here, after the module name.

```
>       module Types ( Tree(Leaf,Node),
>                      Bit(L,R),
>                      HCode ,
>                      Table ) where
```

Trees to represent the relative frequencies of characters
and therefore the Huffman codes.

```
>       data Tree = Leaf Char Int |
>                   Node Int Tree Tree
```

The types of bits, Huffman codes and tables of Huffman codes.

```
>       data Bit = L | R deriving (Eq,Show)

>       type HCode = [Bit]

>       type Table = [ (Char,HCode) ]
```

Figure 15.1 The file Types.lhs.

Note that we have given a full description of what is exported by the module, by
listing the items after the module name. For the data types which are exported, Tree
and Bit, the constructors are exported explicitly; this could also be done by following
their names with (..). This interface information could have been omitted, but we
include it here as useful documentation of the interface to the module.

Coding and decoding – Coding.lhs

This module uses the types in Types.lhs, and so imports them with

import Types (Tree(Leaf,Node), Bit(L,R), HCode, Table)

We have chosen to list the names imported here; the statement import Types would
have the same effect, but would lose the extra documentation.

The purpose of the module is to define functions to code and decode messages: we
export only these, and not the auxiliary function(s) which may be used in their definition.
Our module therefore begins

module Coding (codeMessage , decodeMessage)

To code a message according to a table of codes, we look up each character in the table, and concatenate the results.

```
codeMessage :: Table -> [Char] -> HCode

codeMessage tbl = concat . map (lookupTable tbl)
```

It is interesting to see that the function level definition here gives an exact implementation of the description which precedes it; using partial application and function composition has made the definition clearer.

We now define `lookupTable`, which is a standard function to look up the value corresponding to a 'key' in a table.

```
lookupTable :: Table -> Char -> HCode

lookupTable [] c = error "lookupTable"
lookupTable ((ch,n):tb) c
  | ch==c       = n
  | otherwise   = lookupTable tb c
```

Because of the `module` statement, this definition is not exported.

To decode a message, which is a sequence of bits, that is an element of HCode, we use a `Tree`.

```
decodeMessage :: Tree -> HCode -> [Char]
```

We saw in Section 15.3 that decoding according to the tree `tr` has two main cases.

● If we are at an internal `Node`, we choose the sub-tree dictated by the first bit of the code.

● If at a leaf, we read off the character found, and then begin to decode the remainder of the code at the top of the tree `tr`.

When the code is exhausted, so is the decoded message.

```
decodeMessage tr
  = decodeByt tr
    where
    decodeByt (Node n t1 t2) (L:rest)
      = decodeByt t1 rest
    decodeByt (Node n t1 t2) (R:rest)
      = decodeByt t2 rest
    decodeByt (Leaf c n) rest
      = c : decodeByt tr rest
    decodeByt t [] = []
```

The locally defined function is called `decodeByt` because it decodes 'by t'.

The first coding tree and example message of Section 15.3 can be given by

```
exam1 = Node 0 (Leaf 'a' 0)
                (Node 0 (Leaf 'b' 0) (Leaf 't' 0))
mess1 = [R,L,L,R,R,R,R,L,R,R]
```

and decoding of this message begins thus

```
decodeMessage exam1 mess1
⤳   decodeByt exam1 mess1
⤳   decodeByt exam1 [R,L,L,R,R,R,R,L,R,R]
⤳   decodeByt (Node 0 (Leaf 'b' 0) (Leaf 't' 0))
                                    [L,L,R,R,R,R,L,R,R]
⤳   decodeByt (Leaf 'b' 0) [L,R,R,R,R,L,R,R]
⤳   'b' : decodeByt exam1 [L,R,R,R,R,L,R,R]
⤳   'b' : decodeByt (Leaf 'a' 0) [R,R,R,R,L,R,R]
⤳   'b' : 'a' : decodeByt exam1 [R,R,R,R,L,R,R]
```

Before looking at the implementation any further, we look at how to construct the Huffman coding tree, given a text.

Exercises

15.6 Complete the calculation of decodeMessage exam1 mess1 begun above.

15.7 With the table

```
table1 = [ ('a',[L]) , ('b',[R,L]) , ('t',[R,R]) ]
```

give a calculation of

```
codeMessage table1 "battab"
```

15.5 Building Huffman trees

Given a text, such as "battat", how do we find the tree giving the optimal code for the text? We explain it in a number of stages following Section 17.3 of Cormen, Leiserson and Rivest (1990).

● We first find the frequencies of the individual letters, in this case giving

```
[('b',1),('a',2),('t',3)]
```

● The main idea of the translation is to build the tree by taking the two characters occurring least frequently, and making a *single* character (or *tree*) of them. This process is repeated until a single tree results; the steps which follow give this process in more detail.

● Each of ('b',1), ... is turned into a tree, giving the list of trees

```
[ Leaf 'b' 1 , Leaf 'a' 2 , Leaf 't' 3 ]
```

which is sorted into frequency order.

● We then begin to *amalgamate together* trees: we take the two trees of lowest frequency, put them together, and insert the result in the appropriate place to preserve the frequency order.

```
[ Node 3 (Leaf 'b' 1) (Leaf 'a' 2) , Leaf 't' 3 ]
```

● This process is repeated, until a single tree results

```
Node 6 (Node 3 (Leaf 'b' 1) (Leaf 'a' 2)) (Leaf 't' 3)
```

which is pictured thus

● This tree can then be turned into a Table

```
[ ('b',[L,L]) , ('a',[L,R]) , ('t',[R]) ]
```

We now look at how the system is implemented in Haskell.

15.6 Design

Implementing the system will involve us in designing various modules to perform the stages given above. We start by deciding what the modules will be and the functions that they will implement. This is the equivalent at the larger scale of **divide and conquer**; we separate the problem into manageable portions, which can be solved separately, and which are put together using the import and module statements. We design these **interfaces** before implementing the functions.

The three stages of conversion are summarized in Figure 15.2, which shows the module directives of the three component files. We have added as comments the types of objects to be exported, so that these directives contain enough information for the exported functions in the files to be used without knowing *how* they are defined.

In fact the component functions frequency and makeTree will never be used separately, and so we compose them in the module MakeCode.lhs when bringing the three files together. This is given in Figure 15.3.

Our next task is to implement each module in full and we turn to that now.

```
        Frequency.lhs

>       module Frequency ( frequency )  -- [Char] -> [(Char,Int)]


        MakeTree.lhs


>       module MakeTree ( makeTree )    -- [(Char,Int)] -> Tree
>       import Types


        CodeTable.lhs

>       module CodeTable ( codeTable )  -- Tree -> Table
>       import Types
```

Figure 15.2 Module directives for Huffman tree formation.

```
        MakeCode.lhs

        Huffman coding in Haskell.

>       module MakeCode ( codes, codeTable ) where

>       import Types
>       import Frequency ( frequency )
>       import MakeTree   ( makeTree )
>       import CodeTable ( codeTable )
```

Putting together frequency calculation and tree conversion

```
>       codes :: [Char] -> Tree

>       codes = makeTree . frequency
```

Figure 15.3 The module MakeCode.lhs.

15.7 Implementation – II

In this section we discuss in turn the three implementation modules.

Counting characters — Frequency.lhs

The aim of the function frequency is to take a text such as "battat" to a list of characters, in increasing frequency of occurrence, [('b',1),('a',2),('t',3)]. We do this in three stages:

● First we pair each character with the count of 1, giving

    [('b',1),('a',1),('t',1),('t',1),('a',1),('t',1)]

● Next, we sort the list on the characters, bringing together the counts of equal characters.

    [('a',2),('b',1),('t',3)]

● Finally, we sort the list into increasing frequency order, to give the list above.

The function uses two different sorts – one on character, one on frequency – to achieve its result. Is there any way we can define a single sorting function to perform both sorts?

We can give a general merge sort function, which works by **merging**, in order, the results of sorting the front and rear halves of the list.

```
mergeSort :: ([a]->[a]->[a]) -> [a] -> [a]

mergeSort merge xs
  | length xs < 2  = xs
  | otherwise
      = merge (mergeSort merge first)
              (mergeSort merge second)
        where
        first  = take half xs
        second = drop half xs
        half   = (length xs) `div` 2
```

The first argument to mergeSort is the merging function, which takes two sorted lists and merges their contents in order. It is by making this operation a *parameter* that the mergeSort function becomes reusable.

In sorting the characters, we amalgamate entries for the same character

```
alphaMerge :: [(Char,Int)] -> [(Char,Int)] -> [(Char,Int)]

alphaMerge xs [] = xs
alphaMerge [] ys = ys
```

```
alphaMerge ((p,n):xs) ((q,m):ys)
  | (p==q)      = (p,n+m) : alphaMerge xs ys
  | (p<q)       = (p,n) : alphaMerge xs ((q,m):ys)
  | otherwise   = (q,m) : alphaMerge ((p,n):xs) ys
```

while when sorting on frequency we compare frequencies; when two pairs have the same frequency, we order according to the character ordering.

```
freqMerge :: [(Char,Int)] -> [(Char,Int)] -> [(Char,Int)]
```

```
freqMerge xs [] = xs
freqMerge [] ys = ys
freqMerge ((p,n):xs) ((q,m):ys)
  | (n<m || (n==m && p<q))
    = (p,n) : freqMerge xs ((q,m):ys)
  | otherwise
    = (q,m) : freqMerge ((p,n):xs) ys
```

We can now give the top-level definition of frequency

```
frequency :: [Char] -> [ (Char,Int) ]
```

```
frequency
  = mergeSort freqMerge . mergeSort alphaMerge . map start
    where
    start ch = (ch,1)
```

which we can see is a direct combination of the three stages listed in the informal description of the algorithm.

Note that of all the functions defined in this module, only frequency is exported.

Making the Huffman tree – MakeTree.lhs

We have two stages in making a Huffman tree from a list of characters with their frequencies.

```
makeTree :: [ (Char,Int) ] -> Tree
makeTree = makeCodes . toTreeList
```

where

```
toTreeList :: [ (Char,Int) ] -> [Tree]
makeCodes  :: [Tree] -> Tree
```

The function toTreeList converts each character-number pair into a tree, thus

```
toTreeList = map (uncurry Leaf)
```

where note that we use the prelude function uncurry to make an uncurried version of the constructor function Leaf.

The function makeCodes amalgamates trees successively into a single tree

```
makeCodes [t] = t
makeCodes ts  = makeCodes (amalgamate ts)
```

How are trees amalgamated? We have to pair together the first two trees in the list (since the list is kept in ascending order of frequency) and then insert the result in the list preserving the frequency order. Working top-down, we have

```
amalgamate :: [ Tree ] -> [ Tree ]
```

```
amalgamate (t1:t2:ts) = insTree (pair t1 t2) ts
```

When we pair two trees, we need to combine their frequency counts, so

```
pair :: Tree -> Tree -> Tree
```

```
pair t1 t2 = Node (v1+v2) t1 t2
             where
             v1 = value t1
             v2 = value t2
```

where the value of a tree is given by

```
value :: Tree -> Int
```

```
value (Leaf _ n)   = n
value (Node n _ _) = n
```

The definition of insTree, which is similar to that used in an insertion sort, is left as an exercise. Again, the definition of the exported function uses various others whose definitions are not visible to the 'outside world'.

The code table – CodeTable.lhs

Here we give the function codeTable which takes a Huffman tree into a code table. In converting the tree Node n t1 t2 we have to convert t1, adding L at the front of the code, and t2 with R at the head. We therefore write the more general conversion function

```
convert :: HCode -> Tree -> Table
```

whose first argument is the 'path so far' into the tree. The definition is

```
convert cd (Leaf c n)
     = [(c,cd)]
convert cd (Node n t1 t2)
     = (convert (cd++[L]) t1) ++ (convert (cd++[R]) t2)
```

The codeTable function is given by starting the conversion with an empty code string

```
codeTable :: Tree -> Table
codeTable = convert []
```

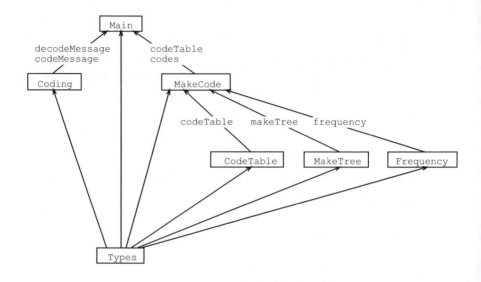

Figure 15.4   The modules of the Huffman coding system.

Consider the calculation of

```
codeTable (Node 6 (Node 3 (Leaf 'b' 1) (Leaf 'a' 2))
                  (Leaf 't' 3))
⤳   convert [] (Node 6 (Node 3 (Leaf 'b' 1) (Leaf 'a' 2))
                        (Leaf 't' 3))
⤳   convert [L] (Node 3 (Leaf 'b' 1) (Leaf 'a' 2)) ++
    convert [R] (Leaf 't' 3)
⤳   convert [L,L] (Leaf 'b' 1) ++
    convert [L,R] (Leaf 'a' 2) ++
    [ ('t',[R]) ]
⤳   [ ('b',[L,L]) , ('a',[L,R]) , ('t',[R]) ]
```

The top-level file – Main.lhs

We can now pull all the parts of the system together into a top-level file.

```
module Main (main) where

import Types    ( Tree(Leaf,Node), Bit(L,R), HCode , Table )
import Coding   ( codeMessage , decodeMessage )
import MakeCode ( codes, codeTable )
```

In this file we can include representative examples, using the major functions listed in the import statements.

The structure of the system is given in Figure 15.4. Modules are represented by boxes, and an arrow from A to B indicates that A.lhs is imported into B.lhs. An arrow is marked to indicate the functions exported by the included module, so that, for example, `codes` and `codeTable` are exported from `MakeCode.lhs` to `Main.lhs`.

If this coding system were to be used as a component of a larger system, a `module` directive could be used to control which of the four functions and the types are exported, after the module had been renamed. It is important to realize that the types will need to be exported (or be included in the file including `Main.lhs`) if the functions are to be used.

Exercises

15.8 Give a definition of merge sort which uses the built-in ordering '`<=`'. What is its type?

15.9 Modifying your previous answer if necessary, give a version of merge sort which removes duplicate entries.

15.10 Give a version of merge sort which takes an ordering function as a parameter:

```
ordering :: a -> a -> Ordering
```

Explain how to implement `mergeSort freqMerge` using this version of merge sort, and discuss why you *cannot* implement `mergeSort alphaMerge` this way.

15.11 Define the `insTree` function, used in the definition of `makeTree`.

15.12 Give a calculation of

```
makeTree   [('b',2),('a',2),('t',3),('e',4)]
```

15.13 Define functions

```
showTree  :: Tree  -> String
showTable :: Table -> String
```

which give printable versions of Huffman trees and code tables. One general way of printing trees is to use indentation to indicate the structure. Schematically, this looks like

```
    left sub tree,  indented by 4 characters
value(s) at Node
    right sub tree, indented by 4 characters
```

Summary

When writing a program of any size, we need to divide up the work in a sensible way. The Haskell module system allows one script to be included in another. At the boundary, it is possible to control exactly which definitions are exported from one module and imported into another.

We gave a number of guidelines for the design of a program into its constituent modules. The most important advice is to make each module perform one clearly defined task, and for only as much information as is needed to be exported – the principle of **information hiding**. This principle is extended in the next chapter when we examine abstract data types.

The design principles were put into practice in the Huffman coding example. In particular, it was shown for the file MakeCode.lhs and its three sub-modules that design can begin with the design of modules and their **interfaces** – that is the definitions (and their types) which are exported. Thus the design process starts *before* any implementation takes place.

Chapter 16

Abstract data types

The Haskell module system allows definitions of functions and other objects to be **hidden** when one file is included in another. Those definitions hidden are only of use in defining the exported functions, and hiding them makes clearer the exact interface between the two files: only those features of the module which are needed will be visible.

This chapter shows that information hiding is equally applicable for types, giving what are known as **abstract data types**, or **ADT**s. We explain the abstract data type mechanism here, as well as providing a number of examples of ADTs, including queues, sets, relations and the fundamental types belonging to a simulation case study.

16.1 Type representations

We begin our discussion with a scenario which is intended to show both the purpose and the operation of the abstract data type mechanism.

Suppose we are to build a calculator for numerical expressions, like those given

299

```
┌─────────────────────────────────────────────────────────────┐
│                                                               │
│     USER                                                      │
│                                                               │
│     ┌───────────────────────────────────────────────────┐    │
│     │  initial :: Store                                  │    │
│     │  value   :: Store -> Var -> Int                    │    │
│     │  update  :: Store -> Var -> Int -> Store           │    │
│     └───────────────────────────────────────────────────┘    │
│                                                               │
│     IMPLEMENTOR                                               │
│                                                               │
└─────────────────────────────────────────────────────────────┘
```

Figure 16.1 The Store abstract data type.

by the Expr type of Section 14.2, but with variables included. The calculator is to provide the facility to set the values of variables, as well as for variables to form parts of expressions.

As a part of our system, we need to be able to model the current values of the variables, which we might call the **store** of the calculator. How can this be done? A number of models present themselves, including:

● a list of integer/variable pairs: [(Int,Var)]; and

● a function from variables to integers: (Var -> Int).

Both models allow us to look up and update the values of variables, as well as set a starting value for the store. These operations have types as follows.

```
initial :: Store
value   :: Store -> Var -> Int                              (StoreSig)
update  :: Store -> Var -> Int -> Store
```

but each model allows more than that: we can, for instance, reverse a list, or compose a function with others. In using the type Store we intend only to use the three operations given, but it is always possible to use the model in unintended ways.

How can we give a better model of a store? The answer is to define a type which **only** has the operations initial, value and update, so that we cannot abuse the representation. We therefore hide the information about how the type is actually implemented, and only allow the operations (StoreSig) to manipulate objects of the type.

When we provide a limited interface to a type by means of a specified set of operations we call the type an **abstract data type** (or ADT). Since the 'concrete' type itself is no longer accessible and we may only access the type by means of the operations provided, these operations give a more 'abstract' view of the type.

Figure 16.1 illustrates the situation, and suggests that as well as giving a natural representation of the type of stores, there are two other benefits of type abstraction.

● The type declarations in (StoreSig) form a clearly defined **interface**, which is called the **signature** of the ADT, between the user of the type and its implementer.

The only information that they have to agree on is the signature; once this is agreed, they can work independently. This is therefore another way of breaking a complex problem into simpler parts; another aspect of the 'divide and conquer' method.

● We can **modify** the implementation of the Store without having any effect on the user. Contrast this with the situation where the implementation is visible to the user. In particular, if the implementation is an algebraic type then any change in the implementation will mean that all definitions that use pattern matching will have to be changed. These will include not just those in the signature, but also any user-defined functions which use pattern matching.

We shall see both aspects illustrated in the sections to come; first we look at the details of the Haskell abstract data type mechanism.

(16.2) The Haskell abstract data type mechanism

When we introduced the Haskell module system in Chapter 15 we saw that there were two ways in which we could export a data type, called Data say. If we include Data(..) in the export list of the module, the type is exported with its constructors; if we include Data then the constructors are *not* exported, and so we can only operate over the type using the other operations of the signature.

In the case of the Store type, our module header would be

```
module Store ( Store, initial, value, update ) where
```

which shows that we can access the type only through the three functions mentioned. In this book we will adopt the convention that we will also include as comments in the module header the types of the exported functions, giving in the case of Store the following header.

```
module Store
  ( Store,
    initial,      -- Store
    value,        -- Store -> Var -> Int
    update        -- Store -> Var -> Int -> Store
  ) where
```

Now, the module must contain a definition of the Store type and the functions over it.

If the implementation type was a data type, then this would complete the realization of the abstract data type. However, in our running example of stores, we suggested earlier that we would use a list of pairs, [(Int,Var)], to model the type, and so we will have to define a new data type, called Store

```
data Store = Sto [ (Int,Var) ]
```

which has a single constructor which we call Sto. This is the function which converts a list into an element of the Store type; we can think of it as 'wrapping up' a list to make it into a Store.

We now have to define the functions `initial`, `value` and `update` over the `Store` type. One approach is to define the analogous functions over `[(Int,Var)]` and then to adapt those. We can say

```
init :: [(Int,Var)]
init = []

val :: [(Int,Var)] -> Var -> Int
val [] v         = 0
val ((n,w):sto) v
  | v==w         = n
  | otherwise    = val sto v

upd :: [(Int,Var)] -> Var -> Int -> [(Int,Var)]
upd sto v n   = (n,v):sto
```

The initial store, `init`, is represented by an empty list; the value of `v` is looked up by finding the first pair `(n,v)` in the list, and the store is updated by adding a new `(Int,Var)` at the front of the list.

These functions then have to be converted to work over the type `Store`, so that arguments and results are of the form `Sto xs` with `xs::[(Int,Var)]`. The definitions become

```
initial :: Store
initial = Sto []

value   :: Store -> Var -> Int
value (Sto []) v           = 0
value (Sto ((n,w):sto)) v
  | v==w                  = n
  | otherwise             = value (Sto sto) v

update  :: Store -> Var -> Int -> Store
update (Sto sto) v n = Sto ((n,v):sto)
```

where we can see that the pattern of the definitions is similar, except that we have to 'unwrap' arguments of the form `(Sto sto)` on the left-hand side, and 'wrap up' results using `Sto` on the right-hand side. We look at a general mechanism for 'wrapping up' functions in the example of the Set ADT in Section 16.8.

What happens if we try to break the abstraction barrier and deal with a `Store` as having the form `(Sto xs)`? On typing

```
initial == Sto []
```

in a module importing `Store` we get the type error message

```
ERROR: Undefined constructor function "Sto"
```

The fact that `initial` is indeed implemented as `Sto []` is irrelevant, since the implementation is not visible outside the `Store` module.

The `newtype` construction

In fact in this case rather than using a data type we will define

```
newtype Store = Sto [ (Int,Var) ]
```

which has the same effect as declaring a data type with one unary constructor but which is implemented in a more efficient fashion.

Another possible way of implementing the type would be to say

```
newtype Store = Store [ (Int,Var) ]
```

using the same name for the type and its constructor. Unfortunately, at the time of writing, this has the effect in Hugs of making the constructor visible, despite the instruction to the contrary in the module header. The same remarks apply to data declarations of this form in Hugs.

Type classes: showing values and equality

We can declare types as belonging to particular type classes such as Show and Eq, and this applies equally well to abstract data types. In the case of Store we can say

```
instance Eq Store where
  (Sto sto1) == (Sto sto2)  = (sto1 == sto2)

instance Show Store where
  show n (Sto sto)      = show n sto
```

Note, however, that once declared, these instances **cannot be hidden**, so that even though they are not named in the export list, the functions over Store which are defined by means of these instance declarations will be available whenever the module Store is imported. Of course, we can choose *not* to declare these instances, and so not to provide an equality or a show function over Stores.

Stores as functions

A different implementation of Store is given by the type of functions from variables to integers.

```
newtype Store = Sto (Var -> Int)

initial :: Store
initial = Sto (\v -> 0)

value :: Store -> Var -> Int
value (Sto sto) v = sto v

update  :: Store -> Var -> Int -> Store
update (Sto sto) v n
  = Sto (\w -> if v==w then n else sto w)
```

Under this implementation,

- the `initial` store maps every variable to 0;
- to look up a `value` of a variable v the store function `sto` is applied to v, and
- in the case of an `update`, a function returned is identical to `sto` except on the variable whose value is changed.

Exercises

16.1 Give an implementation of `Store` using lists whose entries are ordered according to the variable names. Discuss why this might be preferable to the original list implementation, and also its disadvantages, if any.

16.2 For the implementation of `Store` as a list type `[(Int,Var)]`, give a definition of equality which equates any two stores which give the same values to each variable. Can this operation be defined for the second implementation? If not, give a modification of the implementation which allows it to be defined.

16.3 In this question you should use the type `Maybe a`. Suppose it is an error to look up the `value` of a variable which does not have a value in the given store. Explain how you would modify both the signature of `Store` and the two implementations.

16.4 Rather than giving an error when looking up a variable which does not have a value in the particular store, extend the signature to provide a test of whether a variable has a value in a given store, and explain how you would modify the two implementations to define the test.

16.5 Suppose you are to implement a fourth operation over `Store`

```
setAll :: Int -> Store
```

so that `setAll n` is the store where every variable has the value n. Can you do this for both the example implementations? Show how if you can, and explain why, if not.

16.6 Design an ADT for the library database, first examined in Chapter 5.

16.3 Queues

A queue is a 'first in, first out' structure. If first `Flo` and then `Eddie` joins an initially empty queue, the first person to leave will be `Flo`. As an abstract data type, we expect to be able to add items and remove items as well as there being an empty queue.

```
module Queue
  ( Queue ,
    emptyQ ,        --   Queue a
    isEmptyQ ,      --   Queue a -> Bool
```

```
      addQ ,          -- a -> Queue a -> Queue a
      remQ            -- Queue a -> ( a , Queue a )
    ) where
```

The function `remQ` returns a pair – the item removed together with the part of the queue that remains – if there are any items in the queue. If not, the standard function `error` is called.

A list can be used to model a queue: we add to the end of the list, and remove from the front, giving

```
newtype Queue a = Qu [a]

emptyQ = Qu []

isEmptyQ (Qu []) = True
isEmptyQ _        = False

addQ x (Qu xs) = Qu (xs++[x])

remQ q@(Qu xs)
  | not (isEmptyQ q)    = (head xs , Qu (tail xs))
  | otherwise           = error "remQ"
```

The definition of `remQ` uses an aspect of pattern matching which we have not seen so far. We use the pattern `q@(Qu xs)`, where we can read '@' as 'as', to match the input. The variable `q` matches the whole input, while it is also matched against `Qu xs`, so that `xs` gives us access to the list from which it is built. This means that we can refer directly to the whole input *and* to its components in the definition. Without this, the alternative would be

```
remQ (Qu xs)
  | not (isEmptyQ (Qu xs))   = (head xs , Qu (tail xs))
  | otherwise                = error "remQ"
```

in which we have to rebuild the original queue from `xs`.

Rather than adding elements at the end of the list, we can add them at the beginning. This leaves `emptyQ` and `isEmptyQ` unchanged, and gives

```
addQ x (Qu xs) = Qu (x:xs)

remQ q@(Qu xs)
  | not (isEmptyQ q)    = (last xs , Qu (init xs))
  | otherwise           = error "remQ"
```

where the built-in functions `last` and `init` take the last element and the remainder of a list.

Although we have not said exactly how to calculate the cost of evaluation (a topic we take up in Chapter 19), we can see that in each implementation one of the operations is 'cheap' and the other is 'expensive'. The 'cheap' functions – `remQ` in the first

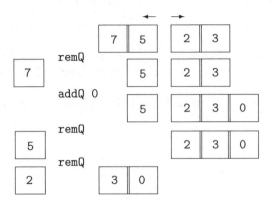

Figure 16.2   A two-list queue in action.

implementation and addQ in the second – can be evaluated in one step, while in both cases the 'expensive' function will have to run along a list xs one step per element, and so will be costly if the list is long.

Is there any way of making both operations 'cheap'? The idea is to make the queue out of *two* lists, so that both adding and removing an element can take place at the head of a list. The process is illustrated in Figure 16.2, which represents a number of queues. Initially the queue containing the elements 7, 5, 2 and 3 is shown. Subsequently we see the effect of removing an element, adding the element 0, and removing two further elements. In each case the queue is represented by two lists, where the left-hand list grows to the left, and the right-hand to the right.

The function remQ removes elements from the head of the left-hand list, and addQ adds elements to the head of the right. This works until the left-hand list is empty, when the elements of the right-hand queue have to be transferred to the left (the picture might be misleading here: remember that the two lists grow in opposite directions).

This case in which we have to transfer elements is expensive, as we have to run along a list to reverse it, but we would not in general expect to perform this every time we remove an element from the queue. The Haskell implementation follows now.

```
data Queue a = Qu [a] [a]

emptyQ = Qu [] []

isEmptyQ (Qu [] []) = True
isEmptyQ _          = False

addQ x (Qu xs ys) = Qu xs (x:ys)
```

```
remQ (Qu (x:xs) ys)   = (x , Qu xs ys)
remQ (Qu [] (y:ys))   = remQ (Qu (reverse (y:ys)) [])
remQ (Qu [] [])       = error "remQ"
```

As we commented for the Store types, the behaviour of this implementation will be indistinguishable from the first two, as far as the operations of the abstract data type are concerned. On the other hand, the implementation will be substantially more efficient than the single list implementations, as we explained above. A thorough examination of recent work on the efficient implementation of data structures in functional languages can be found in Okasaki (1998).

Exercises

16.7 Give calculations of

```
"abcde" ++ "f"
init "abcdef"
last "abcdef"
```

where

```
init x = take (length x-1) x
last x = x !! (length x-1)
```

16.8 Explain the behaviour of the three queue models if you are asked to perform the following sequence of queue operations: add 2, add 1, remove item, add 3, remove item, add 1, add 4, remove item, remove item.

16.9 A double-ended queue, or deque, allows elements to be added or removed from either end of the structure. Give a signature for the ADT Deque a, and give two different implementations of the deque type.

16.10 A unique queue can contain only one occurrence of each entry (the one to arrive earliest). Give a signature for the ADT of these queues, and an implementation of the ADT.

16.11 Each element of a priority queue has a numerical priority. When an element is removed, it will be of the highest priority in the queue. If there is more than one of these, the earliest to arrive is chosen. Give a signature and implementation of the ADT of priority queues.

16.12 [Harder] Examine how priority queues could be used to implement the Huffman coding system in Chapter 15.

(16.4) Design

This section examines the design of Haskell abstract data types, and how the presence of this mechanism affects design in general.

General principles

In building a system, the choice of types is fundamental, and affects the subsequent design and implementation profoundly. If we use abstract data types at an early stage we hope to find 'natural' representations of the types occurring in the problem. Designing the abstract data types is a three-stage process.

- First we need to identify and **name** the types in the system.
- Next, we should give an **informal description** of what is expected from each type.
- Using this description we can then move to writing the **signature** of each abstract data type.

How do we decide what should go in the signature? This is the $64,000 question, of course, but there are some general questions we can ask of any abstract data type signature.

- Can we create objects of the type? For instance, in the Queue a type, we have the object emptyQ, and in a type of sets, we might give a function taking an element to the 'singleton' set containing that element alone. If there are no such objects or functions, something is wrong!
- Can we check what sort of object we have? In a tree ADT we might want to check whether we have a leaf or a node, for instance.
- Can we extract the components of objects, if we so require? Can we take the head of a Queue a, say?
- Can we transform objects: can we reverse a list, perhaps, or add an item to a queue?
- Can we combine objects? We might want to be able to join together two trees, for example.
- Can we collapse objects? Can we take the sum of a numerical list, or find the size of an object, say?

Not all these questions are appropriate in every case, but the majority of operations we perform on types fall into one of these categories. All the operations in the following signature for binary trees can be so classified, for instance.

```
module Tree
  (Tree,
   nil,        -- Tree a
   isNil,      -- Tree a -> Bool
   isNode,     -- Tree a -> Bool
   leftSub,    -- Tree a -> Tree a
   rightSub,   -- Tree a -> Tree a
   treeVal,    -- Tree a -> a
   insTree,    -- Ord a => a -> Tree a -> Tree a
   delete,     -- Ord a => a -> Tree a -> Tree a
   minTree     -- Ord a => Tree a -> Maybe a
  ) where
```

Other functions might be included in the signature; in the case of `Tree a` we might want to include the `size` function. This function can be defined using the other operations.

```
size :: Tree a -> Int
size t
  | isNil t     = 0
  | otherwise   = 1 + size (leftSub t) + size (rightSub t)
```

This definition of `size` is **independent** of the implementation, and so would not have to be reimplemented if the implementation type for `Tree a` changed. This is a good reason for leaving `size` out of the signature, and this is a check we can make for any signature: are all the functions in the signature needed? We come back to this point, and the tree type, later in the chapter. Now we look at a larger-scale example.

Exercises

16.13 Are all the operations in the `Tree a` signature necessary? Identify those which can be implemented using the other operations of the signature.

16.14 Design a signature for an abstract type of library databases, as first introduced in Chapter 5.

16.15 Design a signature for an abstract type of indexes, as examined in Section 10.8.

16.5 Simulation

We first introduced the simulation example in Section 14.5, where we designed the algebraic types `Inmess` and `Outmess`. Let us suppose, for ease of exposition, that the system time is measured in minutes.

The `Inmess No` signals no arrival, while `Yes 34 12` signals the arrival of a customer at the 34th minute, who will need 12 minutes to be served.

The `Outmess Discharge 34 27 12` signals that the person arriving at time 34 waited 27 minutes before receiving their 12 minutes of service.

Our aim in this section is to design the ADTs for a simple simulation of queueing. We start by looking at a single queue. Working through the stages, we will call the type `QueueState`, and it can be described thus.

> There are two main operations on a queue. The first is to add a new item, an `Inmess`, to the queue. The second is to process the queue by a one-minute step; the effect of this is to give one minute's further processing to the item at the head of the queue (if there is such a thing). Two outcomes are possible: the item might have its processing completed, in which case an `Outmess` is generated, or further processing may be needed.

> Other items we need are an empty queue, an indication of the length of a queue and a test of whether a queue is empty.

This description leads directly to a signature declaration

```
module QueueState
  ( QueueState ,
    addMessage,       -- Inmess -> QueueState -> QueueState
    queueStep,        -- QueueState -> ( QueueState , [Outmess] )
    queueStart,       -- QueueState
    queueLength,      -- QueueState -> Int
    queueEmpty        -- QueueState -> Bool
  ) where
```

The queueStep function returns a pair: the QueueState after a step of processing, and a **list** of Outmess. A list is used, rather than a single Outmess, so that in the case of no output an empty list can be returned.

The QueueState type allows us to model a situation in which all customers are served by a single processor (or bank clerk). How can we model the case where there is more than one queue? We call this a **server** and it is to be modelled by the ServerState ADT.

A server consists of a collection of queues, which can be identified by the integers 0, 1 and so on. It is assumed that the system receives one Inmess each minute: at most one person arrives every minute, in other words.

There are three principal operations on a server. First, we should be able to add an Inmess to one of the queues. Second, a processing step of the server is given by processing each of the constituent queues by one step: this can generate a list of Outmess, as each queue can generate such a message. Finally, a step of the simulation combines a server step with allocation of the Inmess to the shortest queue in the server.

Three other operations are necessary. We have a starting server, consisting of the appropriate number of empty queues, and we should be able to identify the number of queues in a server, as well as the shortest queue it contains.

As a signature, we have

```
module ServerState
  ( ServerState ,
    addToQueue,      -- Int -> Inmess -> ServerState -> ServerState
    serverStep,      -- ServerState -> ( ServerState , [Outmess] )
    simulationStep,  -- ServerState -> Inmess -> ( ServerState ,
                                                        [Outmess] )
    serverStart,     -- ServerState
    serverSize,      -- ServerState -> Int
    shortestQueue    -- ServerState -> Int
  ) where
```

In the next section we explore how to implement these two abstract data types. It is important to realize that users of the ADTs can begin to do their programming now: all the information that they need to know is contained in the signature of the abstract data type.

───── ──

16.16 Are there redundant operations in the signatures of the ADTs `QueueState` and `ServerState`?

16.17 Design a signature for **round-robin** simulation, in which allocation of the first item is to queue 0, the second to queue 1, and so on, starting again at 0 after the final queue has had an element assigned to it.

16.6 Implementing the simulation

This section gives an implementation of the ADTs for a queue and a server. The `QueueState` is implemented from scratch, while the `ServerState` implementation builds on the `QueueState` ADT. This means that the two implementations are independent; modifying the implementation of `QueueState` has no effect on the implementation of `ServerState`.

The queue

In the previous section, we designed the interfaces for the ADT; how do we proceed with implementation? First we ought to look again at the description of the `QueueState` type. What information does this imply the type should contain?

- There has to be a **queue** of `Inmess` to be processed. This can be represented by a list, and we can take the item at the head of the list as the item currently being processed.

- We need to keep a record of the processing time given to the head item, up to the particular time represented by the state.

- In an `Outmess`, we need to give the waiting time for the particular item being processed. We know the time of arrival and the time needed for processing – if we also know the current time, we can calculate the waiting time from these three numbers.

It therefore seems sensible to define

```
data QueueState = QS Time Service [Inmess]
                     deriving (Eq, Show)
```

where the first field gives the current time, the second the service time so far for the item currently being processed, and the third the queue itself. Now we look at the operations one by one. To add a message, it is put at the end of the list of messages.

```
addMessage  :: Inmess -> QueueState -> QueueState

addMessage im (QS time serv ml) = QS time serv (ml++[im])
```

The most complicated definition is of `queueStep`. As was explained informally, there are two principal cases, when there is an item being processed.

```
queueStep    :: QueueState -> ( QueueState , [Outmess] )

queueStep (QS time servSoFar (Yes arr serv : inRest))
  | servSoFar < serv
    = (QS (time+1) (servSoFar+1) (Yes arr serv : inRest) , [])
  | otherwise
    = (QS (time+1) 0 inRest , [Discharge arr (time-serv-arr) serv])
```

In the first case, when the service time so far (servSoFar) is smaller than is required (serv), processing is not complete. We therefore add one to the time, and the service so far, and produce no output message.

If processing is complete – which is the otherwise case – the new state of the queue is QS (time+1) 0 inRest. In this state the time is advanced by one, processing time is set to zero and the head item in the list is removed. An output message is also produced in which the waiting time is given by subtracting the service and arrival times from the current time.

If there is nothing to process, then we simply have to advance the current time by one, and produce no output.

```
queueStep (QS time serv []) = (QS (time+1) serv [] , [])
```

Note that the case of an input message No is not handled here since these messages are filtered out by the server; this is discussed below.

The three other functions are given by

```
queueStart   :: QueueState
queueStart   =  QS 0 0 []

queueLength :: QueueState -> Int
queueLength (QS _ _ q) = length q

queueEmpty  :: QueueState -> Bool
queueEmpty (QS _ _ q)  = (q==[])
```

and this completes the implementation.

Obviously there are different possible implementations. We might choose to take the item being processed and hold it separately from the queue, or to use an ADT for the queue part, rather than a 'concrete' list.

The server

The server consists of a collection of queues, accessed by integers from 0; we choose to use a **list** of queues.

```
newtype ServerState = SS [QueueState]
                            deriving (Eq, Show)
```

Note that the implementation of this ADT builds on another ADT; this is not unusual. Now we take the functions in turn.

Adding an element to a queue uses the function addMessage from the QueueState abstract type.

```
addToQueue :: Int -> Inmess -> ServerState -> ServerState

addToQueue n im (SS st)
  = SS (take n st ++ [newQueueState] ++ drop (n+1) st)
    where
    newQueueState = addMessage im (st!!n)
```

A step of the server is given by making a step in each of the constituent queues, and concatenating together the output messages they produce.

```
serverStep :: ServerState -> ( ServerState , [Outmess] )

serverStep (SS [])
  = (SS [],[])
serverStep (SS (q:qs))
  =  (SS (q':qs') , mess++messes)
    where
    (q' , mess)        = queueStep  q
    (SS qs' , messes) = serverStep (SS qs)
```

In making a simulation step, we perform a server step, and then add the incoming message, if it indicates an arrival, to the shortest queue.

```
simulationStep
  :: ServerState -> Inmess -> ( ServerState , [Outmess] )

simulationStep servSt im
  = (addNewObject im servSt1 , outmess)
    where
    (servSt1 , outmess) = serverStep servSt
```

Adding the message to the shortest queue is done by addNewObject, which is not in the signature. The reason for this is that it can be defined using the operations addToQueue and shortestQueue.

```
addNewObject :: Inmess -> ServerState -> ServerState

addNewObject No servSt = servSt

addNewObject (Yes arr wait) servSt
  = addToQueue (shortestQueue servSt) (Yes arr wait) servSt
```

It is in this function that the input messages No are not passed to the queues, as was mentioned above.

The other three functions of the signature are standard.

```
serverStart :: ServerState
serverStart = SS (replicate numQueues queueStart)
```

where numQueues is a constant to be defined, and the standard function replicate returns a list of n copies of x when applied thus: replicate n x.

```
serverSize :: ServerState -> Int
serverSize (SS xs) = length xs
```

In finding the shortest queue, we use the queueLength function from the QueueState type.

```
shortestQueue :: ServerState -> Int

shortestQueue (SS [q]) = 0
shortestQueue (SS (q:qs))
  | (queueLength (qs!!short) <= queueLength q)   = short+1
  | otherwise                                    = 0
      where
      short = shortestQueue (SS qs)
```

This concludes the implementation of the two simulation ADTs. The example is intended to show the merit of designing in stages. First we gave an informal description of the operations on the types, then a description of their signature, and finally an implementation. Dividing the problem up in this way makes each stage easier to solve.

The example also shows that types can be implemented **independently**: since ServerState uses only the abstract data type operations over QueueState, we can reimplement QueueState without affecting the server state at all.

Exercises

16.18 Give calculations of the expressions

```
queueStep (QS 12 3 [Yes 8 4])
queueStep (QS 13 4 [Yes 8 4])
queueStep (QS 14 0 [])
```

16.19 If we let

```
serverSt1 = SS [ (QS 13 4 [Yes 8 4]) , (QS 13 3 [Yes 8 4]) ]
```

then give calculations of

```
serverStep serverSt1
simulationStep (Yes 13 10) serverSt1
```

16.20 Explain why we cannot use the function type (Int -> QueueState) as the representation type of ServerState. Design an extension of this type which will represent the server state, and implement the functions of the signature over this type.

16.21 Given the implementations of the ADTs from this section, is your answer to the question of whether there are redundant operations in the signatures of queues and servers any different?

16.22 If you have not done so already, design a signature for round-robin simulation, in which allocation of the first item is to queue 0, the second to queue 1, and so on.

16.23 Give an implementation of the round-robin simulation which *uses* the `ServerState` ADT.

16.24 Give a different implementation of the round-robin simulation which *modifies* the implementation of the type `ServerState` itself.

(16.7) Search trees

A binary search tree is an object of type `Tree a` whose elements are **ordered**. A general binary tree is implemented by the algebraic data type `Tree`:

```
data Tree a = Nil | Node a (Tree a) (Tree a)
```

When is a tree ordered? The tree (`Node val t₁ t₂`) is ordered if

- all values in t_1 are smaller than `val`,
- all values in t_2 are larger than `val`, and
- the trees t_1 and t_2 are themselves ordered;

and the tree `Nil` is ordered.

Search trees are used to represent sets of elements, for instance. How can we create a type of search trees? The concrete (algebraic) type `Tree a` will not serve, as it contains elements like `Node 2 (Node 3 Nil Nil) Nil`, which are not ordered.

The answer is to build elements of the type `Tree a` using only operations which create or preserve order. We ensure that only these 'approved' operations are used by making the type an abstract data type.

The abstract data type for search trees

We discussed the signature of the abstract data type earlier, in Section 16.4, but we repeat it here.

```
module Tree
  (Tree,
   nil,          -- Tree a
   isNil,        -- Tree a -> Bool
   isNode,       -- Tree a -> Bool
   leftSub,      -- Tree a -> Tree a
```

```
    rightSub,       -- Tree a -> Tree a
    treeVal,        -- Tree a -> a
    insTree,        -- Ord a => a -> Tree a -> Tree a
    delete,         -- Ord a => a -> Tree a -> Tree a
    minTree         -- Ord a => Tree a -> Maybe a
  ) where
```

As we have said, the implementation type is

```
data Tree a = Nil | Node a (Tree a) (Tree a)
```

and the standard operations to discriminate between different sorts of tree and to extract components are defined by

```
nil :: Tree a
nil = Nil

isNil :: Tree a -> Bool
isNil Nil = True
isNil _   = False

isNode :: Tree a -> Bool
isNode Nil = False
isNode _   = True

leftSub :: Tree a -> Tree a
leftSub Nil             = error "leftSub"
leftSub (Node _ t1 _) = t1

rightSub :: Tree a -> Tree a
rightSub Nil             = error "rightSub"
rightSub (Node _ _ t2) = t2

treeVal  :: Tree a -> a
treeVal Nil             = error "treeVal"
treeVal (Node v _ _)   = v
```

Figure 16.3 contains the definitions of the insertion, deletion and join functions. The function join is used to join two trees with the property that all elements in the left are smaller than all in the right; that will be the case for the call in delete where it is used. It is not exported, as it can break the ordered property of search trees if it is applied to an arbitrary pair of search trees.

Note that the types of insTree, delete, minTree and join contain the context Ord a. Recall from Chapter 12 that this constraint means that these functions can only be used over types which carry an ordering operation, <=. It is easy to see from the definitions of these functions that they do indeed use the ordering, and given the definition of search trees it is unsurprising that we use an ordering in these operations. Now we look at the definitions in Figure 16.3 in turn.

```
insTree :: Ord a => a -> Tree a -> Tree a

insTree val Nil = (Node val Nil Nil)

insTree val (Node v t1 t2)
  | v==val        = Node v t1 t2
  | val > v       = Node v t1 (insTree val t2)
  | val < v       = Node v (insTree val t1) t2

delete :: Ord a => a -> Tree a -> Tree a

delete val (Node v t1 t2)
  | val < v       = Node v (delete val t1) t2
  | val > v       = Node v t1 (delete val t2)
  | isNil t2      = t1
  | isNil t1      = t2
  | otherwise     = join t1 t2

minTree :: Ord a => Tree a -> Maybe a

minTree t
  | isNil t       = Nothing
  | isNil t1      = Just v
  | otherwise     = minTree t1
      where
      t1 = leftSub t
      v  = treeVal t

--      join is an auxiliary function, used in delete;
--      it is not exported.

join :: Ord a => Tree a -> Tree a -> Tree a

join t1 t2
  = Node mini t1 newt
    where
    (Just mini) = minTree t2
    newt        = delete mini t2
```

Figure 16.3 Operations over search trees.

Inserting an element which is already present has no effect, while inserting an element smaller (larger) than the value at the root causes it to be inserted in the left (right) subtree. The diagram shows 3 being inserted in the tree

```
(Node 7 (Node 2 Nil Nil) (Node 9 Nil Nil))
```

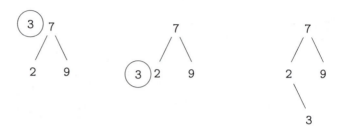

Deletion is straightforward when the value is smaller (larger) than the value at the root node: the deletion is made in the left (right) sub-tree. If the value to be deleted lies at the root, deletion is again simple if either sub-tree is `Nil`: the other sub-tree is returned. The problem comes when both sub-trees are non-`Nil`. In this case, the two sub-trees have to be joined together, keeping the ordering intact.

To `join` two non-`Nil` trees `t1` and `t2`, where it is assumed that `t1` is smaller than `t2`, we pick the minimum element, `mini`, of `t2` to be the value at the root. The left sub-tree is `t1`, and the right is given by deleting `mini` from `t2`. The picture shows the deletion of 7 from

```
(Node 7 (Node 2 Nil Nil) (Node 9 (Node 8 Nil Nil) Nil))
```

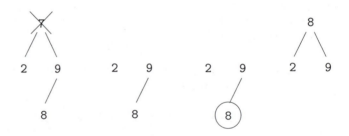

The `minTree` function returns a value of type `Maybe a`, since a `Nil` tree has no minimum. The `Just` constructor therefore has to be removed in the `where` clause of `join`.

Modifying the implementation

Given a search tree, we might be asked for its nth element,

```
indexT :: Int -> Tree a -> a
```

```
indexT n t                                        (indexT)
  | isNil t      = error "indexT"
  | n < st1      = indexT n t1
  | n == st1     = v
  | otherwise    = indexT (n-st1-1) t2
    where
    v   = treeVal t
    t1  = leftSub t
    t2  = rightSub t
    st1 = size t1
```

where the size is given by

```
size :: Tree a -> Int
size t
  | isNil t      = 0
  | otherwise    = 1 + size (leftSub t) + size (rightSub t)
```

If we are often asked to index elements of a tree, we will repeatedly have to find the size of search trees, and this will require computation.

We can think of making the size operation more efficient by *changing the implementation* of Tree a, so that an extra field is given in an Stree to hold the size of the tree:

```
data Stree a = Nil | Node a Int (Stree a) (Stree a)
```

What will have to be changed?

● We will have to redefine all the operations in the signature, since they access the implementation type, and this has changed. For example, the insertion function has the new definition

```
insTree val Nil = (Node val 1 Nil Nil)

insTree val (Node v n t1 t2)
  | v==val      = Node v n t1 t2
  | val > v     = Node v (1 + size t1 + size nt2) t1 nt2
  | val < v     = Node v (1 + size nt1 + size t2) nt1 t2
    where
    nt1 = insTree val t1
    nt2 = insTree val t2
```

● We will have to add size to the signature, and redefine it thus:

```
size Nil            = 0
size (Node _ n _ _) = n
```

to use the value held in the tree.

Nothing else needs to be changed, however. In particular, the definition of indexT given in (indexT) is unchanged. This is a powerful argument in favour of using abstract data type definitions, and against using pattern matching. If (indexT) had used a pattern match over its argument, then it would have to be rewritten if the underlying type changed. This shows that ADTs make programs more easily modifiable, as we argued at the start of the chapter.

In conclusion, it should be said that these search trees form a model for a collection of types, as they can be modified to carry different sorts of information. For, example, we could carry a count of the number of times an element occurs. This would be increased when an element is inserted, and reduced by one on deletion. Indeed any type of additional information can be held at the nodes – the insertion, deletion and other operations use the ordering on the elements to structure the tree irrespective of whatever else is held there. An example might be to store indexing information together with a word, for instance. This would form the basis for a reimplementation of the indexing system of Section 10.8.

Exercises

16.25 Explain how you would *test* the implementations of the functions over search trees. You might need to augment the signature of the type with a function to print a tree.

16.26 Define the functions

```
successor :: Ord a => a -> Tree a -> Maybe a
closest   :: Int -> Tree Int -> Int
```

The successor of v in a tree t is the smallest value in t larger than v, while the closest value to v in a numerical tree t is a value in t which has the smallest difference from v. You can assume that closest is always called on a non-Nil tree, so always returns an answer.

16.27 Redefine the functions of the Tree a signature over the Stree implementation type.

16.28 To speed up the calculation of maxTree and other functions, you could imagine storing the maximum and minimum of the sub-tree at each node. Redefine the functions of the signature to manipulate these maxima and minima, and redefine the functions maxTree, minTree and successor to make use of this extra information stored in the trees.

16.29 You are asked to implement search trees with a count of the number of times an element occurs. How would this affect the signature of the type? How would you implement the operations? How much of the previously written implementation could be re-used?

16.30 Using a modified version of search trees instead of lists, reimplement the indexing software of Section 10.8.

16.31 Design a polymorphic abstract data type

```
Tree a b c
```

so that entries at each node contain an item of type a, on which the tree is ordered, and an item of type b, which might be something like the count, or a list of index entries.

On inserting an element, information of type c is given (a single index entry in that example); this information has to be combined with the information already present. The method of combination can be a functional parameter. There also needs to be a function to describe the way in which information is transformed at deletion.

As a test of your type, you should be able to implement the count trees and the index trees as instances.

(16.8) Sets

A finite set is a collection of elements of a particular type, which is both like and unlike a list. Lists are, of course, familiar, and examples include

```
[Joe,Sue,Ben]      [Ben,Sue,Joe]
[Joe,Sue,Sue,Ben]  [Joe,Sue,Ben,Sue]
```

Each of these lists is different – not only do the elements of a list matter, but also the **order** in which they occur and the number of times that each element occurs (its **multiplicity**) are significant.

In many situations, order and multiplicity are irrelevant. If we want to talk about the collection of people going to a birthday party, we just want the names; a person is either there or not and so multiplicity is not important and the order in which we might list them is also of no interest. In other words, all we want to know is the **set** of people coming. In the example above, this is the set consisting of Joe, Sue and Ben.

Like lists, queues, trees and so on, sets can be combined in many different ways: the operations which combine sets form the signature of the abstract data type. The search trees we saw earlier provide operations which concentrate on elements of a single ordered set: 'what is the successor of element e in set s?' for instance.

In this section we focus on the combining operations for sets. The signature for sets is as follows. We explain the purpose of the operations at the same time as giving their implementation.

```
module Set
  ( Set ,
    empty              , -- Set a
    sing               , -- a -> Set a
    memSet             , -- Ord a => Set a -> a -> Bool
    union,inter,diff   , -- Ord a => Set a -> Set a -> Set a
```

```
    eqSet              , -- Eq a  => Set a -> Set a -> Bool
    subSet             , -- Ord a => Set a -> Set a -> Bool
    makeSet            , -- Ord a => [a] -> Set a
    mapSet             , -- Ord b => (a -> b) -> Set a -> Set b
    filterSet          , -- (a->Bool) -> Set a -> Set a
    foldSet            , -- (a -> a -> a) -> a -> Set a -> a
    showSet            , -- (a -> String) -> Set a -> String
    card                 -- Set a -> Int
  ) where
```

There are numerous possible signatures for sets, some of which assume certain properties of the element type. To test for elementhood, we need the elements to belong to a type in the Eq class; here we assume that the elements are in fact from an ordered type, which enlarges the class of operations over Set a. This gives the contexts Ord a and Ord b, which are seen in some of the types in the signature above.

Implementing the type and operations

We choose to represent a set as an **ordered list of elements without repetitions**:

```
newtype Set a = SetI [a]
```

The principal definitions over Set a are given in Figures 16.4 and 16.5. At the start of the file we see that we import the library List, but as there is a definition of union in there we have to hide this on import, thus,

```
import List hiding ( union )
```

Also at the start of the file we give the instance declarations for the type. It is important to list these at the start because there is no explicit record of them in the module header.

   We now run through the individual functions as they are implemented in Figures 16.4 and 16.5. In our descriptions we use curly brackets '{', '}', to represent sets in examples – this is emphatically not part of Haskell notation.
   The empty set {} is represented by an empty list, and the singleton set {x}, consisting of the single element x, by a one-element list.
   To test for membership of a set, we define memSet. It is important to see that we exploit the ordering in giving this definition. Consider the three cases where the list is non-empty. In (memSet.1), the head element of the set, x, is smaller than the element y which we seek, and so we should check recursively for the presence of y in the tail xs. In case (memSet.2) we have found the element, while in case (memSet.3) the head element is larger than y; since the list is ordered, all elements will be larger than y, so it cannot be a member of the list. This definition would not work if we chose to use arbitrary lists to represent sets.
   The functions union, inter, diff give the union, intersection and difference of two sets. The union consists of the elements occurring in either set (or both), the intersection of those elements in both sets and the difference of those elements in the first but not the second set – we leave the definition of diff as an exercise for the reader. For example,

```
import List hiding ( union )

instance Eq a => Eq (Set a) where
  (==) = eqSet
instance Ord a => Ord (Set a) where
  (<=) = leqSet


newtype Set a = SetI [a]

empty :: Set a
empty = SetI []

sing :: a -> Set a
sing x = SetI [x]

memSet :: Ord a => Set a -> a -> Bool
memSet (SetI []) y      = False
memSet (SetI (x:xs)) y
  | x<y            = memSet (SetI xs) y          (memSet.1)
  | x==y           = True                        (memSet.2)
  | otherwise      = False                       (memSet.3)

union :: Ord a => Set a -> Set a -> Set a
union (SetI xs) (SetI ys) = SetI (uni xs ys)

uni :: Ord a => [a] -> [a] -> [a]
uni [] ys        = ys
uni xs []        = xs
uni (x:xs) (y:ys)
  | x<y            = x : uni xs (y:ys)
  | x==y           = x : uni xs ys
  | otherwise      = y : uni (x:xs) ys

inter :: Ord a => Set a -> Set a -> Set a
inter (SetI xs) (SetI ys) = SetI (int xs ys)

int :: Ord a => [a] -> [a] -> [a]
int [] ys        = []
int xs []        = []
int (x:xs) (y:ys)
  | x<y            = int xs (y:ys)
  | x==y           = x : int xs ys
  | otherwise      = int (x:xs) ys
```

Figure 16.4   Operations over the set abstract data type, part 1.

```
subSet :: Ord a => Set a -> Set a -> Bool
subSet (SetI xs) (SetI ys) = subS xs ys

subS :: Ord a => [a] -> [a] -> Bool
subS [] ys        = True
subS xs []        = False
subS (x:xs) (y:ys)
  | x<y           = False
  | x==y          = subS xs ys
  | x>y           = subS (x:xs) ys

eqSet :: Eq a => Set a -> Set a -> Bool
eqSet (SetI xs) (SetI ys) = (xs == ys)

leqSet :: Ord a => Set a -> Set a -> Bool
leqSet (SetI xs) (SetI ys) = (xs <= ys)

makeSet :: Ord a => [a] -> Set a
makeSet = SetI . remDups . sort
          where
          remDups []      = []
          remDups [x]     = [x]
          remDups (x:y:xs)
            | x < y       = x : remDups (y:xs)
            | otherwise   = remDups (y:xs)

mapSet :: Ord b => (a -> b) -> Set a -> Set b
mapSet f (SetI xs) = makeSet (map f xs)

filterSet :: (a -> Bool) -> Set a -> Set a
filterSet p (SetI xs) = SetI (filter p xs)

foldSet :: (a -> a -> a) -> a -> Set a -> a
foldSet f x (SetI xs) = (foldr f x xs)

showSet :: (a->String) -> Set a -> String
showSet f (SetI xs) = concat (map ((++"\n") . f) xs)

card :: Set a -> Int
card (SetI xs) = length xs
```

Figure 16.5   Operations over the set abstract data type, part 2.

```
union {Joe,Sue} {Sue,Ben} =  {Joe,Sue,Ben}
inter {Joe,Sue} {Sue,Ben} =  {Sue}
diff  {Joe,Sue} {Sue,Ben} =  {Joe}
```

In making these definitions we again exploit the fact that the two arguments are ordered. We also define the functions by 'wrapping up' a function over the 'bare' list type. For instance, in defining union we first define

```
uni :: Ord a => [a] -> [a] -> [a]
```

which works directly over ordered lists, and then make a version which works over Set,

```
union :: Ord a => Set a -> Set a -> Set a
union (SetI xs) (SetI ys) = SetI (uni xs ys)
```

Recall that the brackets '{', '}' are not a part of Haskell; we can see them as shorthand for Haskell expressions as follows.

```
{e₁, ... ,en} = makeSet [e₁, ... ,en]
```

To test whether the first argument is a subset of the second, we use subSet; x is a subset of y if every element of x is an element of y.

Two sets are going to be equal if their representations as ordered lists are the same – hence the definition of eqSet as list equality; note that we require equality on a to define equality on Set a. The function eqSet is exported as part of the signature, but also we declare an instance of the Eq class, binding == to eqSet thus

```
instance Eq a => Eq (Set a) where
  (==) = eqSet
```

The ADT equality will not in general be the equality on the underlying type: if we were to choose arbitrary lists to model sets, the equality test would be more complex, since [1,2] and [2,1,2,2] would represent the same set.

We also export list ordering as an ordering over Set.

```
instance Ord a => Ord (Set a) where
  (<=) = leqSet
```

The subset ordering is not bound to <= since it is customary for the <= in Ord to be a total order, that is for all elements x and y, either x<=y or y<=x will hold. The subset ordering is not a total order, while the lexicographic ordering over (ordered) lists is total. Some examples for comparison are given in the exercises.

To form a set from an arbitrary list, makeSet, the list is sorted, and then duplicate elements are removed, before it is wrapped with SetI. The definition of sort is imported from the List library.

mapSet, filterSet and foldSet behave like map, filter and foldr except that they operate over sets. The latter two are essentially given by filter and foldr; in mapSet duplicates have to be removed after mapping.

showSet f (SetI xs) gives a printable version of a set, one item per line, using the function f to give a printable version of each element.

```
showSet f (SetI xs) = concat (map ((++"\n") . f) xs)
```

The cardinality of a set is the number of its members. The function `card` gives this, as it returns the `length` of the list.

In the next section we build a library of functions to work with relations and graphs which uses the `Set` library as its basis.

Exercises

16.32 Compare how the following pairs of sets are related by the orderings `<=` and `subSet`.

{3}	{3,4}
{2,3}	{3,4}
{2,9}	{2,7,9}

16.33 Define the function `diff` so that `diff s1 s2` consists of the elements of `s1` which do not belong to `s2`.

16.34 Define the function

```
symmDiff :: Ord a => Set a -> Set a -> Set a
```

which gives the **symmetric difference** of two sets. This consists of the elements which lie in one of the sets but not the other, so that

```
symmDiff {Joe,Sue} {Sue,Ben} = {Joe,Ben}
```

Can you use the function `diff` in your definition?

16.35 How can you define the function

```
powerSet :: Ord a => Set a -> Set (Set a)
```

which returns the set of all subsets of a set defined? Can you give a definition which uses only the operations of the abstract data type and not the concrete implementation?

16.36 How are the functions

```
setUnion :: Ord a => Set (Set a) -> Set a
setInter :: Ord a => Set (Set a) -> Set a
```

which return the union and intersection of a set of sets defined using the operations of the abstract data type?

16.37 Can infinite sets (of numbers, for instance) be adequately represented by ordered lists? Can you tell if two infinite lists are equal, for instance?

16.38 The abstract data type `Set a` can be represented in a number of different ways. Alternatives include arbitrary lists (rather than ordered lists without repetitions) and Boolean valued functions, that is elements of the type `a -> Bool`. Give implementations of the type using these two representations.

16.39 Give an implementation of the `Set` abstract data type using search trees.

16.40 Give an implementation of the search tree abstract data type using ordered lists. Compare the behaviour of the two implementations.

(16.9) Relations and graphs

We now use the `Set` abstract data type as a means of implementing relations and, taking an alternative view of the same objects, graphs.

Relations

A binary relation relates together certain elements of a set. A family relationship can be summarized by saying that the `isParent` relation holds between Ben and Sue, between Ben and Leo and between Sue and Joe. In other words, it relates the **pairs** `(Ben,Sue)`, `(Ben,Leo)` and `(Sue,Joe)`, and so we can think of this particular relation as the set

```
isParent = {(Ben,Sue) , (Ben,Leo) , (Sue,Joe)}
```

In general we say

```
type Relation a = Set (a,a)
```

This definition means that all the set operations are available on relations. We can test whether a relation holds of two elements using `memSet`; the `union` of two relations like `isParent` and `isSibling` gives the relationship of being either a parent *or* a sibling, and so on.

   We look at two particular examples of **family relations**, based on a relation `isParent` which we assume is given to us. We first set ourselves the task of defining the function `addChildren` which adds to a set of people all their children; we then aim to define the `isAncestor` relation. The full code for the functions discussed here is given in Figure 16.6.

Examples

1.   Working bottom-up, we first ask how we find all elements related to a given element: who are all Ben's children, for instance? We need to find all pairs beginning with Ben, and then return their second halves. The function to perform this is `image` and the set of Ben's children will be

```
image isParent Ben = {Sue,Leo}
```

Now, how can we find all the elements related to a *set* of elements? We find the `image` of each element separately and then take the union of these sets. The union of a set of sets is given by folding the binary union operation into the set.

```
image :: Ord a => Relation a -> a -> Set a
image rel val = mapSet snd (filterSet ((==val).fst) rel)

setImage :: Ord a => Relation a -> Set a -> Set a
setImage rel = unionSet . mapSet (image rel)

unionSet :: Ord a => Set (Set a) -> Set a
unionSet = foldSet union empty

addImage :: Ord a => Relation a -> Set a -> Set a
addImage rel st = st 'union' setImage rel st

addChildren :: Set People -> Set People
addChildren = addImage isParent
```

```
compose :: Ord a => Relation a -> Relation a -> Relation a
compose rel1 rel2
   =  mapSet outer (filterSet equals (setProduct rel1 rel2))
      where
      equals ((a,b),(c,d)) = (b==c)
      outer  ((a,b),(c,d)) = (a,d)

setProduct :: (Ord a,Ord b) => Set a -> Set b -> Set (a,b)
setProduct st1 st2 = unionSet (mapSet (adjoin st1) st2)

adjoin :: (Ord a,Ord b) => Set a -> b -> Set (a,b)
adjoin st el = mapSet (addEl el) st
              where
              addEl el el' = (el',el)

tClosure :: Ord a => Relation a -> Relation a
tClosure rel = limit addGen rel
              where
              addGen rel' = rel' 'union' (rel' 'compose' rel)

limit:: Eq a => (a -> a) -> a -> a
limit f x
   | x == next    = x
   | otherwise    = limit f next
     where
     next = f x
```

Figure 16.6 Functions over the type of relations, Relation a.

```
unionSet {s₁, ... ,sₙ}
  = s₁ ∪ ... ∪ sₙ
  = s₁ 'union' ... 'union' sₙ
```

Now, how do we add all the children to a set of people? We find the image of the set under isParent, and combine it with the set itself. This is given by the function addChildren.

2. The second task we set ourselves was to find the isAncestor relation. The general problem is to find the transitive closure of a relation, the function tClosure of Figure 16.6. We do this by closing up the relation, so we add grandparenthood, great-grandparenthood and so forth to the relation until nothing further is added. We explain transitive closure formally later in this section.

How do we get the isGrandparent relation? We match together pairs like

```
(Ben,Sue)    (Sue,Joe)
```

and see that this gives that Ben is a grandparent of Joe. We call this the **relational composition** of isParent with itself. In general,

```
isGrandparent
  = isParent 'compose' isParent
  = {(Ben,Joe)}
```

In defining compose we have used the setProduct function to give the **product** of two sets. This is formed by pairing every element of the first set with every element of the second. For instance,

```
setProduct {Ben,Suzie} {Sue,Joe}
  = { (Ben,Sue) , (Ben,Joe) , (Suzie,Sue) , (Suzie,Joe) }
```

setProduct uses the function adjoin to pair each element of a set with a given element. For instance,

```
adjoin Joe {Ben,Sue} = { (Ben,Joe) , (Sue,Joe) }
```

A relation rel is **transitive** if for all (a,b) and (b,c) in rel, (a,c) is in rel. The **transitive closure** of a relation rel is the smallest relation extending rel which is transitive. We compute the transitive closure of rel, tClosure rel, by repeatedly adding one more 'generation' of rel, using compose, until nothing more is added.

To do this, we make use of the limit function, a polymorphic higher-order function of general use. limit f x gives the **limit** of the sequence

```
x , f x , f (f x) , f (f (f x)) , ...
```

The limit is the value to which the sequence settles down if it exists. It is found by taking the first element in the sequence whose successor is equal to the element itself.

As an example, take Ben to be Sue's father, Sue to be Joe's mother, who himself has no children. Now define

```
addChildren :: Set Person -> Set Person
```

to add to a set the children of all members of the set, so that for instance

```
addChildren {Joe,Ben} = {Joe,Sue,Ben}
```

Now we can give an example calculation of a `limit` of a function over sets.

```
limit addChildren {Ben}
  ??  {Ben}=={Ben,Sue} ↝ False
↝   limit addChildren {Ben,Sue}
  ??  {Ben,Sue}=={Ben,Joe,Sue} ↝ False
↝   limit addChildren {Ben,Joe,Sue}
  ??  {Ben,Joe,Sue}=={Ben,Joe,Sue} ↝ True
↝   {Ben,Joe,Sue}
```

Context simplification

The functions of Figure 16.6 give an interesting example of context simplification for type classes. The `adjoin` function requires that the types a and b carry an ordering. Haskell contains the instance declaration

```
instance (Ord a, Ord b) => Ord (a,b) ....                        (pair)
```

and so this is sufficient to ensure `Ord (a,b)`, which is required for the application of `mapSet` within `adjoin`.

Similarly, in defining `compose` we require an ordering on the type `((a,a),(a,a))`; again, knowing `Ord a` is sufficient to give this, since (pair) can be used to derive the ordering on `((a,a),(a,a))`.

Graphs

Another way of seeing a relation is as a directed **graph**. For example, the relation

```
graph1 = { (1,2) , (1,3) , (3,2) , (3,4) , (4,2) , (2,4) }
```

can be pictured thus

where we draw an arrow joining a to b if the pair `(a,b)` is in the relation. What then does the transitive closure represent? Two points a and b are related by `tClosure graph1` if there is a **path** from a to b through the graph. For example, the pair `(1,4)` is in the closure, since a path leads from 1 to 3 then to 2 and finally to 4, while the pair `(2,1)` is not in the closure, since no path leads from 2 to 1 through `graph1`.

Strongly connected components

A problem occurring in many different application areas, including networks and compilers, is to find the **strongly connected components** of a graph. Every graph can have its nodes split into sets or components with the property that every node in a component is connected by a path to all other nodes in the same component. The components of graph1 are {1}, {3} and {2,4}.

We solve the problem in two stages:

● we first form the relation which links points in the same component, then

● we form the components (or equivalence classes) generated by this relation.

There is a path from x to y and vice versa if both (x,y) and (y,x) are in the closure, so we define

```
connect :: Ord a => Relation a -> Relation a
connect rel = clos 'inter' solc
            where
            clos = tClosure rel
            solc = inverse clos

inverse :: Ord a => Relation a -> Relation a
inverse = mapSet swap
        where
        swap (x,y) = (y,x)
```

Now, how do we form the components given by the relation graph1? We start with the set

{{1},{2},{3},{4}}

and repeatedly add the images under the relation to each of the classes, until a fixed point is reached. In general this gives

```
classes :: Ord a => Relation a -> Set (Set a)
classes rel
  = limit (addImages rel) start
    where
    start = mapSet sing (eles rel)
```

where the auxiliary functions used are

```
eles :: Ord a => Relation a -> Set a
eles rel = mapSet fst rel 'union' mapSet snd rel

addImages :: Ord a => Relation a -> Set (Set a) -> Set (Set a)
addImages rel = mapSet (addImage rel)
```

Searching in graphs

Many algorithms require us to **search** through the nodes of a graph: we might want to find a shortest path from one point to another, or to count the number of paths between two points.

Two general patterns of search are depth-first and breadth-first. In a depth-first search, we explore all elements below a given child before moving to the next child; a breadth-first search examines all the children before examining the grandchildren, and so on. In the case of searching below node 1 in graph1, the sequence [1,2,4,3] is depth-first (4 is visited before 3), while [1,2,3,4] is breadth-first. These examples show that we can characterize the searches as transformations

```
breadthFirst :: Ord a => Relation a -> a -> [a]
depthFirst   :: Ord a => Relation a -> a -> [a]
```

with breadthFirst graph1 1 = [1,2,3,4], for instance. The use of a list in these functions is crucial – we are not simply interested in finding the nodes below a node (tClosure does this), we are interested in the *order* in which they occur.

A crucial step in both searches is to find all the descendants of a node which have not been visited so far. We can write

```
newDescs :: Ord a => Relation a -> Set a -> a -> Set a
newDescs rel st v = image rel v 'diff' st
```

which returns the **set** of descendants of v in rel which are not in the set st. Here we have a problem; the result of this function is a set and not a list, but we require the elements in some order. One solution is to add to the Set abstract data type a function

```
flatten :: Set a -> [a]                                    (setList)
flatten (SetI xs) = xs
```

which breaks the abstraction barrier in the case of the ordered list implementation. An alternative is to supply as a parameter a function

```
minSet :: Set a -> Maybe a
```

which returns the minimum of a non-empty set and which can be used in flattening a set to a list without breaking the abstraction barrier. Unconcerned about its particular definition, we assume the existence of a flatten function of type (setList). Then we can say

```
findDescs :: Ord a => Relation a -> [a] -> a -> [a]
findDescs rel xs v = flatten (newDescs rel (makeSet xs) v)
```

Breadth-first search

A breadth-first search involves repeatedly applying findDescs until a limit is reached. The limit function discussed earlier will find this, so we define

```
breadthFirst :: Ord a => Relation a -> a -> [a]
breadthFirst rel val
= limit step start
  where
  start = [val]
  step xs = xs ++ nub (concat (map (findDescs rel xs) xs))
```

A step performs a number of operations:

- First, all the descendants of elements in xs which are not already in xs are found. This is given by mapping (findDescs rel xs) along the list xs.

- This list of lists is then concatenated into a single list.

- Duplicates can occur in this list, as a node may be a descendant of more than one node, and so any duplicated elements must be removed. This is the effect of the library function nub :: Eq a => [a] -> [a], which removes all but the first occurrence of each element in a list.

Depth-first search

How does depth-first search proceed? We first generalize the problem to

```
depthSearch :: Ord a => Relation a -> a -> [a] -> [a]
depthFirst rel v = depthSearch rel v []
```

where the third argument is used to carry the list of nodes already visited, and which are therefore not to appear in the result of the function call.

```
depthSearch rel v used
        = v : depthList rel (findDescs rel used' v) used'
          where
          used' = v:used
```

Here we call the auxiliary function depthList, which finds all the descendants of a list of nodes.

```
depthList :: Ord a => Relation a -> [a] -> [a] -> [a]

depthList rel [] used = []

depthList rel (val:rest) used
  = next ++ depthList rel rest (used++next)
    where
    next = if   elem val used
           then []
           else depthSearch rel val used
```

The definition has two equations, the first giving the trivial case where no nodes are to be explored. In the second there are two parts to the solution:

- next gives the part of the graph accessible below val. This may be [], if val is a member of the list used, otherwise depthSearch is called.

- depthList is then called on the tail of the list, but with next appended to the list of nodes already visited.

This pair of definitions is a good example of definition by **mutual recursion**, since each calls the other. It is possible to define a single function to perform the effect of the two, but this pair of functions seems to express the algorithm in the most natural way.

Exercises

16.41 Calculate

```
classes (connect graph1)
classes (connect graph2)
```

where graph2 = graph1 $\cup$ {(4,3)}.

16.42 Give calculations of

```
breadthFirst graph2 1
depthFirst graph2 1
```

where graph2 is defined in the previous question.

16.43 Using the searches as a model, give a function

```
distance :: Eq a => Relation a -> a -> a -> Int
```

which gives the length of a shortest path from one node to another in a graph. For instance,

```
distance graph1 1 4 = 2
distance graph1 4 1 = 0
```

0 is the result when no such path exists, or when the two nodes are equal.

16.44 A weighted graph carries a numerical **weight** with each edge. Design a type to model this. Give functions for breadth-first and depth-first search which return lists of pairs. Each pair consists of a node, together with the length of a shortest path to that node from the node at the start of the search.

16.45 A **heterogeneous** relation relates objects of different type. An example might be the relation relating a person to their age. Design a type to model these relations; how do you have to modify the functions defined over Relation a to work over this type, if it is possible?

(16.10) Commentary

This section explores a number of issues raised by the introduction of ADTs into our repertoire.

First, we have not yet said anything about verification of functions over abstract data types. This is because there is nothing new to say about the *proof* of theorems: these are proved for the implementation types exactly as we have seen earlier. The theorems valid for an abstract data type are precisely those which obey the type constraints on the functions in the signature. For a queue type, for instance, we will be able to prove that

```
remQ (addQ x emptyQ) = (x , emptyQ)
```

by proving the appropriate result about the implementation. What would not be valid would be an equation like

```
emptyQ = Qu []
```

since this breaks the information-hiding barrier and reveals something of the implementation itself.

Next we note that our implementation of sets gives rise to some properties which we ought to prove, often called **proof obligations**. We have assumed that our sets are implemented as ordered lists without repetitions; we ought to prove that each operation over our implementation preserves this property.

Finally, observe that both classes and abstract data types use signatures, so it is worth surveying their similarities and differences.

- Their purposes are different: ADTs are used to provide information hiding, and to structure programs; classes are used to overload names, to allow the same name to be used over a class of different types.

- The signature in an ADT is associated with a single implementation type, which may be monomorphic or polymorphic. On the other hand, the signature in a class will be associated with multiple instances; this is the whole point of including classes, in fact.

- The functions in the signature of an ADT provide the only access to the underlying type. There is no such information hiding over classes: to be a member of a class, a type must provide at least the types in signature.

- ADTs can be polymorphic, so we can have a polymorphic type of search trees, for instance. Classes classify single types rather than polymorphic families of types; constructor classes as discussed in Chapter 18 extend classes to do exactly that.

Summary

The abstract data types of this chapter have three important and related properties.

- They provide a natural representation of a type, which avoids being over-specific. An abstract data type carries precisely the operations which are naturally associated with the type and nothing more.

● The signature of an abstract data type is a firm interface between the user and the implementer: development of a system can proceed completely independently on the two sides of the interface.

● If the implementation of a type is to be modified, then only the operations in the signature need to be changed; any operation using the signature functions can be used unchanged. We saw an example of this with search trees, when the implementation was modified to include size information.

We saw various examples of ADT development. Most importantly we saw the practical example of the simulation types being designed in the three stages suggested. First the types are named, then they are described informally and finally a signature is written down. After that we are able to implement the operations of the signature as a separate task.

One of the difficulties in writing a signature is being sure that all the relevant operations have been included; we have given a check-list of the kinds of operations which should be present, and against which it is sensible to evaluate any candidate signature definitions.

Lazy programming

In our calculations so far we have said that the order in which we make evaluation steps will not affect the results produced – it may only affect whether the sequence leads to a result. This chapter describes precisely the **lazy evaluation** strategy which underlies Haskell. Lazy evaluation is well named: a lazy evaluator will only evaluate an argument to a function if that argument's value is **needed** to compute the overall result. Moreover, if an argument is structured (a list or a tuple, for instance), only those parts of the argument which are needed will be examined.

Lazy evaluation has consequences for the style of programs we can write. Since an intermediate list will only be generated **on demand**, using an intermediate list will not necessarily be expensive computationally. We examine this in the context of a series of examples, culminating in a case study of parsing.

To build parsers we construct a **toolkit** of polymorphic, higher-order functions which can be combined in a flexible and extensible way to make language processors of all sorts. One of the distinctive features of a functional language is the collection of facilities it provides for defining such sets of building blocks.

We also take the opportunity to extend the **list comprehension** notation. This does not allow us to write any new programs, but does make a lot of list processing programs

– especially those which work by generating and then testing possible solutions – easier to express and understand.

Another consequence of lazy evaluation is that it is possible for the language to describe **infinite** structures. These would require an infinite amount of time to evaluate fully, but under lazy evaluation, only parts of a data structure need to be examined. Any recursive type will contain infinite objects; we concentrate on lists here, as infinite lists are by far the most widely used infinite structures.

After introducing a variety of examples, such as infinite lists of prime and random numbers, we discuss the importance of infinite lists for **program design**, and see that programs manipulating infinite lists can be thought of as processes consuming and creating `streams' of data. Based on this idea, we explore how to complete the simulation case study.

The chapter concludes with an update on program **verification** in the light of lazy evaluation and the existence of infinite lists; this section can only give a flavour of the area, but contains references to more detailed presentations.

Sections 17.1 and 17.2 are essential reading, but it is possible to follow as much of the remainder as you like: the chapters which follow do not depend upon it.

17.1 Lazy evaluation

Central to evaluation in Haskell is function application. The basic idea behind this is simple; to evaluate the function f applied to arguments a_1, a_2, ..., a_k, we simply **substitute** the expressions a_i for the corresponding variables in the definition of the function. For instance, if

```
f x y = x+y
```

then

```
f (9-3) (f 34 3)
⤳   (9-3)+(f 34 3)
```

since we replace x by (9-3) and y by (f 34 3). The expressions (f 34 3) and (9-3) are not evaluated before they are passed to the function.

In this case, for evaluation to continue, we need to evaluate the arguments to '+', giving

```
⤳   6+(34+3)
⤳   6+37
⤳   43
```

In this example, both of the arguments are evaluated eventually, but this is not always the case. If we define

```
g x y = x+12
```

then

```
g (9-3) (g 34 3)
⤳   (9-3)+12
⤳   6+12
⤳   18
```

Here (9-3) is substituted for x, but as y does not appear on the right-hand side of the equation, the argument (g 34 3) will not appear in the result, and so is not evaluated. Here we see the first advantage of lazy evaluation – an argument which is not needed will not be evaluated. This example is rather too simple: why would we write the second argument if its value is never needed? A rather more realistic example is

```
switch :: Int -> a -> a -> a
switch n x y
   | n>0          = x
   | otherwise    = y
```

If the integer n is positive, the result is the value of x; otherwise it is the value of y. Either of the arguments x and y might be used, but in the first case y is not evaluated and in the second x is not evaluated. A third example is

```
h x y = x+x
```

so that

```
h (9-3) (h 34 3)                                        (h-eval)
⤳   (9-3)+(9-3)
```

It appears here that we will have to evaluate the argument (9-3) twice since it is duplicated on substitution. Lazy evaluation ensures that **a duplicated argument is never evaluated more than once**. This can be modelled in a calculation by doing the corresponding steps simultaneously, thus

```
h (9-3) 17
⤳   (9-3)+(9-3)
⤳   6+6
⤳   12
```

In the implementation, there is no duplicated evaluation because calculations are made over **graphs** rather than trees to represent the expressions being evaluated. For instance, instead of duplicating the argument, as in (i) below, the evaluation of (h-eval) will give a graph in which on both sides of the plus there is the *same* expression. This is shown in (ii).

A final example is given by the pattern matching function,

```
pm (x,y) = x+1
```

applied to the pair (3+2,4-17).

```
pm (3+2,4-17)
 ↝    (3+2)+1
 ↝    6
```

The argument is examined, and part of it is evaluated. The second half of the pair remains unevaluated, as it is not needed in the calculation. This completes the informal introduction to lazy evaluation, which can be summarized in the three points:

- arguments to functions are evaluated only when this is necessary for evaluation to continue;
- an argument is not necessarily evaluated fully: only the parts that are needed are examined;
- an argument is evaluated at most only once. This is done in the implementation by replacing expressions by graphs and calculating over them.

We now give a more formal account of the calculation rules which embody lazy evaluation.

17.2 Calculation rules and lazy evaluation

As we first saw in Section 3.7, the definition of a function consists of a number of conditional equations. Each conditional equation can contain multiple clauses and may have a number of local definitions given in a where clause. Each equation will have on its left-hand side the function under definition applied to a number of patterns.

```
f p₁ p₂ ··· pₖ
   | g₁              = e₁
   | g₂              = e₂
   ...
   | otherwise       = eᵣ
     where
       v₁ a₁,₁ ··· = r₁
       ....
f q₁ q₂ ··· qₖ
   = ...
```

In calculating f a_1 ... a_k there are three aspects.

Calculation – pattern matching

In order to determine which of the equations is used, the arguments are evaluated. The arguments are not evaluated fully, rather they are evaluated sufficiently to see whether they match the corresponding patterns. If they match the patterns p_1 to p_k, then evaluation proceeds using the first equation; if not, they are checked against the second equation, which may require further evaluation. This is repeated until a match is given, or until there are no more equations (which would generate a `Program error`). For instance, given the definition

```
f :: [Int] -> [Int] -> Int
f [] ys          = 0                                          (f.1)
f (x:xs) []      = 0                                          (f.2)
f (x:xs) (y:ys) = x+y                                         (f.3)
```

the evaluation of f [1 .. 3] [1 .. 3] proceeds thus

```
f [1 .. 3] [1 .. 3]                                            (1)
⤳   f (1:[2 .. 3]) [1 .. 3]                                    (2)
⤳   f (1:[2 .. 3]) (1:[2 .. 3])                                (3)
⤳   1+1                                                        (4)
```

At stage (1), there is not enough information about the arguments to determine whether there is a match with (f.1). One step of evaluation gives (2), and shows there is not a match with (f.1).

The first argument of (2) matches the first pattern of (f.2), so we need to check the second. One step of calculation in (3) shows that there is no match with (f.2), but that there is with (f.3); hence we have (4).

Calculation – guards

Suppose that the first conditional equation matches (simply for the sake of explanation). The expressions a_1 to a_k are substituted for the patterns p_1 to p_k throughout the conditional equation. We must next determine which of the clauses on the right-hand side applies. The guards are evaluated in turn, until one is found which gives the value `True`; the corresponding clause is then used. If we have

```
f :: Int -> Int -> Int -> Int
f m n p
  | m>=n && m>=p          = m
  | n>=m && n>=p          = n
  | otherwise             = p
```

then

```
f (2+3) (4-1) (3+9)
  ??   (2+3)>=(4-1) && (2+3)>=(3+9)
  ??      ⤳   5>=3 && 5>=(3+9)
  ??      ⤳   True && 5>=(3+9)
  ??      ⤳   5>=(3+9)
  ??      ⤳   5>=12
  ??      ⤳   False
  ??   3>=5 && 3>=12
```

```
??      ⤳   False && 3>=12
??      ⤳   False
??  otherwise ⤳   True
⤳   12
```

We leave it as an exercise for the reader to work out which parts of the calculation above are shared.

Calculation – local definitions

Values in where clauses are calculated on demand: only when a value is needed does calculation begin. Given the definitions

```
f :: Int -> Int -> Int

f m n
  | notNil xs     = front xs
  | otherwise     = n
    where
    xs = [m .. n]

front (x:y:zs) = x+y
front [x]      = x

notNil []      = False
notNil (_:_) = True
```

the calculation of f 3 5 will be

```
f 3 5
  ?? notNil xs
  ?? |   where
  ?? |   xs = [3 .. 5]
  ?? |      ⤳   3:[4 .. 5]                              (1)
  ?? ⤳  notNil (3:[4 .. 5])
  ?? ⤳  True
⤳   front xs
    |   where
    |   xs = 3:[4 .. 5]
    |      ⤳   3:4:[5]                                   (2)
⤳   3+4                                                  (3)
⤳   7
```

To evaluate the guard notNil xs, evaluation of xs begins, and after one step, (1) shows that the guard is True. Evaluating front xs requires more information about xs, and so we evaluate by one more step to give (2). A successful pattern match in the definition of front then gives (3), and so the result.

Operators and other expression formers

The three aspects of evaluating a function application are now complete; we should now say something about the built-in operators. If they can be given Haskell definitions, such as

```
True  && x = x
False && x = False
```

then they will follow the rules for Haskell definitions. The left-to-right order means that '&&' will not evaluate its second argument in the case that its first is False, for instance. This is unlike many programming languages, where the 'and' function will evaluate both its arguments.

The other operations, such as the arithmetic operators, vary. Plus needs both its arguments to return a result, but the equality on lists can return False on comparing [] and (x:xs) without evaluating x or xs. In general the language is implemented so that no manifestly unnecessary evaluation takes place.

Recall that if ... then ... else ...; cases; let and lambda expressions can be used in forming expressions. Their evaluation follows the form we have seen for function applications. Specifically, if ... then ... else ... is evaluated like a guard, cases like a pattern match, let like a where clause and a lambda expression like the application of a named function such as f above.

Finally, we turn to the way in which a choice is made between applications.

Evaluation order

What characterizes evaluation in Haskell, apart from the fact that no argument is evaluated twice, is the **order** in which applications are evaluated when there is a choice.

- Evaluation is **from the outside in**. In a situation like

$$\underline{f_1 \ e_1 \ (f_2 \ e_2 \ 17)}$$

where one application encloses another, as seen in the expression, the outer one, $f_1 \ e_1 \ (f_2 \ e_2 \ 17)$, is chosen for evaluation.

- Otherwise, evaluation is **from left to right**. In the expression

$$\underline{f_1 \ e_1} \ + \ \underline{f_2 \ e_2}$$

the underlined expressions are both to be evaluated. The left-hand one, $f_1 \ e_1$, will be examined first.

These rules are enough to describe the way in which lazy evaluation works. In the sections to come we look at the consequences of a lazy approach for functional programming.

(17.3) List comprehensions revisited

The list comprehension notation does not add any new programs to the Haskell language, but it does allow us to (re-)write programs in a new and clearer way. Building on the introduction in Section 5.5, the notation lets us combine multiple maps and filters together in a single expression. Combinations of these functions allow us to write algorithms which generate and test: all the elements of a particular form are generated and combinations of them are tested, before results depending upon them are returned. We begin the section with a re-examination of the syntax of the list comprehension, before giving some simple illustrative examples. After that we give the rules for calculating with list comprehensions, and we finish the section with a series of longer examples.

Syntax

A list comprehension has the form

```
[ e | q1 , ... , qk ]
```

where each **qualifier** q_i has one of two forms.

- It can be a **generator**, p <- lExp, where p is a pattern and lExp is an expression of list type.
- It can be a **test**, bExp, which is a boolean expression.

An expression lExp or bExp appearing in qualifier q_i can refer to the variables used in the patterns of qualifiers q_1 to q_{i-1}.

Simpler examples

Multiple generators allow us to combine elements from two or more lists

```
pairs :: [a] -> [b] -> [(a,b)]
pairs xs ys = [ (x,y) | x<-xs , y<-ys ]
```

This example is important as it shows the way in which the values x and y are chosen.

```
pairs [1,2,3] [4,5]
↝   [(1,4),(1,5),(2,4),(2,5),(3,4),(3,5)]
```

The first element of xs, 1, is given to x, and then *for this fixed value* all possible values of y in ys are chosen. This process is repeated for the remaining values x in xs, namely 2 and 3.

This choice is not accidental, since if we have

```
triangle :: Int -> [(Int,Int)]
triangle n = [ (x,y) | x <- [1 .. n] , y <- [1 .. x] ]
```

the second generator, y <- [1 .. x] depends on the value of x given by the first generator.

```
triangle 3
⤳  [(1,1),(2,1),(2,2),(3,1),(3,2),(3,3)]
```

For the first choice of x, 1, the value of y is chosen from [1 .. 1], for the second choice of x, the value of y is chosen from [1 .. 2], and so on.

Three positive integers form a **Pythagorean triple** if the sum of squares of the first two is equal to the square of the third. The list of all triples with all sides below a particular bound, n, is given by

```
pyTriple n
  = [ (x,y,z) | x <- [2 .. n] , y <- [x+1 .. n] ,
                z <- [y+1 .. n] , x*x + y*y == z*z ]
```

```
pyTriple 100
⤳  [(3,4,5),(5,12,13),(6,8,10),...,(65,72,97)]
```

Here the test combines values from the three generators.

Calculating with list comprehensions

How can we describe the way in which the results of list comprehensions are obtained? One way is to give a translation of the comprehensions into applications of map, filter and concat. We give a different approach here, of calculating *directly* with the expressions.

Before we do this, we introduce one piece of very helpful notation. We write $e\{f/x\}$ for the expression e in which every occurrence of the variable x has been replaced by the expression f. This is the **substitution** of f for x in e. If p is a pattern, we use $e\{f/p\}$ for the substitution of the appropriate parts of f for the variables in p. For instance,

```
[ (x,y) | x<-xs ]{[2,3]/xs}   = [ (x,y) | x<-[2,3] ]
```

```
(x + sum xs){(2,[3,4])/(x,xs)} = 2 + sum [3,4]
```

since 2 matches x, and [3,4] matches xs when (2,[3,4]) is matched against (x,xs).

We now explain list comprehensions. The notation looks a bit daunting, but the effect should be clear. The generator v <- [a_1,...,a_n] has the effect of setting v to the values a_1 to a_n in turn. Setting the value appears in the calculation as **substitution** of a value for a variable.

```
[ e | v <- [a₁,...,aₙ] , q₂ , ... , qₖ ]
⤳  [ e{a₁/v} | q₂{a₁/v} , ... , qₖ{a₁/v} ]
    ++ ... ++
    [ e{aₙ/v} | q₂{aₙ/v} , ... , qₖ{aₙ/v} ]
```

As a running example for this section we take

```
[ x+y | x <- [1,2] , isEven x , y <- [x .. 2*x] ]
⤳  [ 1+y | isEven 1 , y <- [1 .. 2*1] ] ++
    [ 2+y | isEven 2 , y <- [2 .. 2*2] ]
```

where the values 1 and 2 are substituted for x. The rules for tests are simple,

```
[ e | True  , q2 , ... , qk ]
~> [ e | q2 , ... , qk ]

[ e | False , q2 , ... , qk ]
~> []
```

so that our example is

```
~> [ 1+y | False , y <- [1 .. 2*1] ] ++
   [ 2+y | True , y <- [2 .. 2*2] ]
~> [ 2+y | y <- [2,3,4] ]
~> [ 2+2 | ] ++ [ 2+3 | ] ++ [ 2+4 | ]
```

and when there are no qualifiers,

```
[ e | ] = [ e ]
```

Completing the example, we have

```
[ x+y | x <- [1,2] , isEven x , y <- [x .. 2*x] ]
~> [4,5,6]
```

Now we consider some more examples.

```
triangle 3
~> [ (x,y) | x <- [1 .. 3] , y <- [1 .. x] ]
~> [ (1,y) | y <- [1 .. 1] ] ++
   [ (2,y) | y <- [1 .. 2] ] ++
   [ (3,y) | y <- [1 .. 3] ]
~> [ (1,1) | ] ++
   [ (2,1) | ] ++ [ (2,2) | ] ++
   [ (3,1) | ] ++ [ (3,2) | ] ++ [ (3,3) | ]
~> [(1,1),(2,1),(2,2),(3,1),(3,2),(3,3)]
```

as we argued above. Another example contains a test:

```
[ m*m | m <- [1 .. 10] , m*m<50 ]
~> [ 1*1 | 1*1<50 ] ++ [ 2*2 | 2*2<50 ] ++ ...
   [ 7*7 | 7*7<50 ] ++ [ 8*8 | 8*8<50 ] ++ ...
~> [ 1  | True ] ++ [ 4  | True ] ++ ...
   [ 49 | True ] ++ [ 64 | False ] ++ ...
~> [1,4,...49]
```

We now look at two longer examples, the solutions for which are aided by the list comprehension style.

Example

_____

List permutations

A permutation of a list is a list with the same elements in a different order. The `perms` function returns a list of all permutations of a list.

```
perms :: Eq a => [a] -> [[a]]
```

The empty list has one permutation, itself. If xs is not empty, a permutation is given by picking an element x from xs and putting x at the front of a permutation of the remainder xs\\[x]. (The operation '\\' returns the difference of two lists: xs\\ys is the list xs with each element of ys removed, if it is present.) The definition is therefore

```
perms [] = [[]]
perms xs = [ x:ps | x <- xs , ps <- perms (xs\\[x]) ]
```

Example evaluations give, for a one-element list,

```
perms [2]
↝   [x:ps| x <- [2] , ps <- perms [] ]
↝   [x:ps| x <- [2] , ps <- [[]] ]
↝   [2:ps| ps <- [[]] ]
↝   [2:[] | ]
↝   [[2]]
```

for a two-element list,

```
perms [2,3]
↝   [ x:ps | x <- [2,3] , ps <- perms([2,3]\\[x]) ]
↝   [ 2:ps | ps <- perms [3] ] ++ [ 3:ps | ps <- perms [2] ]
↝   [ 2:[3] ] ++ [ 3:[2] ]
↝   [ [2,3] , [3,2] ]
```

and finally for a three-element list,

```
perms [1,2,3]
↝   [ x:ps | x <- [1,2,3] , ps <- perms([1,2,3]\\[x]) ]
↝   [ 1:ps | ps <- perms [2,3]] ++...++ [ 3:ps | ps <- perms [1,2]]
↝   [ 1:ps | ps<-[[2,3],[3,2]]] ++...++ [ 3:ps | ps<-[[1,2],[2,1]]]
↝   [[1,2,3],[1,3,2],[2,1,3],[2,3,1],[3,1,2],[3,2,1]]
```

There is another algorithm for permutations: in this, a permutation of a list (x:xs) is given by forming a permutation of xs, and by inserting x into this somewhere. The possible insertion points are given by finding all the possible *splits* of the list into two halves.

```
perm :: [a] -> [[a]]

perm []     = [[]]
perm (x:xs) = [ ps++[x]++qs | rs <- perm xs ,
                              (ps,qs) <- splits rs ]
```

We get the list of all possible `splits` of a list `xs` after seeing that on splitting `(y:ys)`, we either split at the front of `(y:ys)`, or somewhere inside `ys`, as given by a split of `ys`.

```
splits :: [a]->[([a],[a])]
```

```
splits []    = [ ([],[]) ]
splits (y:ys) = ([],y:ys) : [ (y:ps,qs) | (ps,qs) <- splits ys]
```

Before moving on, observe that the type of `perms` requires that `a` must be in the class Eq. This is needed for the list difference operator `\\` to be defined over the type `[a]`. There is no such restriction on the type of `perm`, which uses a different method for calculating the permutations.

Vectors and matrices

In this section we give one model for vectors and matrices of real numbers; others exist, and are suitable for different purposes.

A vector is a sequence of real numbers, `[2.1,3.0,4.0]`, say.

```
type Vector = [Float]
```

The scalar product of two vectors (assumed to be the same length) is given by multiplying together corresponding elements and taking the total of the results.

```
scalarProduct [2.0,3.1] [4.1,5.0]
⤳   2.0*4.1 + 3.1*5.0
⤳   23.7
```

As a first attempt we might write

```
mul xs ys = sum [ x*y | x<-xs , y<-ys ]
```

but this gives

```
mul [2.0,3.1] [4.1,5.0]
⤳   sum [8.2,10.0,12.71,15.5]
⤳   46.41
```

since *all* combinations of pairs from the lists are taken. In order to multiply together corresponding pairs, we first `zip` the lists together:

```
scalarProduct :: Vector -> Vector -> Float
scalarProduct xs ys = sum [ x*y | (x,y) <- zip xs ys ]
```

and a calculation shows that this gives the required result. (It is also possible to use `zipWith` to define `scalarProduct`.) A matrix like

$$\begin{pmatrix} 2.0 & 3.0 & 4.0 \\ 5.0 & 6.0 & -1.0 \end{pmatrix}$$

can be thought of as a list of rows or a list of columns; we choose a list of rows here.

```
type Matrix = [Vector]
```

The example matrix is

```
[[2.0,3.0,4.0],[5.0,6.0,-1.0]]
```

Two matrices M and P are multiplied by taking the scalar products of rows of M with columns of P.

$$\begin{pmatrix} 2.0 & 3.0 & 4.0 \\ 5.0 & 6.0 & -1.0 \end{pmatrix} \times \begin{pmatrix} 1.0 & 0.0 \\ 1.0 & 1.0 \\ 0.0 & -1.0 \end{pmatrix} = \begin{pmatrix} 5.0 & -1.0 \\ 11.0 & 7.0 \end{pmatrix}$$

We therefore define

```
matrixProduct :: Matrix -> Matrix -> Matrix
matrixProduct m p
  = [ [scalarProduct r c | c <- columns p] | r <- m ]
```

where the function `columns` gives the representation of a matrix as a list of columns.

```
columns :: Matrix -> Matrix

columns y = [ [ z!!j | z <- y ] | j <- [0 .. s] ]
            where
            s = length (head y)-1
```

The expression `[ z!!j | z <- y ]` picks the jth element from each row z in y; this is exactly the jth column of y. `length (head y)` is the length of a row in y, and so the indices j will be in the range 0 to s = `length (head y)-1`. Another variant of the columns function is `transpose` which is in the library `List.hs`.

Refutable patterns in generators

Some patterns are **refutable**, meaning that an attempt to pattern-match against them may fail. If a refutable pattern is used on the left-hand side of an '`<-`', its effect is to filter from the list only the elements matching the pattern. For example,

```
[ x | (x:xs) <- [[],[2],[],[4,5]] ]  ~>  [2,4]
```

The rules for calculation with generators containing a refutable pattern on their left-hand side are similar to those given above, except that before performing the substitution for the pattern, the list is filtered for the elements which match the pattern. The details are left as an exercise.

Exercises

17.1 Give a calculation of the expression

```
[ x+y | x <- [1 .. 4] , y <- [2 .. 4] , x>y ]
```

17.2 Using the list comprehension notation, define the functions

```
subLists,subSequences :: [a] -> [[a]]
```

which return all the sublists and subsequences of a list. A sublist is obtained by omitting some of the elements of a list; a subsequence is a continuous block from a list. For instance, both [2,4] and [3,4] are sublists of [2,3,4], but only [3,4] is a subsequence.

17.3 Give calculations of the expressions

```
perm [2]
perm [2,3]
perm [1,2,3]
```

and of the matrix multiplication

```
matrixProduct [[2.0,3.0,4.0],[5.0,6.0,-1.0]]
              [[1.0,0.0],[1.0,1.0],[0.0,-1.0]]
```

17.4 Give a definition of scalarProduct using zipWith.

17.5 Define functions to calculate the determinant of a square matrix and, if this is non-zero, to invert the matrix.

17.6 The calculation rules for list comprehensions can be re-stated for the two cases [] and (x:xs), instead of for the arbitrary list $[a_1,\ldots,a_n]$. Give these rules by completing the equations

```
[ e | v <- []      , q2 , ... , qk ] ⤳ ...
[ e | v <- (x:xs) , q2 , ... , qk ] ⤳ ...
```

17.7 Give the precise rules for calculating with a generator containing a refutable pattern, like (x:xs) <- lExp. You might need to define auxiliary functions to do this.

17.8 List comprehensions can be translated into expressions involving map, filter and concat by the following equations.

```
[ x | x<-xs ]                = xs
[ f x | x<-xs ]              = map f xs
[ e | x<-xs , p x , ... ]  = [ e | x <- filter p xs , ... ]
[ e | x<-xs , y<-ys , .. ] = concat [ [e|y<-ys, ..] | x<-xs]
```

Translate the expressions

```
[ m*m | m <- [1 .. 10] ]
[ m*m | m <- [1 .. 10] , m*m<50 ]
[ x+y | x <- [1 .. 4] , y <- [2 .. 4] , x>y ]
[ x:p | x <- xs , p <- perms (xs\\[x]) ]
```

using these equations; you will need to define some auxiliary functions as a part of your translation.

17.4 Data-directed programming

The data structures manipulated by a program will be generated on demand, and indeed may never appear explicitly. This makes possible a style of programming, **data-directed programming**, in which complex data structures are constructed and manipulated. Take the example of finding the sum of fourth powers of numbers from 1 to n. A data-directed solution is to

● build the list of numbers [1 .. n];

● take the power of each number, giving $[1, 16, \ldots, n^4]$, and

● find the sum of this list.

As a program, we have

```
sumFourthPowers n = sum (map (^4) [1 .. n])
```

How does the calculation proceed?

```
sumFourthPowers n
~>   sum (map (^4) [1 .. n])
~>   sum (map (^4) (1:[2 .. n]))
~>   sum ((^4) 1 : map (^4) [2 .. n])
~>   (1^4) + sum (map (^4) [2 .. n])
~>   1 + sum (map (^4) [2 .. n])
~>   ...
~>   1 + (16 + sum (map (^4) [3 .. n]))
~>   ...
~>   1 + (16 + (81 + ... + n^4))
```

As can be seen, none of the intermediate lists is created in this calculation. As soon as the head of the list is created, its fourth power is taken, and it becomes a part of the sum which produces the final result.

Examples

1. List minimum

A more striking example is given by the problem of finding the minimum of a list of numbers. One solution is to sort the list, and take its head! This would be ridiculous if the whole list were sorted in the process, but, in fact we have, using the definition of insertion sort from Chapter 7,

```
iSort [8,6,1,7,5]
~>   ins 8 (ins 6 (ins 1 (ins 7 (ins 5 []))))
~>   ins 8 (ins 6 (ins 1 (ins 7 [5])))
~>   ins 8 (ins 6 (ins 1 (5 : ins 7 [])))
~>   ins 8 (ins 6 (1 : (5 : ins 7 [])))
~>   ins 8 (1 : ins 6 (5 : ins 7 []))
~>   1 : ins 8 (ins 6 (5 : ins 7 []))
```

As can be seen from the underlined parts of the calculation, each application of `ins` calculates the minimum of a larger part of the list, since the head of the result of `ins` is given in a single step. The head of the whole list is determined in this case without us working out the value of the tail, and this means that we have a sensible algorithm for minimum given by (`head . iSort`).

2. Routes through a graph

A graph can be seen as an object of type `Relation` a, as defined in Section 16.9. How can we find a route from one point in a graph to another? For example, in the graph

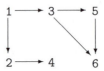

```
graphEx = makeSet  [(1,2),(1,3),(2,4),(3,5),(5,6),(3,6)]
```

a route from 1 to 4 is the list [1,2,4].

We solve a slightly different problem: find the list of *all* routes from x to y; our original problem is solved by taking the head of this list. Note that as a list is returned, the algorithm allows for the possibility of there being *no* route from x to y – the empty list of routes is the answer in such a case. This method, which is applicable in many different situations, is often called the **list of successes** technique: instead of returning one result, or an error if there is none, we return a list; the error case is signalled by the empty list. The method also allows for multiple results to be returned, as we shall see.

How do we solve the new problem? For the present we assume that the graph is **acyclic**: there is no circular path from any node back to itself.

- The only route from x to x is [x].

- A route from x to y will start with a step to one of x's neighbours, z say. The remainder will be a path from z to y.

We therefore look for all paths from x to y going through z, for each neighbour z of x.

```
routes :: Ord a => Relation a -> a -> a -> [[a]]
routes rel x y
    | x==y        = [[x]]
    | otherwise   = [ x:r | z <- nbhrs rel x ,
                            r <- routes rel z y ]
```

The nbhrs function is defined by

```
nbhrs :: Ord a => Relation a -> a -> [a]
nbhrs rel x = flatten (image rel x)
```

where `flatten` turns a set into a list. Now consider the example, where we write `routes'` for `routes graphEx` and `nbhrs'` for `nbhrs graphEx`, to make the calculation more readable:

```
routes' 1 4
↝   [ 1:r | z <- nbhrs' 1 , r <- routes' z 4 ]
↝   [ 1:r | z <- [2,3] , r <- routes' z 4 ]
↝   [ 1:r | r <- routes' 2 4 ] ++
    [ 1:r | r <- routes' 3 4 ]                              (†)
↝   [ 1:r | r <- [ 2:s | w <- nbhrs' 2 , s <- routes' w 4 ]]++...
↝   [ 1:r | r <- [ 2:s | w <- [4] , s <- routes' w 4 ] ] ++ ...
↝   [ 1:r | r <- [ 2:s | s <- routes' 4 4 ] ] ++ ...        (‡)
↝   [ 1:r | r <- [ 2:s | s <- [[4]] ] ] ++ ...
↝   [ 1:r | r <- [ [2,4] ] ] ++ ...
↝   [[1,2,4]] ++ ...
```

The head of the list is given by exploring only the first neighbour of 1, namely 2, and its first neighbour, 4. In this case the search for a route leads directly to a result. This is not always so. Take the example of

```
routes' 1 6 = ...
↝   [ 1:r | r <- routes' 2 6 ] ++
    [ 1:r | r <- routes' 3 6 ]                              (†)
↝   ...
↝   [ 1:r | r <- [ 2:s | s <- routes' 4 6 ] ] ++
    [ 1:r | r <- routes' 3 6 ]                              (‡)
```

Corresponding points in the calculations are marked by (†) and (‡). The search for routes from 4 to 6 will *fail*, though, as 4 has no neighbours – we therefore have

```
↝   [] ++ [ 1:r | r <- routes' 3 6 ] = ...
↝   [ 1:r | r <- [ 3:s | s <- routes' 5 6 ] ] ++ ...
↝   [[1,3,5,6]] ++ ...
```

The effect of this algorithm is to **backtrack** when a search has failed: there is no route from 1 to 6 via 2, so the other possibility of going through 3 is explored. This is done *only* when the first possibility is exhausted, however, so lazy evaluation ensures that this search through 'all' the paths turns out to be an efficient method of finding a single path.

We assumed at the start of this development that the graph was acyclic, so that we have no chance of a path looping back on itself, and so of a search going into a loop. We can make a simple addition to the program to make sure that only paths without cycles are explored, and so that the program will work for an arbitrary graph. We add a list argument for the points not to be visited (again), and so have

```
routesC :: Ord a => Relation a -> a -> a -> [a] -> [[a]]
routesC rel x y avoid
  | x==y        = [[x]]
  | otherwise   = [ x:r | z <- nbhrs rel x \\ avoid ,
                          r <- routesC rel z y (x:avoid) ]
```

Two changes are made in the recursive case.

● In looking for neighbours of x we look only for those which are not in the list `avoid`;

● in looking for routes from z to y, we exclude visiting both the elements of `avoid` and the node x itself.

A search for a route from x to y in `rel` is given by `routesC rel x y []`.

17.9 Defining graphEx2 to be

```
makeSet [(1,2),(2,1),(1,3),(2,4),(3,5),(5,6),(3,6)]
```

try calculating the effect of the original definition on

```
routes graphEx 1 4
```

Repeat the calculation with the revised definition which follows:

```
routes rel x y
  | x==y       = [[x]]
  | otherwise  = [ x:r | z <- nbhrs rel x ,
                         r <- routes rel z y ,
                         not (elem x r) ]
```

and explain why this definition is not suitable for use on cyclic graphs. Finally, give a calculation of

```
routesC graphEx 1 4 []
```

17.5 Case study: parsing expressions

We have already seen the definition of `Expr`, the type of arithmetic expressions, in Section 14.2 and in a revised version given on page 255:

```
data Expr = Lit Int | Var Var | Op Ops Expr Expr
data Ops  = Add | Sub | Mul | Div | Mod
```

and showed there how we could calculate the results of these expressions using the function `eval`. Chapter 16 began with a discussion of how to represent the values held in the variables using the abstract data type `Store`. Using these components, we can build a calculator for simple arithmetical expressions, but the input is unacceptably crude, as we have to enter members of the `Expr` type, so that to add 2 and 3, we are forced to type

```
Op Add (Lit 2) (Lit 3)                                          (exp)
```

What we need to make the input reasonable is a function which performs the reverse of show: it will take the text "(2+3)" and return the expression (exp).

Constructing a parser for a type like Expr gives a read function which essentially gives the functionality of the Read class, introduced in Section 12.4 above. Note, however, that the derived definition of read for Expr will parse strings of the form "Op Add (Lit 2) (Lit 3)" rather than the more compact form which we read with our parser.

The type of parsers: Parse

In building a library of parsing functions, we first have to establish the type we shall use to represent parsers. The problem of parsing is to take a list of objects – of type a and characters in our example "(2+3)" – and from it to extract an object of some other type, b, in this case Expr. As a first attempt, we might define the type of parsers thus:

```
type Parse1 a b = [a] -> b
```

Suppose that bracket and number are the parsers of this type which recognize brackets and numbers then we have

```
bracket "(xyz"  ⤳   '('
number  "234"   ⤳   2 or 23 or 234?
bracket "234"   ⤳   no result?
```

The problem evident here is that a parser can return more than one result – as in number "234" – or none at all, as seen in the final case. Instead of the original type, we suggest

```
type Parse2 a b = [a] -> [b]
```

where a list of results is returned. In our examples,

```
bracket "(xyz"  ⤳   ['(']
number  "234"   ⤳   [2 , 23 , 234]
bracket "234"   ⤳   []
```

In this case an empty list signals failure to find what was sought, while multiple results show that more than one successful parse was possible. We are using the 'list of successes' technique again, in fact.

Another problem presents itself. What if we look for a bracket *followed by* a number, which we have to do in parsing our expressions? We need to know the part of the input which remains after the successful parse. Hence we define

```
type Parse a b = [a] -> [(b,[a])]
```

and our example functions will give

```
bracket "(xyz"  ⤳   [('(' , "xyz")]
number  "234"   ⤳   [(2,"34") , (23,"4") , (234,"")]
bracket "234"   ⤳   []
```

Each element in the output list represents a successful parse. In number "234" we see three successful parses, each recognizing a number. In the first, the number 2 is recognized, leaving "34" unexamined, for instance.

The type ReadS b, which appears in the standard prelude and is used in defining the Read class, is a special case of the type Parse a b in which [a] is replaced by String, that is, a is replaced by Char.

Some basic parsers

Now we have established the type we shall use, we can begin to write some parsers. These and the parser-combining functions are illustrated in Figure 17.1; we go through the definitions now.

The first is a parser which always fails, so accepts nothing. There are no entries in its output list.

```
none :: Parse a b
none inp = []
```

On the other hand, we can succeed immediately, without reading any input. The value recognized is a parameter of the function.

```
succeed :: b -> Parse a b
succeed val inp = [(val,inp)]
```

More useful is a parser to recognize a single object or token, t, say. We define

```
token :: Eq a => a -> Parse a a
token t (x:xs)
   | t==x        = [(t,xs)]
   | otherwise   = []
token t []        = []
```

More generally, we can recognize (or spot) objects with a particular property, as represented by a Boolean-valued function.

```
spot :: (a -> Bool) -> Parse a a
spot p (x:xs)
   | p x         = [(x,xs)]
   | otherwise   = []
spot p []         = []
```

These parsers allow us to recognize single characters like a left bracket, or a single digit,

```
bracket = token '('
dig     = spot isDigit
```

and indeed, we can define token from spot:

```
token t = spot (==t)
```

If we are to build parsers for complex structures like expressions we will need to be able to combine these simple parsers into more complicated ones to, for instance, recognize numbers consisting of lists of digits.

```
infixr 5 >*>

type Parse a b = [a] -> [(b,[a])]

none :: Parse a b
none inp = []

succeed :: b -> Parse a b
succeed val inp = [(val,inp)]

token :: Eq a => a -> Parse a a
token t = spot (==t)

spot :: (a -> Bool) -> Parse a a
spot p (x:xs)
  | p x         = [(x,xs)]
  | otherwise   = []
spot p []       = []

alt :: Parse a b -> Parse a b -> Parse a b
alt p1 p2 inp = p1 inp ++ p2 inp

(>*>) :: Parse a b -> Parse a c -> Parse a (b,c)
(>*>) p1 p2 inp
  = [((y,z),rem2) | (y,rem1) <- p1 inp , (z,rem2) <- p2 rem1 ]

build :: Parse a b -> (b -> c) -> Parse a c
build p f inp = [ (f x,rem) | (x,rem) <- p inp ]

list :: Parse a b -> Parse a [b]
list p = (succeed []) 'alt'
         ((p >*> list p) 'build' (uncurry (:)))
```

Figure 17.1 The major parsing functions.

Combining parsers

Here we build a library of higher-order polymorphic functions, which we then use to give our parser for expressions. First we have to think about the ways in which parsers need to be combined.

Looking at the expression example, an expression is *either* a literal, *or* a variable *or* an operator expression. From parsers for the three sorts of expression, we want to build a single parser for expressions. For this we use alt

```
alt :: Parse a b -> Parse a b -> Parse a b
```

```
alt p1 p2 inp = p1 inp ++ p2 inp
```

The parser combines the results of the parses given by parsers p1 and p2 into a single list, so a success in either is a success of the combination. For example,

```
(bracket 'alt' dig) "234"
~>   [] ++ [(2,"34")]
```

the parse by bracket fails, but that by dig succeeds, so the combined parser succeeds.

For our second function, we look again at the expression example. In recognizing an operator expression we see a bracket *then* a number. How do we put parsers together so that the second is applied to the input that remains after the first has been applied?

We make this function an operator, as we find that it is often used to combine a sequence of parsers, and an infix form with defined associativity is most convenient for this.

```
infixr 5 >*>
```

```
(>*>) :: Parse a b -> Parse a c -> Parse a (b,c)
```

```
(>*>) p1 p2 inp
  = [((y,z),rem2) | (y,rem1) <- p1 inp , (z,rem2) <- p2 rem1 ]
```

The values (y,rem1) run through the possible results of parsing inp using p1. For each of these, we apply p2 to rem1, which is the input which is unconsumed by p1 in that particular case. The results of the two successful parses, y and z, are returned as a pair.

As an example, assume that number recognizes non-empty sequences of digits, and look at (number >*> bracket) "24(". Applying number to the string "24(" gives two results,

```
number "24(" ~>   [(2,"4(") , (24,"(")]
```

and so (y,rem1) runs through two cases

```
(number >*> bracket) "24("
~>   [((y,z),rem2) | (y,rem1) <- [(2,"4(") , (24,"(")] ,
                     (z,rem2)   <- bracket rem1 ]
~>   [((2,z),rem2)  | (z,rem2)   <- bracket "4(" ] ++
     [((24,z),rem2) | (z,rem2)   <- bracket "(" ]
```

Now, bracket "4(" ~> [], so fails, giving

```
~>   [] ++ [((24,z),rem2) | (z,rem2)   <- bracket "(" ]
```

and

```
bracket "(" ~>   [('(',"")]
```

which signals success, and finally gives

```
~>   [((24,z),rem2) | (z,rem2)   <- [(')(','"")] ]
~>   [ ((24,'(') , "") ]
```

This shows we have one successful parse, in which we have recognized the number 24 followed by the left bracket '('.

Our final operation is to change the item returned by a parser, or to build something from it. Consider the case of a parser, digList, which returns a list of digits. Can we make it return the number which the list of digits represents? We apply conversion to the results, thus

```
build :: Parse a b -> (b -> c) -> Parse a c
```

```
build p f inp = [ (f x,rem) | (x,rem) <- p inp ]
```

so in an example, we have

```
(digList 'build' digsToNum) "21a3"
~>   [ (digsToNum x,rem) | (x,rem) <- digList "21a3" ]
~>   [ (digsToNum x,rem) | (x,rem) <- [("2","1a3"),("21","a3")]]
~>   [ (digsToNum "2" , "1a3") , (digsToNum "21" , "a3") ]
~>   [ (2,"1a3") , (21,"a3")]
```

Using the three operations or **combinators** alt, >*> and build together with the primitives of the last section we will be able to define all the parsers we require.

As an example, we show how to define a parser for a **list** of objects, when we are given a parser to recognize a single object. There are two sorts of list:

● A list can be empty, which will be recognized by the parser succeed [].

● Any other list is non-empty, and consists of an object followed by a list of objects. A pair like this is recognized by p >*> list p; we then have to turn this pair (x,xs) into the list (x:xs), for which we use build, applied to the uncurried form of (:), which takes its arguments as a pair, and thus converts (x,xs) to (x:xs).

```
list :: Parse a b -> Parse a [b]
```

```
list p = (succeed []) 'alt'
           ((p >*> list p) 'build' (uncurry (:)))
```

Exercises

17.10 Define the functions

```
neList   :: Parse a b -> Parse a [b]
optional :: Parse a b -> Parse a [b]
```

so that neList p recognizes a non-empty list of the objects which are recognized by p, and optional p recognizes such an object *optionally* – it may recognize an object or succeed immediately.

17.11 Define the function

```
nTimes :: Int -> Parse a b -> Parse a [b]
```

so that `nTimes n p` recognizes n of the objects recognized by p.

A parser for expressions

Now we can describe our expressions and define the parser for them. Expressions have three forms:

- Literals: 67, ~89, where '~' is used for unary minus.
- Variables: 'a' to 'z'.
- Applications of the binary operations +, *, -, /, %, where % is used for mod, and / gives integer division. Expressions are fully bracketed, if compound, thus: (23+(34-45)), and white space not permitted.

The parser has three parts

```
parser :: Parse Char Expr
parser = litParse 'alt' varParse 'alt' opExpParse
```

corresponding to the three sorts of expression. The simplest to define is

```
varParse :: Parse Char Expr
varParse = spot isVar 'build' Var

isVar :: Char -> Bool
isVar x = ('a' <= x && x <= 'z')
```

(Here the constructor Var is used as a function taking a character to the type Expr.)
An operator expression will consist of two expressions joined by an operator, the whole construct between a matching pair of parentheses:

```
opExpParse
  = (token '(' >*>
     parser    >*>
     spot isOp >*>
     parser    >*>
     token ')')
    'build' makeExpr
```

where the conversion function takes a nested sequence of pairs, like

```
('(',(Lit 23,('+',(Var 'x',')'))))
```

into the expression Op Add (Lit 23) (Var 'x'), thus

```
makeExpr (_,(e1,(bop,(e2,_)))) = Op (charToOp bop) e1 e2
```

Defining the functions isOp and charToOp is left as an exercise.

Finally, we look at the case of literals. A number consists of a non-empty list of digits, with an optional '~' at the front. We therefore use the functions from the exercises of the previous section to say

```
litParse
  = ((optional (token '~')) >*>
    (neList (spot isDigit))
    'build' (charlistToExpr . uncurry (++))
```

Left undefined here is the function charlistToExpr which should convert a list of characters to a literal integer; this is an exercise for the reader.

Exercises

17.12 Define the functions

```
isOp     :: Char -> Bool
charToOp :: Char -> Ops
```

used in the parsing of expressions.

17.13 Define the function

```
charlistToExpr :: [Char] -> Expr
```

so that

```
charlistToExpr "234" ⤳ Lit 234
charlistToExpr "~98" ⤳ Lit (-98)
```

which is used in parsing literal expressions.

17.14 A command to the calculator to assign the value of expr to the variable var is represented thus

```
var:expr
```

Give a parser for these commands.

17.15 How would you change the parser for numbers if decimal fractions are to be allowed in addition to integers?

17.16 How would you change the parser for variables if names longer than a single character are to be allowed?

17.17 Explain how you would modify your parser so that the *whitespace* characters space and tab can be used in expressions, but would be ignored on parsing. (Hint: there is a simple pre-processor which does the trick!)

17.18 (Note: this exercise is for those familiar with Backus-Naur notation for grammars.)

Expressions without bracketing and allowing the multiplicative expressions higher binding power are described by the grammar

```
Expr   ::= Int | Var | (Expr Ops Expr) |
               Lexpr Mop Mexpr | Mexpr Aop Expr
Lexpr  ::= Int | Var | (Expr Ops Expr)
Mexpr  ::= Int | Var | (Expr Ops Expr) | Lexpr Mop Mexpr
Mop    ::= '*' | '/' | '%'
Aop    ::= '+' | '-'
Ops    ::= Mop | Aop
```

Give a Haskell parser for this grammar. Discuss the associativity of the operator '−' in this grammar.

The top-level parser

The parser defined in the last section, `parser` is of type

```
[Char] -> [ (Expr,[Char]) ]
```

yet what we need is to convert this to a function taking a string to the expression it represents. We therefore define the function

```
topLevel :: Parse a b -> [a] -> b
topLevel p inp
  = case results of
       [] -> error "parse unsuccessful"
       _  -> head results
    where
    results = [ found | (found,[]) <- p inp ]
```

The parse `p inp` is successful if the result contains at least one parse (the second case) in which all the input has been read (the test given by the pattern match to (`found,[]`)). If this happens, the first value `found` is returned; otherwise we are in error.

We can define the type of commands thus

```
data Command = Eval Expr | Assign Var Expr | Null
```

which are intended to cause

- the evaluation of the expression,
- the assignment of the value of the expression to the variable, and
- no effect.

If the assignment command takes the form `var:expr`, then it is not difficult to design a parser for this type,

```
commandParse :: Parse Char Command
```

We will assume this has been built when we revisit the calculator example below.

Conclusions

The type of parsers `Parse a b` with the functions

```
none     :: Parse a b
succeed  :: b -> Parse a b
spot     :: (a -> Bool) -> Parse a a
alt      :: Parse a b -> Parse a b -> Parse a b
>*>      :: Parse a b -> Parse a c -> Parse a (b,c)
build    :: Parse a b -> (b -> c) -> Parse a c
topLevel :: Parse a b -> [a] -> b
```

allow us to construct so-called recursive descent parsers in a straightforward way. It is worth looking at the aspects of the language we have exploited.

- The type `Parse a b` is represented by a function type, so that all the parser combinators are higher order functions.

- Because of polymorphism, we do not need to be specific about either the input or the output type of the parsers we build.

   In our example we have confined ourselves to inputs which are strings of characters, but they could have been *tokens* of any other type, if required: we might take the tokens to be *words* which are then parsed into sentences, for instance.

   More importantly in our example, we can return objects of any type using the same combinators, and in the example we returned lists and pairs as well as simple characters and expressions.

- Lazy evaluation plays a role here also. The possible parses we build are generated *on demand* as the alternatives are tested. The parsers will backtrack through the different options until a successful one is found.

Building general libraries like this parser library is one of the major advantages of using a modern functional programming language with the facilities mentioned above. From a toolkit like this it is possible to build a whole range of parsers and language processors which can form the front ends of systems of all sorts.

We will return to a discussion of parsing in Chapter 18; note also that we could make the type of `Parse a b` into an abstract data type, along the lines discussed in Chapter 16. On the other hand, it would also be useful to leave the implementation open to extension by users, which is the way in which other Haskell libraries are made available.

Exercises

17.19 Define a parser which recognizes strings representing Haskell lists of integers, like `"[2,-3,45]"`.

17.20 Define a parser to recognize simple sentences of English, with a subject, verb and object. You will need to provide some vocabulary, `"cat"`, `"dog"`, and so on, and a parser to recognize a string. You will also need to define a function

```
tokenList :: Eq a => [a] -> Parse a [a]
```

so that, for instance,

```
tokenList "Hello" "Hello Sailor"  ⤳  [ ("Hello"," Sailor") ]
```

17.21 Define the function

```
spotWhile :: (a -> Bool) -> Parse a [a]
```

whose parameter is a function which tests elements of the input type, and returns the longest initial part of the input, all of whose elements have the required property. For instance

```
spotWhile digit "234abc"  ⤳  [ ("234","abc") ]
spotWhile digit "abc234"  ⤳  [ ([],"abc234") ]
```

(17.6) Infinite lists

One important consequence of lazy evaluation is that it is possible for the language to describe **infinite** structures. These would require an infinite amount of time to evaluate fully, but under lazy evaluation it is possible to compute with only portions of a data structure rather than the whole object. Any recursive type will contain infinite objects; we concentrate on lists here, as these are by far the most widely used infinite structures.

In this section we look at a variety of examples, starting with simple one-line definitions and moving to an examination of random numbers to be used in our simulation case study. The simplest examples of infinite lists are constant lists like

```
ones = 1 : ones
```

Evaluation of this in a Haskell system produces a list of ones, indefinitely. This can be **interrupted** in Hugs by typing Ctrl-C or in the Hugs Windows interface by hitting the 'Stop' button. In either case this produces the result

```
[1, 1, 1, 1, 1, 1, 1^C{Interrupted!}
```

We can sensibly evaluate functions applied to ones. If we define

```
addFirstTwo :: [Int] -> Int
addFirstTwo (x:y:zs) = x+y
```

then applied to ones we have

```
addFirstTwo ones
⤳   addFirstTwo (1:ones)
⤳   addFirstTwo (1:1:ones)
⤳   1+1
⤳   2
```

Built into the system are the lists [n ..], [n,m ..], so that

```
[3 .. ]    = [3,4,5,6,...
[3,5 .. ] = [3,5,7,9,...
```

We can define these ourselves:

```
from :: Int -> [Int]
from n         = n : from (n+1)

fromStep :: Int -> Int -> [Int]
fromStep n m = n : fromStep (n+m) m
```

and an example evaluation gives

```
fromStep 3 2
↝   3 : fromStep 5 2
↝   3 : 5 : fromStep 7 2
↝   ...
```

These functions are also defined over any instance of Enum; details can be found in Prelude.hs.

List comprehensions can also define infinite lists. The list of *all* Pythagorean triples is given by selecting z in [2 ..], and then selecting suitable values of x and y below that.

```
pythagTriples =
   [ (x,y,z) | z <- [2 .. ] , y <- [2 .. z-1] ,
              x <- [2 .. y-1] , x*x + y*y == z*z ]
pythagTriples
= [(3,4,5),(6,8,10),(5,12,13),(9,12,15),(8,15,17),(12,16,20),...]
```

The powers of an integer are given by

```
powers :: Int -> [Int]
powers n = [ n^x | x <- [0 .. ] ]
```

and this is a special case of the prelude function iterate, which gives the infinite list

```
[ x , f x , .. , fⁿ x , ..
```

```
iterate :: (a -> a) -> a -> [a]
iterate f x = x : iterate f (f x)
```

Examples

1. Generating prime numbers

A positive integer greater than one is **prime** if it is divisible only by itself and one. The *Sieve of Eratosthenes* – an algorithm known for over two thousand years – works by

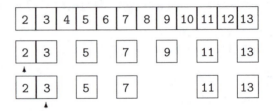

Figure 17.2 The Sieve of Eratosthenes.

cancelling out all the multiples of numbers, once they are established as prime. The primes are the only elements which remain in the list. The process is illustrated in Figure 17.2.

We begin with the list of numbers starting at 2. The head is 2, and we remove all the multiples of 2 from the list. The head of the remainder of the list, 3, is prime, since it was not removed in the sieve by 2. We therefore sieve the remainder of the list of multiples of 3, and repeat the process indefinitely. As a Haskell definition, we write

```
primes :: [Int]

primes       = sieve [2 .. ]
sieve (x:xs) = x : sieve [ y | y <- xs , y 'mod' x > 0]
```

where we test whether x divides y by evaluating y 'mod' x; y is a multiple of x if this value is zero. Beginning the evaluation, we have

```
primes
~→  sieve [2 .. ]
~→  2 : sieve [ y | y <- [3 .. ] , y 'mod' 2 > 0]
~→  2 : sieve (3 : [ y | y <- [4 .. ] , y 'mod' 2 > 0])
~→  2 : 3 : sieve [ z | z <- [ y | y <- [4 .. ] , y 'mod' 2 > 0],
                   z 'mod' 3 > 0]
~→  ...
~→  2 : 3 : sieve [ z | z <- [5,7,9...] , z 'mod' 3 > 0]
~→  ...
~→  2 : 3 : sieve [5,7,11,...]
~→  ...
```

Can we use primes to test for a number being a prime? If we evaluate member primes 7 we get the response True, while member primes 6 gives no answer. This is because an infinite number of elements have to be checked before we conclude that 6 is not in the list. The problem is that member cannot use the fact that primes is ordered. This we do in memberOrd.

```
memberOrd :: Ord a => [a] -> a -> Bool
memberOrd (x:xs) n
```

```
| x<n           = memberOrd xs n
| x==n          = True
| otherwise     = False
```

The difference here is in the final case: if the head of the list (x) is greater than the element we seek (n), the element cannot be a member of the (ordered) list. Evaluating the test again,

```
memberOrd [2,3,5,7,11,...] 6
↝   memberOrd [3,5,7,11,...] 6
↝   memberOrd [5,7,11,...] 6
↝   memberOrd [7,11,...] 6
↝   False
```

2. Generating random numbers

Many computer systems require us to generate 'random' numbers, one after another. Our queuing simulation is a particular example upon which we focus here, after looking at the basics of the problem.

No Haskell program can produce a truly random sequence; after all, we want to be able to predict the behaviour of our programs, and randomness is inherently unpredictable. What we can do, however, is generate a **pseudo-random** sequence of natural numbers, smaller than modulus. This **linear congruential method** works by starting with a seed, and then by getting the next element of the sequence from the previous value thus

```
nextRand :: Int -> Int
nextRand n = (multiplier*n + increment) 'mod' modulus
```

A (pseudo-)random sequence is given by iterating this function,

```
randomSequence :: Int -> [Int]
randomSequence = iterate nextRand
```

Given the values

```
seed       = 17489
multiplier = 25173
increment  = 13849
modulus    = 65536
```

the sequence produced by randomSequence seed begins

```
[17489,59134,9327,52468,43805,8378,...
```

The numbers in this sequence, which range from 0 to 65535, all occur with the same frequency. What are we to do if instead we want the numbers to come in the (integer) range a to b inclusive? We need to scale the sequence, which is achieved by a map:

```
scaleSequence :: Int -> Int -> [Int] -> [Int]
scaleSequence s t
  = map scale
    where
    scale n = n 'div' denom + s
    range   = t-s+1
    denom   = modulus 'div' range
```

The original range of numbers 0 to modulus-1 is split into range blocks, each of the same length. The number s is assigned to values in the first block, s+1 to values in the next, and so on.

In our simulation example, we want to generate for each arrival the length of service that person will need on being served. For illustration, we suppose that they range from 1 to 6 minutes, but that they are supposed to happen with different probabilities.

Waiting time	1	2	3	4	5	6
Probability	0.2	0.25	0.25	0.15	0.1	0.05

We need a function to turn such a distribution into a transformer of infinite lists. Once we have a function transforming individual values, we can map it along the list.

We can represent a distribution of objects of type a by a list of type [(a,Float)], where we assume that the numeric entries add up to one. Our function transforming individual values will be

```
makeFunction :: [(a,Float)] -> (Float -> a)
```

so that numbers in the range 0 to 65535 are transformed into items of type a. The idea of the function is to give the following ranges to the entries for the list above.

Waiting time	1	2	3	...
Range start	0	(m*0.2)+1	(m*0.45)+1	...
Range end	m*0.2	m*0.45	m*0.7	...

where m is used for modulus. The definition follows:

```
makeFunction dist = makeFun dist 0.0

makeFun ((ob,p):dist) nLast rand
  | nNext >= rand && rand > nLast
      = ob
  | otherwise
      = makeFun dist nNext rand
        where
        nNext = p*fromInt modulus + nLast
```

The makeFun function has an extra argument, which carries the position in the range 0 to modulus-1 reached so far in the search; it is initially zero. The fromInt function used here converts an Int to an equivalent Float.

The transformation of a list of random numbers is given by

```
map (makeFunction dist)
```

and the random distribution of waiting times we require begins thus

```
map (makeFunction dist . fromInt) (randomSequence seed)
= [2,5,1,4,3,1,2,5,4,2,2,2,1,3,2,5,...
```

with 6 first appearing at the 35th position.

Another random number generator is given in the library Random.hs.

Note: Infinite list generators

The list comprehension pythagTriples2, intended to produce the list of all Pythagorean triples, instead produces *no* output to the prompt.

```
pythagTriples2 =
  = [ (x,y,z) | x <- [2 .. ] ,
                y <- [x+1 .. ] ,
                z <- [y+1 .. ] ,
                x*x + y*y == z*z ]
```

The problem is in the order of choice of the elements. The first choice for x is 2, and for y is 3; given this, there are an infinite number of values to try for z: 4, 5 and so on, indefinitely. We therefore never try any of the other choices for x or y, among which the triples lie.

Two options present themselves. First we can redefine the solution, as in the original pythagTriples, so that it involves only one infinite list. Alternatively, we can try to write a function which returns all pairs of elements from two infinite lists:

```
infiniteProduct :: [a] -> [b] -> [(a,b)]
```

This is left as an exercise. Using such a function it is possible to adapt the definition of pythagTriples2 to make it give all the Pythagorean triples.

Exercises

17.22 Define the infinite lists of factorial and Fibonacci numbers,

```
factorial = [1,1,2,6,24,120,720,...]
fibonacci = [0,1,1,2,3,5,8,13,21,...]
```

17.23 Give a definition of the function

```
factors :: Int -> [Int]
```

which returns a list containing the factors of a positive integer. For instance,

```
factors 12 = [1,2,3,4,6,12]
```

Using this function or otherwise, define the list of numbers whose only prime factors are 2, 3 and 5, the so-called **Hamming numbers**:

```
hamming = [1,2,3,4,5,6,8,9,10,12,15,...
```

17.24 Define the function

```
runningSums :: [Int] -> [Int]
```

which calculates the running sums

$$[0,a_0,a_0+a_1,a_0+a_1+a_2,\ldots$$

of a list

$$[a_0,a_1,a_2,\ldots]$$

17.25 Define the function `infiniteProduct` specified above, and use it to correct the definition of `pythagTriples2`.

17.7 Why infinite lists?

Haskell supports infinite lists and other infinite structures, and we saw in the last section that we could define a number of quite complicated lists, like the list of prime numbers, and lists of random numbers. The question remains, though, of whether these lists are anything other than a curiosity. There are two arguments which show their importance in functional programming.

First, an infinite version of a program can be more **abstract**, and so simpler to write. Consider the problem of finding the nth prime number, using the Sieve of Eratosthenes. If we work with finite lists, we need to know in advance how large a list is needed to accommodate the first n primes; if we work with an infinite list, this is not necessary: only that part of the list which is needed will be generated as computation proceeds.

In a similar way, the random numbers given by `randomSequence seed` provided an unlimited resource: we can take as many random numbers from the list as we require. There needs to be no decision at the start of programming as to the size of sequence needed. (These arguments are rather like those for **virtual memory** in a computer. It is often the case that predicting the memory use of a program is possible, but tiresome; virtual memory makes this unnecessary, and so frees the programmer to proceed with other tasks.)

The second argument is of wider significance, and can be seen by re-examining the way in which we generated random numbers. We generated an infinite list by means of `iterate`, and we transformed the values using map; these operations are pictured

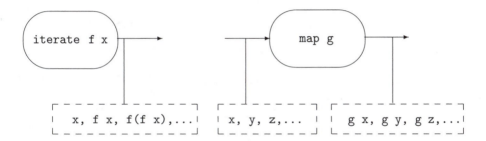

Figure 17.3 A generator and a transformer.

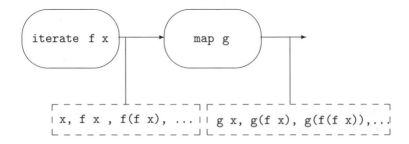

Figure 17.4 Linking processes together.

in Figure 17.3 as a generator of and a transformer of lists of values. These values are shown in the dashed boxes. These components can then be linked together, giving more complex combinations, as in Figure 17.4.   This approach **modularizes** the generation of values in a distribution in an interesting way. We have separated the generation of the values from their transformation, and this means we can change each part independently of the other.

Once we have seen the view of infinite lists as the links between processes, other combinations suggest themselves, and in particular we can begin to write process-style programs which involve **recursion**.

Among the exercises in the last section was the problem of finding the running sums

$[0,a_0,a_0+a_1,a_0+a_1+a_2,\ldots$

of the list $[a_0,a_1,a_2,\ldots.$ Given the sum up to a_k, say, we get the next sum by adding the next value in the input, a_{k+1}. It is as if we *feed the sum back* into the process to have the value a_{k+1} added. This is precisely the effect of the network of processes in Figure 17.5, where the values passing along the links are shown in the dotted boxes.

The first value in the output `out` is 0, and we get the remaining values by adding the next value in `iList` to the previous sum, appearing in the list `out`. This is translated into Haskell as follows. The output of the function on input `iList` is `out`. This is

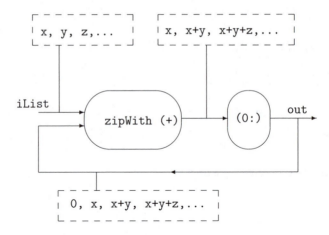

Figure 17.5 A process to compute the running sums of a list.

itself got by adding 0 to the front of the output from the zipWith (+), which itself has inputs iList and out. In other words,

```
listSums :: [Int] -> [Int]

listSums iList = out
                 where
                 out = 0 : zipWith (+) iList out
```

where we recall that zipWith is defined by

```
zipWith f (x:xs) (y:ys) = f x y : zipWith f xs ys
zipWith f _       _        = []
```

and the operator section (0:) puts a zero on the front of a list. We give a calculation of an example now.

```
listSums [1 .. ]
⤳    out
⤳    0 : zipWith (+) [1 .. ] out
⤳    0 : zipWith (+) [1 .. ] (0:...)                      (1)
⤳    0 : 1+0 : zipWith (+) [2 .. ] (1+0:...)              (2)
⤳    0 : 1 : 2+1 : zipWith (+) [3 .. ] (2+1:...)  ⤳  ...
```

In making this calculation, we replace the occurrence of out in line (1) with the incomplete list (0:...). In a similar way, we replace the tail of out by (1+0:...) in line (2).

The definition of listSums is an example of the general function scanl1', which combines values using the function f, and whose first output is st.

```
scanl1' :: (a -> b -> b) -> b -> [a] -> [b]
scanl1' f st iList
  = out
    where
    out = st : zipWith f iList out
```

The function listSums is given by scanl1' (+) 0, and a function which keeps a running sort of the initial parts of list is sorts = scanl1' ins [], where ins inserts an element in the appropriate place in a sorted list. The list of factorial values, [1,1,2,6,...] is given by scanl1' (*) 1 [1 ..], and taking this as a model, any primitive recursive function can be described in a similar way.

The definition we give here is a minor variant of the prelude function scanl, but we choose to give the definition here because of its close correspondence to the process networks for running sums given in Figure 17.5.

<hr>

Exercises

17.26 Give a definition of the list [2^n | n <- [0 ..]] using a process network based on scanl1'. (Hint: you can take the example of factorial as a guide.)

17.27 How would you select certain elements of an infinite list? For instance, how would you keep running sums of the *positive* numbers in a list of numbers?

17.28 How would you *merge* two infinite lists, assuming that they are sorted? How would you remove duplicates from the list which results? As an example, how would you merge the lists of powers of 2 and 3?

17.29 Give definitions of the lists of Fibonacci numbers [0,1,1,2,3,5,...] and Hamming numbers [1,2,3,4,5,6,8,9,...] (defined on page 370) using networks of processes. For the latter problem, you may find the merge function of the previous question useful.

(17.8) Case study: simulation

We are now in a position to put together the ingredients of the queue simulation covered in

- Section 14.5, where we designed the algebraic types Inmess and Outmess,
- Section 16.5, where the abstract types QueueState and ServerState were introduced, and in
- Section 17.6, where we showed how to generate an infinite list of pseudo-random waiting times chosen according to a distribution over the times 1 to 6.

As we said in Section 14.5, our top-level simulation will be a function from a series of input messages to a series of output messages, so

```
doSimulation :: ServerState -> [Inmess] -> [Outmess]
```

where the first parameter is the state of the server at the start of the simulation. In Section 16.5 we presented the function performing one step of the simulation,

```
simulationStep :: ServerState ->
                  Inmess ->
                  (ServerState, [Outmess])
```

which takes the current server state, and the input message arriving at the current minute and returns the state after one minute's processing, paired with the list of the output messages produced by the queues that minute (potentially every queue could release a customer at the same instant, just as no customers might be released.)

The output of the simulation will be given by the output messages generated in the first minute, and after those the results of a new simulation beginning with the updated state:

```
doSimulation servSt (im:messes)
  = outmesses ++ doSimulation servStNext messes
    where
    (servStNext , outmesses) = simulationStep servSt im
```

How do we generate an input sequence? From Section 17.6 we have the sequence of times given by

```
randomTimes
  = map (makeFunction dist . fromInt) (randomSequence seed)
  ↝  [2,5,1,4,3,1,2,5,...
```

We are to have arrivals of one person per minute, so the input messages we generate are

```
simulationInput
  = zipWith Yes [1 .. ] randomTimes
  ↝  [ Yes 1 2 , Yes 2 5 , Yes 3 1 , Yes 4 4 , Yes 5 3 ,...
```

What are the outputs produced when we run the simulation on this input with four queues, by setting the constant numQueues to 4? The output begins

```
doSimulation serverStart simulationInput
  ↝  [Discharge 1 0 2, Discharge 3 0 1, Discharge 6 0 1,
      Discharge 2 0 5, Discharge 5 0 3, Discharge 4 0 4,
      Discharge 7 2 2,...
```

The first six inputs are processed without delay, but the seventh requires a waiting time of 2 before being served.

The infinite number of arrivals represented by simulationInput will obviously generate a corresponding infinite number of output messages. We can make a finite approximation by giving the input

```
simulationInput2 = take 50 simulationInput ++ noes
noes = No : noes
```

where after one arrival in each of the first 50 minutes, no further people arrive. Fifty output messages will be generated, and we define this list of outputs thus:

```
take 50 (doSimulation serverStart simulationInput2)
```

Experimenting

We now have the facilities to begin experimenting with different data, such as the distribution and the number of queues. The total waiting time for a (finite) sequence of Outmess is given by

```
totalWait :: [Outmess] -> Int
totalWait = sum . map waitTime
            where
            waitTime (Discharge _ w _) = w
```

For simulationInput2 the total waiting time is 29, going up to 287 with three queues and down to zero with five. We leave it to the reader to experiment with the **round robin** simulation outlined in the exercises of Section 16.5.

A more substantial project is to model a set-up with a single queue feeding a number of bank clerks – one way to do this is to extend the serverState with an extra queue which feeds into the individual queues: an element leaves the feeder queue when one of the small queues is empty. This should avoid the unnecessary waiting time we face when making the wrong choice of queue, and the simulation shows that waiting times are reduced by this strategy, though by less than we might expect if service times are short.

17.9 Proof revisited

After summarizing the effect that lazy evaluation has on the types of Haskell, we examine the consequences for reasoning about programs. Taking lists as a representative example, we look at how we can prove properties of infinite lists, and of all lists, rather than simply the set of finite lists, which was the scope of the proofs we looked at in Chapters 8, 10 and 14.

This section cannot give complete coverage of the issues of verification; we conclude with pointers to further reading.

Undefinedness

In nearly every programming language, it is possible to write a program which fails to terminate, and Haskell is no exception. We call the value of such programs the **undefined** value, as it gives no result to a computation.

The simplest expression which gives an undefined result is

```
undef :: a
undef = undef                                          (undef.1)
```

which gives a non-terminating or undefined value of every type, but of course we can write an undefined program without intending to, as in

```
fak n = (n+1) * fak n
```

where we have confused the use of n and n+1 in attempting to define the factorial function. The value of `fak n` will be the same as `undef`, as they are both non-terminating.

We should remark that we are using the term 'undefined' in two different ways here. The **name** undef is given a definition by (undef.1); the **value** that the definition gives it is the undefined value, which represents the result of a calculation or evaluation which fails to terminate (and therefore fails to define a result).

The existence of these undefined values has an effect on the type of lists. What if we define, for example, the list

```
list1 = 2:3:undef
```

The list has a well-defined head, 2, and tail `3:undef`. Similarly, the tail has a head, 3, but its tail is undefined. The type `[Int]` therefore contains **partial** lists like `list1`, built from the undefined list, `undef`, parts of which are defined and parts of which are not.

Of course, there are also undefined integers, so we also include in `[Int]` lists like

```
list2 = undef:[2,3]
list3 = undef:4:undef
```

which contain undefined values, and might also be partial. Note that in `list3` the first occurrence of `undef` is at type `Int` while the second is at type `[Int]`.

What happens when a function is applied to `undef`? We use the rules for calculation we have seen already, so that the `const` function of the standard prelude satisfies

```
const 17 undef ↝  17
```

If the function applied to `undef` has to pattern match, then the result of the function will be `undef`, since the pattern match has to look at the structure of `undef`, which will never terminate. For instance, for the functions used in Chapter 8,

```
sum undef       ↝   undef                              (sum.u)
doubleAll undef ↝   undef                          (doubleAll.u)
```

In writing proofs earlier in the book we were careful to state that in some cases the results hold only for **defined** values.

An integer is defined if it is not equal to `undef`; a list is defined if it is a finite list of defined values; using this as a model it is not difficult to give a definition of the defined values of any algebraic type.

A finite list as we have defined it may contain undefined values. Note that in some earlier proofs we stipulated that the results hold only for (finite) lists of defined values, that is for defined lists.

List induction revisited

As we said above, since there is an undefined list, `undef`, in each list type, lists can be built up from this; there will therefore be two base cases in the induction principle.

Proof by structural induction: fp-lists

To prove the property `P(xs)` for all finite or partial lists (**fp-lists**) `xs` we have to do three things:

Base cases   Prove `P([])` and `P(undef)`.
Induction step Prove `P(x:xs)` assuming that `P(xs)` holds already.

Among the results we proved by structural induction in Chapter 8 were the equations

```
sum (doubleAll xs) = 2 * sum xs                    (sum-double)
xs ++ (ys ++ zs)   = (xs ++ ys) ++ zs              (assoc++)
reverse (xs ++ ys) = reverse ys ++ reverse xs      (reverse++)
```

for all **finite** lists `xs`, `ys` and `zs`. For these results to hold for all fp-lists, we need to show that

```
sum (doubleAll undef) = 2 * sum undef              (sum-double.u)
undef ++ (ys ++ zs)   = (undef ++ ys) ++ zs        (assoc++.u)
reverse (undef ++ ys) = reverse ys ++ reverse undef  (reverse++.u)
```

as well as being sure that the induction step is valid for all fp-lists. Now, by (`sum.u`) and (`doubleAll.u`) the equation (`sum-double.u`) holds, and so (`sum-double`) holds for all fp-lists. In a similar way, we can show (`assoc++.u`). More interesting is (`reverse++.u`). Recall the definition of `reverse`:

```
reverse []     = []
reverse (x:xs) = reverse xs ++ [x]
```

It is clear from this that since there is a pattern match on the parameter, `undef` as the first parameter will give an `undef` result, so

```
reverse undef = undef
```

Taking a defined list, like `[2,3]` for `ys` in (`reverse++.u`) gives

```
reverse (undef ++ [2,3])
  = reverse undef
  = undef
```

```
reverse [2,3] ++ reverse undef
  = [3,2] ++ undef
```

This is enough to show that (`reverse++.u`) does not hold, and that we cannot infer that (`reverse++`) holds for all fp-lists. Indeed the example above shows exactly that (`reverse++`) is not valid.

Infinite lists

Beside the fp-lists, there are **infinite** members of the list types. How can we prove properties of infinite lists? A hint is given by our discussion of printing the results of evaluating an infinite list. In practice what happens is that we interrupt evaluation by hitting Ctrl-C after some period of time. We can think of what we see on the screen as an **approximation** to the infinite list.

If what we see are the elements $a_0, a_1, a_2, \ldots, a_n$, we can think of the approximation being the list

```
a0:a1:a2:...:an:undef
```

since we have no information about the list beyond the element a_n.

More formally, we say that the partial lists

```
undef,  a0:undef,  a0:a1:undef,  a0:a1:a2:undef,  ...
```

are approximations to the infinite list $[a_0, a_1, a_2, \ldots, a_n, \ldots]$.

Two lists xs and ys are equal if all their approximants are equal, that is for all natural numbers n, take n xs = take n ys. (The take function gives the defined portion of the nth approximant, and it is enough to compare these parts.) A more usable version of this principle applies to infinite lists only.

Infinite list equality

A list xs is infinite if for all natural numbers n, take n xs $\neq$ take (n+1) xs.
Two infinite lists xs and ys are equal if for all natural numbers n, xs!!n = ys!!n.

> **Example** ──

Two factorial lists

Our example here is inspired by the process-based programs of Section 17.7. If fac is the factorial function

```
fac :: Int -> Int
fac 0 = 1                                              (fac.1)
fac m = m * fac (m-1)                                   (fac.2)
```

one way of defining the infinite list of factorials is

```
facMap = map fac [0 .. ]                               (facMap.1)
```

while a process-based solution is

```
facs = 1 : zipWith (*) [1 .. ] facs                    (facs.1)
```

Assuming these lists are infinite (which they clearly are), we have to prove for all natural numbers n that

```
facMap!!n = facs!!n                                    (facMap.!!)
```

Proof In our proof we will assume for all natural numbers n the results

```
(map f xs)!!n        = f (xs!!n)                          (map.!!)
(zipWith g xs ys)!!n = g (xs!!n) (ys!!n)                  (zipWith.!!)
```

which we discuss again later in this section.

(facMap.!!) is proved by mathematical induction, that is we prove the result for 0 outright, and we prove the result for a positive n assuming the result for n-1.

Base We start by proving the result at zero. Examining the left-hand side first,

```
facMap!!0
  = (map fac [0 .. ])!!0                                  by (facMap.1)
  = fac ([0 .. ]!!0)                                       by (map.!!)
  = fac 0                                           by def of [0 .. ],!!
  = 1                                                       by (fac.1)
```

The right-hand side is

```
facs!!0
  = (1 : zipWith (*) [1 .. ] facs)!!0                     by (facs.1)
  = 1                                                     by def of !!
```

thus establishing the base case.

Induction In the induction case we have to prove (facMap.!!) using the induction hypothesis:

```
facMap!!(n-1) = facs!!(n-1)                               (hyp)
```

The left-hand side of (facMap.!!) is

```
facMap!!n
  = (map fac [0 .. ])!!n                                  by (facMap.1)
  = fac ([0 .. ]!!n)                                       by (map.!!)
  = fac n                                           by def of [0 .. ],!!
  = n * fac (n-1)                                           by (fac.2)
```

It is not hard to see that we have facMap !! (n-1) = fac (n-1) by a similar argument to the first three steps here and so,

```
  = n * (facMap!!(n-1))
```

The right-hand side of (facMap.!!) is

```
facs!!n
  = (1 : zipWith (*) [1 .. ] facs)!!n                     by (facs.1)
  = (zipWith (*) [1 .. ] facs)!!(n-1)                    by def of !!
  = (*) ([1 .. ]!!(n-1)) (facs!!(n-1))                 by (zipWith.!!)
  = ([1 .. ]!!(n-1)) * (facs!!(n-1))                     by def of (*)
  = n * (facs!!(n-1))                              by def of [1 .. ],!!
  = n * (facMap!!(n-1))                                     by (hyp)
```

The final step of this proof is given by the induction hypothesis, and completes the proof of the induction step and the result itself. ∎

Proofs for infinite lists

When are results we prove for all fp-lists valid for all lists? If a result holds for all fp-lists, then it holds for all *approximations* to infinite lists. For some properties it is enough to know the property for all approximations to know that it will be valid for all infinite lists as well. In particular, this is true for all *equations*. This means that, for example, we can assert that for *all* lists xs,

```
(map f . map g) xs = map (f.g) xs
```

and therefore by the principle of extensionality for functions,

```
map f . map g = map (f.g)
```

Many other of the equations we proved initially for finite lists can be extended to proof for the fp-lists, and therefore to all lists. Some of these are given in the exercises which follow.

Further reading

The techniques we have given here provide a flavour of how to write proofs for infinite lists and infinite data structures in general. We cannot give the breadth or depth of a full presentation, but refer the reader to Paulson (1987) for more details. An alternative approach to proving the factorial list example is given in Thompson (1999), which also gives a survey of proof in functional programming.

Exercises

17.30 Show that for all fp-lists ys and zs,

```
undef ++ (ys ++ zs)  = (undef ++ ys) ++ zs
```

to infer that ++ is associative over all lists.

17.31 If rev xs is defined to be shunt xs [], as in Section 8.7, show that

```
rev (rev undef) = undef                                    (rev-rev.1)
```

In Chapter 8 we proved that

```
rev (rev xs) = xs                                          (rev-rev.2)
```

for all finite lists xs.

Why can we not infer from (rev-rev.1) and (rev-rev.2) that the equation rev (rev xs) = xs holds for all fp-lists xs?

17.32 Prove for all natural numbers m, n and functions f :: Int -> a that

```
(map f [m .. ])!!n = f (m+n)
```

[Hint: you will need to choose the right variable for the induction proof.]

17.33 Prove that the lists

```
facMap = map fac [0 .. ]
facs = 1 : zipWith (*) [1 .. ] facs
```

are infinite.

17.34 If we define indexing thus

```
(x:_)!!0   = x
(_:xs)!!n = xs!!(n-1)
[]!!n      = error "Indexing"
```

show that for all functions f, fp-lists xs and natural numbers n,

```
(map f xs)!!n = f (xs!!n)
```

and therefore infer that the result is valid for all lists xs. State and prove a similar result for zipWith.

17.35 Show that the following equations hold between functions.

```
filter p . map f      = map f . filter (p . f)
filter p . filter q  = filter (q &&& p)
concat . map (map f) = map f . concat
```

where the operator &&& is defined by

```
(q &&& p) x = q x && p x
```

Summary

Lazy evaluation of Haskell expressions means that we can write programs in a different style. A data structure created within a program execution will only be created on demand, as we saw with the example of finding the sum of fourth powers. In finding routes through a graph we saw that we could explore just that part of the graph which is needed to reveal a path. In these and many more cases the advantage of lazy evaluation is to give programs whose purpose is clear and whose execution is efficient.

We re-examined the list comprehension notation, which makes many list processing programs easier to express; we saw this in the particular examples of route finding and parsing.

A design principle exploited in this chapter involved the use of lazy lists: if a function can return multiple results it is possible to represent this as a list; using lazy evaluation, the multiple results will only be generated one-by-one, as they are required. Also, we are able to represent 'no result' by the empty list, []. This 'list of successes' method is useful in a variety of contexts.

Exploiting this principle as well as higher-order functions, polymorphism and list comprehensions we gave a library of parsing functions, which we saw applied to the type of arithmetical expressions, Expr. This showed one of the strengths of modern functional programming languages, whose constructs are especially well suited to describing general toolkits of this sort.

Rather than being simply a curiosity, this chapter has shown that we can exploit infinite lists for a variety of purposes.

- In giving an *infinite* list of prime or random numbers we provide an unlimited resource: we do not have to know how much of the resource we need while constructing the program; this *abstraction* makes programming simpler and clearer.

- Infinite lists provide a mechanism for process-based programming in a functional setting.

The chapter concluded with a discussion of how proofs could be lifted to the partial and infinite elements of the list type: criteria were given in both cases and we gave examples and counter-examples in illustration.

Chapter 18

Programming with actions

The programs we have written so far in this book have been self-contained. However, most larger-scale programs have some interaction with the `world outside'. This can take many forms.

● A program, like the Hugs interpreter itself, can read from a terminal and write to a terminal.

● A mail system reads and writes from files as well as standard terminal channels.

● An operating system executes programs in parallel, as well as controlling devices like printers, CD-ROM readers and terminals.

This chapter explores how the simplest kinds of programs, reading and writing to a terminal, can be developed in Haskell. The model we describe forms the foundation for more complex interactions like those in a mail system or an operating system.

We begin the chapter by discussing how in the past I/O has been a problem for the users of a functional language. The solution in Haskell is to introduce the types IO a, which we can think of as **programs** that do some input/output before returning a value of type a. These programs include simple operations to read and write information, as well complex programs which are built from a number of IO programs sequenced into one by means of the do construct.

We show a number of examples of interactive programs, including an interactive version of the calculator case study, and also discuss some of the more general I/O facilities in the standard prelude and libraries.

The sequential nature of the IO a types is not peculiar to I/O and in the second half of the chapter we show how these types are simply one example of the more general phenomenon of a **monad**; other examples include side-effects, error-handling and non-determinacy.

We argue that monads provide a powerful structuring mechanism for functional programs incorporating these effects, as well as providing an interface between the functional and imperative worlds. We illustrate this versatility by showing that two substantially different programs over a tree will have the same top-level structure if they are programmed in a monadic style.

(18.1) Why is I/O an issue?

A functional program consists of a number of definitions, such as

```
val :: Int
val = 42

function :: Int -> Int
function n = val + n
```

The effect of these definitions is to associate a fixed value with each name; in the case of val the value is an integer and in the case of function it is a function from integers to integers. How is an input or an output action to fit into this model?

One approach – taken in Standard ML (Milner *et al.* 1997), for instance – is to include operations like

```
inputInt :: Int
```

whose effect is to read an integer from the input; the value read in becomes the value given to inputInt. Each time inputInt is evaluated it will be given a new value, and so it is not a fixed integer value as it ought to be according to our original model.

Allowing this operation into our language may not seem to cause too big a problem, but examining the example of

```
inputDiff = inputInt - inputInt                          (inputDiff)
```

shows how it has two important consequences for our model of functional programming.

- Suppose that the first item input is 4, and that the next is 3. Depending upon the order in which the arguments to '-' are evaluated, the value of inputDiff will be either 1 or -1.

- More seriously, (inputDiff.1) breaks the model of reasoning which we have used. We would hitherto have expected that subtracting a value from itself would have given a result of 0, but that is *not* the case here.

  The reason for this is precisely that the meaning of an expression is no longer determined by looking only at the meanings of its parts, since we cannot give a meaning to inputInt without knowing where it occurs in a program; as we saw in the previous point, the first and second occurrences of inputInt in inputDiff will generally have different values.

As the second point shows, if we take this approach then it will be substantially more difficult to understand the meaning of any program. This is because *any* definition in a program may be affected by the presence of the I/O operations. An example is the function

```
funny :: Int -> Int
funny n = inputInt + n
```

from whose definition we can see the dependence on I/O, but potentially any function may be affected in a similar way.

Because of this, I/O proved to be a thorny issue for functional programmers for some considerable time, and there have been a number of attempts to find the right model for I/O – indeed, earlier versions of Haskell included two of these. An illuminating history and overview of functional I/O is given in Gordon (1994).

This chapter describes the **monadic** approach, which has proved to be a robust model that extends easily to other sorts of interaction with the 'world outside'. The basic idea of monadic I/O is to control how programs that perform I/O are built, and in particular to limit the way that the I/O operations affect functions in general. This is the topic of the next section.

(18.2) The basics of input/output

In thinking about **input/output** or **I/O** it makes more sense to think of **actions happening in sequence**. For instance, first some input might be read, and then on the basis of that some further input might be read, or output might be produced.

Haskell provides the types IO a of **I/O actions of type** a or **I/O programs of type** a. An object belonging to IO a is a **program** which will do some I/O and then return a value of type a. Built into Haskell are some primitive I/O programs, as well as a mechanism to sequence these I/O programs.

One way of looking at the IO a types is that they provide a simple imperative programming language for writing I/O programs on top of Haskell, without compromising the functional model of Haskell itself.

The best way to understand how IO a works is to look at some representative examples of objects in IO a which come from the standard prelude. We then examine how to put these components together using the do notation to form more complex I/O programs.

Reading input

The operation which reads a line of text from the standard input does some I/O and returns a `String` which is the line just read. According to the explanation above, this should be an object of type `IO String`, and indeed, the built-in function

```
getLine :: IO String
```

reads a line from the standard input. In a similar way,

```
getChar :: IO Char
```

will read a single character from the input.

The one-element type

Haskell contains the type `()`, which contains one element only. This element is also written `()`. A value of this type can convey no useful information and so the type is not often used. However, it *is* useful in performing `IO`, as there are cases of IO programs whose only significance is their I/O actions and not the results they return. Programs of that sort will have type

```
IO ()
```

and they will return the value `()` as their result.

Writing `Strings`

The operation of writing the string `"Hello, World!"` will be an object which performs some I/O, but which has nothing of significance to pass back to the program. It is therefore of type `IO ()`.

The general operation to print a text string will be a **function** which takes the string to be written, and gives back the I/O object which writes that string:

```
putStr :: String -> IO ()
```

and using this we can write our 'hello, world' program.

```
helloWorld :: IO ()
helloWorld = putStr "Hello, World!"
```

Using `putStr` we can define a function to write a line of output.

```
putStrLn :: String -> IO ()
putStrLn = putStr . (++ "\n")
```

The effect of this is to add a newline to the end of its input before passing it to `putStr`.

Writing values in general

The Haskell prelude provides the class Show with the function

```
show :: Show a => a -> String
```

which can be used to write values of many types. For example, we can define a general print function from the standard prelude thus

```
print :: Show a => a -> IO ()
print = putStrLn . show
```

Returning a value: return

Suppose we want to write an I/O action which does no I/O but does return a value – we will see examples of this in due course. This is achieved by the built-in function

```
return :: a -> IO a
```

The effect of IO x is to do no I/O, but simply to return the result x.

Running an I/O program

We have written a simple I/O program, namely helloWorld; how is it run? In Hugs we can evaluate it at the prompt:

```
Main> helloWorld
Hello, World!
Main> ...
```

Strictly speaking, the main definition of a Haskell program should be of type IO a for some a. In Hugs, if we ask to evaluate an expression e of type b then it is wrapped up as an object of type IO () by applying the print function.

This completes our introduction to the basic I/O functions in the standard prelude as well as the method by which IO a programs are run.

We now need to look at how programs are sequenced, and also how to use the values read in by means of input programs like getLine; this is the topic of the next section.

(18.3) The do notation

The do notation is a flexible mechanism which supports two things:

● it is used to sequence I/O programs, and
● it is used to 'capture' the values returned by IO actions and so to pass these values to actions which follow them in the program.

Together these ideas make a do expression appear like a simple imperative program, containing a sequence of commands and assignments; although this analogy is not complete – we examine how it breaks down in the next section – it shows that the model of I/O given by the IO types is a familiar one, albeit in a different guise.

Sequencing I/O actions

One purpose of the do construct is to sequence I/O actions and we show how it is used through a series of examples.

1. We begin by looking at the definition of putStrLn from the standard prelude. The effect of putStrLn str is to do two things: first the string str is output, then a newline. This is accomplished by

```
putStrLn :: String -> IO ()
putStrLn str = do putStr str
                  putStr "\n"
```

Here we see the effect of do is to sequence a number of IO actions into a single action. The syntax of do is governed by the offside rule, and do can take any number of arguments. We see an example of more arguments next.

2. We can write an I/O program to print something four times. The first version of this is

```
put4times :: String -> IO ()
put4times str
  = do putStrLn str
       putStrLn str
       putStrLn str
       putStrLn str
```

3. Rather than 'hard wiring' the number of times to output the string, we can make this a parameter of the program,

```
putNtimes :: Int -> String -> IO ()
putNtimes n str
  = if n <= 1
       then putStrLn str
       else do putStrLn str
               putNtimes (n-1) str
```

and using this we can give another definition of put4times,

```
put4times = putNtimes 4
```

4. We have only seen examples of output, but we can also make inputs a part of a sequence of actions. For instance, we can read two lines of input and then output the message "Two lines read." thus:

```
read2lines :: IO ()
read2lines
  = do getLine
       getLine
       putStrLn "Two lines read."
```

and by analogy with Example 3 it is not difficult to see that we could write an I/O program which reads an arbitrary number of lines.

Capturing the values read

As was apparent in Section 18.1, it is necessary to be careful in the way that the results of input actions are handled. The operation inputInt :: Int was shown to be too powerful to fit into the functional model, but some mechanism to handle input values is required. This is the second purpose of the do notation; it is only possible to use the result of an input within a do expression, and this limitation prevents the I/O actions from 'contaminating' the whole program.

The sequence of examples continues by examining this aspect of the do notation.

Examples

5. The last example read two lines, but did nothing with the results of the getLine actions. How can we use these lines in the remainder of the I/O program? As part of a do program we can **name** the results of IO a actions. A program to read a line and then write that line is given by

```
getNput :: IO ()
getNput = do line <- getLine
             putStrLn line
```

where the 'line <-' names the result of the getLine.

If you are familiar with imperative programming you can think of this as like an assignment to a variable, as in

```
line := getLine
```

but you should be aware that there are important differences between the names in a Haskell I/O program and the variables in an imperative program. The essential difference is that each 'var <-' creates a *new* variable var, and so the language permits '**single** assignment' rather than the 'updatable assignment' familiar from the vast majority of modern imperative languages; we will say more about this difference in Section 18.4.

6. We are not forced simply to output the lines we have read, unchanged, so that we might define

```
reverse2lines :: IO ()
reverse2lines
  = do line1 <- getLine
       line2 <- getLine
       putStrLn (reverse line2)
       putStrLn (reverse line1)
```

In this example, we read two lines, and then write them in the opposite order, reversed.

Local definitions in a do expression

The notation var <- getLine names the output of the getLine, and so acts like a definition. It is also possible to make local definitions within a do expression so that we can revisit the last example, as follows.

(**Example**)────────────────────────────────

7. Example 6 can be redefined to contain local definitions of the reversed lines

```
reverse2lines :: IO ()
reverse2lines
  = do line1 <- getLine
       line2 <- getLine
       let rev1 = reverse line1
       let rev2 = reverse line2
       putStrLn rev2
       putStrLn rev1
```

Reading values in general

Haskell contains the class Read with the function

```
read :: Read a => String -> a
```

which can be used to parse a string representing a value of a particular type into that value.

(**Example**)────────────────────────────────

8. As an example, suppose that we want to write an I/O program to read in an integer value. To read an integer from a line of input we start by saying

```
do line <- getLine
```

but then we need to sequence this with an I/O action to return the line interpreted as an Int. We can convert the line to an integer by the expression

```
read line :: Int
```

What we need is the `IO Int` action which returns this value – this is the purpose of `return` introduced in the previous section. Our program to read an `Int` is therefore

```
getInt :: IO Int
getInt = do line <- getLine
            return (read line :: Int)
```

Summary

This section has shown that a do expression provides a context in which to do sequential programming. It is possible to program complicated I/O interactions, by sequencing simpler I/O programs. Moreover, the '<-' allows us to name the value returned by an action and then to use this named value in the remainder of the I/O program. It is also possible to make these programs more readable by judicious use of `let` definitions to name intermediate calculations.

In the next section we look at how to write repetitive I/O programs, reading all the lines in the input, for example. We shall see that this can be done by defining a looping construct recursively. We also discuss the way in which '<-' behaves differently from the usual assignment operator.

Exercises

18.1 Write an I/O program which will read a line of input and test whether the input is a palindrome. The program should 'prompt' for its input and also output an appropriate message after testing.

18.2 Write an I/O program which will read two integers, each on a separate line, and return their sum. The program should prompt for input and explain its output.

18.3 Write an I/O program which will first read a positive integer, n say, and then read n integers and write their sum. The program should prompt appropriately for its inputs and explain its output.

18.4 Iteration and recursion

In this section we examine how to build I/O programs with a repetitive nature; this will involve us building a general `while`-loop operation, as well as seeing the difference between variables and the names used in do expressions.

A `while` loop

Suppose that we want to repeat an `IO ()` action *while* a **condition** is true. The condition will depend upon the I/O system, and so will be of type

```
IO Bool
```

An example of this, which is provided in the library module IO.hs, is a test for the end of input,

```
isEOF :: IO Bool
```

This discussion means that our while-loop construct will have the type

```
while :: IO Bool -> IO () -> IO ()
```

and the function itself is given by

```
while test action
  = do res <- test
       if res then do action
                      while test action
              else return ()
```

which is a sequence of two IO actions. In the first we perform the test, and its Boolean result is named res. The second action is conditional on the value of res; if res is True then the action performed is

```
do action
   while test action
```

This means that in the then case the effect is first to perform the action and then to repeat the loop. On the other hand, if the condition is False the effect of the program should be to 'do nothing'. The null I/O action is

```
return ()
```

since it returns the single value of type () without performing any I/O.

Copying input to output

Now we look at an example of the while loop in practice. If we want to copy the input to the output, line by line, we can write this as a while loop. Informally,

```
while -- not end of file
         -- read and write a line
```

How to test for not being the end of file? We want to perform the test isEOF but to return the negation of the result. This we do by writing

```
do res <- isEOF
   return (not res)
```

What action do we want to do if there is still input to be read? We read then write, as we saw earlier,

```
do line <- getLine
   putStrLn line
```

Putting this together we have the program

```
copyInputToOutput :: IO ()
copyInputToOutput
  = while (do res <- isEOF
              return (not res))
          (do line <- getLine
              putStrLn line)
```

where it should be noted that the parentheses are necessary.

An important example

Suppose now that we want to copy lines of input until we hit a line which is empty, when we stop. A first attempt might be

```
goUntilEmpty :: IO ()
goUntilEmpty
  = do line <- getLine                          (1)
       while (return (line /= []))              (2)
             (do putStrLn line                  (3)
                 line <- getLine                (4)
                 return ())                     (5)
```

where the lines have been numbered to make discussion easier. The apparent effect of this program is as follows. At (1) a line is read, and named `line`; while this line is not empty – the test `return (line /= [])` at (2) – we output `line` at (3) and read another line into `line` at (4).

The effect of this program is repeatedly to write out the *first line* of the input; that is the `line` read in at (1) and used in (2) and (3). In (4) we create a **new variable** `line` and associate the value read with it, but this is not a re-assignment to the original variable, and so the test in (2) and the print in (3) still refer to the first line. It is in this way that these variables differ from the variables of an imperative programming language: if we think of

```
line <- getLine
```

as an assignment `line := getLine` then it is a *single assignment* to a variable which cannot be updated: every occurrence of `line <- ...` creates a new variable. In other words, the variables here do not change their values.

How can we think of writing a correct program to this specification? The key is to think recursively.

```
goUntilEmpty :: IO ()
goUntilEmpty
  = do line <- getLine                          (1)
       if (line == [])                          (2)
         then return ()                         (3)
         else (do putStrLn line                 (4)
                  goUntilEmpty)                 (5)
```

The effect here is to get a line, (1), and if that line is empty, (2), the I/O actions halt with the `return ()` in (3). On the other hand, if the `line` is not empty it is output at (4). This is followed by the whole program being reinvoked, and when this is done, the next line read is called `line`, and if that is not empty, (2), (4) and (5) are repeated for this new `line`.

Adding a sequence of integers

Now suppose we want to write an interactive program to sum integers supplied one per line until zero is input. We will write an I/O program

```
sumInts :: IO Int
```

which returns this sum. In writing the program there are two cases: if we read zero then the result must be zero; if not, we get the result by adding the number just read to the sum of the remaining lines, which is given by calling `sumInts` again. This gives the program

```
sumInts
  = do n <- getInt
       if n==0
          then return 0
          else (do m <- sumInts
                   return (n+m))
```

where we use the `getInt` function defined earlier to read a single `Int` on a line of its own. It is interesting with compare this with the recursion in

```
sum [] = 0
sum (n:ns)
   = n + sum ns
```

or especially with a modified definition of sum

```
sum [] = 0
sum (n:ns)
   = let m = sum ns
     in (n + m)
```

We can also put the `sumInts` program inside a 'wrapper' which explains its purpose and prints the sum at the end.

```
sumInteract :: IO ()
sumInteract
   = do putStrLn "Enter integers one per line"
        putStrLn "These will be summed until zero is entered"
        sum <- sumInts
        putStr "The sum was "
        print sum
```

18.4 Write a program which repeatedly reads lines and tests whether they are palindromes until an empty line is read. The program should explain clearly to the user what input is expected and output is produced.

18.5 Write a program which repeatedly reads integers (one per line) until finding a zero value and outputs a sorted version of the inputs read. Which sorting algorithm is most appropriate in such a case?

18.6 Give a definition of the function

```
mapF :: (a -> b) -> IO a -> IO b
```

the effect of which is to transform an interaction by applying the function to its result. You should define it using the do construct.

18.7 Define the function

```
repeat ::  IO Bool -> IO () -> IO ()
```

so that `repeat test oper` has the effect of repeating `oper` until the condition `test` is True.

18.8 Give a generalization of `while` in which the condition and the operation work over values of type a. Its new type is

```
whileG :: (a -> IO Bool) -> (a -> IO a) -> (a -> IO a)
```

18.9 Using the function `whileG` or otherwise, define an interaction which reads a number, n say, and then reads a further n numbers and finally returns their average.

18.10 Modify your answer to the previous question so that if the end of file is reached before n numbers have been read, a message to that effect is printed.

18.11 Define a function

```
accumulate :: [IO a] -> IO [a]
```

which performs a sequence of interactions and accumulates their result in a list. Also give a definition of the function

```
sequence :: [IO a] -> IO ()
```

which performs the interactions in turn, but discards their results. Finally, show how you would sequence a series, passing values from one to the next:

```
seqList :: [a -> IO a] -> a -> IO a
```

What will be the result on an empty list?

(18.5) **The calculator**

The ingredients of the calculator are contained in three places in the text.

● In Section 14.2 we saw the introduction of the algebraic type of expressions, Expr, which we subsequently revised in Section 17.5, giving

```
data Expr = Lit Int | Var Var | Op Ops Expr Expr
data Ops  = Add | Sub | Mul | Div | Mod
type Var  = Char
```

We revise the evaluation of expressions after discussing the store below.

● In Chapter 16 we introduced the abstract type Store, which we use to model the values of the variables currently held. The signature of the abstract data type is

```
initial :: Store
value   :: Store -> Var -> Int
update  :: Store -> Var -> Int -> Store
```

● In Section 17.5 we looked at how to parse expressions and commands,

```
data Command = Eval Expr | Assign Var Expr | Null
```

and defined the ingredients of the function

```
commLine :: String -> Command
```

which is used to parse each line of input into a Command. For instance,

```
commLine "(3+x)"   = (Eval (Op Add (Lit 3) (Var 'x')))
commLine "x:(3+x)" = (Assign 'x' (Op Add (Lit 3) (Var 'x')))
commLine ""        = Null
```

Expressions are evaluated by

```
eval :: Expr -> Store -> Int

eval (Lit n) st = n
eval (Var v) st = value st v
eval (Op op e1 e2) st
  = opValue op v1 v2
    where
    v1 = eval e1 st
    v2 = eval e2 st
```

where the opValue function of type Ops->Int->Int->Int interprets each operator, such as Add, as the corresponding function, like (+).

What is the effect of a command? An expression should return the value of the expression in the current store; an assignment will change the store, and a null command will do nothing. We therefore define a function which returns both a value and a store,

```
command :: Command -> Store -> (Int,Store)

command Null st     = (0 , st)
command (Eval e) st = (eval e st , st)
command (Assign v e) st
  = (val , newSt)
    where
    val   = eval e st
    newSt = update st v val
```

A single step of the calculator will take a starting Store, and read an input line, evaluate the command in the line, print some output and finally return an updated Store,

```
calcStep :: Store -> IO Store

calcStep st
  = do line <- getLine
       let comm          = commLine line            (1)
           (val,newSt) = command comm st            (2)
       print val
       return newSt
```

In lines (1) and (2) of the definition of calcStep we see an example of the use of let within a do expression. Line (1),

```
let comm          = commLine line
```

gives comm the value of parsing the line, and this is subsequently used in (2),

```
(val,newSt) = command comm st
```

which simultaneously gives val and newSt the value of the expression read and the new state. Note that the let extends over multiple lines, and that it is terminated by the symbol 'print'. In the lines that follow the let, the value val is printed and the new state newSt is returned as the overall result of the interaction.

A sequence of calculator steps is given by

```
calcSteps :: Store -> IO ()

calcSteps st
  = while notEOF
          (do newSt <- calcStep st
              calcSteps newSt)
```

where the looping test `notEOF` is given by

```
notEOF :: IO Bool
notEOF = do res <- isEOF
            return (not res)
```

and the main I/O program for the calculator is given by starting off `calcSteps` with the `initial` store.

```
mainCalc :: IO ()
mainCalc = calcSteps initial
```

In the exercises various extensions and modifications of the calculator program are discussed.

Exercises

18.12 How would you add initial and final messages to the output of the calculator?

18.13 If the calculator is not given a valid command, then an error message will be generated by the function `topLevel`, and evaluation stops. Discuss how you would add an extra argument to `topLevel` to be used in the error case, so that evaluation with the calculator does not halt.

18.14 Discuss how you would have to modify the system to allow variables to have arbitrarily long names, consisting of letters and numbers, starting with a letter.

18.15 How would you extend the calculator to deal with decimal floating-point numbers as well as integers?

18.16 Discuss how you would modify the calculator so that it could read input commands split over more than one line. You will need to decide how this sort of split is signalled by the user – maybe by \ at the end of the line – and how to modify the interaction program to accommodate this. Alternatively, you might let the user do this without signalling; can you modify the program to do that?

18.17 How would you modify the parser so that 'white space' is permitted in the input commands, as in the example

```
"   x : (2\t+3)      "
```

which parses to the `Command`

```
(Assign 'x' (Op Add (Lit 2) (Lit 3)))
```

18.6 Further I/O

In this section we survey further features of Haskell I/O.

File I/O

So far we have seen that we can read from the terminal – the 'standard input' – and write to the screen – the 'standard output'. The Haskell I/O model also provides for reading from and writing and appending to files, by means of the functions

```
readFile   :: FilePath -> IO String
writeFile  :: FilePath -> String -> IO ()
appendFile :: FilePath -> String -> IO ()
```

where

```
type FilePath = String
```

and files are specified by the text strings appropriate to the implementation in question.

Errors

I/O programs can raise errors, which belong to the system-dependent data type IOError. The function

```
ioError :: IOError -> IO a
```

builds an I/O action which fails giving the appropriate error, and the program

```
catch :: IO a -> (IOError -> IO a) -> IO a
```

will catch an error raised by the first argument and handle it using the second argument, which gives a handler – that is an action of type IO a – for each possible IOError. More details of error handling can be found in the documentation for the I/O library IO.hs.

Input and output as lazy lists

An alternative view of I/O programs, popular in earlier lazy functional programming languages, was to see the input and output as Strings, that is as lists of characters. Under that model an I/O program is a function

```
listIOprog :: String -> String
```

This obviously makes sense in a 'batch' program, where all the input is read before any output is produced, but in fact it also works for interactive programs where input and output are interleaved, if the language is **lazy**. This is because in a lazy language we can begin to print the result of a computation – the output of the interactive program here – before the argument – the interactive input – is fully evaluated. As an example, repeatedly to reverse lines of input under this model one can write

```
unlines . map reverse . lines
```

The drawback of this approach is in scaling it up. It is often difficult to predict in advance the way in which the input and output are interleaved: often output comes after it is expected, and sometimes even before; the IO approach in Haskell avoids such problems. Nevertheless, support for this style is available, using

```
getContents :: IO String
```

a primitive to get the contents of the standard input, and which is used in

```
interact :: (String -> String) -> IO ()
interact f = do s <- getContents
                putStr (f s)
```

The IO.hs library

A more sophisticated library for manipulating files and their contents appears in IO.hs. It is based on the principles introduced here, and is covered in the Library documentation.

Exercises

18.18 Write file-handling versions of the programs goUntilEmpty and sumInts.

18.19 Write lazy-list versions of the programs goUntilEmpty and sumInts.

18.20 [Harder] Write a lazy-list version of the calculator program.

18.7 The do construct revisited

We have seen that the type IO a comes with various functions, including

```
return  :: a -> IO a
putStr  :: String -> IO ()
getLine :: IO String
```

but also items of the IO a type can be sequenced using the do construct. In this section we look 'under the bonnet' to see how the do works, as this will lead to us seeing IO as just one example of a general phenomenon.

The key to understanding the do is the operation (>>=), which is often pronounced 'then', which sequences two operations, one after the other, passing the result of the first as a parameter to the second.

```
(>>=) :: IO a -> (a -> IO b) -> IO b
```

What is the effect of this operation? It combines an IO a

with a **function** taking the result of this (of type a) into an IO b, that is an object of type a -> IO b,

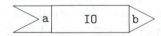

We can join them together, passing the result of the first as an argument to the second, thus:

The result of putting them together is something which does some I/O before returning a value of type b:

in other words, an object of type IO b.

How does this relate to the do notation? We look at an example by way of explanation. Consider what happens in the program

```
addOneInt :: IO ()
addOneInt
  = do line <- getLine
       putStrLn (show (1 + read line :: Int))
```

The value returned by getLine is called line and then used in the subsequent interaction. Using (>>=) we have to sequence the interaction with a function expecting an argument of type String, so we write

```
addOneInt
  = getLine >>= \line ->
    putStrLn (show (1 + read line :: Int))
```

where recall that \x -> e is the function which takes the parameter x to result e, so here the parameter is called line, and used just as above. More complex examples are translated in a similar way.

We will continue to use the do notation, but will note that it rests on the existence of a function (>>=) which does the work of sequencing I/O programs.

Exercise

18.21 Repeat some of the earlier examples and exercises using the >>= operator instead of a do expression.

18.8 Monads for functional programming

As research and experience in functional programming have increased, certain styles of programming have shown themselves to be particularly elegant and powerful. Among these is the **monadic** style, which extends beyond I/O to cover a number of fields. This section contains an introductory discussion of the approach; further details of this and other advanced techniques can be found in Jeuring and Meijer (1995).

As we have already seen, a characteristic of monads is that they make explicit the sequence in which operations take place. It is the do construct, which is itself based on the combinator >>= which sequences the operations of a general monad m.

```
(>>=) :: m a -> (a -> m b) -> m b
```

When is such a sequencing necessary? Consider the example of the numeric expression

```
e - f
```

As this is simply an expression, we can choose to evaluate the arguments to -, e and f, in either order, or indeed in parallel. Suppose, however, that the expressions e and f cause some I/O to take place, or cause some store to be changed. Then we need to say in which order the evaluation takes place, since different orders will give different results. A simple example, first discussed in Section 18.1, is

```
inputInt - inputInt
```

If the input is 7 followed by 4, evaluation left-to-right gives 3, while right-to-left gives −3; parallel evaluation has an unpredictable effect!

How do we achieve an explicit sequence? The operation

```
do e <- getInt
   f <- getInt
   return (e-f)
```

clearly inputs the left-hand value before the right, where getInt :: IO Int performs integer input.

This sort of explicit sequencing is, as we said, a feature of many kinds of programming where **side-effects** accompany a computation. The novel feature of the monadic approach is that these side-effects can be incorporated into a **pure** functional programming language by means of monads.

We should now say formally what a monad is.

What is a monad?

A monad is a family of types m a, based on a polymorphic type constructor m, with functions return, (>>=), (>>), and fail:

```
class Monad m where
  (>>=)  :: m a -> (a -> m b) -> m b
  return :: a -> m a
  (>>)   :: m a -> m b -> m b
  fail   :: String -> m a
```

This is an example of a **constructor class**, which is like a type class, except that the things which belong to a constructor class are **type constructors** – that is functions which build types from types – rather than types. Examples of type constructors are 'list', written [] in Haskell, and IO as we have seen already.

The definition of Monad also contains default declarations for >> and fail:

```
m >> k = m >>= \_ -> k
fail s = error s
```

From this definition it can be seen that >> acts like >>=, except that the value returned by the first argument is discarded rather than being passed to the second argument.

In order properly to be a monad, the functions return and (>>=) and the value zero should have some simple properties. Informally we can state the requirements as follows.

- The operation return x should simply return the value x, without any additional computational effect, such as input or output in the case of the IO monad.
- The sequencing given by >>= should be irrelevant of the way that expressions are bracketed.
- The value fail s corresponds to a computation which **fails**, giving the error message s.

The laws are much clearer when stated in terms of a derived operator, >@>.

```
(>@>) :: Monad m => (a -> m b) ->
                    (b -> m c) ->
                    (a -> m c)
```

```
f >@> g = \x -> (f x) >>= g
```

This operator generalizes function composition[1] in that it composes objects

to give

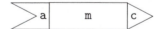

Note also that return is of this shape, as its type is a -> m a.

Now we can state formally the rules that the operations of a monad should satisfy. First, return is an **identity** for the operator >@>:

```
return >@> f = f                                            (M1)
f >@> return = f                                            (M2)
```

and the operator >@> should be **associative**:

```
(f >@> g) >@> h = f >@> (g >@> h)                           (M3)
```

The derived sequencing operator, >>, is also associative.

Of course, there is no way that we can make the requirements (M1)–(M3) a part of the Haskell definition of Monad.

We can also restate the rules in terms of do, since

---

[1] In category theory, this operation is called **Kleisli composition**.

```
m >>= f  =  do x <- m
               f x
```

The first two rules become

```
do y <- return x  =  f x
   f y
do x <- m          =  m
   return x
```

and the third is implicit in the fact that the do construct is associative.

Some examples of monads

We said earlier that we can think of a monad m a as representing some sort of computation, with elements of m a being 'computations' which perform actions of some sort before returning a value of type a. Here we look at a number of examples and explain their computational interpretation.

The identity monad

The identity monad, which takes a type to itself, is the simplest example of a monad, with the definitions

```
m >>= f = f m
return  = id
```

Under this interpretation, >@> becomes forward composition of functions, >.>, which is indeed associative and has id as its identity. An undefined computation sequenced with any other computation will be undefined.

Computationally, this monad represents the trivial state in which no actions are performed, and values are returned immediately.

The input/output monad

We have already seen the example of the IO monad in Section 18.2.

Other examples come from **collections** of objects.

The list monad

We can build a monad from lists

```
instance Monad [] where
  xs >>= f  = concat (map f xs)
  return x  = [x]
  fail s    = []
```

The computational interpretation of the list monad is of non-deterministic computation: an element of [a] represents *all* the results of a potentially non-deterministic computation. In this case the return gives a single answer, while >>= applies the function f to every possible outcome in xs, and concatenates the results to give a single list of overall outcomes. The value fail s corresponds to there being no result of the non-deterministic computation; a **failure** to give a result, in other words.

The Maybe *monad*

Another instance of a monad is given by the 'maybe' type, Maybe a, whose values are 'just' members of a or the single value Nothing – they *maybe* contain a value of type a:

```
instance Monad Maybe where
  (Just x) >>= k  =  k x
  Nothing  >>= k  =  Nothing
  return          =  Just
  fail s          =  Nothing
```

The computational interpretation here is of computations which might produce a result, but that might also produce an error; this was discussed at some length in Section 14.4.

The parsing *monad*

A fifth example is given by parsing, where we can show that Parse a is a monad. To make a formal declaration of this we need to wrap it in a new data constructor, SParse, whose inclusion clutters the definition somewhat.

```
data SParse a b = SParse (Parse a b)

instance Monad (SParse a) where
  return x = SParse (succeed x)
  fail s   = SParse none
  (SParse pr) >>= f
    = SParse (\st -> concat [ sparse (f x) rest | (x,rest) <- pr st ])

sparse :: SParse a b -> Parse a b
sparse (SParse pr) = pr
```

The crux of the definition of (>>=) is like that of (>*>) – a parse is done by one parser, pr, and the remains of the input are passed to a second parser f, here dependent on the result of the first parse, and so a result of the first parse, x, is passed to f to give a second parser, which is applied to the remaining input, rest.

The state *monad*

Later in this chapter we will give an example of a **state** monad, State a b. An operation of this type can change the state (of type a) before returning a value of type b.

Combining monads

The monads here can be combined to give more complex effects, so that one can build computations which perform I/O and manipulate a state value, for instance. A full account of how this can be done in a systematic way is given in Liang, Hudak and Jones (1995).

Some standard functions

We can define some standard functions over every monad. Their types should be familiar from the list case

```
mapF  :: Monad m => (a -> b) -> m a -> m b
joinM :: Monad m => m (m a) -> m a
```

and their definitions are

```
mapF f m
  = do x <- m
       return (f x)
joinM m
  = do x <- m
       x
```

Over lists these functions are called `map` and `concat`; many of the properties of `map` and `concat` over lists lift to these functions. For instance, we can show using properties (M1) to (M3) that for all `f` and `g`

$$mapF\ (f.g)\ =\ mapF\ f\ .\ mapF\ g \qquad\qquad (M4)$$

Exercises

18.22 Show that sets and binary trees can be given a monad structure, as can the type:

```
data Error a = OK a | Error String
```

18.23 For the monads `Id`, `[]` and `Maybe` prove the rules (M1) to (M3). Also show that these rules hold for your implementations in the previous exercise.

18.24 Prove the property (M4) using the laws (M1) to (M3).

18.25 Prove the following properties using the monad laws:

```
joinM return = joinM . mapF return
joinM return = id
```

18.26 Can you define a different monad structure over lists from that given above? Check that your definition has properties (M1) to (M3).

18.27 Write down the definitions of map and join over lists using list comprehensions. Compare them with the definitions of mapF and joinM given in the do notation in this section.

18.28 Reimplement the parser for the calculator using the do construct (based on >>=) rather than (>*>) and build. Contrast the two approaches.

(18.9) Example: monadic computation over trees

We now illustrate how computations over the type of

```
data Tree a = Nil | Node a (Tree a) (Tree a)
```

can be given a monadic structure. We first look at a simple example, and then we look at a rather more realistic one.

We see that with a monadic approach the top-level structure of the two solutions is exactly the same. This structure guides the way that we build the implementation of the second example, as we shall see.

The moral of these examples is that monads provide an important structuring mechanism for program construction, as they encourage a **separation of concerns**. The top-level structure of the computation is given in terms of a monad whose specific properties are only touched upon. Within the monad itself is the appropriate computational behaviour to, for example, maintain a state or to perform some IO (or both); the particular sequencing operation of the monad will ensure that values are passed between the parts of the program in an appropriate way.

This separation of concerns comes into its own when changes are required in the details of the computation: it is usually possible to change the monad implementing a computation with at most minimal changes required at the top level. This is in stark contrast to a non-monadic computation in which data representations are visible: a wholesale restructuring is often required in such a situation.

Summing a tree of integers

Suppose we are asked to give the sum of a tree of integers,

```
sTree :: Tree Int -> Int
```

A direct recursive solution is

```
sTree Nil             = 0
sTree (Node n t1 t2) = n + sTree t1 + sTree t2
```

In writing this we give no explicit sequence to the calculation of the sum: we could calculate sTree t1 and sTree t2 one after the other, or indeed in parallel. How might a monadic solution proceed?

```
sumTree :: Tree Int -> St Int
```

where St is a monad which we have yet to define. In the Nil case,

```
sumTree Nil = return 0
```

while in the case of a Node we calculate the parts in a given order:

```
sumTree (Node n t1 t2)                              (sumTree)
  = do num <- return n
        s1  <- sumTree t1
        s2  <- sumTree t2
        return (num + s1 + s2)
```

How is the definition structured? We put the operations in sequence, using do. First we return the value n, giving it the name num. Next we calculate sumTree t1 and sumTree t2, naming their results s1 and s2. Finally we return the result, which is the sum num+s1+s2.

Now, since all we are doing here is calculating values and not trying to do any I/O or other side-effecting operation, we make the monad St the *identity* monad Id which we mentioned earlier. Its formal definition is

```
data Id a = Id a

instance Monad Id where
  return        = Id
  (>>=) (Id x) f = f x
```

This means that we could say

```
sumTree :: Tree Int -> Id Int
```

There is a remarkable similarity between the definition (sumTree) and an imperative program, bearing in mind that do performs a sequencing and j <- ... gives (or assigns) a value to j. In an imperative setting, we might well write

```
num := n ;
s1   := sumTree t1 ;
s2   := sumTree t2 ;
return (num + s1 + s2) ;
```

where 'num :=' corresponds to the '<-' and do puts a sequence of commands one after the other, as does the semi-colon.

To give a function of type Tree Int -> Int we compose with the extract function to give

```
extract . sumTree
```

where

```
extract :: Id a -> a
extract (Id x) = x
```

takes the wrapper off an element Id x to give the element x. In the next section we tackle a more complex problem, but see the same monadic structure repeated.

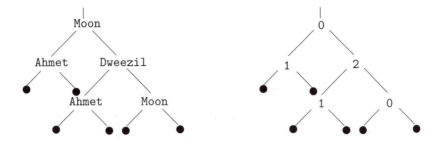

Figure 18.1   Replacing the elements of a tree with natural numbers.

Using a state monad in a tree calculation

Building on the experience of the last section in defining `sumTree` we tackle here a rather more tricky problem. We want to write a function

```
numTree :: Eq a => Tree a -> Tree Int
```

so that given an arbitrary tree we transform it to a tree of integers in which the original elements are replaced by natural numbers, starting from 0. An example is given in Figure 18.1. The same element has to be replaced by the same number at every occurrence, and when we meet an as-yet-unvisited element we have to find a 'new' number to match it with.

How does our definition appear? We give the function a type,

```
numberTree :: Eq a => Tree a -> State a (Tree Int)
```

in which the monad `State` a will have to carry about enough information to allow us to replace the elements in the correct way. The structure of the program then is

```
numberTree Nil = return Nil

numberTree (Node x t1 t2)                                    (numberTree)
  = do num <- numberNode x
       nt1 <- numberTree t1
       nt2 <- numberTree t2
       return (Node num nt1 nt2)
```

The structure here is exactly the same as that of (`sumTree`) on page 408; we perform the operations on the components `x`, `t1` and `t2` (for the subtrees we use recursion) and then combine them in the result (`Node num nt1 nt2`).

What else do we have to define to give the result? We need to identify the monad `State` a and to define the function which replaces an individual entry,

```
numberNode :: Eq a => a -> State a Int
```

We now have to think about the implementation of the monad. We have called it `State` since it keeps a record of the state, that is of which values are associated with which numbers. This we do in a table:

```
type Table a = [a]
```

where the table [True,False] indicates that True is associated with 0 and False with 1.

What then is the state monad? It consists of functions

```
data State a b = State (Table a -> (Table a , b))
```

which, after we strip off the constructor State, we can think of as taking the state *before* doing the operation to the state *after* the operation, together with its result. In other words, we return a value of type b, but perhaps we change the value of the state of type Table a as a side-effect.

Next we have to define the two monad operations.

```
instance Monad (State a) where
```

To return a value, we leave the state unchanged.

```
    return x = State (\tab -> (tab,x))
```

How do we sequence the operations? The intended effect here is to do st, pass its result to f and then do the resulting operation.

In more detail, to perform st, we pass it the table tab; the output of this is a new state, newTab, and a value y. This y is passed to f, giving an object of type State a b; this is then performed starting with the *new* state newTab.

```
(State st) >>= f
  = State (\tab -> let
                     (newTab,y)    = st tab
                     (State trans) = f y
                   in
                     trans newTab)
```

Here we can see that the operations are indeed done in sequence, leading from one state value to the next. This has given us the monad; all that remains is to define the function numberNode. Our definition is

```
numberNode :: Eq a => a -> State a Int
numberNode x = State (nNode x)

nNode :: Eq a => a -> (Table a -> (Table a , Int))
nNode x table
  | elem x table      = (table      , lookup x table)
  | otherwise         = (table++[x] , length table)
```

If x is an element of table, we return its position in the table, given by lookup; if it is not, we add it to the end of the table, and return its position, which is length table. The definition of

```
lookup :: Eq a => a -> Table a -> Int
```

is standard, and we leave it as an exercise for the reader.

Standing back, we can see that we have completed our definition of the function

```
numberTree :: Eq a => Tree a -> State a (Tree Int)
```

but one ingredient of the solution is still needed. If we form

```
numberTree exampleTree
```

for some `exampleTree` of the tree type, we have an object in

```
State a (Tree Int)
```

In order to `extract` the result, we have to write a function

```
extract :: State a b -> b
```

This has to perform the calculation, starting with some initial table, and return the resulting value of type u. The definition is

```
extract :: State a b -> b
extract (State st) = snd (st [])
```

where we see that `st` is applied to the initial state `[]`. The result of this is a pair, from which we select the second part, of type b. Now we can define our function

```
numTree :: Eq a => Tree a -> Tree Int
numTree = extract . numberTree
```

which has the effect we require.

To conclude, we have shown how a complex calculation over a tree, (`numberTree`), can be structured in exactly the same way as a simple one, (`sumTree`). In the case of a tree type the advantage is tangible, but for more complex types a monadic structure becomes almost essential if we are to follow a computation with complicated side-effects.

Exercises

18.29 Show how to look up the position of an element in a list

```
lookup :: Eq a => a -> Table a -> Int
```

You might find it useful to define a function

```
look :: Eq a => a -> Table a -> Int -> Int
```

where the extra integer parameter carries the current 'offset' into the list.

18.30 Show how you can use a `State`-style monad in a computation to replace each element in a tree by a random integer, generated using the techniques of Section 17.6.

18.31 We can use monads to extend the case study of the calculator in a variety of ways. Consider how you would

- add exceptions or messages to be given on an attempt to divide by zero;
- count the number of steps taken in a calculation; and
- combine the two.

Summary

Looking at the examples we have covered, we can conclude that the advantages of structuring a computation using a monad are threefold:

- We follow a well-defined strategy for writing **sequential** programs, which has strong similarities with imperative programming.

- There is an advantage in **abstraction**: we can change the underlying monad yet retain the overall structure of the computation.

- Finally, we have seen that various properties can be inferred automatically once we have a monad. As we saw above, (M4) is a consequence of the monad properties (M1) to (M3).

We have also seen that many different sort of computational **effects** like IO, state, errors (as implemented by the Maybe type) and non-determinism, as given by the list monad, are all described by means of monads. On the one hand this means that we can make models in a functional language of these effects, but on the other we can use monads as a way of building an **interface** between a pure functional language like Haskell and systems with effects; this approach appears to be very fruitful, allowing Haskell programs to call foreign-language functions, and indeed allowing Haskell programmers to inter-work with programmers in C and Java. We give some pointers to this work and also to further work on programming in a monadic style in the concluding chapter.

Chapter 19

Time and space behaviour

This chapter explores not the values which programs compute, but the way in which those values are reached; we are interested here in program **efficiency** rather than program correctness.

We begin our discussion by asking how we can measure complexity in general, before asking how we measure the time and space behaviour of our functional programs. We work out the time complexity of a sequence of functions, leading up to looking at various implementations of the Set abstype.

The **space** behaviour of lazy programs is complex: we show that some programs use less space than we might predict, while others use more. This leads into a discussion of **folding** functions into lists, and we introduce the foldl' function, which folds from the left, and gives more space-efficient versions of folds of operators which need their arguments – the **strict** operations. In contrast to this, foldr gives better performance on lazy folds, in general.

In many algorithms, the naive implementation causes recomputation of parts of the solution, and thus a poor performance. In the final section of the chapter we show how to exploit lazy evaluation to give more efficient implementations, by **memoizing** the partial results in a table.

(19.1) Complexity of functions

If we are trying to measure the behaviour of functions, one approach is to ask how much time and space are consumed in evaluations for different input values. We might, for example, given a function `fred` over the natural numbers, count the number of steps taken in calculating the value of `fred` n for natural numbers n. This gives us a function, call it `stepsFred`, and then we can ask how complex that function is.

One way of estimating the complexity of a function is to look at how fast it grows for large values of its argument. The idea of this is that the essential behaviour of a function becomes clearer for large values. To start with, we examine this idea through an example. How fast does the function

$$f\ n\ =\ 2*n^2\ +\ 4*n\ +\ 13$$

grow, as n gets large? The function has three components:

- a constant 13,
- a term 4*n, and
- a term, $2*n^2$. (Note that here we use the mathematical notation for powers, n^2, rather than the Haskell notation, n^2.)

As the values of n become large, how do these components behave?

- The constant 13 is unchanged;
- the term 4*n grows like a straight line; but
- a square term, $2*n^2$, will grow the most quickly.

For 'large' values of n the square term is greater than the others, and so we say that f is of **order** n^2, $O(n^2)$. In this case the square dominates for any n greater than or equal to 3; we shall say exactly what is meant by 'large' when we make the definition of order precise. As a rule of thumb we can say that order classifies how functions behave when all but the fastest-growing components are removed, and constant multipliers are ignored; the remainder of the section makes this precise, but this explanation should be sufficient for understanding the remainder of the chapter.

The notation n^2 is the usual way that mathematicians write down 'the function that takes n to n^2'. This is the notation which is generally used in describing complexity, and so we use it here. In a Haskell program to describe the function we would either write \n -> n^2 or use the operator section (^2).

In the remainder of this section we make the idea of order precise, before examining various examples and placing them on a scale for measuring complexity.

The big-Oh and Theta notation – upper bounds

A function f `:: Int -> Int` is O(g), '*big-Oh g*', if there are positive integers m and d, so that for all n≥m,

$$f\ n\ \le\ d*(g\ n)$$

The definition expresses the fact that when numbers are large enough $(n \geq m)$ the value of f is no larger than a multiple of the function g, namely $(d*).g$.

For example, f above is $O(n^2)$ since, for n greater than or equal to 1,

$$2*n^2 + 4*n + 13 \leq 2*n^2 + 4*n^2 + 13*n^2 = 19*n^2$$

so the definition is satisfied by taking m as 1 and d as 19.

Note that the measure gives an upper bound, which may be an overestimate; by similar reasoning, f is $O(n^{17})$ as well. In most cases we consider the bound will in fact be a tight one. One way of expressing that g is a tight bound on f is that in addition to f being $O(g)$, g is $O(f)$; we then say that f is $\Theta(g)$, '*Theta* g'. Our example f is in fact $\Theta(n^2)$.

A scale of measurement

We say that $f \ll g$ if f is $O(g)$, but g is not $O(f)$; we also use $f \equiv g$ to mean that f is $O(g)$ and simultaneously g is $O(f)$.

We now give a scale by which function complexity can be measured. Constants which are $O(n^0)$ grow more slowly than **linear** – $O(n^1)$ – functions, which in turn grow more slowly than **quadratic** functions of order $O(n^2)$. This continues through the powers, and all the powers (n^k) are bounded by exponential functions, such as 2^n.

$$n^0 \ll n^1 \ll n^2 \ll \ldots \ll n^k \ll \ldots \ll 2^n \ll \ldots$$

Two other points ought to be added to the scale. The logarithm function, log, grows more slowly than any positive power, and the product of the functions n and log n, $n(\log n)$ fits between linear and quadratic, thus

$$n^0 \ll \log n \ll n^1 \ll n(\log n) \ll n^2 \ll \ldots$$

Counting

Many of the arguments we make will involve counting. In this section we look at some general examples which we will come across in examining the behaviour of functions below.

Examples

1. The first question we ask is – given a list, how many times can we **bisect** it, before we cut it into pieces of length one? If the length is n, after the first cut, the length of each half is $n/2$, and after p cuts, the length of each piece is $n/(2^p)$. This number will be smaller than or equal to one when

$$(2^p) \geq n > (2^{(p-1)})$$

which when we take $\log_2$ of each side gives

$$p \geq \log_2 n > p-1$$

The function giving the number of steps in terms of the length of the list, n, will thus be $\Theta(\log_2 n)$.

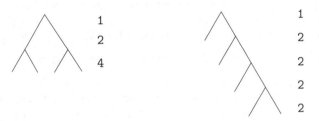

Figure 19.1   Counting the nodes of trees.

2.   The second question concerns trees. A tree is called **balanced** if all its branches are the same length. Suppose we have a balanced binary tree, whose branches are of length b; how many nodes does the tree have? On the first level it has 1, on the second 2, on the kth it has $2^{(k-1)}$, so over all b+1 levels it has

$$1 + 2 + 4 + \ldots + 2^{(k-1)} + \ldots + 2^b = 2^{(b+1)} - 1$$

as illustrated in Figure 19.1.

We thus see that the size of a balanced tree is $\Theta(2^b)$ in the length of the branches, b; taking logarithms, a balanced tree of size n will therefore have branches of length $\Theta(\log_2 n)$ in the size of the tree. If a tree is not balanced, the length of its longest branch can be of the same order as the size of the tree itself; see Figure 19.1 for an example.

3.   Our final counting question concerns taking **sums**. If we are given one object every day for n days, we have n at the end; if we are given n each day, we have n^2; what if we are given 1 on the first day, 2 on the second, and so on? What is the sum of the list [1 .. n], in other words? Writing the list backwards, as well as forwards, we have

```
1       + 2     + 3     +  ...  + (n-1) + n +
n       + (n-1) + (n-2) +  ...  + 2     + 1
```

adding *vertically* at each point we have a sum of (n+1),

```
(n+1) + (n+1) + (n+1) +   ...   + (n+1) + (n+1)
```

and this sum occurs n times, so

```
sum [1 .. n] = n*(n+1) 'div' 2
```

which makes it $\Theta(n^2)$, or quadratic. In a similar way, the sum of the squares is $\Theta(n^3)$, and so on.

Exercises

19.1 Show that the example

$$f\ n\ =\ 2*n^2\ +\ 4*n\ +\ 13$$

is $\Theta(n^2)$.

19.2 Give a table of the values of the functions n^0, $\log\ n$, n^1, $n(\log\ n)$, n^2, n^3 and 2^n for the values

0 1 2 3 4 5 10 50 100 500 1000 10000 100000 10000000

19.3 By giving the values of d, m and c (when necessary), show that the following functions have the complexity indicated.

$f1\ n\ =\ 0.1*n^5\ +\ 31*n^3\ +\ 1000$	$O(n^6)$
$f2\ n\ =\ 0.7*n^5\ +\ 13*n^2\ +\ 1000$	$\Theta(n^5)$

19.4 Show that $n^k \ll 2^n$ for all positive k. By taking logarithms of both sides, show that $\log\ n \ll n^k$ for all positive k.

19.5 Show that

$$\log\ \equiv\ \ln\ \equiv\ \log_2$$

and in fact that logarithms to any base have the same rate of growth.

19.6 The function fib is defined by

```
fib 0 = 0
fib 1 = 1
fib m = fib (m-2) + fib (m-1)
```

Show that $n^k \ll$ fib n for all k.

19.7 Show that $\ll$ is transitive – that is $f \ll g$ and $g \ll h$ together imply that $f \ll h$. Show also that $\equiv$ is an equivalence relation.

19.8 If f is $O(g)$, show that any constant multiple of f is also of the same order. If f1 and f2 are $O(g)$, show that their sum and difference are also $O(g)$. Are the same results valid with Θ replacing O?

19.9 If f1 is $O(n^{k1})$ and f2 is $O(n^{k2})$, show that their product,

$$f\ n\ =\ f1\ n\ *\ f2\ n$$

is $O(n^{(k1+k2)})$.

19.10 Prove by induction over the natural number n that

```
1 + 2 + 4 + ... + 2ⁿ = 2(n+1) - 1
1 + 2 + ... + n      = n*(n+1) 'div' 2
1² + 2² + ... + n²   = n*(n+1)*(2*n+1) 'div' 6
1³ + 2³ + ... + n³   = (n*(n+1) 'div' 2)²
```

19.2 The complexity of calculations

How can we measure the complexity of the functions we write? One answer is to use an implementation of Haskell, which can be expected to produce some diagnostic information about evaluation. In Hugs we use the command `:set +s` to achieve this. While this gives some information, we opt for a cleaner **model** of what is going on, and we choose to analyse the **calculations** we have been using. There are three principal measures we can use.

- The **time** taken to compute a result is given by the number of steps in a calculation which uses lazy evaluation.

- The **space** necessary for the computation can be measured in two ways. First, there is a lower limit on the amount of space we need for a calculation to complete successfully. During calculation, the expression being calculated grows and shrinks; obviously, we need enough space to hold the *largest* expression built during the calculation. This is often called the **residency** of the computation, we shall call it the **space complexity**.

- We can also make a measure of the **total space** used by a computation, which in some way reflects the total area of the calculation; it is of interest to implementers of functional languages but for users (and for us) the first two are the crucial measures.

How then do we measure the complexity of a function?

Complexity measures

We measure the complexity of the function f by looking at the time and space complexity as described above, as *functions* of the *size* of the inputs to f. The size of a number is the number itself, while the size of a list is given by its length, and of a tree by the number of nodes it contains. We now look at a series of examples.

Examples

1. Let us start with the example of `fac`.

```
fac :: Int -> Int
fac 0 = 1
fac n = n * fac (n-1)
```

Working through a calculation, we have

```
fac n
⤳   n * fac (n-1)
⤳   ...
⤳   n * ((n-1) * ... * (2 * (1 * 1)) ...)          (facMax)
⤳   n * ((n-1) * ... * (2 * 1) ...)
⤳   n * ((n-1) * ... * 2 ...)
⤳   ...
⤳   n!
```

The calculation contains 2*n+1 steps, and the largest expression, (facMax), contains n multiplication symbols. This makes the time and space complexity both $\Theta(n^1)$, or linear.

2.   Next we look at insertion sort. Recall that

```
iSort []     = []
iSort (x:xs) = ins x (iSort xs)

ins x [] = [x]
ins x (y:ys)
   | (x<=y)        = x:y:ys
   | otherwise     = y:ins x ys
```

A general calculation will be

```
iSort [a1,a2,...,an-1,an]
  ~>   ins a1 (iSort [a2,...,an-1,an])
  ~>   ...
  ~>   ins a1 (ins a2 ( ... (ins an-1 (ins an []))...))
```

followed by the calculation of the n ins's. What sort of behaviour does ins have? Take the general example of

```
ins a [a1,a2,...,an-1,an]
```

where we assume that $[a_1, \ldots, a_n]$ is sorted. There are three possibilities:

- In the *best* case, when a<=a₁, the calculation takes 1 step.
- In the *worst* case, when a>aₙ, the calculation takes n steps.
- In an *average* case, the calculation will take n/2 steps.

What does this mean for iSort?

- In the *best* case, each ins will take one step, and the calculation will therefore take a further n steps, making it $O(n^1)$ in this case.
- On the other hand, in the *worst* case, the first ins will take one step, the second two, and so on. By our counting argument in Section 19.1 the calculation will take $O(n^2)$ steps.
- In an *average* case, the ins's will take a total of

```
1/2 + 2/2 + ... + (n-1)/2 + n/2
```

steps, whose sum is again $O(n^2)$, by our observation in Section 19.1 about the size of the sum 1+2...n.

We therefore see that in most cases the algorithm takes quadratic time, but in some exceptional cases, when sorting an (almost) sorted list, the complexity is linear in the length of the list. In all cases the space usage will also be linear.

3. Before looking at another sorting algorithm, we look at the time taken to join together two lists, using ++.

```
[a1,a2,...,an-1,an] ++ x
⤳    a1 : ([a2,...,an-1,an] ++ x)
⤳    a1 : (a2 : [a3,...,an-1,an] ++ x)
⤳    ... n-3 steps ...
⤳    a1 : (a2 : ... : (an:x)...)
```

The time taken is *linear* in the length of the first list.

4. Our second sorting algorithm, quicksort, is given by

```
qSort []     = []
qSort (x:xs) = qSort [z|z<-xs,z<=x] ++ [x] ++ qSort [z|z<-xs,z>x]
```

When the list is sorted and contains no duplicate elements, the calculation goes thus:

```
qSort [a1,a2,...,an-1,an]
⤳    ... n steps ...
⤳    [] ++ [a1] ++ qSort [a2,...,an-1,an]
⤳    ... n-1 steps ...
⤳    a1 : ([] ++ [a2] ++ qSort [a3,...,an])
⤳    ... n-2 steps ...
⤳    ...
⤳    a1 : (a2 : (a3 : ... an:[])
⤳    [a1,a2,...,an-1,an]
```

Since the number of steps here is $1+2+\ldots n$, we have **quadratic** behaviour in this sorted case. In the *average* case, we split thus

```
qSort [a1,a2,...,an-1,an]
⤳    qSort [b1,...,bn/2] ++ [a1] ++ qSort [c1,...,cn/2]
```

where the list has been bisected. Forming the two sublists will take $O(n^1)$ steps, as will the joining together of the results. As we argued in Section 19.1, there can be $\log_2 n$ bisections before a list is reduced to one-element lists, so we have $O(n^1)$ steps to perform $O(\log n)$ many times; this makes quicksort take $O(n(\log n))$ steps, *on average*, although we saw that it can take quadratic steps in the worst (already sorted!) case.[1]

The logarithmic behaviour here is characteristic of a 'divide and conquer' algorithm: we split the problem into two smaller problems, solve these and then recombine the results. The result is a comparatively efficient algorithm, which reaches its base cases in $O(\log_2 n)$ rather than $O(n^1)$ steps.

---

[1] The explanation we have given here depends upon us rearranging the order of the calculation steps; this is legitimate if we observe that lazy evaluation of combinators is *optimal*, in the sense of taking fewest steps to reach a result; any rearrangement can only give more steps to our calculation, so the bound of $n(\log n)$ holds.

Exercises

19.11 Estimate the time complexity of the two reverse functions given here:

```
rev1 []     = []
rev1 (x:xs) = rev1 xs ++ [x]
```

and

```
rev2           = shunt []
shunt xs []    = xs
shunt xs (y:ys) = shunt (y:xs) ys
```

19.12 We can define multiplication by repeated addition as follows:

```
mult n 0 = 0
mult n m = mult n (m-1) + n
```

'Russian' multiplication is defined by

```
russ n 0 = 0
russ n m
  | (m 'mod' 2 == 0)   = russ (n+n) (m 'div' 2)
  | otherwise          = russ (n+n) (m 'div' 2) + n
```

Estimate the time complexity of these two multiplication algorithms.

19.13 Estimate the time complexity of the Fibonacci function.

19.14 Show that the worst-case time behaviour of the merge sort function below is
O(n(log n)).

```
mSort xs
  | (len < 2)  = xs
  | otherwise  = mer (mSort (take m xs)) (mSort (drop m xs))
    where
    len = length xs
    m   = len 'div' 2

mer (x:xs) (y:ys)
  | (x<=y)       = x : mer xs (y:ys)
  | otherwise    = y : mer (x:xs) ys
mer (x:xs) []    = (x:xs)
mer []    ys     = ys
```

19.3 Implementations of sets

We first saw the Set abstract data type in Section 16.8, where we gave an implementation based on ordered lists without repetitions. Alternatively we can write an implementation based on arbitrary lists whose elements may occur in any order and be repeated.

```
type Set a = [a]

empty       = []
memSet      = member
inter xs ys = filter (member xs) ys
union       = (++)
subSet xs ys = and (map (member ys) xs)
eqSet xs ys = subSet xs ys && subSet ys xs
makeSet     = id
mapSet      = map
```

We can also write an implementation based on the search trees of Section 16.7. We now compare the time complexity of these implementations, and summarize the results in the table which follows.

	Lists	Ordered lists	Search trees (average)
memSet	$O(n^1)$	$O(n^1)$	$O(\log n)$
subSet	$O(n^2)$	$O(n^1)$	$O(n(\log n))$
inter	$O(n^2)$	$O(n^1)$	$O(n(\log n))$
makeSet	$O(n^0)$	$O(n(\log n))$	$O(n(\log n))$
mapSet	$O(n^1)$	$O(n(\log n))$	$O(n(\log n))$

As we can see from the table, there is no clear 'best' or 'worst' choice; depending upon the kind of set operation we intend to perform, different implementations make more sense. This is one more reason for providing the abstract data type boundary beneath which the implementation can be changed to suit the use to which the sets are being put without any need to change the user programs.

Exercises

19.15 Confirm the time complexities given in the table above for the two list implementations of sets.

19.16 Implement the operations subSet, inter, makeSet and mapSet for the search tree implementation, and estimate the time complexity of your implementations.

19.17 Give an implementation of sets as lists without repetitions, and estimate the time complexity of the functions in your implementation.

(19.4) Space behaviour

A rule of thumb for estimating the space needed to calculate a result is to measure the largest expression produced during the calculation. This is accurate if the result being computed is a number or a Boolean, but it is not when the result is a data structure, like a list.

Lazy evaluation

Recall the explanation of lazy evaluation in Section 17.1, where we explained that parts of results are printed as soon as possible. Once part of a result is printed, it need no longer occupy any space. In estimating space complexity, we must be aware of this.

Take the example of the lists [m .. n], defined thus

```
[m .. n]
  | n>=m          = m:[m+1 .. n]
  | otherwise    = []
```

Calculating [1 .. n] gives

```
[1 .. n]
        ?? n>=1
~>   1:[1+1 .. n]
        ??  n>=2
~>   1:[2 .. n]
~>   1:2:[2+1 .. n]
~>   ...
~>   1:2:3:...:n:[]
```

where we have underlined those parts of the result which can be output. To measure the space complexity we look at the non-underlined part, which is of constant size, so the space complexity is $O(n^0)$. The calculation has approximately 2*n steps, giving it linear time complexity, as expected.

Saving values in where clauses

Consider the example of

```
exam1 = [1 .. n] ++ [1 .. n]
```

The time taken to calculate this will be $O(n^1)$, and the space used will be $O(n^0)$, but we will have to calculate the expression [1 .. n] *twice*. Suppose instead that we compute

```
exam2 = list ++ list
        where
        list=[1 .. n]
```

The effect here is to compute the list [1 .. n] once, so that we save its value after calculating it in order to be able to use it again. Unfortunately, this means that after evaluating list, the whole of the list is stored, giving an $O(n^1)$ space complexity.

This is a general phenomenon. If we save something by referring to it in a where clause we have to pay the penalty of the space that it occupies: if the space is available, fair enough; if not, we have turned a working computation into one which fails for lack of space.

This problem can be worse! Take the examples

```
exam3 = [1 .. n] ++ [last [1 .. n]]
exam4 = list ++ [last list]
        where
        list=[1 .. n]
```

in which last returns the last element of a non-empty list. The space required by exam3 is $O(n^0)$, while in exam4 it is $O(n^1)$, since we hold on to the calculated value of list even though we require only one value from it, the last. This feature, of keeping hold of a large structure when we only need part of it, is called a **dragging problem**. In the example here, the problem is clear, but in a larger system the source of a dragging problem can be most difficult to find.

The lesson of these examples must be that while it is *always* sensible not to repeat the calculation of a simple value, saving a compound value like a list or a tuple can increase the space usage of a program.

Saving space?

As we saw in Section 19.2, the naive factorial function has $O(n^1)$ space complexity, as it forms the expression

```
n * ((n-1) * ... * (1 * 1)...)
```

before it is evaluated. Instead, we can perform the multiplications as we go along, using

```
newFac :: Int -> Int
newFac n = aFac n 1

aFac 0 p = p
aFac n p = aFac (n-1) (p*n)
```

and compute the factorial of n using aFac n 1. Now, we examine the calculation

```
newFac n
↝   aFac n 1
↝   aFac (n-1) (1*n)
    ??  (n-1)==0 ↝  False
↝   aFac (n-2) (1*n*(n-1))
↝   ...
↝   aFac 0 (1*n*(n-1)*(n-2)*...*2*1)
↝   (1*n*(n-1)*(n-2)*...*2*1)                              (needVal)
```

so that the effect of this program is exactly the same: it still forms a large unevaluated expression! The reason that the expression is unevaluated is that it is not clear that its value is needed until the step (needVal).

How can we overcome this? We ought to make the intermediate values *needed*, so that they are calculated earlier. We do this here by adding a test; another method is given in Section 19.5.

```
aFac n p
  | p==p        = aFac (n-1) (p*n)
```

Now the calculation of the factorial of 4, say, is

```
aFac 4 1
↝   aFac (4-1) (1*4)
        ??  (4-1)==0       ↝   False
        ??  (1*4)==(1*4) ↝   True                              (eqTest)
↝   aFac (3-1) (4*3)
        ??  (3-1)==0       ↝   False
        ??  (4*3)==(4*3) ↝   True                              (eqTest)
↝   aFac (2-1) (12*2)
↝   ...
↝   aFac 0 (24*1)
↝   (24*1)
↝    24
```

The lines (eqTest) show where the guard p==p is tested, and so where the intermediate multiplications take place. From this we can conclude that this version has better (constant) space behaviour.

Exercises

19.18 Estimate the space complexity of the function

```
sumSquares :: Int -> Int
sumSquares n = sumList (map sq [1 .. n])
```

where

```
sumList = foldr (+) 0
sq n    = n*n
```

and map and [1 .. n] have their standard definitions.

19.19 Give an informal estimate of the complexity of the text processing functions in Chapter 7.

19.5 Folding revisited

One of the patterns of computation which we identified in Chapter 9 is **folding** an operator or function into a list. This section examines the complexity of the two standard folding functions, and discusses how we can choose between them in program design. Before this we make a definition which expresses the fact of a function needing to evaluate an argument. This distinction will be crucial to our full understanding of folding.

Strictness

A function is **strict** in an argument if the result is undefined whenever an undefined value is passed to this argument. For instance, (+) is strict in both arguments, while (&&) is strict in its first only. Recall that it is defined by

```
True  && x = x
False && x = False                                    (andFalse)
```

The pattern match in the first argument forces it to be strict there, but equation (andFalse) shows that it is possible to get an answer from (&&) when the second argument is undef, so it is therefore not strict in the second argument.

    If a function is not strict in an argument, we say that it is **non-strict** or **lazy** in that argument.

Folding from the right

Our definition of folding was given by

```
foldr :: (a -> b -> b) -> b -> [a] -> b

foldr f st []     = st
foldr f st (x:xs) = f x (foldr f st xs)
```

which we saw was of general application. Sorting a list, by insertion sort, was given by

```
iSort = foldr ins []
```

and indeed any primitive recursive definition over lists can be given by applying `foldr`.
    Writing the function applications as infix operations gives

$$\text{foldr f st } [a_1, a_2, \ldots, a_{n-1}, a_n]$$
$$\rightsquigarrow \quad a_1 \text{ `f` } (a_2 \text{ `f` } \ldots \text{ `f` } (a_{n-1} \text{ `f` } (a_n \text{ `f` st}))\ldots) \qquad \text{(foldr)}$$

and shows why the 'r' is added to the name: bracketing is to the right, with the starting value st appearing to the right of the elements also. If f is lazy in its second argument, we can see from (foldr) that given the head of the list, output may be possible. For instance, map can be defined thus

```
map f = foldr ((:).f) []
```

and in calculating map (+2) [1 .. n] we see

```
foldr ((:).(+2)) [] [1 .. n]
⤳  ((:).(+2)) 1 (foldr ((:).(+2)) [] [2 .. n])
⤳  1+2 : (foldr ((:).(+2)) [] [2 .. n])
⤳  3 : (foldr ((:).(+2)) [] [2 .. n])
⤳  ...
```

As in Section 19.4, we see that the space complexity of this will be $O(n^0)$, since the elements of the list will be output as they are calculated. What happens when we fold a strict operator into a list? The definition of fac in Section 19.2 can be rewritten as

```
fac n = foldr (*) 1 [1 .. n]
```

and we saw there that the effect was to give $O(n^1)$ space behaviour, since the multiplications in equation (foldr) cannot be performed until the whole expression is formed, as they are bracketed to the right. We therefore define a function to fold from the left.

Folding from the left

Instead of folding from the right, we can define

```
foldl :: (a -> b -> a) -> a -> [b] -> a
foldl f st []     = st
foldl f st (x:xs) = foldl f (f st x) xs
```

which gives

```
foldl f st [a₁,a₂,...,aₙ₋₁,aₙ]
⤳  (...((st 'f' a₁) 'f' a₂) 'f' ... 'f' aₙ₋₁) 'f' aₙ          (foldl)
```

We can calculate this in the factorial example, the effect being

```
foldl (*) 1 [1 .. n]
⤳  foldl (*) (1*1) [2 .. n]
⤳  ...
⤳  foldl (*) (...((1*1)*2)*...*n) []
⤳  (...((1*1)*2)*...*n)
```

As in Section 19.2, the difficulty is that foldl as we have defined it is not strict in its second argument. Using the standard function seq

```
seq :: a -> b -> b
```

it is possible to make it strict in the second argument. The effect of seq x y is to evaluate x before returning y. We can use seq over every type, since it is a polymorphic function. If we write

```
strict :: (a -> b) -> a -> b
strict f x = seq x (f x)
```

then `strict f` is a **strict** version of the function `f` which evaluates its argument `x` before computing the result `f x`. We can therefore write as a strict version of `foldl` the function `foldl'`,

```
foldl' :: (a -> b -> a) -> a -> [b] -> a
foldl' f st []     = st
foldl' f st (x:xs) = strict (foldl' f) (f st x) xs
```

Now, evaluating the example again,

```
foldl' (*) 1 [1 .. n]
~>  foldl' (*) 1 [2 .. n]
~>  foldl' (*) 2 [3 .. n]
~>  foldl' (*) 6 [4 .. n]
~>  ...
```

Clearly, this evaluation is in constant space, $O(n^0)$. Can we draw any conclusions from these examples?

Designing folds

When we fold in a *strict* function, we will form a list-sized expression with `foldr`, so it will always be worth using `foldl'`. This covers the examples of `(+)`, `(*)` and so forth.

We saw earlier that when `map` was defined using `foldr` we could begin to give output before the whole of the list argument was constructed. If we use `foldl'` instead, we will have to traverse the whole list before giving any output, since any `foldl'` computation follows the pattern

```
foldl' f st1 xs1
~>  foldl' f st2 xs2
~>  ...
~>  foldl' f stk xsk
~>  ...
~>  foldl' f stn []
~>  stn
```

so in the case of `map`, `foldr` is the clear choice of the two.

A more interesting example is given by the function which is `True` only if a list of Booleans consists of `True` throughout. We fold in `(&&)`, of course, but should we use `foldr` or `foldl'`? The latter will give a constant-space version, but will examine the *entire* list. Since `(&&)` is lazy in its second argument, we might not need to examine the value returned from the remainder of the list. For instance,

```
foldr (&&) True (map (==2) [2 .. n])
~>  (2==2) && (foldr (&&) True (map (==2) [3 .. n]))
~>  True && (foldr (&&) True (map (==2) [3 .. n]))
~>  foldr (&&) True (map (==2) [3 .. n])
```

```
↝   (3==2) && (foldr (&&) True (map (==2) [4 .. n]))
↝   False && (foldr (&&) True (map (==2) [4 .. n]))
↝   False
```

This version uses constant space, *and* may not examine the whole list; `foldr` is therefore the best choice.

Beside the examples of (+) and (*), there are many other examples where `foldl'` is preferable, including:

● Reversing a list. To use `foldr` we have to add an element a to the end of a list, x. The operation x++[a] is strict in x, while the 'cons' operation (:) is lazy in its list argument.

● Converting a list of digits "7364" into a number is strict in both the conversion of the front, 736 and the final character, '4'.

Since `foldl'` consumes an entire list before giving any output, it will be of no use in defining functions to work over infinite lists or the partial lists we looked at while writing interactive systems.

Exercises

19.20 Define the functions to reverse a list and to convert a digit list into a number using both `foldr` and `foldl'` and compare their behaviour by means of calculation.

19.21 Is it better to define insertion sort using `foldr` or `foldl'`? Justify your answer.

19.22 How are the results of `foldr` and `foldl'` related? You may like to use the functions `reverse` and `flip` in framing your answer.

19.23 What is the relationship between `foldr` and `foldl'` when the function to be folded is

associative:	a 'f' (b 'f' c) = (a 'f' b) 'f' c;
has st as an identity:	st 'f' a = a = a 'f' st;
commutative:	a 'f' b = b 'f' a;

and what is the relationship when all three hold?

19.6 Avoiding recomputation: memoization

In this section we look at general strategies which allow us to avoid having to recompute results during the course of evaluating an expression. This happens particularly in some recursive solutions of problems, where the solutions to sub-problems can be used repeatedly.

We begin the discussion by looking again at the Fibonacci function.

```
fibP 3
= (y,x+y)
  where
  (x,y) = fibP 2
        = (y₁,x₁+y₁)
          where
          (x₁,y₁) = fibP 1
                  = (y₂,x₂+y₂)
                    where
                    (x₂,y₂) = fibP 0
                            = (0,1)
                  = (1,1)
        = (1,2)
= (2,3)
```

Figure 19.2 Calculating fibP 3.

```
fib :: Int -> Int
fib 0 = 0
fib 1 = 1
fib n = fib (n-2) + fib (n-1)
```

This definition is remarkably inefficient. Computing fib n calls fib (n-2) and fib (n-1) – the latter will call fib (n-2) again, and within *each* call of fib (n-2) there will be two calls to fib (n-3). The time complexity of fib is greater than any power. How might we avoid this recomputation? We explore two ways of augmenting the definition to make it efficient; in the first we return a complex data structure from each call, and in the second we define an infinite list to hold all the values of the function.

First we observe that to get the value at n we need the two previous values; we could therefore return *both* these values in the result.

```
fibP :: Int -> (Int,Int)
fibP 0 = (0,1)
fibP n = (y,x+y)
         where
         (x,y) = fibP (n-1)
```

A calculation is given in Figure 19.2, where different variables x_1, y_1 and so on have been used for the different occurrences of the local variables x and y; this is not necessary but does make the different occurrences clearer.

As an alternative strategy, we can try to define the list of Fibonacci values, fibs, directly. The values of the fib function given above now become values at particular indices:

```
fibs      :: [Int]
```

```
fibs!!0     = 0
fibs!!1     = 1
fibs!!(n+2) = fibs!!n + fibs!!(n+1)
```

This gives a *description* of the list, but it is not executable in this form. The first two lines tell us that `fibs = 0 : 1 : rest`, while the third equation tells us what the rest is. The `(n+2)`nd element of `fibs` is the nth element of `rest`; similarly, the `(n+1)`st element is the nth element of `(tail fibs)`. We therefore have, for every n,

```
rest!!n = fibs!!n + (tail fibs)!!n
```

which says that each element is got by adding the corresponding elements of two lists, that is

```
rest = zipWith (+) fibs (tail fibs)
```

so that putting the parts together, we have

```
fibs ::[Int]
fibs = 0 : 1 : zipWith (+) fibs (tail fibs)
```

a **process network** computing the Fibonacci numbers. This gives a linear time, constant space algorithm for the problem, in contrast to the pair solution which is linear in both time and space, since all the nested calls to `fibP` are built before any result can be given.

Dynamic programming

The example in this section illustrates a general method of solving problems by what is known as **dynamic programming**. Dynamic programming solutions work by breaking a problem into subproblems but, as in the Fibonacci example, the subproblems will not be independent, in general. A naive solution therefore will contain massive redundancy, which we remove by building a *table* of solutions to subproblems.

The example we consider is to find the length of a **maximal common subsequence** of two lists – the subsequences need not have all their elements adjacent. In the examples of

```
[2,1,4,5,2,3,5,2,4,3]        [1,7,5,3,2]
```

the length of 4 is given by the subsequence `[1,5,3,2]`. This problem is not simply a 'toy'; a solution to this can be used to find the common lines in two files, which gives the basis of the Unix `diff` program, which is used, for instance, for comparing different versions of programs stored in separate files.

The naive solution is given by `mLen` in Figure 19.3. The interesting part of the definition is given by the third equation. In the case where the lists have equal first elements, these elements must be in a maximal common subsequence, so we find the overall solution by looking in the tails and adding one to the result. More problematic is the case in which the heads are distinct. We have the choice of excluding either x or y; in this algorithm we try both possibilities and take the maximal result. There,

```
mLen :: Eq a => [a] -> [a] -> Int

mLen xs []        = 0
mLen [] ys        = 0
mLen (x:xs) (y:ys)
   | x==y         = 1 + mLen xs ys
   | otherwise    = max (mLen xs (y:ys)) (mLen (x:xs) ys)




maxLen :: Eq a => [a] -> [a] -> Int -> Int -> Int

maxLen xs ys 0 j = 0                                        (maxLen.1)
maxLen xs ys i 0 = 0                                        (maxLen.2)
maxLen xs ys i j
   | xs!!(i-1) == ys!!(j-1)  = (maxLen xs ys (i-1) (j-1)) + 1
                                                            (maxLen.3)
   | otherwise               = max (maxLen xs ys i (j-1))
                                   (maxLen xs ys (i-1) j)
                                                            (maxLen.4)




maxTab ::  Eq a => [a] -> [a] -> [[Int]]

maxTab xs ys
  = result
    where
    result = [0,0 .. ] : zipWith f [0 .. ] result
    f i prev
        = ans
          where
          ans   = 0 : zipWith g [0 .. ] ans
          g j v
             | xs!!i == ys!!j      = prev!!j + 1
             | otherwise           = max v (prev!!(j+1))
```

Figure 19.3   Three algorithms for the maximum common subsequence.

of course, is the source of the redundant computations – each of these may well give rise to a computation of mLen xs ys. How are we to avoid this situation? We shall store these results in a **table**, which will be represented by a list of lists. Once a result appears in the table, we have no need to recompute it.

As an intermediate step, we rewrite the solution as `maxLen` which uses list indexing, so that

```
maxLen xs ys u v
```

is the longest common subsequence in the lists `take u xs` and `take v ys`. The function is given in Figure 19.3, and the definition is a straightforward adaptation of `mLen`.

Now we aim to define the table `maxTab xs ys` so that

```
(maxTab xs ys)!!u!!v = maxLen xs ys u v
```

This requirement is made specific by equations `(maxLen.1)` to `(maxLen.4)`. The base case is given by `(maxLen.1)`, stating that

```
(maxTab xs ys)!!0!!v = 0
```

for all `v`. In other words,

```
(maxTab xs ys)!!0 = [0,0 .. ]
```

so,

```
result = [0,0 .. ] :  ...
```

The equations `(maxLen.2)` to `(maxLen.4)` tell us how to define the list `maxTab!!(i+1)` from the list `maxTab!!i`, and i, so we can define

```
maxTab xs ys = result
                where
                result = [0,0 .. ] : zipWith f [0 .. ] result
```

where `f :: Int -> [Int] -> [Int]` is the function taking i and the previous value, `maxTab!!i`, to `maxTab!!(i+1)`. Now we have to define this latter, which appears in the solution as `ans`.

Equation `(maxLen.2)` tells us that it starts with 0, and g is the function taking `maxTab!!(i+1)!!j` and j to `maxTab!!(i+1)!!(j+1)`, where we are also able to use the values of `maxTab!!i`, named by `prev`. Using these insights, the definition of g is a straightforward transliteration of `(maxLen.3)` and `(maxLen.4)`:

```
ans   = 0 : zipWith g [0 .. ] ans
g j v
  | xs!!i == ys!!j        = prev!!j + 1
  | otherwise             = max v (prev!!(j+1))
```

The top-level result is given by calling

```
maxTab xs ys !! (length xs) !! (length ys)
```

and this is computed in linear time and space.

Haskell provides arrays which can be used to give a more efficient implementation of a number of algorithms, including this one here. Further details can be found in the library module `Array.hs` and its documentation.

Greedy algorithms

A greedy solution to a dynamic programming problem works by building up the optimal solution by making *local* choices of what appear to be the best solutions of sub-problems. In the common subsequence problem, we can think of searching along the two lists in a single sweep, looking successively for the first points of agreement; we search all pairs of indices smaller than n before looking at n. In an example, the greedy solution gives

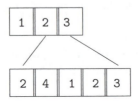

which is *not* optimal: the subsequence [1,2,3] has been missed, since we make the choice of 2 the first element, it is the first point of agreement. This local choice is not part of an optimal global solution, but the algorithm gives reasonable performance.

In many situations, where local choices are always part of a global solution, a greedy solution will work. Examples we have seen thus far include

- the line-splitting algorithm we gave in Chapter 7 is optimal in minimizing the sum of the inter-word spaces when the lines are justified;

- the Huffman codes described in Chapter 15 are optimal in the sense of giving the shortest possible codings of files. We did not search all possible sets of codes in giving the Huffman code, rather we built it up from locally sensible choices.

Exercises

19.24 Give an implementation of the greedy solution to the maximal common subsequence problem, and show that it behaves as explained above on the lists [1,2,3] and [2,4,1,2,3] above.

19.25 Can you give an improvement of the maximal common subsequence solution along the lines of fibP, returning a complex (finite) data structure as the result of a function call, rather than simply one value?

19.26 Finding the 'edit distance' between two strings was first discussed in Section 14.5 where we gave a dynamic programming solution to the problem. Show how you can give an efficient implementation of this algorithm using the techniques of this section, and also how you give a greedy solution to the problem. How do the two solutions compare?

19.27 Based on the examples of this section, provide a program which gives the difference between two files, matching the corresponding lines and giving the output in a suitable form, such as a list of the pairs of matching line numbers or a form copied from the Unix diff program.

Summary

In this chapter we have examined the efficiency of lazy functional programs. We saw that we are able to analyse the time complexity of many of our more straightforward functions without too much difficulty. To analyse the space behaviour is more difficult, but we have shown how the space consumption of lazy programs can be estimated from our calculations.

The introduction of `foldl` brings the space issue into focus, and the distinction we made between strict and lazy functions allows us to analyse the different behaviour of the two folds.

We concluded the discussion with an application of lazy infinite lists to memoizing results for reuse; the transition from naive to efficient was done in a systematic way, which can be carried over to other application areas.

This chapter has provided an introduction to the study of functional program behaviour; much more information – particularly about functional data structures – can be found in Okasaki (1998).

Chapter 20

Conclusion

This book has covered the basics of functional programming in the lazy language Haskell. It has shown how to craft programs, both by giving extensive examples as each new aspect of the language was introduced, and also by giving general advice on how to design programs, in a distinct phase between giving a precise specification of the problem and writing a solution in Haskell.

The power of functional programming

A functional programmer models the real world at a high level of abstraction, concentrating on what relationships there are between values, embodied in function definitions. This contrasts with a lower-level view in which the details of how items are related predominate. For instance, in Haskell lists are simply values, whereas in C or C++ they become data structures built from pointers, and even in Java it is difficult to present a suitably abstract model of lists. This higher-level approach has a number of consequences, which have come out in the course of the book.

- Higher-order functions and polymorphism combine to support the construction of general-purpose libraries of functions, such as the list functions in the Haskell standard prelude and library. The map function, for instance,

```
map :: (a -> b) -> [a] -> [b]
```

embodies the 'pattern' of applying the same transformation to every element in a list, which will be **reused** in a host of applications of lists.

Also supporting reuse through **overloading** are type classes, used for instance in giving the function

```
elem :: Eq a => a -> [a] -> Bool
```

which tests for membership of a list using the overloaded equality function.

- The definitions of functions are equations which express properties of the functions defined. From the definitions of map and function composition, '.', for example, it is possible to **prove** that for all functions f and g,

```
map (f . g) = map f . map g
```

Proof provides a user with assurance about how a program behaves on all arguments, in contrast to testing which can only give direct information about its behavour on a – hopefully representative – subset of inputs.

● Data structures can be introduced in a directly recursive manner, giving trees, queues and so forth without having to look at their representations. Algorithms are written at the same level as they would be described informally, in contrast with more traditional approaches which make the representation very clear.

A text like this can only provide an introduction to a subject as rich and developed as functional programming; the rest of this concluding chapter discusses other aspects of the subject, as well as giving pointers to other sources on the Web and in books and articles.

Further Haskell

The purpose of this text is to introduce functional programming ideas using the Haskell language. It covers the important aspects of the language, but does not aim to be complete. Among the topics omitted are data types with labelled fields, which resemble records or structures in other languages; strictness annotations, which are used to make data type constructors strict in some or all of their arguments; details of the Read class and the numeric types and classes.

Further information about all these can be found in the Haskell language report (Peyton Jones and Hughes 1998), and the 'Gentle Introduction' of Hudak, Fasel and Peterson (1997) also contains useful information about some of them, as well as providing an overview of the language for an experienced functional programmer. Both of these, as well as many other Haskell resources, can be found at the Haskell home page, http://www.haskell.org/

The text has discussed many of the most important functions in the standard prelude but on the whole has avoided discussing the contents of the libraries, which are documented in Peyton Jones and Hughes (1998). These libraries fall into two classes. First there are libraries of utilities, such as List.hs which contains a multitude of list-manipulating functions. These are in libraries, which can be included or not by the programmer at will, so as not to clutter up the name space of the language.

Other libraries contain extensions of the language, including a library of arrays, Array.hs, as well as facilities for file creation and management, Directory.hs, and for system links, System.hs. These libraries come with all Haskell implementations; each implementation will also come with particular extensions, usually available in the form of library modules.

Haskell in the future

Haskell was first defined in 1987, and has been modified and extended since then. This text is written in Haskell 98, which is meant to provide a stable base system consisting of tried and tested features. The progress of research in functional programming makes it clear that a language like Haskell will not stand still forever and at the time of writing there is an initiative under way to design Haskell 2, which will extend and modify the language in a number of significant ways. Nevertheless, it is likely that systems will continue to support the features of Haskell 98 as outlined in this text. The Haskell home page can be relied upon to contain up-to-date information on the status of Haskell.

Extending Haskell

As it has been introduced in this text, Haskell is a general-purpose, high-level programming language. Many real-world applications require programs to, for instance, manipulate computer graphics, modify the state of a machine, or operate in parallel, and Haskell as it stands does not provide these facilities directly.

However, there have been extensions to particular Haskell implementations to perform tasks like this. Information about a great number of applications and extensions of Haskell can be found on the home page

```
http://www.haskell.org/libraries.html                    (libraries)
```

or in the documentation for particular implementations, as detailed on the Haskell home page and in Appendix E.

Often languages are not used in isolation, and so links to external libraries and programming languages are important. These interfacing issues are discussed in Finne *et al.* (1998) and Meijer (1998). A variety of graphical user interfaces for Haskell programs have been written; details of these can be found on the (libraries) page.

Other specific extensions include a library to write CGI scripts, which are used to extend the interactive capabilities of Web pages,

```
http://www.cse.ogi.edu/~erik/Personal/cgi.htm
```

to provide a language for describing graphical animations which interact with users (Elliott and Hudak 1997),

```
http://www.research.microsoft.com/~conal/Fran/
```

to give efficient implementations of functional data structures (Okasaki 1998),

```
http://www.cs.columbia.edu/~cdo/edison/
```

to describe musical notation in Haskell (Hudak *et al.* 1996),

```
http://www.haskell.org/haskore/
```

and to support a concurrent version of the language Glasgow Parallel Haskell,

```
http://www.dcs.gla.ac.uk/fp/software/gph/
```

Using a monadic view it is also possible to integrate mutable state into the Haskell model. This is discussed in Peyton Jones and Wadler (1993) and Launchbury and Peyton Jones (1994) and implemented in the Glasgow Haskell Compiler.

Haskell and functional programming on the Web

There are now many resources on Haskell and functional programming to be found on the World Wide Web. This text itself has a home page at

```
http://www.cs.ukc.ac.uk/people/staff/sjt/craft2e/
```

which lists all the links given here. The Haskell home page is at

```
http://www.haskell.org/
```

and information about the Haskell mailing list can also be found there.

The Haskell language was named in honour of Haskell Brooks Curry. A short biography and photograph of Curry can be found at

```
http://www-groups.dcs.st-and.ac.uk/~history/Mathematicians/Curry.html
```

For functional programming in general, the first place to start is the 'FAQ',

```
http://www.cs.nott.ac.uk/Department/Staff/gmh/faq.html
```

which gives details of all functional programming languages, as well as more general information and indeed answers to frequently asked questions about the basics of functional programming.

Information about a number of real-world applications of functional programming can be found at

```
http://www.cs.bell-labs.com/~wadler/realworld/
```

Jon Mountjoy has a web page on functional programming,

```
http://carol.wins.uva.nl/~jon/func.html
```

and Claus Reinke makes available his functional programming bookmarks,

```
http://www.cs.nott.ac.uk/~czr/FP.html
```

Functional programming languages are used in many universities and other institutions, and resources on functional languages in education are accessible from

```
http://www.cs.kun.nl/fple/
```

A final resource is the Internet newsgroup

```
news:comp.lang.functional
```

devoted to discussion of functional programming in general.

Other functional programming languages

Haskell is a lazy, strongly typed functional programming language; another is Miranda (Turner 1986; Thompson 1995). In this text laziness is only examined explicitly in

Chapter 17, and up to that point it looks at aspects of functional programming which are broadly shared with Standard ML (Milner *et al.* 1997; Appel 1993), the best known and most widely used strict and strongly typed functional language, for which Paulson (1996) provides an introduction. It is possible to model lazy evaluation within a strict language, and Haskell provides facilities to make evaluation strict, so the two schools are very close indeed.

A different style of functional programming, eschewing variables as much as possible, was introduced in Backus (1978). Bird and de Moor (1997) is a recent text which emphasizes the benefits of this style in supporting program transformation and also advocates a 'relational' style of programming which extends the functional.

LISP is the oldest established functional lanaguage, but it differs from Haskell and SML in not being strongly typed. An excellent tutorial introduction to programming in the Scheme dialect of LISP is given in Abelson, Sussman and Sussman (1996). An imperative language with similiarities to LISP and used for telephone switching and other real-time applications is Erlang (Armstrong, Virding and Williams 1993).

Two recent surveys of applications of functional programming languages in large-scale projects are Runciman and Wakeling (1995) and Hartel and Plasmeijer (1995b), and there is also information about this on the Web, as cited above.

In the last ten years, powerful techniques of implementation of especially lazy functional languages have been developed. The twin texts (Peyton Jones 1987; Peyton Jones and Lester 1992) describe these in lucid detail.

Where is functional programming going?

The material in this text is an introduction to modern functional programming in a typed, lazy, language. As the field develops, new techniques and approaches are continually being developed; a good place to start in learning about these is the proceedings of two summer schools in Advanced Functional Programming (Jeuring and Meijer 1995; Launchbury, Meijer and Sheard 1996). To see the ways in which functional langauges are being used in education, the proceedings of a meeting on Functional Languages in Education appear in Hartel and Plasmeijer (1995a), and these have been followed up with the creation of the FPLE Web site mentioned above. Research in functional programming is reported in the *Journal of Functional Programming*

http://www.dcs.gla.ac.uk/jfp/

and at the annual International Conference in Functional Programming (Hudak and Queinnec 1998), as well as at other meetings detailed at the Web sites mentioned above.

It is difficult to predict future directions in a field like computing, but it is clear that one fruitful direction for functional programming is in forming a **component of larger systems**. The Fran system (Elliott and Hudak 1997) uses a functional language to describe animations which are ultimately produced at a lower level using a library written in C++. The opening up of functional systems, so that it is no longer a choice of 'either functional or non-functional, but not both', means that functional languages can take their place in the programmer's toolkit of techniques and prove their worth alongside object-oriented and other languages. This opening up is enabled by systems such as H/Direct (Finne *et al.* 1998) and ActiveHaskell, which links Haskell to COM components; details of this can be found on the (libraries) Web page.

Another direction is in **strengthening type systems** for functional languages, so that only terminating programs can be written. At first sight this seems to exclude too many programs to be practical, but with 'co-data' (Turner 1995), and dependent types – where the type of a result depends upon the value of an argument (Augustsson 1998) – it appears that practical languages can be defined. The advantage of languages like these is that they make reasoning much more straightforward, as well as allowing a programmer to express more of their intuitions about how a program behaves as a part of the program. This text has already shown how a strongly typed language allows for the capture of many errors at compile time, and strengthening the type system can only help this.

A third issue is that of providing **tool support** for developers of functional programs. As was evident in the discussion of lazy evaluation, it is often very difficult indeed to predict the space behaviour of lazy programs; interesting work on this is reported in Runciman and Röjemo (1996).

These are only three of the possible directions for functional languages, and it is clear that they provide a fertile approach to programming which will remain an important element of computing science in years to come.

Functional, imperative and OO programming

In this appendix we compare programming in Haskell to more traditional notions in imperative languages like Pascal and C and object-oriented (OO) languages such as C++ and Java.

Values and states

Consider the example of finding the sum of squares of natural numbers up to a particular number. A functional program describes the values that are to be calculated, directly.

```
sumSquares :: Int -> Int
sumSquares 0 = 0
sumSquares n = n*n + sumSquares (n-1)
```

These equations state what the sum of squares is for a natural number argument. In the first case it is a direct description; in the second it states that the sum to non-zero n is got by finding the sum to n-1 and adding the square of n.

A typical imperative program might solve the problem thus

```
s := 0 ;
i := 0 ;
while i<n do begin
    i := i+1 ;
    s := i*i + s ;
end {while}
```

The sum is the final value of the variable s, which is changed repeatedly during program execution, as is the 'count' variable, i. The effect of the program can only be seen by following the sequence of changes made to these variables by the commands in the program, while the functional program can be read as a series of equations defining the sum of squares. This meaning is **explicit** in the functional program, whereas the imperative program has an overall effect which is not obvious from the program itself.

A more striking algorithm still is one which is completely explicit: 'to find the sum of squares, build the list of numbers 1 to n, square each of them, and sum the result'. This program, which uses neither complex control flow, as does the imperative example, nor recursion as seen in the function sumSquares, can be written in a functional style, thus:

```
newSumSq :: Int -> Int
newSumSq n = sum (map square [1 .. n])
```

where square x = x*x, the operation map applies its first argument to every member of a list, and sum finds the sum of a list of numbers. More examples of this sort of **data-directed** programming can be seen in the body of the text.

Functions and variables

An important difference between the two styles is what is meant by some of the terminology. Both 'function' and 'variable' have different interpretations.

As was explained earlier, a function in a functional program is simply something which returns a value which depends upon some inputs. In imperative and object-oriented languages like Pascal, C, C++ and Java a function is rather different. It will return a value depending upon its arguments, but in general it will also change the values of variables. Rather than being a pure function it is really a procedure which returns a value when it terminates.

In a functional program a variable stands for an **arbitrary** or **unknown** value. Every occurrence of a variable in an equation is interpreted in the same way. They are just like variables in logical formulas, or the mathematical variables familiar from equations like

$$a^2 - b^2 = (a-b)(a+b)$$

In any particular case, the value of all three occurrences of a will be the same. In exactly the same way, in

```
sumSquares n = n*n + sumSquares (n-1)
```

all occurrences of n will be interpreted by the same value. For example

```
sumSquares 7 = 7*7 + sumSquares (7-1)
```

The crucial motto is 'variables in functional programs *do not vary*'.

On the other hand, the value of a variable in an imperative program changes throughout its lifetime. In the sum of squares program above, the variable s will take the values 0,1,5,... successively. Variables in imperative programs *do* vary over time, on the other hand.

Program verification

Probably the most important difference between functional and imperative programs is logical. As well as being a program, a functional definition is a logical equation describing a **property** of the function. Functional programs are **self-describing**, as it were. Using the definitions, other properties of the functions can be deduced.

To take a simple example, for all n>0, it is the case that

```
sumSquares n > 0
```

To start with,

```
sumSquares 1
= 1*1 + sumSquares 0
= 1*1 + 0
= 1
```

which is greater than 0. In general, for n greater than zero,

```
sumSquares n = n*n + sumSquares (n-1)
```

Now, n*n is positive, and if sumSquares (n-1) is positive, their sum, sumSquares n, must be. This proof can be formalized using **mathematical induction**. The body of the text contains numerous examples of proofs by induction over the structure of data structures like lists and trees, as well as over numbers.

Program verification is possible for imperative programs as well, but imperative programs are not self-describing in the way functional ones are. To describe the effect of an imperative program, like the 'sum of squares' program above, we need to add to the program logical formulas or assertions which describe the state of the program at various points in its execution. These methods are both more indirect and more difficult, and verification seems very difficult indeed for 'real' languages like Pascal and C. Another aspect of program verification is **program transformation** in which programs are transformed to other programs which have the same effect but better performance, for example. Again, this is difficult for traditional imperative languages.

Records and tuples

In Chapter 5 the tuple types of Haskell are introduced. In particular we saw the definition

```
type Person = (String,String,Int)
```

This compares with a Pascal declaration of a record

```
type Person = record
  name  : String;
  phone : String;
  age   : Integer
end;
```

which has three fields which have to be named. In Haskell the fields of a tuple can be accessed by pattern matching, but it is possible to define functions called **selectors** which behave in a similar way, if required:

```
name   :: Person -> String
name (n,p,a) = n
```

and so on. If `per :: Person` then `name per :: String`, similarly to `r.name` being a string variable if `r` is a variable of type `Person` in Pascal.

Haskell 98 also contains records with named fields, rather more like those of Pascal. For further details, see the Haskell Report (Peyton Jones and Hughes 1998).

Lists and pointers

Haskell contains the type of lists built in, and other recursive types such as trees can be defined directly. We can think of the type of linked lists given by pointers in Pascal as an **implementation** of lists, since in Haskell it is not necessary to think of pointer values, or of storage allocation (`new` and `dispose`) as it is in Pascal. Indeed, we can think of Haskell programs as **designs** for Pascal list programs. If we define

```
type list = ^node;
type node = record
   head : value;
   tail : list
end;
```

then we have the following correspondence, where the Haskell `head` and `tail` functions give the head and tail of a list.

```
         []                    nil
         head ys               ys^.head
         tail ys               ys^.tail
         (x:xs)                cons(x,xs)
```

The function `cons` in Pascal has the definition

```
function cons(y:value;ys:list):list;
  var xs:list;
  begin
    new(xs);
    xs^.head := y;
    xs^.tail := ys;
    cons := xs
  end;
```

Functions such as

```
sumList []     = 0
sumList (x:xs) = x + sumList xs
```

can then be transferred to Pascal in a straightforward way.

```
function sumList(xs:list):integer;
```

```
begin
  if xs=nil
    then sumList := 0
    else sumList := xs^.head + sumList(xs^.tail)
end;
```

A second example is

```
doubleAll []     = []
doubleAll (x:xs) = (2*x) : doubleAll xs
```

where we use cons in the Pascal definition of the function

```
function doubleAll(xs:list):list;
  begin
    if xs=nil
      then doubleAll := nil
      else doubleAll := cons( 2*xs^.head , doubleAll(xs^.tail) )
  end;
```

If we define the functions

```
function head(xs:list):value;     function tail(xs:list):list;
  begin                             begin
    head := xs^.head                  tail := xs^.tail
  end;                              end;
```

then the correspondence is even clearer:

```
function doubleAll(xs:list):list;
  begin
    if xs=nil
      then doubleAll := nil
      else doubleAll := cons( 2*head(xs) , doubleAll( tail(xs) ) )
  end;
```

This is strong evidence that a functional approach can be useful even if we are writing in an imperative language: the functional language can be the high-level *design* language for the imperative implementation. Making this separation can give us substantial help in finding imperative programs – we can think about the design and the lower level implementation *separately*, which makes each problem smaller, simpler and therefore easier to solve.

Higher-order functions

Traditional imperative languages give little scope for higher-order programming; Pascal, Java and C allow functions as arguments, so long as those functions are not themselves higher-order, but has no facility for returning functions as results. In C++ it is possible to return objects which represent functions by overloading the function application operator! This underlies the genericity hailed in the C++ Standard Template Library, which requires advanced features of the language to implement functions like map and filter.

Control structures like if-then-else bear some resemblance to higher-order functions, as they take commands, c_1, c_2 etc. into other commands,

```
if b then c₁ else c₂       while b do c₁
```

just as map takes one function to another. Turning the analogy around, we can think of higher-order functions in Haskell as **control structures** which we can define ourselves. This perhaps explains why we form libraries of polymorphic functions: they are the control structures we use in programming particular sorts of system. Examples in the text include libraries for building parsers (Section 17.5) and interactive I/O programs (Chapter 18), as well as the built-in list-processing functions.

Polymorphism

Again, this aspect is poorly represented in many imperative languages; the best we can do in Pascal, say, is to use a text editor to copy and modify the list processing code from one type of lists for use with another. Of course, we then run the risk that the different versions of the programs are not modified in step, unless we are very careful to keep track of modifications, and so on.

Polymorphism in Haskell is what is commonly known as **generic** polymorphism: the same 'generic' code works over a whole collection of types. A simple example is the function which reverses the elements in a list.

Haskell classes support what is known as 'ad hoc' polymorphism, or in object-oriented terminology simply 'polymorphism', in which different programs implement the same operation over different types. An example of this is the Eq class of types carrying an equality operation: the way in which equality is checked is completely different at different types. Another way of viewing classes is as **interfaces** which different types can implement in different ways; in this way they resemble the interfaces of object-oriented languages like Java.

As is argued in the text, polymorphism is one of the mechanisms which helps to make programs *reusable* in Haskell; it remains to be seen whether this will also be true of advanced imperative languages.

Defining types and classes

The algebraic type mechanism of Haskell, explained in Chapter 14, subsumes various traditional type definitions. Enumerated types are given by algebraic types all of whose constructors are 0-ary (take no arguments); variant records can be implemented as algebraic types with more then one constructor, and **recursive** types usually implemented by means of pointers become recursive algebraic types.

Just as we explained for lists, Haskell programs over trees and so on can be seen as *designs* for programs in imperative languages manipulating the pointer implementations of the types.

The abstract data types, introduced in Chapter 16, are very like the abstract data types of Modula-2 and so on; the design methods we suggest for use of abstract data types mirror aspects of the **object-based** approach advocated for modern imperative languages such as Ada.

The Haskell class system also has object-oriented aspects, as we saw in Section 14.6. It is important to note that Haskell classes are in some ways quite different from the classes of, for instance, C++. In Haskell classes are made up of types, which themselves have members; in C++ a class is like a type, in that it contains objects. Because of this many of the aspects of object-oriented design in C++ are seen as issues of type design in Haskell.

List comprehensions

List comprehensions provide a convenient notation for **iteration** along lists: the analogue of a for loop, which can be used to run through the indices of an array. For instance, to sum all pairs of elements of xs and ys, we write

```
[ a+b | a <- xs , b <- ys ]
```

The order of the iteration is for a value a from the list xs to be fixed and then for b to run through the possible values from ys; this is then repeated with the next value from xs, until the list is exhausted. Just the same happens for a **nested** for loop

```
for i:=0 to xLen-1 do
  for j:=0 to yLen-1 do                          (twoFor)
    write( x[i]+y[j] )
```

where we fix a value for i while running through all values for j.

In the for loop, we have to run through the indices; a list generator runs through the values directly. The indices of the list xs are given by

```
[0 .. length xs - 1]
```

and so a Haskell analogue of (twoFor) can be written thus:

```
[ xs!!i + ys!!j | i <- [0 .. length xs - 1] ,
                  j <- [0 .. length ys - 1] ]
```

if we so wish.

Lazy evaluation

Lazy evaluation and imperative languages do not mix well. In Pascal, for instance, we can write the function definition

```
function succ(x : integer):integer;
begin
  y    := y+1;
  succ := x+1
end;
```

This function adds one to its argument, but also has the **side-effect** of increasing y by one. If we evaluate f(y,succ(z)) we cannot predict the effect it will have.

● If f evaluates its second argument first, y will be increased before being passed to f;

● on the other hand, if f needs its first argument first (and perhaps its second argument not at all), the value passed to f will not be increased, even if it is increased before the function call terminates.

In general, it will not be possible to predict the behaviour of even the simplest programs. Since evaluating an expression can cause a change of the state, the order of expression evaluation determines the overall effect of a program, and so a lazy implementation can behave differently (in unforeseen ways) from the norm.

State, infinite lists and monads

Section 17.6 introduced infinite lists, and one of the first examples given there was an infinite list of random numbers. This list could be supplied to a function requiring a supply of random numbers; because of lazy evaluation, these numbers will only be generated on demand.

If we were to implement this imperatively, we would probably keep in a variable the last random number generated, and at each request for a number we would update this store. We can see the infinite list as supplying *all the values that the variable will take* as a single structure; we therefore do not need to keep the state, and hence have an **abstraction** from the imperative view.

We have seen in Section 18.8 that there has been recent important work on integrating side-effecting programs into a functional system by a monadic approach.

Conclusion

Clearly there are parallels between the functional and the imperative, as well as clear differences. The functional view of a system is often higher-level, and so even if we ultimately aim for an imperative solution, a functional design or **prototype** can be most useful.

We have seen that monads can be used to give an interface to imperative features within a functional framework. Many of the Haskell implementations offer these facilities, and so give a method of uniting the best features of two important programming paradigms without compromising the purity of the language. Other languages, including Standard ML (Milner, Tofte and Harper 1990), combine the functional and the imperative, but these systems tend to lose their pure functional properties in the process.

It is interesting to see the influence of ideas from modern functional programming languages in the design of Java extensions. One of the main drawbacks of Java is that it lacks a generic mechanism; the Pizza language (Odersky and Wadler 1997) adds this, together with Haskell-style pattern matching, and Pizza is a forerunner of the Generic Java extension, GJ, www.cs.bell-labs.com/who/wadler/pizza/gj/.

Glossary

We include this glossary to give a quick reference to the most widely used terminology in the book. Words appearing in **bold** in the descriptions have their own entries. Further references and examples are to be found by consulting the index.

Abstract type   An abstract type definition consists of the type name, the **signature** of the type, and the implementation equations for the names in the signature.

Algebraic type   An algebraic type definition states what are the **constructors** of the type. For instance, the declaration

```
data Tree = Leaf Int |
            Node Tree Tree
```

says that the two constructors of the Tree type are Leaf and Node, and that their types are, respectively,

```
Leaf :: Int->Tree
Node :: Tree->Tree->Tree
```

Application   This means giving values to (some of) the arguments of a function. If an n-argument function is given fewer than n arguments, this is called a **partial application**. Application is written using **juxtaposition**.

Argument   A **function** takes one or more arguments into an **output**.

Arguments are also known as **inputs** and **parameters**.

Associativity   The way in which an expression involving two applications of an operator is interpreted. If x#y#z is interpreted as (x#y)#z then # is left associative, if as x#(y#z) it is right associative; if both bracketings give the same result then # is called associative.

Base types   The types of numbers, including Int and Float, **Booleans**, Bool, and **characters**, Char.

Binding power   The 'stickiness' of an operator, expressed as an integer; the higher the number the stickier the operator. For example, 2+3*4 is interpreted as 2+(3*4) as '*' has higher binding power – binds more tightly – than '+'.

Booleans   The type containing the two 'truth values' True and False.

Calculation   A calculation is a line-by-line **evaluation** of a Haskell **expression** on paper. Calculations use the **definitions** which are contained in a **script** as well as the built-in definitions.

Cancellation   The rule for finding the type of a partial application.

Character   A single letter, such as `'s'` or `'\t'`, the tab character. They form the `Char` type.

Class   A collection of types. A class is defined by specifying a **signature**; a type is made an **instance** of the class by supplying an implementation of the definitions of the signature over the type.

Clause   A clause is one of the alternatives making up a **conditional equation**. A clause consists of a **guard** followed by an **expression**. When evaluating a function application, the first clause whose guard evaluates to `True` is chosen.

Combinator   Another name for a **function**.

Comment   Part of a **script** which plays no computational role; it is there for the reader to read and observe. Comments are specified in two ways: the part of the line to the right is made a comment by the symbol `--`; a comment of arbitrary length is enclosed by `{-` and `-}`.

Complexity   A measurement of the time or space behaviour of a function.

Composition   The combination of two functions by passing the **output** of one to the **input** of the other.

Concatenate   To put together a number of lists into a single list.

Conditional equation   A conditional equation consists of a left-hand side followed by a number of **clauses**. Each clause consists of a **guard** followed by an expression which is to be equated with the left-hand side of the **equation** if that particular clause is chosen during evaluation. The clause chosen is the first whose guard evaluates to `True`.

Conformal pattern match   An equation in which a pattern appears on the left-hand side of an equation, as in

`(x,y) = ....`

Constructor   An **algebraic type** is specified by its constructors, which are the functions which build elements of the algebraic type.

   In the example in the entry for algebraic types, elements of the type are constructed using `Leaf` and `Node`; the elements are `Leaf n` where `n::Int` and `Node s t` where s and t are trees.

Context   The hypotheses which appear before `=>` in type and class declarations. A context `M a` means that the type a must belong to the class M for the function or class definition to apply. For instance, to apply a function of type

`Eq a => [a] -> a -> Bool`

to a list and object, these must come from types over which equality is defined.

Curried function   A function of at least two arguments which takes its arguments one at a time, so having the type

`t1 -> t2 -> ... -> t`

in contrast to the *uncurried* version

`(t1,t2,...) -> t`

The name is in honour of Haskell B. Curry, after whom the Haskell language is also named.

Declaration   A **definition** can be accompanied by a statement of the **type** of the object defined; these are often called type declarations.

Default   A default holds in the absence of any other definition. Used in `class` definitions to give definitions of some of the operations in terms of others; an example is the definition of /= in the Eq class.

Definition   A definition associates a **value** or a **type** with a **name**.

Design   In writing a system, the effort expended *before* implementation is started.

Derived class instance   An instance of a standard class which is derived by the system, rather than put in explicitly by the programmer.

Enumerated type   An **algebraic type** with each constructor having no arguments.

Equation   A **definition** in Haskell consists of a number of equations. On the left-hand side of the equation is a **name** applied to zero or more **patterns**; on the right-hand side is a value. In many cases the equation is **conditional** and has two or more **clauses**. Where the meaning is clear we shall sometimes take 'equation' as shorthand for 'equation or conditional equation'.

Evaluation   Every **expression** in Haskell has a value; evaluation is the process of finding that value. A **calculation** evaluates an expression, as does an interactive Haskell system when that expression is typed to the prompt.

Export   The process of defining which definitions will be visible when a module is **imported** by another.

Expression   An expression is formed by applying a **function** or **operator** to its arguments; these arguments can be **literal** values, or expressions themselves. A simple numerical expression is

(2+8)-10

in which the operator '-' is applied to two arguments.

Extensionality   The principle of proof which says that two functions are equal if they give equal results for every input.

Filter   To pick out those elements of a list which have a particular property, represented by a **Boolean**-valued function.

Floating-point number   A number which is given in decimal (e.g. 456.23) or exponent (e.g. 4.5623e+2) form; these numbers form the type Float.

Fold   To combine the elements of a list using a binary **operation**.

Forward composition   Used for the operator '>.>' with the definition

f >.> g = g . f

f >.> g can be read 'f then g'.

Function   A function is an object which returns a **value**, called the **output** or **result** when it is applied to its **inputs**. The inputs are also known as its **parameters** or **arguments**. Examples include the square root function, whose input and output are numbers, and the function which returns the borrowers (output) of a book (input) in a database (input).

Function types   The type of a **function** is a function type, so that, for instance, the function which checks whether its integer argument is even has type Int->Bool. This is the type of functions with **input** type Int and **output** type Bool.

Generalization   Replacing an object by something of which the original object is an instance.

This might be the replacement of a function by a polymorphic function from which the original is obtained by passing the appropriate parameter, or replacing a logical formula by one which implies the original.

Guard   The **Boolean** expression appearing to the right of '|' and to the left of '=' in a **clause** of a **conditional equation** in a Haskell **definition**.

Higher-order function   A **function** is higher-order if either one of its **arguments** or its **result**, or both, are functions.

Identifier   Another word for **name**.

Implementation   The particular **definitions** which make a design concrete; for an **abstract data type**, the definitions of the objects named in the **signature**.

Import   The process of including the **exported** definitions of one module in another.

Induction   The name for a collection of methods of proof, by which statements of the form 'for all x ...' are proved.

Infix   An **operation** which appears between its **arguments**. Infix functions are called **operators**.

Inheritance   One **class** inherits the operations of another if the first class is in the **context** of the definition of the second. For instance, of the standard classes, Ord inherits (in)equality from Eq.

Input   A **function** takes one or more inputs into an **output**. Inputs are also known as **arguments** and **parameters**. The 'square' function takes a single numerical input, for instance.

Instance   The term 'instance' is used in two different ways in Haskell.

An instance of a **type** is a type which is given by **substituting** a type expression for a type **variable**. For example,

[(Bool,b)] is an instance of [a], given by substituting the type (Bool,b) for the variable a.

An instance of a **class**, such as Eq (a,b), is given by declaring how the function(s) of the class, in this case ==, are defined over the given type (here (a,b)). Here we would say

```
(x,y) == (z,w)
  = (x==z) && (y==w)
```

Integers   The positive and negative whole numbers. In Haskell the type Int represents the integers in a fixed size, while the type Integer represents them exactly, so that evaluating 2 to the power 1000 will give a result consisting of some three hundred digits.

Interactive program   A program which reads from and writes to the terminal; reading and writing will be *interleaved*, in general.

Interface   The common information which is shared between two program modules.

Juxtaposition   Putting one thing next to another; this is the way in which function application is written down in Haskell.

Lambda expression   An **expression** which denotes a **function**. After a '\' we list the arguments of the function, then an '->' and then the result. For instance, to add a number to the length of a list we could write

```
\xs n -> length xs + n
```

The term 'lambda' is used since '\' is close to the Greek letter 'λ', or lambda, which is used in a similar way in Church's lambda calculus.

Lazy evaluation   The sort of expression **evaluation** in Haskell. In a function application only those arguments whose values are *needed* will be evaluated, and moreover, only the parts of structures which are needed will be examined.

Linear complexity   Order 1, $O(n^1)$, behaviour.

Lists   A list consists of a collection of elements of a particular type, given in some order, potentially containing a particular item more than once. The list [2,1,3,2] is of type [Int], for example.

Literal   Something that is 'literally' a value: it needs no **evaluation**. Examples include 34, [23] and "string".

Local definitions   The definitions appearing in a where clause or a let expression. Their **scope** is the equation or expression to which the clause or let is attached.

Map   To apply an operation to every element of a list.

Mathematical induction   A method of proof for statements of the form 'for all natural numbers n, the statement P(n) holds'.

   The proof is in two parts: the base case, at zero, and the induction step, at which P(n) is proved on the assumption that P(n-1) holds.

Memoization   Keeping the value of a sub-computation (in a list, say) so that it can be reused rather than recomputed, when it is needed.

Module   Another name for a **script**; used particularly when more than one script is used to build a program.

Monad   A monad consists of a type with (at least) two functions, return and >>=. Informally, a monad can be seen as performing some sorts of action before returning an object. The two monad functions respectively return a value

without any action, and sequence two monadic operations.

Monomorphic   A type is **monomorphic** if it is not **polymorphic**.

Most general type   The most general type of an expression is the type t with the property that every other type for the expression is an **instance** of t.

Mutual recursion   Two definitions, each of which depends upon the other.

Name   A **definition** associates a name or **identifier** with a value. Names of **classes**, **constructors** and **types** must begin with capital letters; names of **values**, **variables** and **type variables** begin with small letters. After the first letter, any letter, digit, '' ' or '_' can be used.

Natural numbers   The non-negative whole numbers: 0, 1, 2, ...

Offside rule   The way in which the end of a part of a definition is expressed using the *layout* of a **script**, rather than an explicit symbol for the end.

Operation   Another name for **function**.

Operator   A **function** which is written in infix form, between its **arguments**. The function f is made infix thus: ` f `.

Operator section   A partially applied operator.

Output   When a **function** is applied to one or more **inputs**, the resulting value is called the output, or **result**. Applying the 'square' function to (-2) gives the output 4, for example.

Overloading   The use of the same **name** to mean two (or more) different things, at different types. The equality operation, ==, is an example. Overloading is supported in Haskell by the **class** mechanism.

Parameter   A **function** takes one or more parameters into an **output**. Parameters are also known as **arguments** and **inputs**, and applying a function to its inputs is sometimes known as 'passing its parameters'.

Parsing   Revealing the structure of a sentence in a formal language.

Partial application   A **function** of type t_1->t_2->$...$->t_n->t can be applied to n arguments, or less. In the latter case, the **application** is partial, since the result can itself be passed further parameters.

Pattern   A pattern is either a **variable**, a **literal**, a **wild card** or the application of a **constructor** to other patterns.

The term 'pattern' is also used as short for a 'pattern of computation' such as 'applying an operation to every member of a list', a pattern which in Haskell is realised by the map function.

Polymorphism   A type is polymorphic if it contains type **variables**; such a type will have many **instances**.

Prefix   An **operation** which appears before its **arguments**.

Primitive recursion   Over the natural numbers, defining the values of a function outright at zero, and at n greater than zero using the value at n-1. Over an **algebraic type** defining the function by cases over the constructors; recursion is permitted at arguments to a constructor which are of the type in question.

Proof   A logical argument which leads us to accept a logical statement as being valid.

Pure programming language   A functional programming language is pure if it does not allow **side-effects**.

Quadratic complexity   Order two, $O(n^2)$, behaviour.

Recursion   Using the name of a value or type in its own **definition**.

Result   When a **function** is applied to one or more **inputs**, the resulting value is called the result, or **output**.

Scope   The area of a program in which a **definition** or definitions are applicable. In Haskell the scope of top-level definitions is by default the whole **script** in which they appear; it may be extended by importing the module into another. More limited scopes are given by **local definitions**.

Script   A script is a file containing **definitions**, **declarations** and module statements.

Set   A collection of objects for which the order of elements and the number of occurrences of each element are irrelevant.

Side-effect   In a language like Pascal, evaluating an expression can cause other things to happen besides a value being computed. These might be I/O operations, or changes in values stored. In Haskell this does not happen, but a **monad** can be used to give a similar effect, without compromising the simple model of evaluation underlying the language. Examples are IO and State.

Signature   A sequence of type **declarations**. These declarations state what are the types of the operations (or functions) over an **abstract type** or a **class** which can be used to manipulate elements of that type.

Stream   A stream is a channel upon which items arrive in sequence; in Haskell we can think of **lazy** lists in this way, so it becomes a synonym for lazy list.

String   The type String is a **synonym** for lists of characters, [Char].

Structural induction   A method of proof for statements of the form 'for all finite lists xs, the statement P(xs) holds of xs'. The proof is in two parts: the base case, at [], and the induction step, at which P(y:ys) is proved on the assumption that P(ys) holds.
Also used of the related principle for any algebraic type.

Substitution   The replacement of a **variable** by an **expression**. For example, (9+12) is given by substituting 12 for n in (9+n). Types can also be substituted for type variables; see the entry for **instance**.

Synonym   Naming a type is called a type synonym. The keyword type is used for synonyms.

Syntax   The description of the properly formed programs (or sentences) of a language.

Transformation   Turning one program into another program which computes identical results, but with different behaviour in other respects such as time or space efficiency.

Tuples   A tuple type is built up from a number of component types. Elements of the type consist of tuples of elements of the component types, so that

(2,True,3) :: (Int,Bool,Int)

for instance.

Type   A collection of values. Types can be built from the **base** types using **tuple**, list and **function types**. New types can be defined using the **algebraic** and **abstract** type mechanisms, and types can be named using the type **synonym** mechanism.

Type variable   A **variable** which appears in a **polymorphic type**. An **identifier** beginning with a small letter can be used as a type variable; in this text we use the letters at the start of the alphabet, a, b, c and so on.

Undefinedness   The result of an expression whose evaluation continues forever, rather than giving a *defined* result.

Unification   The process of finding a common **instance** of two (type) expressions containing (type) variables.

Value   A value is a member of some **type**; the value of an **expression** is the result of **evaluating** the expression.

Variable   A variable stands for an *arbitrary* value, or in the case of type variables, an arbitrary type. Variables and type variables have the same syntax as **names**.

Verification   Proving that a function or functions have particular logical properties.

Where clause   Definitions **local** to a (conditional) **equation**.

Wild card   The name for the pattern '_', which is matched by any value of the appropriate type.

Haskell operators

The Haskell operators are listed below in decreasing order of binding power: see Section 3.7 for a discussion of associativity and binding power.

	Left associative	Non-associative	Right associative
9	`!, !!, //`		`.`
8			`**, ^, ^^`
7	`*, /, 'div', 'mod', 'rem', 'quot'`		
6	`+, -`	`:+`	
5		`\\`	`:, ++`
4		`/=, <, <=, ==, >, >=, 'elem', 'notElem'`	
3			`&&`
2			`||`
1	`>>, >>=`	`:=`	
0			`$, 'seq'`

Also defined in this text are the operators

9	`>.>`		
5			`>*>`

The restrictions on names of operators, which are formed using the characters

`! # $ % & * + . / < = > ? \ ^ | : - ~`

are that operators must not start with a colon; this character starts an infix constructor. The operators `-` and `!` can be user-defined, but note that they have a special meaning in certain circumstances – the obvious advice here is not to use them. Finally, certain combinations of symbols are reserved, and cannot be used: `.. :: => = @ \ | ^ <- ->`.

To change the associativity or binding power of an operator, `&&&` say, we make a declaration like

```
infixl 7 &&&
```

which states that `&&&` has binding power 7, and is a left associative operator. We can also declare operators as non-associative (`infix`) and right associative (`infixr`). Omitting the binding power gives a default of 9. These declarations can also be used for back-quoted function names, as in

```
infix 0 `poodle`
```

Understanding programs

This appendix is included to offer help to readers confronted with an unfamiliar function definition. There are various things we can do with the definition, and these are examined in turn here. Given a functional program like

```
mapWhile :: (a -> b) -> (a -> Bool) -> [a] -> [b]

mapWhile f p []     = []                          (mapWhile.1)
mapWhile f p (x:xs)
   | p x            = f x : mapWhile f p xs        (mapWhile.2)
   | otherwise      = []                           (mapWhile.3)
```

we can understand what it means in various complementary ways. We can read the program itself, we can write calculations of examples using the program, we can prove properties of the program, and we can estimate its space and time complexity,

Reading the program

Besides any comments which might accompany a program, the program itself is its most important documentation.

The type declaration gives information about the input and output types: for mapWhile, we have to supply three arguments:

- a function, f say, of arbitrary type, a -> b;
- a **property** of objects of type a; that is a function taking an a to a Boolean value; and,
- a list of items of type a.

The output is a list of elements of type b – the output type of f.

The function definition itself is used to give values of mapWhile, but also can be read directly as a description of the program.

- On [], the result is [].

- On a non-empty list, if the head x has property p, then according to (mapWhile.2), we have f x as the first element of the result, with the remainder given by a recursive call on xs.

- If the property p fails of x, the result is terminated, as it were, by returning the empty list [].

In the definition we have a complete description of how the program behaves, but we can animate this by trying specific examples.

Calculating with the program

A more concrete view of what the program does is given by calculating particular examples. For instance,

```
mapWhile (2+) (>7) [8,12,7,13,16]
  ⤳   2+8 : mapWhile (2+) (>7) [12,7,13,16]          by (mapWhile.2)
  ⤳   10 : 2+12 : mapWhile (2+) (>7) [7,13,16]       by (mapWhile.2)
  ⤳   10 : 14 : []                                   by (mapWhile.3)
  ⤳   [10,14]
```

Other examples include

```
mapWhile (2+) (>2) [8,12,7,13,16]  ⤳  [10,14,9,15,18]
mapWhile (2+) (>2) []              ⤳  []
```

Note that in these examples we use mapWhile at the instance

```
(Int -> Int) -> (Int -> Bool) -> [Int] -> [Int]
```

of its polymorphic type, given by replacing the type variables a and b by the type Int.

Reasoning about the program

We can get a deeper understanding about a program by **proving** properties that the program might have. For mapWhile, we might prove that for all f, p and finite lists xs,

```
mapWhile f p xs            = map f (takeWhile p xs)    (mapWhile.4)
mapWhile f (const True) xs = map f xs                  (mapWhile.5)
mapWhile id p xs           = takeWhile p xs            (mapWhile.6)
```

where we can, in fact, see (mapWhile.5) and (mapWhile.6) as consequences of the characterization of mapWhile given by property (mapWhile.4).

Program behaviour

It is not hard to see that the program will at worst take time linear (that is $O(n^1)$) in the
length (n) of the list argument assuming $O(n^0)$ behaviour of f and p, as it runs through
the elements of the list once, if at all.

The **space** behaviour is more interesting; because we can output the head of a list
once produced, the space required will be constant, as suggested by underlining the
parts which can be output in the calculation above.

```
mapWhile (2+) (>7) [8,12,7,13,16]
↝   2+8 : mapWhile (2+) (>7) [12,7,13,16]
↝   10 : 2+12 : mapWhile (2+) (>7) [7,13,16]
↝   10 : 14 : []
↝   [10,14]
```

Getting started

Each view of the program gives us a different understanding of its behaviour, but when
we are presented with an unfamiliar definition we can begin to understand what its effect
is by calculating various small examples. If we are given a collection of functions, we
can test out the functions from the bottom up, building one calculation on top of another.

The important thing is to realize that rather than being stuck, we can get started by
calculating representative examples to show us the way.

Implementations of Haskell

Implementations of Haskell have been built at various sites around the world. This text discusses the Hugs interpreter, which was developed in a joint effort by staff at the Universities of Nottingham in the UK and Yale in the USA. Compilers have been developed at the University of Glasgow, UK, and Chalmers Technical University, Goteborg, Sweden.

Hugs

Hugs is available from

```
http://www.haskell.org/hugs/
```

For the Unix version of Hugs you should follow the installation notes.

> **Note: Downloading Hugs for Windows**
>
> If you want to download the standard installation of Hugs which will set up the appropriate registry entries, you should download one of the
>
> ```
> selfinstall.exe
> selfinstall.zip
> ```
>
> files which will run an InstallShield script to make the appropriate settings and so on. If you download the **binaries**, you will have to make these settings and so forth for yourself.

You can choose to set the default editor for Hugs. The most straightforward way of doing this under Windows is to run WinHugs and to change the settings there. These changes persist to future invocations of both Hugs and WinHugs. The Programmer's File Editor is a freely available editor for Windows systems:

`http://www.lancs.ac.uk/people/cpaap/pfe/`

For the Macintosh, there is a port of Hugs 1.4 to the Power Macintosh OS at

```
ftp://haskell.org/pub/haskell/hugs/mac
  /hugs-June98-MacPPC-binary.sea.bin
```

which has been made by Hans Aberg.

The developers of Hugs recommend it as a Haskell program development system because of its fast compilation cycle, but it cannot offer the speed of execution of the various compilers.

Other Haskell systems

These include the Glasgow Haskell compiler

`http://www.dcs.gla.ac.uk/fp/software/ghc/`

developed at the University of Glasgow, the HBC/HBI system

`http://www.cs.chalmers.se/~augustss/hbc/hbc.html`

developed at Chalmers Technical University. NHC13

`http://www.cs.york.ac.uk/fp/nhc13/`

is a 'lightweight' compiler designed with implementation experimentation in mind.

Further information

Up-to-date information about future developments of these and any other implementations will be available from the Haskell home page,

`http://www.haskell.org/implementations.html`

Hugs errors

This appendix examines some of the more common programming errors in Haskell, and shows the error messages to which they give rise in Hugs.

The programs we write all too often contain errors. On encountering an error, the system either halts, and gives an **error message**, or continues, but gives a **warning message** to tell us that something unusual has happened, which might signal that we have made an error. In this appendix, we look at a selection of the messages output by Hugs; we have chosen the messages which are both common and require some explanation; messages like

```
Program error: {head []}
```

are self-explanatory. The messages are classified into roughly distinct areas. Syntax errors show up malformed programs, while type errors show well-formed programs in which objects are used at the wrong types. In fact, an ill-formed expression can often show itself as a type error and not as a syntax error, so the boundaries are not clear.

Syntax errors

A Haskell system attempts to match the input we give to the syntax of the language. Commonly, when something goes wrong, we type something *unexpected*. Typing '2==3)' will provoke the error message

```
ERROR: Syntax error in input (unexpected ')')
```

If a part of a definition is missing, as in

```
fun x
fun 2 = 34
```

we receive the message

```
Syntax error in declaration (unexpected ';')
```

The ';' here is an indication of the end of a definition – the error message therefore tells us that a definition has been ended unexpectedly, as there is no right-hand side corresponding to the fun x.

The inclusion of a type definition in a where clause is signalled by

```
Syntax error in declaration (unexpected keyword "type")
```

The syntax of patterns is more restricted than the full expression syntax, and so we get error messages like

```
Repeated variable "x" in pattern
```

when we use the same variable more than once within a pattern.

In specifying constants, we can make errors: floating-point numbers can be too large, and characters specified by an out-of-range ASCII code:

```
Inf.0
ERROR: Decimal character escape out of range
```

Not every string can be used as a name; some words in Haskell are **keywords** or **reserved identifiers**, and will give an error if used as an identifier. The keywords are

```
case class data default deriving do else if import in infix
infixl infixr instance let module newtype of then type where
```

The special identifiers as, qualified and hiding have special meanings in certain contexts but can be used as ordinary identifiers.

The final restriction on names is that names of constructors and types must begin with a capital letter; nothing else can do so, and hence we get error messages like

```
Undefined constructor function "Montana"
```

if we try to define a function called Montana.

Type errors

As we have seen in the body of the text, the main type error we meet is exemplified by the response to typing 'c' && True to the Hugs prompt:

```
ERROR: Type error in application
*** expression    : 'c' && True
*** term          : 'c'
*** type          : Char
*** does not match : Bool
```

which is provoked by using a Char where an Bool is expected. Other type errors, such as

```
True + 4
```

provoke the error message

```
ERROR: Bool is not an instance of class "Num"
```

This comes from the class mechanism: the system attempts to make `Bool` an instance of the class `Num` of numeric types over which '+' is defined. The error results since there is no such instance declaration making `Bool` belong to the class `Num`.

As we said before, we can get type errors from syntax errors. For example, writing `abs -2` instead of `abs (-2)` gives the error message

```
ERROR: a -> a is not an instance of class "Num"
```

because it is parsed as 2 subtracted from `abs::a->a`, and the operator '−' expects something in the class `Num`, rather than a function of type `a->a`. Other common type errors come from confusing the roles of ' : ' and '++' as in `2++[2]` and `[2]:[2]`.

We always give type declarations for our definitions; one advantage of this is to spot when our definition does not conform to its declared type. For example,

```
myCheck :: Int -> Bool
myCheck n = ord n == 6
```

gives the error message

```
ERROR "error.hs" (line 8): Type error in function binding
*** term            : myCheck
*** type            : Char -> Bool
*** does not match : Int -> Bool
```

Without the type declaration the definition would be accepted, only to give an error (presumably) when it is used. A final error related to types is given by definitions like

```
type Fred = (Fred,Int)                                           (Fred)
```

a **recursive** type synonym; these are signalled by

```
ERROR "error.hs" (line 11): Recursive type synonym "Fred"
```

The effect of (Fred) can be modelled by the algebraic type definition

```
data Fred = Node Fred Int
```

which introduces the **constructor** `Node` to identify objects of this type.

Program errors

Once we have written a syntactically and type correct script, and asked for the value of an expression which is itself acceptable, other errors can be produced during the **evaluation** of the expression.

The first class of errors comes from missing cases in definitions. If we have written a definition like

```
bat [] = 45
```

and applied it to [34] we get the response

```
Program error: {bat {dict} [Num_Int_fromInt 34]}
```

which shows the point at which evaluation can go no further, since there is no case in the definition of bat to cover a non-empty list. Similar errors come from built-in functions, such as head.

Other errors happen because an **arithmetical constraint** has been broken. These include an out-of-range list index, division by zero, using a fraction where an integer is expected and floating-point calculations which go out of range; the error messages all have the same form:

```
Program error: PreludeList.!!: index too large
Program error: {primDivInt 3 0}
```

If we make a conformal definition, like

```
[a,b] = [1 .. 10]
```

this will fail with a lengthy message

```
Program error: {b_v851_v850_v852 [1, 2, 3] ++ takeWhile (flip (Ord_<= {dict}) 10)
            (_strict (numericEnumFrom {dict}) (Num_Int_+ 3 (Num_Int_fromInt 1)))}
```

which reveals the implementation of this sort of definition.

Evaluation in Haskell is by need, and so a script which uses a name with no corresponding definition for the name will not be in error; only if the value of that name is required, will we get the message

```
ERROR: Undefined variable "cat"
```

Module errors

The module and import statements can provoke a variety of error messages: files may not be present, or may contain errors; names may be included more than once, or an alias on inclusion may cause a name clash. The error messages for these and other errors are self-explanatory.

System messages

In response to some commands and interrupts, the system generates messages, including

```
^C{Interrupted!}
```

signalling the interruption of the current task,

```
ERROR: Garbage collection fails to reclaim sufficient space
```

which shows that the space consumption of the evaluation exceeds that available. One way around this is to increase the size of the heap. To see the current size of the heap and the other settings of the system type

```
:set
```

The message given there shows how the heap size can be changed, as well as how to affect other system parameters.

If the option +s is set, the system prints diagnostic information of the form

```
(2 reductions, 8 cells)
```

The number of reductions corresponds to the number of steps in our calculations and the cells to the total space usage.

A measure of the space complexity of a function, as described in Chapter 19, is given by the size of the smallest heap in which the evaluation can take place; there is no direct measure of this given by the system.

Bibliography

Abelson, H., G. J. Sussman and J. Sussman (1996). *The Structure and Interpretation of Computer Programs* (2nd edn). MIT Press.

Appel, A. (1993). A critique of Standard ML. *Journal of Functional Programming*, **3**.

Armstrong, J., R. Virding and M. Williams (1993). *Concurrent Programming in ERLANG*. Prentice-Hall.

Augustsson, L. (1998). Cayenne – a language with dependent types. See Hudak and Queinnec (1998).

Backus, J. (1978). Can programming be liberated from the Von Neumann style? *Communications of the ACM*, **21**(8).

Bird, R. and O. de Moor (1997). *Algebra of Programming*. Prentice-Hall.

Cormen, T. H., C. E. Leiserson and R. L. Rivest (1990). *Introduction to Algorithms*. MIT Press.

Elliott, C. and P. Hudak (1997). Functional reactive animation. In *Proceedings of the 1997 ACM SIGPLAN International Conference on Functional Programming (ICFP97)*. ACM Press.

Finne, S., D. Leijen, E. Meijer and S. Peyton Jones (1998). H/direct: A binary foreign language interface for Haskell. See Hudak and Queinnec (1998).

Gordon, A. J. (1994). *Functional Programming and Input/Output*. British Computer Society Distinguished Dissertations in Computer Science. Cambridge University Press.

Peyton Jones, S. and J. Hughes (eds) (1998). *Standard Libraries for the Haskell 98 Programming Language*. http://www.haskell.org/library/.

Hartel, P. and R. Plasmeijer (eds) (1995a). *Functional Programming Languages in Education (FPLE)*. Springer-Verlag, Lecture Notes in Computer Science, 1022.

Hartel, P. and R. Plasmeijer (1995b). Special issue on state-of-the-art applications of pure functional programming languages. *Journal of Functional Programming*, **5**.

Hudak, P., T. Makucevich, S. Gadde and B. Whong (1996). Haskore music notation – An algebra of music. *Journal of Functional Programming*, **6**.

Hudak, P., J. H. Fasel and J. Peterson (1997). A gentle introduction to Haskell. `http://www.haskell.org/tutorial/`

Hudak, P. and C. Queinnec (eds) (1998). *The 1998 International Conference on Functional Programming*. ACM Press.

Hugs (1998). The Hugs System. Available from `http://www.haskell.org/hugs/`

Humphrey, W. S. (1996). *Introduction to the Personal Software Process*. Addison-Wesley.

Jeuring, J. and E. Meijer (eds) (1995). *Advanced Functional Programming*. Springer-Verlag, Lecture Notes in Computer Science, 925.

Läufer, K. (1996). Type classes with existential types. *Journal of Functional Programming*, **6**.

Launchbury, J., E. Meijer and T. Sheard (eds) (1996). *Advanced Functional Programming*. Springer Verlag, Lecture Notes in Computer Science, 1129.

Launchbury, J. and S. Peyton Jones (1994). Lazy functional state threads. In *Programming Languages Development and Implementation*. ACM Press.

Liang, S., P. Hudak and M. Jones (1995). Monad transformers and modular interpreters. In *22nd ACM SIGPLAN-SIGACT Symposium on Principles of Programming Languages (POPL)*. ACM Press.

Meijer, E. (1998). Calling hell from heaven and heaven from hell. See Hudak and Queinnec (1998).

Milner, R., M. Tofte and R. Harper (1990). *The Definition of Standard ML*. MIT Press.

Milner, R., M. Tofte, R. Harper and D. MacQueen (1997). *The Definition of Standard ML* (revised edn). MIT Press.

Odersky, M. and P. Wadler (1997). Pizza into Java: Translating theory into practice. In *24th ACM SIGPLAN-SIGACT Symposium on Principles of Programming Languages*. ACM Press.

Okasaki, C. (1998). *Purely Functional Data Structures*. Cambridge University Press.

Paulson, L. C. (1987). *Logic and Computation — Interactive Proof with Cambridge LCF*. Cambridge University Press.

Paulson, L. C. (1996). *ML for the Working Programmer* (2nd edn). Cambridge University Press.

Peyton Jones, S. (1987). *The Implementation of Functional Programming Languages*. Prentice-Hall.

Peyton Jones, S. and J. Hughes (eds) (1998). *Report on the Programming Language Haskell 98*. `http://www.haskell.org/report/`

Peyton Jones, S. and D. Lester (1992). *Implementing functional languages*. Prentice-Hall.

Peyton Jones, S. and P. Wadler (1993). Imperative functional programming. In *20th ACM SIGPLAN-SIGACT Symposium on Principles of Programming Languages*. ACM Press.

Polya, G. (1988). *How To Solve It* (reissued edn). Princeton University Press.

Runciman, C. and N. Röjemo (1996). New dimensions in heap profiling. *Journal of Functional Programming*, **6**.

Runciman, C. and D. Wakeling (eds) (1995). *Applications of Functional Programming*. UCL Press.

Thompson, S. (1995). *Miranda: The Craft of Functional Programming*. Addison-Wesley.

Thompson, S. (1999). Proof for functional programming. In K. Hammond and G. Michaelson (eds), *Research Directions in Parallel Functional Programming*. Springer Verlag.

Turner, D. (1995). Elementary strong functional programming. In P. Hartel and R. Plasmeijer (eds), *FPLE*, Lecture Notes in Computer Science, Springer Verlag, 1022.

Turner, D. A. (1986). An overview of Miranda. *SIGPLAN Notices*, **21**.

Index